THE REPUBLIC COMES OF AGE
1789-1841

SIX-VOLUME SET

THE REPUBLIC
COMES OF AGE
1789-1841

DUMAS MALONE
COLUMBIA UNIVERSITY
and UNIVERSITY OF VIRGINIA

•

BASIL RAUCH
BARNARD COLLEGE
COLUMBIA UNIVERSITY

APPLETON-CENTURY-CROFTS

DIVISION OF MEREDITH PUBLISHING COMPANY

New York

COVER ILLUSTRATIONS

FRONT: *Top,* A "Grasshopper" Engine, 1835
Baltimore & Ohio Railroad

Right, Detail from Portrait of Thomas Jefferson, by Rembrandt Peale
The New-York Historical Society

Left, Detail from Portrait of Andrew Jackson, by Asher B. Durand
The New-York Historical Society

Bottom, Battle of Lake Erie, War of 1812
Culver Service

BACK: *Top,* The Virginia State Capitol, Richmond

Right, Detail from Portrait of Alexander Hamilton, by John Trumbull
Museum of Fine Arts, Boston

Left, Detail from Portrait of John Adams, by Asher B. Durand after original by Gilbert Stuart
The New-York Historical Society

Bottom, The First Successful McCormick Reaper, 1831
State Historical Society, Wisconsin

To

the students we have been privileged to teach —at COLUMBIA, BARNARD, YALE, the UNIVERSITY OF VIRGINIA, the UNITED STATES NAVAL ACADEMY, and elsewhere—*we gratefully dedicate this book.*

PREFACE

THIS IS ONE OF SIX PORTIONS OF OUR WORK OF HISTORY WHICH WAS FIRST published in two volumes under the title, *Empire For Liberty: The Genesis and Growth of the United States of America*. Extended to include the Kennedy-Johnson administration, and also brought up to date in other respects, the work is now presented in six paperbound books for the convenience of students and the public.

Each of these books represents a chronological segment of American history and is a self-contained unit—with bibliography, appendices, and index. To each book we have given a descriptive title because, besides being usable in any combination with the others, it stands alone.

In preparing a new edition we have corrected such errors as were reported to us by those who have used the work and have availed ourselves of various helpful suggestions. The treatment of recent events, of course, is fresh, and minor changes have been made in the text elsewhere as a result of further study. There have been numerous additions to and some omissions from the original bibliographies.

Remaining mindful of the continuity as well as the variety of the American story, we repeat here parts of the original preface in which we tried to sum things up.

We believe that if history is to come alive in the minds of readers it must be presented primarily as a story. Therefore, this work is predominantly narrative in form. Within the inexorable limits of space, we have tried to do justice to all the important aspects of American history—political, economic, constitutional, diplomatic, social, religious, artistic, and intellectual.

In the process of selection, we have laid emphasis on two themes of special interest today. The course of world affairs in our century has magnified the importance of American foreign policy, and in this work we have emphasized international relations. In response to the crucial importance of ideology and movements of thought in our time, we have also given special attention to these. But we do not forget that the American story is one of human beings rather than impersonal forces. We have paid special attention to the people and their leaders in all fields at each stage.

We are wedded to no single thesis, knowing of none by which the whole of our history can be adequately explained. But we do see, as a thread running through the entire fabric, the idea of the free individual. And we repeat, as designating a major historic goal of our growing society, the Jeffersonian quotation from the original titlepage: "Such an Empire for Liberty as She has never surveyed since the Creation." (To Madison, April 27, 1809).

As used here, the word "empire" connotes no exploitation of subject regions on this continent or anywhere else. Its meaning has been newly illustrated by the admission of Alaska and Hawaii as full-bodied members of the Union of self-governing states. The vision of a better life for every human being, with faith that it would result from maximum liberty compatible with public order, inspired all the most fruitful public and private actions of Americans from the beginnings of English settlement. If this vision was temporarily blurred after the Civil War, it has gained renewed life because of events in the twentieth century, especially the rise of totalitarianism in the world.

The threat to the free individual that is implicit in the consolidating tendencies of our generation, both at home and abroad, intensifies the need to grasp the meaning of the American experience. Americans and all others who believe that man fulfills himself in conditions of political, social, economic, and cultural freedom should understand that American history is less important as a success story in material terms than as a struggle to fulfill human potentiality. The authors will be grateful to readers who accept this work as an effort to contribute to such understanding.

In the preface to the first edition, after expressing our gratitude to all those who had helped us through the years to understand our country better, we named a number of individuals who had rendered us special services. The list of helpful friends has now become so long that we must content ourselves with a general expression of thanks, without reference to particular persons. We should be remiss, however, if we did not say that we are more grateful than ever for the good counsel of our publishers.

Since the labor and judgment of both authors have gone into all parts of this history, no precise apportionment of responsibility between them is possible. In the full meaning of the term this is a joint product. In restudying and resurveying the whole of our country's past we have enjoyed a very great experience. We hope that this book will serve as an invitation to others to explore that past and share that experience.

D. M.

B. R.

CONTENTS

Part II: Nationalism, Sectionalism, and Democracy, 1815–1841

CONTENTS

MAPS and CHARTS

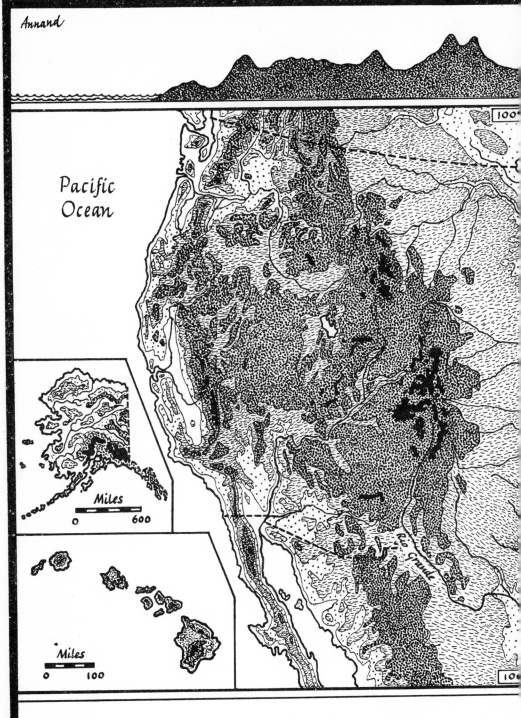

Annand

Pacific
Ocean

Miles
0   600

Miles
0   100

100°

Rio Grande

100°

PHYSIOGRAPHIC

Profile

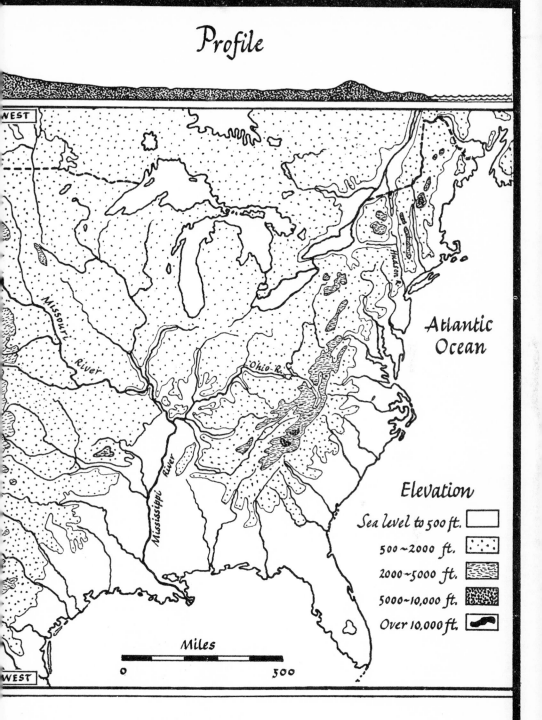

WEST

Atlantic
Ocean

Missouri River

Mississippi River

Ohio R.

Hudson R.

Elevation

Sea level to 500 ft.
500~2000 ft.
2000~5000 ft.
5000~10,000 ft.
Over 10,000 ft.

Miles

0   500

WEST

UNITED STATES

Part I

ESTABLISHING THE REPUBLIC
1789-1815

CHAPTER 1

Launching a New Government
1789-1793

THE FIRST CONGRESS UNDER THE CONSTITUTION WAS supposed to convene in New York on March 4, 1789, but it was April 1 before the House of Representatives attained a quorum. Without waiting for a quorum the Senate chose a temporary presiding officer, whose constitutional function it was to open the electoral votes. John Langdon of New Hampshire opened them on April 6 in joint session, announcing that George Washington had been unanimously elected President and that John Adams of Massachusetts, with the next highest vote, had been elected Vice-President.

The long-time secretary of the Continental Congress, Charles Thomson, had the honor of conveying the news to Mount Vernon, where the President-elect was immersed in spring. It took Thomson a week to get there, and a couple of days later Washington started northward. Friends and admirers addressed him in Alexandria and Baltimore; he was given a public banquet in Philadelphia; he passed through a triumphal arch at Trenton; he was received by the president and faculty of the college at Princeton; he crossed the Hudson in a specially constructed barge, rowed by thirteen pilots; and on April 23 he reached New York. John Adams had already taken his seat and started presiding over the Senate.

A week after Washington's arrival he was inaugurated in Federal Hall, in the presence of both houses of Congress, the occasion being marked by severe simplicity. He took the oath at the hands of Chancellor Livingston of New York on the gallery outside the hall; then he stepped back inside and delivered the first Inaugural Address, never taking his eyes off his paper. "This great man was agitated and embarrassed more than ever he was by the leveled cannon or pointed musket,"

3

said one Senatorial observer. His delivery was halting, but the first President inspired confidence throughout the land as the new government slowly got under way.

THE UNITED STATES UNDER WASHINGTON

The territory of the Republic, as defined by the Treaty of 1783, was not fully under American control in the spring of 1789, and a major task of the new government was to enter into undisputed possession of the whole of it. On the north the country extended to British North America and on the south to Spanish Florida, but in each case the boundary line was uncertain. Furthermore, the British still had posts in the Northwest and both they and the Spaniards were conniving with the Indians. The western boundary was the Mississippi, but the Spaniards controlled the mouth of that mighty stream and had not conceded to Americans its free navigation.

All of the eleven states that Washington presided over at first were along the coast, though there were considerable settlements beyond the mountains and below the Ohio. North Carolina ratified the Constitution in 1789 and Rhode Island in the next year, restoring the original thirteen. Three other states joined the Union in the eighteenth century: Vermont (1791), Kentucky (1792), and Tennessee (1796).

Considering the area, the population of the country was small, and it is hard for present-day Americans to realize how sparse and widespread it was. Figures become reasonably full and reliable at just this time, for the first census was that of 1790. The total population in 1790 was about 4,000,000, which was not much more than that of the city of Chicago in the middle of the twentieth century. Slightly more than a fourth of the people were in New England; about the same number were in the middle states, from New York through Delaware; and almost a half were in the southern states, from Maryland through Georgia. Even without her Kentucky counties, Virginia was the largest state in area and much the largest in population. Massachusetts, which then included Maine, was second in population, being followed by Pennsylvania and North Carolina. New York, the future Empire State, was fifth. There is much political significance in the fact that Virginia remained the first state until 1820, when she was passed by New York.

There were slaves in all the states except Massachusetts and Vermont, and the proportion of slaves and free Negroes to the total population was about one to five. This was considerably higher than it was in the middle of the next century, after the tide of European immigration became a flood. In the southern states the proportion was about one to three, about the same as in the 1850's.

In the 1790's the American people were overwhelmingly rural. In-

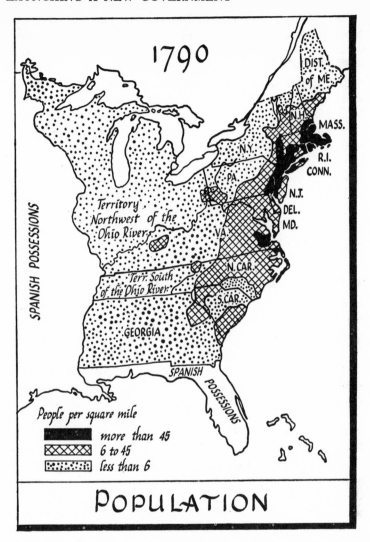

cluding its suburbs, the city of Philadelphia had somewhat more than 42,000 inhabitants, while New York on the island of Manhattan had 33,000. According to the census, Boston had 18,000 people, Charleston a few more than 16,000, and Baltimore 13,500. These were the major marts of commerce but the vast majority of the people were agricultural, living on farms or in small towns.

The English (including the Welsh) comprised some 60 per cent of the white population, and the British group as a whole (including the Scotch and Irish) constituted more than three-fourths. The term "Irish" was then loosely applied to both the Ulstermen or Scotch-Irish, who were really Scottish, and their traditional foes from present-day Ireland. The latter were chiefly to be found in Pennsylvania and the southern states. The Murphy family was more numerous in North Carolina than else-where, while few of the name were as yet in New York and New England. The Scots and Scotch-Irish together were the largest single ethnic group after the English, but they were followed closely by the Germans, who comprised about a twelfth of the total white population. The Irish proper, the Dutch, and the French together were only a little more than that.

The practice of Anglicizing non-British names had long been going on. In part this was a mere matter of practical convenience, but the process also reflected the dominance of the English tradition in American so-ciety. While some advocates of cultural independence resented this, there was in certain quarters a notable recrudescence of pro-British sentiments in the 1790's. It colored domestic politics and entered into the struggle over foreign policy.

The First President and His Court

It has been said that if George Washington should return to earth and not look like the portrait of him by Gilbert Stuart, he would be regarded as an imposter. Everybody would expect him to look just as he does on a dollar bill or a postage stamp. To most of his countrymen today he is a familiar picture, but his lineaments are frozen; he is a statue, a monument, a name; unlike Lincoln he seems unreal as a human being.

His face though not handsome was strong; he was tall and well-proportioned; he had great physical strength and endurance, and he was one of the greatest horsemen of his age. At fifty-seven he believed that he had passed his prime, and actually he had more illness during his first term as President than he had ever had in a comparable period. But he was still a strong and commanding figure. As Abigail Adams said, he looked and acted more like a king than George III.

Everybody stood in some awe of him. It is said that he never smiled during the American Revolution, and those who had witnessed his rare displays of wrath agreed that he was terrifying when aroused. But readers of his letters can find some smiles in them, along with many signs of thoughtful kindness. He was never an autocrat, and the pre-eminent quality of his mind was justness. He lacked the solid learning of John Adams, the brilliant audacity of Hamilton, the rich versatility of Jefferson, but, as a noted Frenchman described him during the Revolution, he was a "perfect whole." The mature judgment of Jefferson on him was expressed in strikingly similar language: "On the whole his character was, in its mass perfect, in nothing bad, in few points in-different; and it may be truly said, that never did nature and fortune combine more perfectly to make a man great." He had no temperamental weakness, seemingly, except extreme sensitivity to criticism, and he made on his contemporaries an ineffaceable impression of high character, sound judgment, and devoted patriotism.

Washington's unusual personal qualifications were enormously enhanced by the symbolic character he had assumed in the minds of his countrymen. During the Revolution he had come to be regarded as the personal embodiment of the American cause. He justified the new Constitution in the minds of many, and in practically all minds he symbolized the Union. That he was unanimously elected in the first place surprised no one; his unanimous re-election in 1792 was a more notable fact but even that was largely taken for granted. Until that time at least he was regarded as indispensable, and in the whole of American history that record is unique.

Since Washington brought dignity and prestige to the new office of President merely by occupying it, there was no point in trying to embellish his title. Yet, in the Senate, John Adams proposed that he be addressed as "His Highness the President of the United States and Protector of Their Liberties." This title, which smacked of royalty, was strongly opposed in the House, and the eventual decision was to designate the Chief Executive simply as the President of the United States. From that day to this he has been addressed simply as "Mr. President." The victory went to the advocates of republican simplicity, but talk about regal forms and monarchical tendencies persisted through the decade. Some of the talk was demagoguery, and at this distance the issue seems unreal, but the people of that time did not know how things were going to turn out. In their world, kingdoms were the rule and a republic was the very rare exception.

To Thomas Jefferson, then in Paris, where he had had abundant opportunity to see monarchy at work, it seemed that his old friend Adams had made himself ridiculous, and in this connection he repeated Franklin's famous characterization of that gentleman: "always an honest man, often a great one, but sometimes absolutely mad." Nobody thought that the President wanted to be a king, but the episode injured Adams, who became both a symbol of formalism and a comic figure. Somebody dubbed that robust patriot "His Rotundity." Aware that he would have to create precedents, Washington had asked suggestions of several men about desirable social policy. In reply Adams had this to say about the presidency:

> The office, by its legal authority, defined in the Constitution has no equal in the world, excepting those only which are held by crowned heads; nor is the royal authority in all cases to be compared to it. . . . If the *state and pomp* essential to this great department are not, in a good degree, preserved, it will be in vain for America to hope for consideration with foreign powers.

Washington was entirely too well-balanced a mind to hold with such an extreme emphasis, but he wanted things to be done with a propriety and dignity that would redound to the credit of the country, and he established a formal court the like of which never surrounded another President. His weekly levees for men, on Tuesdays from three to four, were stiff affairs. But the President was fastidiously polite to everybody, and if he did not bend easily it was not because of pride of office. Mrs. Washington's levees on Fridays for both sexes were more brilliant; and no doubt many a lady and her gallant rejoiced in the thought that this Court was not unlike that of England. The Washingtons were more in character as hosts at the dinners they gave regularly. These were bountiful repasts in the best tradition of generous hospitality.

In social matters Washington set a precedent which his successors, including John Adams, did not maintain. But democratic diatribes on the formalities of these early years were not warranted by the facts. Good social form is not incompatible with republican self-government, and Washington, great gentleman that he was, properly sought to maintain it. If there were dangers to popular rights in these early years, they did not lurk in the presidential drawing room; and if there were some absurdities there, these were unimportant.

The Organization of the New Government

Indispensable as the first President was as a symbol, the carrying of the Constitution into effect was most dependent, at the outset, on the actions of the first Congress. The House of Representatives was the dominant branch, as had been expected, and Madison was the most conspicuous leader in that body at first, as he had been in the Federal Convention. Also, he was on terms of intimacy with Washington.

The most immediate need was for revenue and everybody expected this to come chiefly from duties on imports, which Congress was now empowered to impose. The first tariff act (July 1789) also had some moderate protective features. One sharply disputed question was whether there should be discrimination against countries that did not have commercial treaties with the United States. Madison favored this but Congress disapproved it. Congress did discriminate against foreign shipping in favor of American, however. Tariff duties were reduced on goods imported in American vessels, and the latter were subjected to considerably lower tonnage duties in ports than were imposed on foreign ships. These provisions worked to the distinct advantage of the American carrying trade, which had suffered grievously after the Revolution, and this enjoyed a notable revival during the decade. Also, the actions with respect to revenue had an almost immediate effect in improving American credit abroad.

The Judiciary Act of September 1789 provided for a Supreme Court consisting of a chief justice and five associates, and for circuit and district courts. Late in September, John Jay became the first Chief Justice, but it was some time before the federal judiciary had much to do. The Congressional acts creating the first executive departments were of much more immediate importance.

What the President most needed to gain full respect for his office was not pomp but power and the means to use it. The foundations of presidential power were laid in Article II of the Constitution, but this contains no details of organization. Three departments were provided for during the summer of 1789—State, the Treasury, and War. To head the first of these, Washington appointed Thomas Jefferson, then minister to France, who did not assume his duties until March 1790; in his place John Jay, who had been Secretary for Foreign Affairs under the Confederation and had little to do as Chief Justice, served temporarily. Alexander Hamilton assumed the Secretaryship of the Treasury in September, and Henry Knox, formerly Secretary of War under the Confederation, took over the same office in the new government. Edmund Randolph of Virginia became Attorney General, but he was only the legal adviser of the government on part time.

In the debates on these departments, Madison led the successful fight to make the heads responsible to the President rather than to Congress. Had this crucial question been decided the other way, the President could not have been the real master of his own household, and the executive branch could hardly have been co-ordinate with the legislative as the framers of the Constitution had intended. The expectation was that the department heads would act only in the President's name and would be his assistants. In Washington's first administration his assistants did a large amount of paperwork, but everything was supposed to clear through him and be subject to his approval. This included correspondence. At first Washington conferred with his department heads individually, and when he wanted several opinions he generally asked for them in writing. He was the hub of the wheel, for the departments radiated from him and he supplied unity through his own person. It would be hard to name a President who was a more diligent and effective administrator. He was industrious, prompt, and systematic; he did not spare himself and, without being autocratic, he was exacting of his subordinates. He wanted to gain respect for the new government by making it a good one, and he set a pattern of good administration which persisted through a generation.

It was expected that the Department of the Treasury would be closer to the legislature than the others. Direct reports to Congress were expected from the Secretary. As the law read, he was to "digest and prepare" plans regarding revenue and the public credit, and it was well understood that these were to be presented in writing, not in person, but in a special sense he had access to Congress. The Secretary of State, on the other hand, was expected to be specially close to the President and to have official dealings with Congress only through him. Washington was well informed about foreign affairs and had definite ideas about them, as he did about military affairs. He knew much less about fiscal matters and felt it necessary to give more rein to Hamilton than to Jefferson and Knox.

Hamilton had administrative abilities of the highest order, and in a very short time he built up a departmental organization that dwarfed the others. In his opinion, "most of the important measures of every government are connected with the Treasury," but some critical observers attributed this unparalleled growth to his personal desire for power. He had to gain Washington's consent to legislative proposals but not that of his fellow Secretaries. Circumstances had combined to give Hamilton an unusual opportunity. Yet his vigorous actions and distinguished though controversial public services were no mere accident of circumstance. They were the expressions of his constructive mind, his bold nature, and his particular variety of nationalistic philosophy.

Hamilton and His Financial Policies

Alexander Hamilton, now in his early thirties, was born on the island of Nevis in the British West Indies and came to New York as a youth to pursue his education and seek his fortune. The success that he achieved must be attributed chiefly to his own talents and energies. His marriage to Elizabeth Schuyler, daughter of General Philip Schuyler, allied him as a young man with an aristocratic family, but his ambition never ceased to drive him onward. He was briefly a student at King's College (afterward Columbia) and his precocious mind enabled him to gallop through his courses, but his intellectual interests were far more limited than those of Franklin and John Adams and Jefferson. Concentrating on law, finance, and government, he was masterful in those fields, and he might have become a great military commander had circumstances permitted. As an aide to Washington during the Revolution he gained the confidence of the General which was such an important factor in his later career. Though highly effective in paperwork in headquarters, he chafed under it and eventually resigned as aide, after an altercation with Washington which the General forgave but which revealed the impetuosity of Hamilton's nature. Finally getting an opportunity in the field, he performed brilliantly, emerging from the war as a lieutenant colonel and with a reputation for great personal courage. After that he practiced law and did magnificent service in the fight over the ratification of the Constitution.

His influence had been slight in the framing of the Constitution, because most of his colleagues thought he went to extremes in his advocacy
of a powerful national government. He wanted the President to serve
for life and would have liked to reduce the states virtually to provinces
or departments. Many leaders of the time were dubious of political democracy, but Hamilton was conspicuous in his distrust of popular rule.
It cannot be proved that he ever described the people as a "great Beast,"
but there is significance in the fact that the saying has been so often
attributed to him. He had little faith in ordinary human beings and believed that either force or interest was necessary to cement the government. In the light of the later success of political democracy in the United
States, his philosophy seems cynical, and undoubtedly he liked to exercise power and sought it for himself. But he also coveted it for his
country, believing that without it the new nation would succumb to internal dissension or external force. At a time when the Republic was
emerging from a condition of weakness, he performed an invaluable service in helping to make it strong. This he did, in the first place, by making
it solvent.

Establishing the Public Credit

The responsible leaders of the time were generally agreed on the necessity of establishing the public credit, but Hamilton was notable for the
scope of his proposals. His policies were unfolded in his successive reports
to Congress. These were presented in response to requests from that
body, but he did not follow Congress; he induced it to follow him. The
first Report on the Public Credit was presented on January 9, 1790. This
was followed, about a year later (December 14, 1790), by the Report on
a National Bank. A year after that he submitted (December 5, 1791) a
Report on Manufacturing; and at the end of his service as Secretary of
the Treasury he presented a second Report on the Public Credit (January
1795). Viewed together, these great state papers present a unified policy.
Besides establishing the credit of the new government, this policy was
designed to provide for the financial needs and further the economic
growth of the country. Hamilton gained his strongest support from the
commercial and the rising financial groups, who benefitted most directly
from his measures. There was no industrial group of any consequence as
yet, and his proposals for manufacturing had little immediate result. He
was most opposed by the agricultural groups—to whose interests he was
relatively indifferent.

In his first Report on the Public Credit, Hamilton recommended that
the entire national debt, foreign and domestic, be funded at face value
with arrears of interest, and that the federal government assume the debts
of the various states, which had been largely contracted during the War

for Independence. These proposals generally go by the names of Funding and Assumption.

There never was serious question about the part of the national debt that was owed abroad, amounting to about $12 million. The domestic national debt, which he estimated as amounting to about $42 million, involved more difficult problems. Most of this consisted of certificates of indebtedness, which are not to be confused with the virtually repudiated Continental currency or bills of credit. These certificates had been issued at various times during and after the Revolution; they had passed from hand to hand and had depreciated to the point that Hamilton himself said they might have cost a present owner no more than 15 or 20 per cent of their face value. Yet he wanted to redeem all of them at par, with interest, and he saw no practicable way to distinguish between original and present holders.

So great was the concern of most members of Congress for the sanctity of contracts that there was no serious objection to his recommendation, except on the ground of injustice to the original holders. Madison, the leading critic of the plan, agreed that there must be no repudiation, but proposed that present holders be paid at the current market price and that original holders receive the balance. His motion was defeated in the House, partly on grounds of impracticality. Speculators who now owned many of the certificates therefore stood to profit enormously, and a cry was soon raised against them, but there could be no possible doubt that the credit of the government was going to be firmly established.

Hamilton's recommendation that the federal government assume the state debts ran into much greater difficulty. There was no contractual obligation in this case, but he argued that the state debts had been incurred in a common cause, that they could be provided for in a more orderly and effective way on one plan, rather than on many, and that this action would increase national unity. Some people opposed it on just the ground that it would strengthen the general government and weaken the states by extending the financial sphere of the former, but attitudes were chiefly determined by the advantages and disadvantages to particular states. Virginia and most of the southern states had already paid off a considerable share of their debt, though South Carolina had not, while Massachusetts and Connecticut stood to gain from assumption. A further consideration was that most of the paper representing the southern debt had fallen into the hands of northern financiers and speculators, some of whom had acquired it recently in anticipation of the rise in values that would follow federal action.

The proposals of Hamilton served to draw a line of division between those states and groups that were almost wholly agricultural and those that were relatively more commercial and financial. The former had the greater voting strength and the result was that Assumption was defeated in a test vote. A period of mutual recrimination ensued and the business of Congress was at a standstill. The Secretary and his warmest supporters insisted that Funding and Assumption were inseparable, and for a time his whole program was imperiled. This was the situation in the spring of 1790, soon after the arrival of Thomas Jefferson at the seat of government.

The major objection of Madison and Jefferson to the Assumption proposal was that, in its original form, it was disadvantageous to their state of Virginia by not allowing credit for payments already made on its debt. Meanwhile, another question was pending in which they had more immediate interest: the residence of the federal government. The location of the capital seemed more important in those days of difficult transportation than it does now, and there was keen rivalry between the localities that were regarded as possible contenders. The President had set his heart on a Potomac site, and his fellow Virginians shared his feeling.

Finding his financial program blocked, Hamilton asked Jefferson to use his influence with the Southerners in Congress. In response to this appeal Jefferson brought the Secretary and Madison together for conference. Then a bargain was worked out. Hamilton agreed to a modification of the precise terms of the Assumption bill to make it less unfavorable to Virginia—by specifying the amount to be assumed from each state instead of lumping the existing state debts. Madison agreed to moderate his opposition, and one or the other of them suggested that the permanent seat of the government be on the Potomac. This was to be the sugarcoating of what many Virginians and Southerners would still regard as a bitter pill. Two Congressmen with districts on the Potomac were approached by Jefferson, and the Assumption proposal was adopted by a narrow margin. The Residence Bill, as enacted with Hamilton's co-operation, prescribed that the seat of the government should be for ten years in Philadelphia (1790-1800), and on the Potomac permanently after that. Senator William Maclay from the backwoods of Pennsylvania found consolation in the thought that the removal of the government to the Potomac might "give a preponderance to the agricultural interest." Jefferson himself never regretted the residence decision, but he afterwards reproached himself for having helped Hamilton consolidate his power and become invincible.

The Bank and the Constitution

When Hamilton presented to Congress his second great Report (December 5, 1790), the federal government had moved from New York to Philadelphia. In this strong and luminous paper he recommended the establishment of the Bank of the United States. His purposes were to facilitate the operations of the Treasury, to strengthen the central government, and at the same time to provide more adequately for the financial needs of the country. There were only three banks in the republic—in Boston, New York, and Philadelphia—and each of these had been chartered by a state. The institution he proposed was to be chartered by the federal government and make reports to it, but it was to be "under a *private* not a *public* direction," and was expected to pay profits to its stockholders. Three-fourths of the capital of $10 million might be subscribed by individuals in United States securities, and the government itself was to subscribe $2 million. The Bank was to receive the government deposits, which it could lend out at interest like any other deposits, and was to have authority to issue notes redeemable in specie, which were to be legal tender.

Hamilton thus maintained the initiative by making another bold and constructive proposal and he won a quick victory in the Senate. The chief practical objection raised then in the House of Representatives was that the government would be conferring more benefits on private stockholders than it would receive. The Secretary's plan was welcomed by holders of government securities and by commercial groups, who warmly approved his efforts to make credit more available for expanding business enterprise. Provision was eventually made for branch houses of the Bank, but Hamilton was opposed to these at first and he was charged with ignoring agricultural interests. Farmers required longer credit than this bank could be expected to provide, and suspicion of the rising commercial and financial groups was growing in agricultural districts, especially in the South. This suspicion was coupled with increasing fear of the extension of federal power and distrust of Hamilton, who seemed to be concentrating this power in his own department.

To a greater extent than hitherto, his critics now resorted to constitutional arguments. In the House of Representatives these were advanced most conspicuously by Madison, who asserted that the Federal Convention had rejected a proposal that Congress be empowered to grant charters of incorporation. He claimed, furthermore, that the ratification of the Constitution had been brought about by one set of arguments, while the government was now being administered on another. This was another way of saying that Hamilton as an administrator was trying to establish the sort of centralization that he had vainly advocated at the Federal Convention. There was considerable historical ground for Madison's arguments, but they were unavailing. The bank bill was adopted in the House by a majority of nearly two to one, early in February 1791. "Congress may go home," wrote Senator William Maclay in his Journal. "Mr. Hamilton is all-powerful, and fails in nothing he attempts."

The signature of the President was necessary, however, and Washington was much disturbed by the arguments of Madison, on whom he had long relied in constitutional matters. Therefore, he referred the bill to the

Attorney General, Edmund Randolph, for examination, and he was more confounded when that high official also declared it unconstitutional. Then he passed it on to Jefferson, who took the same position. The President referred these two adverse opinions to Hamilton; and, while waiting for that Secretary's reply, he had Madison draft a veto message in case this should be needed.

It is the opinion of Jefferson, which he drew in skeletonized form for Washington's convenience, that later generations of Americans have regarded as the classic statement of the doctrine of strict construction of the Constitution. He had taken no public stand against the bank bill, but he did not like it and by this time Hamilton had aroused the deep distrust of this lifelong champion of the freedom of the individual, who coupled a fear of governmental power with his faith in human beings. He regarded laws in general and constitutions in particular as "shields against tyranny"; and, while an advocate of the periodical revision of constitutions in the light of experience, he tended to be strict in his interpretation of their provisions while they were still in force.

His argument was based on the sound premise that the federal government under the Constitution is one of enumerated powers, all others being reserved to the states, as is specifically stated in the Tenth Amendment. "To take a single step beyond the boundaries thus specially drawn around the powers of Congress," he said, "is to take possession of a boundless field of power, no longer susceptible of any definition." In the powers specifically enumerated, he could not find the authority to incorporate a bank and to grant it powers historically belonging to the states, nor could he find it in either of the general phrases—the "general welfare" or the "necessary and proper" clauses, both of which he construed rigidly. Alarmed by the extreme claims of national power that had been made by some supporters of the bank bill, he was trying to find a safeguard against the dangers he perceived. He properly contended that large extensions of power should not be made on grounds of minor convenience, but he ran into the insuperable difficulty of finding an unvarying formula which would not put the government in a strait-jacket. In practice, Jefferson himself was not as inflexible as he seemed here, and this abbreviated opinion gives little inkling of his recognition of the necessity of growth and change. He believed that the reserved rights of the states were invaded in this instance. Nevertheless, he said that unless the President's mind was tolerably clear that the bill was unauthorized by the Constitution, "a just respect for the wisdom of the legislature would naturally decide the balance in favor of their opinion."

Hamilton labored on his answer until the last moment, and the lengthy paper that he presented to the President is one of the ablest that he ever wrote. Jefferson's argument in a nutshell was that the Constitution literally meant what it said, and the task of the Secretary of the Treasury was to demonstrate that it meant more than it seemed to. Basing his argument on the sovereignty of the United States within the sphere allotted to it by the Constitution, he proclaimed principles of liberal construction that have gone ringing down the generations. In his opinion, every power vested in the government carries with it the right to employ all means that are requisite and fairly applicable. These means he called "implied powers." In stating his own position with respect to implied powers, he practically took out of the mouth of Madison words that the latter had used a few years earlier, and he chided Jefferson for his extremely restrictive use of terms. Hamilton admitted that there is always chance of error and abuse when the literal meaning of terms is departed from, but he pointed out at the same time that a rigid adherence to the letter of its powers would paralyze the movements of any government. In his opinion, the bank that was proposed had a natural relation to the enumerated powers of collecting taxes, regulating trade, and providing for the common defense, and the bill was therefore constitutional.

Washington was sufficiently persuaded to give the benefit of doubt to Congress and sign the bill. This marked the highest point of Hamilton's success as a constructive statesman. It seemed to a number of his fellows at the time that he was interpreting the Constitution to suit himself and was wielding national power in behalf of the few rather than the many. But the First Bank of the United States justified its creation by its career as a financial institution (1791-1811). Though it did not do much for the agricultural population, it served business interests well. It was of great help to the government, but was not administered as a political institution. It was not subservient to Hamilton even when he was at the height of his influence. The constitutional arguments that he presented in 1791 were not then made public, any more than Jefferson's were, but they were afterward taken up by Chief Justice John Marshall; and to most later commentators it has seemed that Hamilton laid the philosophical foundation for a genuinely effective national government, armed with powers that time has proved to be indispensable.

Within the period of only a little more than a year after he submitted his first Report on the Public Credit, he had won clear title to fame as a master-builder. Until the end of the century this man of small stature, bold imagination, and imperious will was to remain a political Colossus, but his lust for power and lack of restraint were eventually to prove his undoing, and his days of great national achievement were soon past.

HAMILTON AGAINST HIS CRITICS

In the second half of Washington's first term the beginnings of an opposition party could be seen. At this stage it was an informal political grouping rather than an organized party, and it was derided by Hamilton's partisans as a faction. Its members described themselves as republicans, generally without a capital letter, and claimed to carry on the Whig tradition of the American Revolution, characterizing their opponents as monarchists or Tories. They could not properly be called Anti-Federalists since they were not against the Constitution, nor were they against Washington. They objected to certain ideas of John Adams that they labeled as aristocratic, but most of all they were against Hamilton, refusing to recognize him as the embodiment of the government. Out of these quarrels there grew the American two-party political system, which had been quite unforeseen by the framers of the Constitution.

Jefferson and the Opposition

Madison continued to be the most prominent public critic of Hamilton, and he did more than anybody else to organize the opposition to him, but it was Thomas Jefferson who came to be regarded as its personification. He and the Secretary of the Treasury were incompatible in personality and antithetical in philosophy, and he became the historic symbol of anti-Hamiltonianism primarily because of what he stood for and the kind of man he was.

The Secretary of State, who was forty-seven when he took office and considerably older than Hamilton, was undistinguished in physical appearance and had none of the characteristics that we commonly associate with successful politicians, except a marked talent for friendship. At the first meeting he seemed shy, and although an unusually facile writer he had no gift for public speech. His distinguished public services had been rendered primarily to the causes of freedom and equality of opportunity. He had left his mark on history chiefly as a legislator, and his experiences as governor of his own state during the Revolution had accentuated his distaste for personal controversy. In temperament and tastes this amiable man of learning and reason presented a sharp contrast to his ambitious, aggressive, and sometimes ruthless colleague, the Secretary of the Treasury. He was like Hamilton in his unusual capacity for work, however, and he could become passionately aroused in behalf of causes that he regarded as fundamental. Then his language often became extravagant.

He was relatively uncritical of Hamilton's financial policies at the outset. He had strongly urged that adequate provision be made for the foreign debt, and he had no sympathy whatever with repudiationists. At the same time, he was fearful of the growth of public debt and detested all forms of speculation. It seemed to him that Hamilton was extravagant in his policies and played into the hands of manipulators. His own major interest was in agriculture, though he had done much for commerce. He was opposed to the encouragement of manufacturing in

America, because he anticipated ill effects on the human beings laboring in it, and he saw no need to cater to the rising financial class. He
viewed all these economic matters as a conservative who sought to
maintain old values, and he now sounds rather like an old-fashioned
farmer. He followed the philosophy of laissez-faire and was against the
granting of special favors to anybody.

It seemed to him that Hamilton was building for his department and
himself a "phalanx" within Congress. This was not in accord with Jefferson's conception of the separation of powers between the executive and
the legislative branches, and he had occasion for personal annoyance
when Hamilton's followers blocked measures bearing on foreign affairs
and favored by the Secretary of State. The movement, which Madison
had revived, to discriminate against the commerce of countries not having
treaties with the United States was checked at approximately the same
time that the Bank measure received Washington's approval. Furthermore, the Secretary of State now had good reason to be suspicious of
his colleague's intimacy with George Beckwith, the unofficial British
representative.

Jefferson was in close touch with Madison and other Virginians opposed to the policies of the Secretary of the Treasury, but the direct part
he played in organizing the opposition was exaggerated by Hamilton's
partisans and has often been overemphasized by historians. In the
summer of 1791, when Hamilton's success was at full tide, Jefferson and
Madison made a vacation trip from Philadelphia to Lake George and
back through New England. Hamilton and his friends scented in this
trip a political plot to unite northern and southern opponents of the
Secretary of the Treasury. No doubt the two Virginians talked politics
in the course of their journey, but their predominant purpose was to
enjoy a holiday.

More important in the growth of the movement against Hamilton was
the establishment in Philadelphia (October 31, 1791) of the *National
Gazette,* under the editorship of the talented Philip Freneau. Hamilton
had his own organ in Philadelphia, the *Gazette of the United States.*
This was edited by John Fenno, for whom he raised money and to whom
he gave government printing. Freneau was not the only journalist who
spoke for the "republican interest" in this period, but he was the most
effective. He had been at Princeton with Madison, and it was this old
friend who persuaded him to set up a paper in Philadelphia. Former
associates in New York provided the financial backing, while Jefferson
gave him the vacant post of translator in the Department of State—
a part-time job paying $250 a year. This action was the ground for the
later charge of Hamilton that Jefferson had hired Freneau to vilify him.
Freneau proved to be a fiercely independent editor who was much
more extreme in his republican ideas than Madison or Jefferson.

By the spring of 1792, the *National Gazette* was filled with sharp criticisms of the Secretary of the Treasury and his "system." Hamilton seemed more vulnerable than he had previously, for a stock-market panic now followed a period of delirious speculation. The most conspicuous victim of the panic was William Duer of New York, a former Assistant Secretary of the Treasury and friend of Hamilton's whose fantastic career as a promoter and speculator in government securities brought him at last to debtor's prison. Hamilton suffered some discredit from these events, and he was publicly charged by Freneau with responsibility for the rise of speculation, while his "paper system" was sharply attacked in Congress. But his supporters could point to the continuing prosperity of the country as a whole, and it was a matter of more immediate concern to him that his special relationship with the legislative department was strongly challenged, for that was a blow at his power in Congress.

The specific question was whether Congressional requests for information should continue to go straight to him or should go to him through the President, as was the case with requests to the Secretaries of State and War. He won what he regarded as a vote of confidence on this issue, but these proceedings convinced him that Madison, co-operating with Jefferson, was the head of a faction hostile to him and his administration and "subversive of the principles of good government." He identified opposition to his policies and official conduct with opposition to the administration as a whole and sought to stamp it as "subversive." Within the executive branch he identified unity with his own virtual ascendancy, and by summer he concluded that Jefferson must be driven out.

Outbreak of a Feud

Unknown to Hamilton, Jefferson had announced to Washington his intention of retiring at the end of the presidential term. But Washington's idea of the best way to maintain the unity of the country was to keep within his official family representatives of different regions and opinions, and he continued to hope that the Secretary of State would stay. Jefferson, like Madison, was urging the President to stand for re-election. "North and South will hang together," he said, "if they have you to hang on." At the same time he was describing to his chief the causes of public discontent as he interpreted them.

Later in the spring (May 23, 1792) he sent to Washington a paper he had drafted, containing twenty-one "objections" that had been raised against the Treasury "system." Some of these were reported on hearsay and some were stated in extreme language. Jefferson did not advocate the overthrow of the Hamiltonian financial structure, since he believed that would be contrary to public faith. He wanted to check the movement toward arbitrary power which, in his eyes, Hamilton represented.

Concluding that these objections required an answer, Washington sent a copy of them to Hamilton toward the end of the summer, without naming the source. Hamilton immediately recognized it, however, and the document was fuel for the fire that was already blazing. In a newspaper communication signed "T. L." (July 25, 1792) he had charged Jefferson with hiring Freneau to revile the government.

Freneau vigorously asserted his independence and even swore to an affidavit absolving Jefferson, but Hamilton continued the attack on the editor as "the faithful and devoted servant of the head of a party." He was really gunning for the Secretary of State. By referring to certain episodes in Jefferson's career he tried to create the impression that his colleague was hostile to the Constitution and honorable provision for the public debt, and he asserted that the trend of Jefferson's doctrines was toward discredit, disorder, and disunion. After writing half a dozen pieces, he took time out to prepare for Washington a long and powerful reply to the twenty-one "objections."

Hamilton's defense of his financial policies satisfied Washington as to their soundness. What the troubled President feared most was disunity, and he regarded Jefferson's fears of tyranny as largely unwarranted. He himself disliked political criticism of any department of the government in newspapers, and most of all he disliked dissension in his own official family. He valued both Hamilton and Jefferson in their respective fields and saw no way to replace either one of them. Therefore, he now appealed to them in almost identical language to restrain themselves for the sake of the Union. In replying to these moving words, however, each of the rivals described his position and spelled out his indictment in more personal terms. Objective judgment of this feud is exceedingly difficult even now, but one person whom everybody can sympathize with is George Washington.

The battle behind the scenes was indecisive. Jefferson strongly reiterated his determination to retire, while saying that he would certainly not meddle in legislative matters now since he had never done so—except in the case of the bargain over Assumption and Residence which he so deeply regretted. The same could be said for newspaper controversy, into which he did not enter. He left no doubt, however, that he distrusted and detested Hamilton. Hamilton, on the other hand, claimed that he was the deeply injured party and, while admitting that he had had a part in the newspaper attacks on his colleague, he claimed that it was impossible for him to desist as yet.

He wrote at least a dozen more communications to the papers and these surpassed in fury those that had preceded them. He sought to display Jefferson as "the intriguing incendiary, the aspiring, turbulent competitor," comparing the supposedly modest philosopher to Caesar and Catiline. Following a common practice of his time, Hamilton wrote under a series of pseudonyms—"T. L.," "An American," "Amicus," "Catullus," "Scourge." The style and language of these pieces were not those of the superb opinion on the constitutionality of the Bank and the great reports on the public credit; they were those of the scurrilous journalists of the time, and they revealed the lack of self-control which Hamilton showed even more conspicuously later in his famous letter on President John Adams.

The defense of Jefferson by his friends was conducted on a higher plane. James Monroe, now in the Senate, and Madison provided the main reply. The account of the establishment of Freneau's *National Gazette* left some questions unanswered, but the discussion of Jefferson's attitude toward the Constitution and the debt was thoroughly convincing, and on the last day of the year 1792 they had the last word. The result of Hamilton's direct attacks on his colleague was not to drive the latter from an office he already wanted to relinquish, but to build him up in the public mind as an opponent. Hamilton did more than anybody else to make Jefferson the popular symbol of the opposition to himself.

THE VIRGINIANS AGAINST HAMILTON

The outcome of the second presidential election, in 1792, was the same as that of the first one. Washington, who was finally induced to serve again, received all the electoral votes, while John Adams was continued as Vice-President. Governor George Clinton of New York received the second vote of the electors from his own state and Virginia. Madison and Monroe were trying to forge an alliance with opponents of Hamilton in New York, though Jefferson believed that Adams deserved the vice-presidency on the grounds of long and honorable service to his country. Most people still regarded the two highest offices as nonpartisan, but the growth of republican sentiment was reflected in the Congressional elections.

The old Congress lasted until March 1793, however, and in this body Hamilton won a significant personal victory on the eve of Washington's second inauguration. The fight centered in successive resolutions introduced in the House by William Branch Giles of Virginia, a pugnacious debater. Giles was strongly supported by Madison on the floor, and had the spiritual support of James Monroe and John Taylor of Caroline, the two Senators from the Old Dominion, as well as that of Jefferson. The move against Hamilton can be best described as an assault from Virginia, and it reflected the intense hostility in that agricultural state to the Secretary of the Treasury and all his works. It began with a legitimate request for information about certain financial transactions of the Treasury, particularly loans made under authority of acts of Congress. Hamilton resented this request as an intended reflection on his official integrity, which it certainly was in part. There was some justification for the charge that this imperious young man had thrown a cloud of confusion over his complicated operations. He responded with a barrage of communications that revealed anew his extraordinary capacity. It does not appear that he had done anything injurious to the nation, but in his handling of certain foreign loans he seems to have gone somewhat beyond the authority given him by Congressional act.

Apart from partisanship, the point at issue was the discretion that might be allowed the administrative officer in cases of appropriation. Hamilton insisted that, in the public interest, he must be allowed latitude, while his critics argued for executive conformity to the exact letter of the law. This was another dispute over liberal and strict construction. The immediate question was whether or not Hamilton should be rebuked for specific actions as head of the Treasury and for his alleged disregard of Congress. The key resolutions of Giles were defeated by a vote of more than two to one, practically all of the Virginians voting consistently with the minority.

The Hamiltonians afterwards overstated the case when they laid chief blame on Jefferson for this attack, but they were wholly correct in identifying him with it in spirit. He did not instigate it or direct its course, but no doubt he was consulted and he probably drew a draft of the final resolutions—thus departing from his avowed policy of not intermeddling with legislative matters. He believed that Hamilton had exceeded his authority and took the extreme position that the Secretary of the Treasury should be removed from office. His own explanation of the defeat of the Giles Resolutions was that a third of the House was made up of "bank directors and stockjobbers" who acknowledged Hamilton as their chief, and that another third voted in ignorance or blind partisanship.

His charge that there was a "corrupt squadron" has often been dismissed as a partisan exaggeration, and if it be regarded as a reflection on the moral standards of a third of the members of the House it was clearly unjustified. But there can be no question of the great influence of the security-holding interests in politics at this time—when government paper comprised a far larger share of all investments that it ever has since then. Hamilton had carried out his avowed purpose of attaching powerful groups to the new government by ties of financial interest, and he had the strong support of representatives of these groups when he was attacked. Also, he had increasingly aroused the fears of countrymen like Jefferson and John Taylor of Caroline, who were old-fashioned in financial matters and abominated the speculation in government paper which Hamilton condoned. In later years, former President John Adams reinforced their judgment when he said: "The Funding and Banking systems, which are the work of the Federalists, have introduced more corruption and injustice, for what I know, than any other cause."

The Virginians had chosen their immediate issue unwisely and had weakened their case by carrying it to extremes. The Secretary of the Treasury could not be successfully challenged on mere grounds of fiscal administration, and this intemperate attack turned out to be a boomerang. His victory enabled him to regain ground he had lost by his own intemperate attacks on the Secretary of State, and at the end of Washington's first term his dominance of domestic politics was reaffirmed. He concerned himself greatly with foreign affairs, also, but he could not dominate them while Jefferson remained in office.

CHAPTER 2

The New Republic and the Old World, 1789-1793

DURING THE FIRST GENERATION OF GOVERNMENT under the Constitution, foreign relations assumed an importance in American affairs that was not to be approximated until the World War of 1914 ushered in a new era of global conflict and revolution. The scant respect in which the nations of the Old World held the young Republic at the outset was indicated by the scarcity of foreign representatives at its seat. When Jefferson became Secretary of State the emissaries of other governments could have been numbered on the fingers of one hand, and only one of them had a higher rank than that of *chargé d'affaires*. The mighty Empire of Great Britain was wholly without official representation. The foreign problems that Washington's administration inherited from the Confederation had been compounded by the weakness of that government and were accentuated by the continuing tendency of the powers to think of the American states in colonial terms—that is, as fair prey for imperial exploitation. Furthermore, the rivalry of the chief powers, Great Britain and France, constituted a continuing threat to genuine American independence, which required that the young Republic avoid being drawn into either orbit. Another grave danger was that the balance of power between Great Britain and Spain on the North American continent might be upset. The friendship of France, which had no possessions there at that time, could be very useful in this connection. The entire international situation demanded skillful diplomacy on the part of a weak nation.

JEFFERSON AND HIS FOREIGN POLICIES

The first department to be created by act of Congress was that of Foreign Affairs. The name was changed to Department of State soon

24

afterward when certain domestic functions were added to it, giving it even greater dignity and scope, and it has always been the ranking executive department. The Secretary of State was the agent of the President in promulgating laws and issuing commissions and in corresponding with states and territories. Also, he was the official record keeper of the administration and handled copyrights and patents. Yet Jefferson built up no large administrative department, as Hamilton did in the Treasury.

For the conduct of foreign affairs Jefferson was the most experienced man available, since John Adams was now Vice-President, John Jay was Chief Justice, and Franklin soon died. During Jefferson's five years abroad (1784-1789) he had observed Old-World diplomacy at first hand, and had viewed the political systems of Europe with a critical and discerning eye. No American public man of his day was more appreciative of the learning and arts of the Old World, or did quite so much to enable his own countrymen to share their rich fruits. The books and architectural drawings that he sent home, and his lifelong correspondence with European scientists and philosophers, demonstrated his attitude. He had become deeply attached to France and greatly admired her culture. He was delighted with the manners of the French; he relished their cooking and their wines, continuing to order these for himself and his friends— including George Washington—after he got home; and above all things he envied them their music. But he saw nothing in the political institutions of France or her neighboring countries that Americans should emulate, and much that they should consciously avoid. Fully grasping the realities of the power politics of Europe, he believed that the best hope for the young republic lay in the rivalry of the powers, and he hoped to play one against the other in order to gain advantages for the United States.

Consistency in methods cannot be expected of anyone who must adjust himself to the shifting currents of international affairs, but Jefferson was notable in the clearness with which he perceived and the consistency with which he pursued his major objective. This was simply the completion and the maintenance of American independence. On the economic side, he wanted to relieve American external commerce of the obstacles imposed on it by the restrictions of other nations, but he could do little along this line while Secretary of State, and his other immediate objectives now seem more important. These may be summed up under two heads. (1) He wanted to gain for the Republic at the earliest possible moment full possession of its territories, now encroached on by the British and Spanish, and to assure the free navigation of the Mississippi River, which he regarded as indispensable to the retention of the western settlements in the Union. (2) He sought for his country the highest degree of freedom of action that was consonant with existing treaty obligations to France, without subservience to any power.

He was friendly to the French as long as he could be, not merely because they had been friendly to him personally or because he loved their culture and was stirred by their Revolution, but because they had shown far more friendliness to the United States than any other power had, and because he saw no real conflict of interest between these two countries. He was under no illusions about the reasons for past actions of the French; he knew that they valued the United States as a makeweight against the British. He valued them for precisely the same reason, being convinced that the British continued to be the greatest foes of American independence. In his dealings with the latter he manifested a spirit of passionate American patriotism and argued his cases against them like a lawyer for the prosecution. Toward the Spanish he was more bellicose. This was partly because Spain, as a declining power, was more likely to yield to threats; partly because Jefferson believed that the rapidly increasing Westerners could and very probably would attack New Orleans if their desires were not attained by negotiation.

Nootka Sound

His objectives, attitudes, and methods were revealed early in his Secretaryship in connection with the Nootka Sound Affair (1790). The Spanish had seized some British ships in Nootka Sound on the remote Pacific Northwest Coast; and the British, fully realizing Spanish weakness, took this favorable occasion to demand not only an indemnity but a recognition of their rights to trade and settlement on the Pacific Coast. For a time war was threatened and into this France, who was still allied with Spain, might be drawn. If so, the question was whether or not the United States, under the terms of the Treaty of 1778 with France, would be involved. Actually, the affair resulted in a resounding diplomatic victory for the British, since the French declined to support the Spanish and the latter backed down.

Jefferson's greatest fear was that, if war should break out, the British would seize Louisiana and the Floridas from Spain. Since the British controlled Canada on the north and ruled the Atlantic on the east, they would then surround the United States, and he believed they would extinguish the country's independence. If anything would justify American entrance into a general war, he believed that the seizure of these Spanish possessions would. Yet he was fully aware of the advantages of neutrality and hoped by diplomatic means to keep war away from the North American continent. Furthermore, he wanted to seize this favorable opportunity to gain concessions for the United States from one or the other of the conflicting powers.

He was willing to bargain with either Great Britain or Spain. To the former he would have offered neutrality at a price—fair observance by the British of the terms of the Treaty of 1783 and assurance that they would not conquer territory adjacent to the United States. If Britain should refuse, he hinted that the United States might join her enemies. At the same time, he was prepared to hold over the heads of the Spanish the veiled threat of co-operation with the British, as well as that of action by the irate Westerners. But he also offered Spain neutrality for a price: relinquishment to the United States of territories east of the Mississippi. To sweeten the pill, he would guarantee Spanish territories west of the river.

These measures failed because the threatened war between Great Britain and Spain did not occur, but they provided strategy for future reference and proved that Jefferson was ready to favor or oppose any European power for the sake of American advantage. If he was anti-British during most of his public career it was only because he saw in the policies of the old mother country the greatest international danger faced by the young nation. While Secretary of State he had only slight success in his vigorous efforts to effect a modification of British policies, chiefly because the realistic Britishers saw no need for favors to the United States. Furthermore, they knew that his colleague Hamilton supported them in their position.

BRITISH RELATIONS, 1789-1792

Official relations between the governments of the United States and Great Britain were not established until Washington's first term was more than half over. Before Jefferson became Secretary of State, Gouverneur Morris was sent by Washington on an informal mission to England; he was expected to find out what he could about British intentions, and he was provided by the President with proper credentials. But George Beckwith, a young man who flitted between England, Quebec, and the United States (1789-1791), picking up information for the British, had no credentials of any sort. Very properly, Washington would have nothing to do with him; but Beckwith established friendly relations with Hamilton, and the President condoned the latter's conversations with the young Britisher in the hope that something could be learned from them. It is now known from Beckwith's despatches that he connected Hamilton with the "party of the British interest." When Jefferson assumed office in the spring of 1790, he declined to receive an unaccredited representative of a foreign power; and he dated the beginnings of his own breach with Hamilton from the time that he first became aware of his colleague's continued intimacy with Beckwith. Hamilton had revealed to the young Britisher, and therefore to the high officials in London, that he himself favored a different policy from that of the Secretary of State.

The Commercial Question

Differences between Hamilton and Jefferson on commercial policy became clear in the winter of 1790-1791. Jefferson correctly concluded that the British would agree to no treaty of commerce but expected to leave themselves entirely free to impose restrictions on American trade with themselves and their possessions, being confident that the Americans would have to put up with these. As he judged the existing situation, in which about 90 per cent of American commerce had returned to British channels, the only weapon that could be effectively employed against them, and the only threat that might cause them to be more amenable in other and even more important matters, was legislative action against their valuable commerce with the United States. Therefore, he approved the policy of "discrimination."

It might just as well be called a reciprocity policy, since the proposed action against nations not having commercial treaties with the United States was expected to lead to further treaties, based on considerations of mutual advantage. The immediate target, however, was British commerce, and the most immediate effect would be a reduction in British imports. The Secretary of the Treasury counted on the revenue from tariff duties in carrying out his financial program and wanted no decline in British imports. On these financial grounds he opposed this move against the British.

Early in 1791, anti-British sentiment became vocal in Congress. Through the efforts of Madison, a strong bill that had been drawn in imitation of the British navigation laws was favorably reported by a committee of the House. Its opponents, inspired by Hamilton, expressed strong fears that it might lead to war, while its advocates scouted these fears. The wisdom of the policy was never tested and the measure itself was sidetracked, but the mere threat produced some result as the British government decided to send a minister to the United States. The instructions to him left no doubt that his major object was to be the prevention of action against British commerce. Thus it appears that the weapon of retaliatory legislation was the only one in the American arsenal that the British really feared. There would have been dangers in wielding it in 1791, when Hamilton's financial system would have suffered from even a temporary loss of revenue; and perhaps it would have been better never to use it except as a threat. But the fact remains that the foreign policy of the Secretary of State was subordinated in this instance to the financial policy of the Secretary of the Treasury, and that Hamilton deprived his colleague of the best available weapon. Also, he further revealed to the British the sharp division within the administration on the question of foreign policy, and deepened the impression of American weakness they already had.

The Infractions of the Peace Treaty

The first British minister to the United States, George Hammond, aged twenty-eight, arrived in Philadelphia in the autumn of 1791. Soon thereafter the dangerous situation in the Northwest was strikingly illustrated by General St. Clair's defeat (November 4, 1791) by the Indians—whom the British were thought to be supporting. At this psychological moment Jefferson pressed on Hammond the American charge that the British had violated Article VII of the treaty of peace, by which they had agreed to remove their troops from all parts of the United States with all convenient speed, and not to take away American slaves or any other property. Compensation for the lost property in slaves was little more than a talking point with Jefferson. The crucial matter was the presence of British troops on American soil, infringing on the sovereignty and endangering the security of the nation. Supporting his allegations with documents, he challenged Hammond to present the British case in turn.

The British contention was that the Americans had violated Articles IV, V, and VI of the treaty. These stipulated that there should be no lawful impediment to the recovery of previously contracted debts, that Congress should recommend to the states that they make provision for the restitution of the confiscated property of Loyalists and British subjects, and that there should be no future confiscations or prosecutions against such persons. Hammond, who had rather indiscriminately collected the names of about a hundred state legislative acts and court cases, believed that these provided overwhelming proof of American infractions of the treaty; and, following his own instructions from home, he asserted that the British had suspended execution of Article VII because of these previous American violations. That is, the Americans had not only offended but had offended first.

Jefferson collected pertinent materials from the various states with the thoroughness of a scholar and marshalled his arguments with the skill of a great lawyer. Regarding the confiscation of Loyalist property, he showed that many of the actions complained of had taken place before the treaty of peace, and that the acts passed since the treaty related to confiscations made during the war, not after it. As to the restitution of Loyalist property, all that Congress had promised to do, or was constitutionally able to do, was to make recommendations to the states. Such recommendations had been made in good faith, he said, and had been complied with to a greater degree than had actually been expected.

The question of the debts of individual Americans to British creditors was more difficult. Jefferson found on careful examination that relatively few states had imposed legal impediments to the collection of these debts. Congress, moreover, had asked for the repeal of all such measures. What was even more important, treaties superseded the laws of the states under the Constitution, the courts were open, and debts were in process of settlement. Some states had tried to retard the execution of this article of the treaty, but Jefferson found justification for them in the far more serious infraction of the treaty by the British in retaining the Northwest posts, claiming that the British breach of contract came first in point of time.

He asserted that the British government, unlike Congress, had not acted in good faith, correctly concluding that the claim of the previous American infraction of the treaty, as advanced by Hammond, was only a pretext for a policy that was predetermined. The reasons for this policy—in terms of relations with the Indians, control of the fur trade, and the retention of a position in the Northwest—may have seemed sufficient to British officials while the survival of the American Republic was uncertain, but the policy was incompatible with a full recognition of American independence and sovereignty. While overzealous at times in defending his own countrymen, Jefferson made his main point that the prime responsibility for the nonexecution of the treaty was British, and the total impact of his superb paper was terrific.

By any standard that can properly be applied it was an official expression of American policy. Jefferson not only submitted it in draft to Madison and Edmund Randolph but also to Hamilton, and he took advantage of some suggestions of the latter. Washington approved the document as a whole. Hammond rushed to Hamilton as soon as he got Jefferson's "stunning reply." He maintained as intimate relations with the Secretary of the Treasury as Beckwith had, and continued to identify him with the "party of the British interest." According to Hammond's despatches to his home government, Hamilton now lamented the "intemperate violence" of his colleague and stated that Jefferson's paper did not really represent the position of the United States.

It would have been strange if the British officials at home had not interpreted this report to mean that there was no real reason for them to be troubled. Hammond referred Jefferson's paper to them, but they did not reply to it. The international situation changed for the worse before the year was out, and that made them all the more disposed to procrastinate. But they certainly had little reason to respect a government whose Secretary of the Treasury intrigued in secret with a representative of a foreign power to defeat the policy of the Secretary of State and President.

THE UNITED STATES AND THE FRENCH REVOLUTION

The French Revolution, which was destined to shake the Western World, had been going on since the beginning of Washington's first administration, but the course of events in France raised no critical questions of American policy until after Washington's second inauguration. Meanwhile, American interest in French affairs had steadily increased, and some alarmed voices had been heard above the chorus of general approval.

The attitude of the President himself during the first phase of the Revolution is significant. A few weeks after the fall of the Bastille (July 14, 1789), he received from his young friend, the Marquis de Lafayette, the key to that dismantled fortress and described it as "the token of victory gained by liberty over despotism." This prudent man feared that the reformers in France might proceed too fast, as did Jefferson, who was there as the American minister until he sailed home in the autumn; but both of them believed that the French were moving in the right direction. There was little bloodshed, and by adopting the Declaration of the Rights of Man and of the Citizen they seemed to be following the American example. Jefferson put the matter thus: "The appeal to the rights of man, which had been made in the United States, was taken up by the French, first of the European nations."

In Jefferson's judgment the French were not yet prepared for full self-government, and while he was in France he urged Lafayette to aim at a limited monarchy rather than a republic. His own basic opinions about American relations with Lafayette's country were reached before the Revolution and were independent of it. The monarchy was still absolute when he concluded that the maintenance of friendship with France would be to the interest of the United States. His foreign policy was based on his appraisal of the international struggle for power, not on his judgment of French political institutions. Nevertheless, as a philosopher and a human being he greatly rejoiced that the French were now following the Americans on the road toward individual freedom and self-government, and as a statesman he believed that the relations between the two countries would be all the friendlier for that reason.

This was the preponderant American opinion until 1793, when the situation was enormously complicated by world war and the Revolution fell into its bloodiest excesses; but before that date certain American leaders and groups had become alarmed. A conservative reaction had followed the American Revolution, but just as that was a relatively mild revolution the reaction was not extreme, and it led to constructive results in the Constitution. The conservative spirit persisted in many American minds, and as the French Revolution became more drastic there was a revulsion against revolutionary change, in the name of order and tradition.

In the English-speaking world, the classic figure in counterrevolutionary thought was Edmund Burke, who fired an opening salvo in his *Reflections on the Revolution in France* (1790). This was answered in a few weeks by Thomas Paine in the first part of *The Rights of Man*. Paine, whose writings had done so much to precipitate the American Revolution, linked the French Revolution with it. He dedicated the first part of his famous work to George Washington. Paine was an American citizen but he was living in England at this time. Though he was not yet attacking the English government and constitution as severely as he did later, he had joined battle with Burke in the realm of ideas. Thus the issue was drawn between order and tradition on the one hand, and revolutionary change in behalf of human rights on the other.

In the United States, meanwhile, John Adams had made himself a major spokesman of antirevolutionary thought. His *Discourses on Davila* had begun to appear in a newspaper, though this work was much too ponderous for the popular taste and publication was discontinued. It was hard to understand just what Adams was saying but he sounded aristocratic, and he was arrayed on the side opposite Paine when the first part of *The Rights of Man* was published in America in 1791. The publicizing of Jefferson's private endorsement of the work, and his implied criticism of Adams, served to align the Secretary of State in the public mind with the revolutionists and against the traditionalists. Americans generally viewed with satisfaction the progress of the French in the struggle for human rights; in most quarters they hailed Paine and criticized John Adams. Even Hamilton admitted that the episode contributed to the latter's unpopularity. At the same time it served to build up Jefferson in the public mind as a champion of humanity.

During the year 1792, when Jefferson and Hammond were engaged in their diplomatic duel and the feud between Hamilton and Jefferson burst into the newspapers, American sentiment continued to be strongly favorable to France and her Revolution, despite the fact that the tempo of revolution was accelerated and that there was more solid ground for the fears of disquieted conservatives. War broke out between France on the one hand and Austria and Prussia on the other in the spring of 1792. The external foes of France were antirevolutionary, and King Louis XVI was deposed in August on the strong supposition that he was conspiring with them. Gouverneur Morris, the American minister in France, whose indiscreet expression of antirevolutionary sentiments greatly embarrassed his own government, recognized that the question had resolved itself into a choice between an absolute monarchy and a republic. His own sympathies were with the former, but a republic was soon set up, with the accompaniment of considerable bloodshed. Meanwhile, attacks on propertied and religious groups had increased, and these excited in many American minds new fears of "leveling" and atheism.

As distant spectators of the European war, most Americans were still strongly pro-French in sentiment, and they greeted the establishment of the French Republic with great enthusiasm. In the *National Gazette,* Philip Freneau hailed in verse the triumph of freedom, and others confidently predicted that in all Europe the "Reign of Despotism" would not survive the eighteenth century. Even Hamilton admitted that American opinion strongly supported the establishment of a republican government in France, and Jefferson, letting his enthusiasm run away with him, stated that 99 per cent of the American citizens did. In his extreme old age, when he could look back on the full course of the Revolution and the many years of war that followed it, he concluded that his original judgment that the French were not yet ready for a republic was the right one. But at the beginning of the year 1793 he said, in an extravagantly worded private letter: "The liberty of the whole earth was depending on the issue of the contest, and was ever such a prize won with so little innocent blood." John Adams, always more skeptical than his optimistic friend Jefferson, proved to be the better prophet. He was already convinced that the accession to power of each successive revolutionary group would be marked by the destruction of its predecessor, and that force would prevail in the end.

This turned out to be a different sort of revolution from the one that Adams and Jefferson promoted in their own country in 1776. This was partly because it was directed against far greater evils, and in a society untrained in self-government tended toward excess; and partly because the French Revolution was more endangered from without. It was under conditions of external danger that the French deposed their King. They executed him early in 1793, and within a matter of weeks were involved in war with the British, the Dutch, and the Spanish. These events and circumstances had a marked effect on American opinion and forced on the government of the United States grave decisions.

AMERICAN NEUTRALITY, 1793

Americans learned of the execution of King Louis XVI about the middle of March; and the report of war between France and Great Britain was received in April. The news of the execution of the King, who had been so often referred to in diplomatic communications as the "best and greatest friend" of the United States, shocked Americans, who had already been grieved by reports of the imprisonment of a true friend, the Marquis de Lafayette. Opinions varied but the most prevalent one, probably, was that the success of the new French Republic was still greatly to be desired, deeply as the circumstances were to be regretted.

Formulating a Policy

Congress was not in session and the President had gone home to Mount Vernon, expecting to remain a month. The Secretary of State, who had relieved Washington's mind by informing him of his own decision to remain in the government a little longer, was still in Philadelphia. After hearing the news from abroad, the President came back to the seat of government as fast as he could and, on April 22, 1793, he issued the Proclamation of Neutrality, which was destined to serve as a guidepost of American foreign policy for more than a century. This he did on the unanimous recommendation of his department heads. For several months he had been consulting them as a group about foreign affairs.

The spread of the European conflict to include the British meant that war would now be waged on the Atlantic and in the Caribbean, and that American commerce would be affected. That was not the worst of the situation, however. The United States was bound by treaty to France. The entrance of Spain into the war against France a few weeks later complicated things further, for her shift to the British side upset the balance of power on the North American continent by allying the two empires that maintained troops on United States soil. There were dangers in an American policy of complete isolation, but these were not so grave or so immediate as those of involvement in the war, and all the members of the Cabinet wanted to stay out of it. Indeed, a policy of neutrality had been anticipated by tentative instructions that Jefferson had already sent to American representatives abroad.

While there was basic agreement within the government as to national policy, there was considerable difference of opinion about desirable procedure, and a sharp conflict in attitudes toward the war itself. Hamilton was an outspoken admirer of British political institutions and social organization, and he had no sympathy whatever with the ideas that had been loosed by the French Revolution. He would have liked to see the French monarchy restored, and his heart was with the counter-revolutionaries. He was convinced that peace with Great Britain was necessary for the continued success of his financial system. The danger in his attitude lay in the possibility that he would go so far in his efforts to conciliate the British that he would risk an outright break with France.

Jefferson, besides being very conscious of the value of French friendship and more fearful than Hamilton of British dominance, had become increasingly convinced of the bearing that the success of the French Republic had on that of the American experiment in republican self-government. He feared that the counter-revolutionary tide might engulf his own country, and he regarded the enemies of France as "conspirators against human liberty." He could not be indifferent to the outcome of a struggle between republicanism and monarchy which, as he correctly perceived, had world-wide implications. Nevertheless, he was convinced that the United States must play a neutral role in order to survive. He believed the nation could gain more for itself and serve the cause of liberty best by keeping out of this conflict, while maintaining an attitude of benevolence towards France.

Washington differed from his two chief lieutenants in being more moderate and better balanced than either one of them. He had no such admiration of England as Hamilton's, no such love for France as Jefferson's; and this practical man was disposed to minimize the conflict of ideologies. He wanted to keep wholly out of foreign squabbles and believed that nothing less than "imperious necessity" should occasion a breach between the United States and any European nation. On grounds of prudence, if for no other reason, he believed in *real* neutrality.

Chief credit for the promptness in issuing the Proclamation belongs to Hamilton and the President. There was no precedent for a presidential action, and the power to declare war was expressly assigned to Congress by the Constitution. Jefferson raised the question, therefore, whether the President by declaring "no war" would not be infringing on the prerogatives of Congress and limiting its future freedom of action. Hamilton was characteristically impatient with such scruples and Jefferson yielded this point, recognizing that the calling of Congress would have created unnecessary excitement and that Washington had no thought of infringing on the freedom of action of that body when it should meet.

Also, Jefferson saw advantages in delay, since he was hoping to exploit the situation by exacting from the British some concessions as the price of neutrality. From what we now know, however, it seems most unlikely that they would have conceded anything, and Hamilton's judgment that the dangers of the hour would brook no delay appears to have been correct. The pressing danger was that some Americans might enter into privateering or other unneutral activities and unwittingly involve the country. As Jefferson himself put the matter, citizens must be reminded that they were not free "to take side with either party and enrich themselves by depredations on the commerce of the other."

As a concession to Jefferson, the word "neutrality" was not used in the brief Proclamation, which was drafted by Edmund Randolph. This stated that the duty and interest of the United States required "friendly and impartial" conduct toward the belligerent powers, and exhorted and warned the citizens to avoid any actions tending to contravene such disposition. From the beginning everybody called it a Neutrality Proclamation, and it was welcomed as an assurance of the peace that everybody wanted, though some questioned the President's authority to issue it and a good many people wondered how this action could be reconciled with treaty obligations to France. The Cabinet took up that question promptly, and the ensuing debate between Hamilton and Jefferson behind the scenes may be compared to the one on the constitutionality of the Bank. The outcome was just the reverse, however, for Washington accepted Jefferson's interpretation.

French Relations and Fair Neutrality

All of the high executive officials recognized that the treaty of alliance and the treaty of amity and commerce with France, both of which dated back to the American Revolution, might prove embarrassing and limit the freedom of action that they all wanted for their own country. But Hamilton was much more alarmed than Jefferson. The Secretary of the Treasury, scenting grave and immediate danger, proposed a very simple solution of the problem. He would declare the treaties void, or at least suspended, on the ground that they had been made with a royal government no longer in existence. Furthermore, he argued that France was the aggressor in this war and had issued a general invitation to revolution and insurrection, while the alliance with the United States was wholly defensive. In his interpretation of the war he closely followed the British line, he strongly implied that he preferred a monarchical to a republican form of government, and he seemed willing to flout past international commitments for reasons of mere national convenience.

Jefferson had no difficulty in demolishing this extreme position. In the paper that he submitted to Washington (April 28, 1793) he showed that he was as anxious as Hamilton that his own country should escape embarrassment, but he could not agree that one nation is relieved of its treaty obligations to another because of a change in the form of the latter's government. He reasserted the principle on which the American republic had been founded, namely, that any country has a right to form whatever sort of government it likes. Believing that the people not the government constitute a nation, he regarded the treaties as still binding. He recognized the right of a nation to annul a treaty under circumstances of extreme and imminent danger, but such circumstances he did not now perceive.

Specifically, the provisions of the treaties that might cause embarrassment were: (1) the guarantee of French possessions in the New World, that is, the remnant of the French West Indies; (2) the promise to admit the prizes of France to American ports and to deny this privilege to her enemies; (3) the promise that enemy privateers should not be fitted out in American ports, which might be interpreted by the French as granting them this privilege. As to the first of these, Jefferson doubted if the

French would ever invoke the guarantee, since the United States could not possibly defend the French West Indies. As to the second, he saw no reason for the British to object, since they had incorporated similar provisions in their own treaties. As to the third, there was no need to accept the hypothetical French interpretation and he was opposed to doing so, since that would be unneutral. Events were soon to show that difficulties were to center on this third question, but Jefferson stood his ground on that against the French, and his guess that the other two would cause no trouble was borne out. Washington was warranted in accepting this interpretation of American obligations on practical as well as theoretical grounds. If a middle course of genuine independence was to be followed, there was no point in escaping from the embrace of France to fly to the arms of Great Britain.

Further problems were raised by the approach of a new French minister, Edmond Charles Genêt, known as "Citizen Genêt," who represented the French Republic not the King. Washington had already decided to receive him and the Cabinet approved this decision, but Hamilton wanted some reservations about the applicability of the treaties to be expressed. His argument was that non-renunciation of the treaties and unqualified reception of the French minister would be interpreted as siding with France. Jefferson said that nothing of the sort would be implied, but that positive action against the treaties and the minister would unquestionably be interpreted as favoritism to Great Britain and an insult to France. Washington agreed with him.

Even more important than the announcement of the policy of neutrality was the interpretation and application of it, and the chief burden of this fell inevitably on the Secretary of State. The American people were by no means impartial in spirit. As spectators of the European conflict they took sides violently, and their attitudes toward the official policy of the nation were strongly colored by emotions. At first, anti-British sentiment increased. About six weeks after the Proclamation, Jefferson said in a private letter to James Monroe: "The war between France and England seems to be producing an effect not contemplated. All the old spirit of 1776 is being rekindled." Though he was pleased at this, he realized that it would complicate his own official problems. "I wish we may be able to repress the spirits of the people within the limits of a fair neutrality," he said.

There was considerable difference of opinion as to what constituted "fair neutrality." While Jefferson was convinced that Washington would do his best to hold the balance even, he was equally convinced that Hamilton would try to tilt it in the British direction. In view of his own sentiments, it was ironical that his chief difficulties as an official arose from French actions. It was to the irrepressible emissary Genêt that he set forth the "twin principles" of neutrality, as he understood them.

The first and most obvious of these was the *right* of a neutral nation to prevent a warring power from infringing on its sovereignty; the second was the *duty* of a neutral country to prohibit actions that would injure one of the belligerents. The policy that he thus defined was notable for its express recognition of positive obligations, and it set a high standard of conduct for the young republic. A quarter of a century later, George Canning said in the British House of Commons: "If I wished for a guide in a system of neutrality, I should take that laid down by America in the days of the Presidency of Washington and the secretaryship of Jefferson, in 1793." Even in 1793 British officials admitted in private that the American policy was administered in a spirit of commendable fairness. They got more from the Secretary of State than they had anticipated, while Genêt got less than he had expected from an ally.

An Envoy Causes Trouble

Citizen Genêt had been ejected from the court of Catherine II of Russia because of his revolutionary sentiments. He was a well-educated man and an excellent linguist, but what most commended him to the group then in the ascendancy in France, the Girondists, was his ardor. French diplomacy entered a new phase when the Girondists imparted to it missionary zeal. Genêt was expected to be an evangel to the American people; he was to ring the changes on the beautiful words—liberty, equality, and fraternity—while assiduously seeking to advance the interests of a warring nation. He was instructed to observe diplomatic forms, however, and many of his troubles can be attributed to his failure to do so. He landed in Charleston on April 8, 1793, but more than five weeks passed before he presented his credentials in Philadelphia. Meanwhile, on the soil of a foreign country, he freely engaged in independent political and military actions of a grave nature, putting his own interpretation on his country's rights.

Genêt reached the American shore before the issuance of the Proclamation of Neutrality, which he did not anticipate, and he received a friendly reception, Governor William Moultrie of South Carolina being especially cordial and co-operative. The general object of his mission was to identify the United States as much as possible with the French cause, but he had other purposes that were more specifically related to the war. One of these was to use the United States as a vantage point for privateering against British commerce, while another was to send expeditions against the Spanish in Florida and Louisiana. In Charleston he commissioned privateers, which were largely manned by American citizens, and he later boasted that, while minister, he sent out fourteen vessels that took eighty prizes. During his stay in Charleston he set plans afoot for an expedition against Florida, and he left these in charge of the

French consul, Citizen Mangourit, whom he described as an excellent patriot. He hoped to get advance payments on the American debt to France to support his anti-Spanish designs, including an expedition against Louisiana under George Rogers Clark, which he worked on after arriving in Philadelphia.

Genêt himself described his journey northward as an "uninterrupted succession of civic fetes" and his entrance into Philadelphia as a "triumph of liberty." He went overland through the interior, instead of by water, hoping to stir up enthusiasm among the liberty-loving people in the back country, and unquestionably he did so. But he was wholly incorrect in believing that sentiment was against the policy of neutrality. Furthermore, as a foreign diplomat he could not escape the necessity of dealing with the designated officials of the nation. He had a polite but cool reception from Washington and did not find Jefferson demonstrative, though he made a favorable first impression on that apostle of freedom. Jefferson was glad for the Republican Party to benefit from any enthusiasm that Genêt might generate, but as a friend of France he tried to restrain the fiery young Frenchman, and as a responsible official he resisted the actions of his that were incompatible with the policy of the government and dangerous to the safety of the country.

At this time relations between the United States and Spain were strained, and in June the Cabinet believed that war was likely. Jefferson was less suspicious of Genêt's anti-Spanish design than of any other. He wrote a letter of introduction to Governor Shelby of Kentucky for André Michaux, who was going there "in pursuit of objects of natural history." The scientific project unquestionably interested Jefferson, but he also had reason to believe that Michaux had a place in Genêt's plans. Jefferson reminded the French minister that Kentuckians would suffer extreme legal penalties if they attacked Louisiana from American soil, but said that, apart from this consideration, he did not care what insurrections should be excited in Louisiana. In this matter Jefferson was neither neutral in spirit nor discreet in language, but he coveted the mouth of the Mississippi for the United States, not France. He afterward sent warnings to the Governor of Kentucky and other officials, and saw that the forms of neutrality were observed. A further reason for the failure of Genêt's plans against the Spanish was his inability to get advance payments on the debt of the United States to France from Hamilton.

Genêt's actions with respect to prizes and privateers created more difficult and vexatious problems than his designs against Spain did. According to the treaty the French had the right to bring prizes into American ports, and the frigate L'Embuscade brought one to Philadelphia before Genêt himself got there. This was the British merchant ship Grange, whose arrival created great excitement. The enthusiasm of French sympathizers was short-lived, however, since the capture had been made in

Delaware Bay—that is, in American waters—and the restoration of the vessel was promptly ordered. This was a clear case of infringing on American sovereignty, but other cases were more difficult in the lack of a precise statement of the extent of American maritime jurisdiction. It was in the autumn of 1793 that the historic three-mile limit was set. This was supposed to represent the furthest range of a cannon ball. Other difficulties arose when the French set up consular courts in the United States to try prize cases, instead of letting them be handled by American tribunals. Genêt's contention was that the French had the right to do what they pleased with prizes after they brought them in, but the United States could not tolerate such an infringment on its sovereignty. Genêt never backed down, but by means of warnings and threats the government succeeded in deterring the consuls. The worst offender, Vice-Consul Duplaine in Boston, was dismissed.

The recruiting of American sailors for purposes of privateering was forbidden by the United States government, but the latter suffered a rebuff in its effort to punish such enlistment. Gideon Henfield, an American serving on a French privateer, was arrested and tried before the United States Circuit Court sitting in Philadelphia. The jury acquitted him despite the evidence and the judge's charge that the service was punishable. This verdict was acclaimed by Freneau's *National Gazette* and other Republican papers. It strengthened Genêt's delusion that the people were for him even though the government was against him. He continued to arm and outfit privateers, despite the express prohibition of such action, and by midsummer his relations with the high officials reached the breaking point.

The Downfall of Genêt

The most notorious case was that of the *Little Democrat*. When the French captured this former British merchantman (then the *Little Sarah*) the vessel was already partly armed. After she had been further armed and equipped as a privateer in Philadelphia she was about to put to sea when the state and federal authorities were apprised of the situation, at a time when Washington was out of town. Genêt flew into a "great passion" when interviewed by Alexander J. Dallas, secretary of Governor Mifflin of Pennsylvania, threatening an appeal from the President to the people. He was also furious when Jefferson talked with him. Though the vessel dropped a little way down the Delaware River, she did not actually put to sea until after Washington got back (July 11) and took matters in hand. The question was what means the government should or could employ to stop her. Hamilton and Knox favored forcible action, arguing that if there were none the British would have just cause for war. Jefferson opposed such action on the practical ground that it would be ineffective and because he believed that it would bring on war with France, while the failure to employ force would not bring on war with Great Britain. Washington followed Jefferson's judgment, and Genêt merely received a letter telling him that he was expected to detain the vessel. This he did not do. The British, convinced by now of the sincerity of the American government in the matter of neutrality, took the position that the United States had been forced to submit to an indignity because of lack of military preparation. Thus the war threat lifted but Genêt had sealed his doom as an accredited representative.

His private threat to appeal from Washington to the people was brought into the open by Hamilton in the first of a newspaper series signed "No Jacobin" (July 31, 1793), and the public rallied to the support of their President against a foreigner. Meanwhile, there was agreement within the government that Genêt's recall must be requested. Jefferson found it impossible to deal with such an incorrigible person; and he was convinced that Genêt was endangering the neutrality policy, playing into the hands of the pro-British faction, and seriously injuring the Republican interest. As an official, a patriot, and a Republican he wanted to get rid of the French emissary, but at the same time he wanted to reduce the risk of a break with France. Hamilton had informed Hammond that a breach was likely, and he and Knox wanted the request for Genêt's recall to be peremptory. But Washington caused more prudent counsels to prevail. Jefferson dispatched to France a letter which constituted a full exposé of Genêt's conduct and was all the more effective because of its extensive quotation of the emissary's intemperate language. At the same time a clear distinction was drawn between the American attitude toward this envoy and toward the French nation. Genêt was replaced by Fauchet. Rather than risk the chance of death at the hands of the Jacobins now in power in France, he remained in the United States, where he married the daughter of Governor Clinton of New York and lived to a ripe old age. The French government had found Gouverneur Morris as unpalatable as the American officials had found Genêt, and he was replaced in 1794 by James Monroe. These actions on both sides of the Atlantic were favorable to the preservation of American neutrality.

The Success of the Policy

While the incident of the *Little Democrat* was the most flagrant and notorious case of defiance of the government in its efforts to carry out the policy of neutrality, there were many other cases, some of them involving the British and many of them complicated by legal uncertainties. Jefferson, who was overwhelmed by the burden of administering the policy, suggested the reference of disputed questions to the judiciary; and in midsummer, on behalf of the government, he submitted to the Supreme

Court twenty-nine questions, most of which were actually formulated by Hamilton. Chief Justice Jay and his associates set a negative precedent when they declined to pass on these. Soon thereafter the members of the Cabinet themselves drew up a set of rules respecting belligerents, and, for this and other reasons, relatively few difficulties about armed vessels arose afterward.

Viewed as a whole, the neutrality policy of 1793 was not only wise; it was conscientiously and successfully administered. Whether it was more endangered by the British and their partisans on the right, or the French and their zealots on the left, will always be a matter of some dispute; but the government managed to pursue the safe middle course amid strong and changing currents of public opinion. Since Genêt was such a sensational figure, there is danger of overestimating his influence on these. The popular effects of his mission seem to have been at first a stimulation of enthusiasm for France, but later the accentuation of a reaction against her.

The year 1793 was marked by the organization of numerous Democratic or Democratic-Republican societies, and Genêt has often been held responsible for these. The most famous of them, the Democratic Society of Pennsylvania in Philadelphia, was organized about July 4; and it was regarded as the parent organization because it sent out a circular urging the formation of such societies in all parts of the country. These were nuclei for the Republican or Democratic-Republican Party, and more than forty of them were established during the decade, especially in 1793 and 1794. Unquestionably they were stimulated by the enthusiasm for the French Revolution, but these clubs went back in spirit to the American Revolution, and in form to English models as well as French. The claim that they were mere replicas of the Jacobin clubs of France was a partisan exaggeration. They tended to be centers of pro-French sentiment, nevertheless, and intemperate comments on the policy of the government emanated from them, as they did from papers like the *National Gazette.* Philip Freneau now showed how much more extreme he was than his supposed patron, for he continued to support Genêt long after Jefferson found the Frenchman unendurable and urged in private that Republicans disentangle themselves from the wreckage he had wrought.

The rage for Genêt and France and the French Revolution seems to have been greatest in Philadelphia, and John Adams in an extravagant utterance of later years said that only the yellow fever in that city saved the President from the madmen. This fearful epidemic reached its height in September and lasted until frost, paralyzing the operations of the government and carrying off some of the most ardent Republicans. It caused the demise of the *National Gazette,* though not of Freneau himself. The statement of John Adams was proof that there was hysteria on both sides. Essentially the reaction against Genêt was patriotic. It was skillfully exploited by Hamilton to the discredit of the Democratic societies, of the party identified with them, and to some extent of Jefferson. The Secretary of the Treasury remained the chief power in national politics and soon had no rival within the government. After Jefferson relinquished the Secretaryship of State at the end of the year, Washington found it much harder to preserve the balance and maintain a middle course.

CHAPTER 3

Hamilton in the Ascendant 1794-1796

GEORGE WASHINGTON WAS RELUCTANT TO RECOGNIZE the existence of parties, and the high appointments he made on Jefferson's retirement reflected his continuing desire to maintain a balance of opinion within the administration. While the neutrality policy was being carried into effect there was a large area of general agreement, but in cases of disagreement Secretary of War Knox nearly always supported Hamilton against Jefferson. Attorney General Edmund Randolph wavered between the two sides. He succeeded to the Secretaryship of State, and although this makeshift appointment was satisfactory to neither Washington nor Jefferson, Randolph was not regarded by either of them as a partisan of the Secretary of the Treasury. Neither was William Bradford of Pennsylvania, an old college friend of Madison's at Princeton who was named Attorney General in place of Randolph. More significant still was the appointment of James Monroe, a strong Republican partisan, to replace the counterrevolutionary Gouverneur Morris as minister to France. But Hamilton soon gained a control over foreign policy that approximated his dominance in the domestic field. This was specially reflected in the field of British relations. It has been said that Jay's Treaty might just as well be called Hamilton's Treaty.

Hamilton retired from the Secretaryship of the Treasury early in 1795, being succeeded by his assistant, Oliver Wolcott, Jr., of Connecticut, who saw eye to eye with him in all political matters and constantly availed himself of his advice. Knox retired a few weeks earlier and was succeeded as Secretary of War by Timothy Pickering, then of Pennsylvania but more closely identified with Massachusetts, a Federalist of the most extreme sort. In the summer of that year Edmund Randolph resigned the Secretaryship of State under confused circumstances which were exploited by Wolcott and Pickering to his political ruination, and the latter succeeded him. Meanwhile, Monroe let his zeal run away with him in France, and in 1796 he was recalled. Except for the negotiations with Spain, into which partisanship did not enter, foreign matters came to be dominated by persons who followed Hamiltonian lines.

BRITISH RELATIONS: JAY'S TREATY

Despite the satisfaction of the British with the policy of neutrality, Anglo-American relations sharply deteriorated in the winter of 1793-1794 for two main reasons. The situation in the Northwest had grown more critical, and in the course of the war between the British and the French the former took drastic action against American commerce.

In the Northwest the American position was one of great danger after St. Clair's defeat in the autumn of 1791. That demonstration of American weakness emboldened the Indians and gave new life to the British plan to create an Indian buffer state, which would have deprived the republic of all its lands north of the Ohio and a big slice of territory in western and northern New York. No responsible American statesman could consider such dismemberment, and a British proposal to mediate between the United States and the Indians was received coldly. But, while biding their time, the British from their seats in the newly created provinces of Lower and Upper Canada and their posts in American territory supported the Indians in their determination to maintain possession of their lands. A peace conference between American commissioners and western Indians on the northern shore of Lake Erie in the summer of 1793 failed completely, because of utter inability to agree on a boundary line. Colonel John Graves Simcoe, whose anti-American zeal exceeded that of his superiors in England, was now Lieutenant Governor of Upper Canada. A new American military expedition, commanded by "Mad" Anthony Wayne, had winter quarters in 1793-1794 at the site of St. Clair's defeat, and Simcoe strengthened an old fort at the Rapids of the Maumee to protect Detroit, which he believed to be Wayne's objective. Meanwhile, the Governor General of Canada, Lord Dorchester, in a violent speech to a delegation of western Indians (February 10, 1794), predicted war between the United States and Great Britain, after which the Indians might draw any boundary line they liked. News of this provocative speech reached Congress when that body was already seething with resentment because of British actions on the seas.

Infringements by a belligerent on neutral commerce that was thought to benefit the enemy might have been expected in a desperate war and, up to a point, might have been endured. The British were determined to take full advantage of their seapower by driving French shipping from

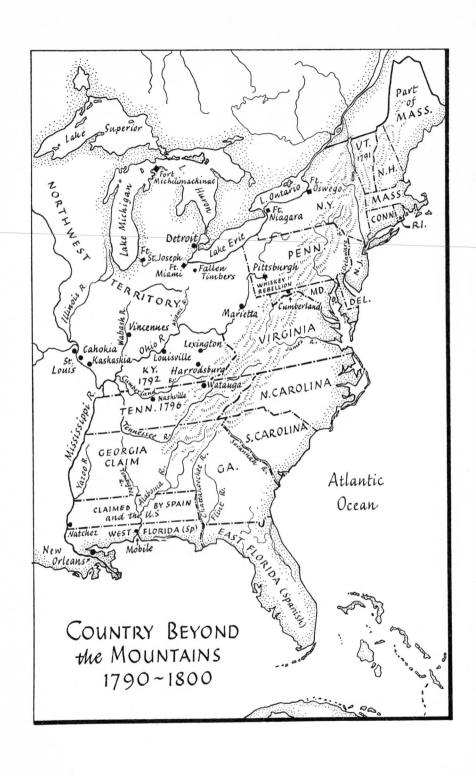

COUNTRY BEYOND
the MOUNTAINS
1790~1800

the seas and preventing its replacement by neutral shipping to their own disadvantage. Furthermore, they interpreted international law according to their own interests. Denying the validity of the principle incorporated by the United States in all its commercial treaties, that free ships make free goods, they asserted the right to take enemy-owned noncontraband goods from neutral-owned ships, and they defined contraband (which everyone agreed could be confiscated even if neutral-owned on a neutral ship) as anything that might aid their enemy, including food. By the Provision Order, issued in England in June 1793 and reported in America late in the summer, naval officers were instructed to bring into British ports neutral vessels carrying food to French ports. Compensation might be had for this, however. They revived the "Rule of 1756," whereby Britain had asserted that trade forbidden in time of peace might not be permitted in time of war (like non-French carrying of sugar from the French West Indies to France). The British policy came to a climax in an order of November 1793 that practically forbade all neutral commerce with the French islands and went far beyond the Rule of 1756. This order was enforced with extreme harshness and without advance notice. Several hundred American ships were detained, while their crews sweated in prison, and many ships were confiscated. The order was soon modified, but news of these ruthless actions created a wave of indignation. Even Hamilton described the order as "atrocious."

Jefferson contributed to anti-British feeling shortly before leaving office by submitting his long-deferred report on commerce (December 16, 1793). It described prewar conditions only, but this able statement of the treatment of American commerce by the various nations was anti-British; and the diplomatic correspondence that was submitted to Congress left no possible doubt of the British policy of obstruction and delay. Jefferson again recommended a policy of discriminatory legislation, and Madison shortly reintroduced the resolutions that the Secretary of the Treasury had caused to be deferred two years before. What with the reports of happenings in the Caribbean and of Dorchester's tirade in the Northwest, the anti-British feeling swelled into a tide which no one could stem. There was talk of sequestering debts to British creditors, and a temporary embargo was declared. Not since the American Revolution had the United States and Great Britain seemed so near to war, though the excitement was chiefly on the American side of the Atlantic.

Hamilton and his partisans executed a flank movement in the effort to preserve the peace. A group of Federalist Senators proposed to Washington that a special envoy be sent to England to negotiate a settlement of the various points at issue between the two countries. This proposal was accepted, but the suggestion that Hamilton be that envoy met with such violent Republican disapproval that it was dropped, and the choice fell on John Jay, who was highly acceptable to the British. Some questioned the propriety of sending the Chief Justice on such a mission, but there could be no question of the dignity of the appointment or of the experience of the appointee.

The Fruits of Jay's Mission

Jay's negotiations with Lord Grenville, the British Secretary of State for Foreign Affairs, extended over several months and the two men signed a treaty on November 19, 1794. Now that the secret archives have been opened up, we are in better position than his contemporaries were to perceive the weakness of Jay's bargaining position. The British knew that he was disposed to accept their contention about the reasons for retaining the western posts rather than that of Jefferson. To all practical purposes he got his instructions from Hamilton, and that anxious advocate of Anglo-American peace revealed to the British minister Hammond at the outset that the American interpretation of international law would not be seriously advocated, though compensation would be sought for the highhanded actions in the West Indies. Hamilton also secretly let the British government know that the United States would not join the Baltic countries in a convention of armed neutrality. The British may not have taken the threat of joint neutral action very seriously, but the treaty signed by Jay after Hamilton gave away his hand was far less favorable to the United States than the draft he had obtained earlier.

The treaty reached Philadelphia in March 1795 after Congress had adjourned, and Washington and Secretary of State Randolph did not like it. It was presented to the Senate in special session in June and discussed behind closed doors. After the elimination of Article XII, providing for limited commerce with the British West Indies but imposing at the same time intolerable restrictions on certain American exports, it was accepted by a bare two-thirds majority. The Senators agreed to keep the terms of the treaty secret, but the French minister caused an extract from it to be published and Senator Stevens Thomson Mason of Virginia released the whole of it. Then the storm broke. Nobody seemed to like the treaty except Hamilton and those closest to him, and he was stoned while making a speech in defense of it. Jay was hanged in effigy, but the main responsibility was unquestionably Hamilton's. Meanwhile, the British had issued another offensive provision order, and Washington hesitated to complete the ratification. He finally yielded to Federalist pressure and attached his signature, having concluded that he had no choice but to make the best of a bad situation.

Contemporary discussion of Jay's Treaty was highly colored by political partisanship but upon its face the settlement looked like a bad bargain. The chief American gain was the agreement of the British to give up the Northwest posts, but they did not agree to discontinue relations with

Indians on the American side of the line, and in return for their physical withdrawal from the posts, the United States government assumed the debts to the collection of which legal obstacles had been imposed by states. One wonders why Jay, the head of the federal judiciary, virtually conceded that serious obstacles to the collection of the debts to English merchants existed when the courts were open to them and decisions upholding British rights under the Treaty of 1783 were to be expected. The Americans also gained the right to appeal to a commission for compensation for shipping losses, and, as things turned out, they got more compensation than the government finally paid in settlement of the debts; hence this was not as great a blow to the pocketbook as had been expected. A principle which was to prove exceedingly important in Anglo-American relations was established by the provision for the settlement of these matters, and of northern boundary questions, by referring them to commissions for arbitration, though the significance of this precedent was not fully recognized at the time. In terms of trade, the only American gain was the opening up of the East Indies.

Besides the assumption of the debts, the price that the Americans paid for a formal settlement with the British was: (1) acceptance of virtually all British interpretations of international law, and (2) a ten-year guarantee against tariff and tonnage discrimination, with the right on the part of the British to levy countervailing duties. It seemed to his critics that Jay had surrendered neutral rights that Americans had long contended for and had bartered away a part of the economic independence of his country. Furthermore, the gains in the Northwest seemed less important than they would have a few months earlier, since the situation there had vastly improved as a consequence of Wayne's victory over the Indians at the battle of Fallen Timbers (August 20, 1794). This was followed a year later by the Treaty of Greenville, by which the western Indians ceded large areas in the present state of Ohio and acknowledged the exclusive protection of the United States. Finally, there was a serious question what effect the treaty would have on relations with France. If the French believed that the United States was being drawn into the British orbit, in violation of the terms or spirit of the treaties of 1778, they might be expected to raise strenuous objection. Thus there would be an increase in danger from that quarter. The strongest argument in favor of Jay's Treaty was that it preserved peace between the United States and Great Britain, with whom war would have been disastrous. Some interpreters of these events have taken the position that almost any treaty was better than none. But this one certainly did not amount to a full recognition of American independence, and even after allowance is made for partisan exaggeration the price of the settlement with England appears to have been unnecessarily high.

The partisan struggle by no means ended when the Senate accepted the treaty. The House of Representatives was called on to make the appropriations necessary to carry it into effect, and heated debate ensued. Important constitutional questions were involved and the alignment on these tended to be partisan. Washington assumed that Congress was obligated to pass the necessary legislation, and by refusing to submit Jay's instructions and other papers relating to the negotiations he upheld the prerogatives of the President and Senate in connection with treaties. The House, while finally voting for the appropriations by a majority of three (April 30, 1796), refused to concede the inevitability of such enabling legislation. According to this historic precedent, the House has the right to block any treaty that requires money or other enabling legislation; but out of respect for the constitutional treaty-making authority it has never exercised this right; instead, it has used it only to win influence in foreign relations.

THE RUIN OF EDMUND RANDOLPH

At the time of Edmund Randolph's appointment one of his friends expressed the fear that he had placed himself on a bed of thorns. Nobody would have found the Secretaryship of State a cozy berth at this juncture, and Randolph's character and circumstances were calculated to make him particularly uncomfortable. His entire public career showed him to be a man of vacillating judgment; and for a variety of reasons, including the long illness of his wife, he was in constant financial difficulty. His position in the administration was anomalous. He was a lifelong friend of Washington, to whom he was intensely loyal, and he had tried to keep himself uncommitted in the partisan struggles of the day. His personal associations were more with the Republicans than the Federalists, however, and he never enjoyed the confidence of the British Minister, George Hammond. Randolph thought it wise and proper to show good will to Fauchet, the new French minister, and went out of his way to be friendly. He was indiscreet at times, though hardly as indiscreet as Hamilton was in talking with Hammond.

Randolph's part in the negotiations with the British was merely nominal, and Jay adopted a patronizing tone toward him. He was in Washington's confidence, however, during the troubled weeks following the receipt of the treaty in America, and he defended it to Monroe, who was getting embarrassing questions from the French. In the summer of 1795, the Secretary of State advised Washington not to sign the treaty until the British had done something about the latest provision order, and while this question was still in the air Hammond intervened.

Hamilton was no longer Secretary of the Treasury, but his successor, Oliver Wolcott, Jr., had inherited his intimacy with Hammond. By that time, Timothy Pickering was Secretary of War in place of Knox. It was to

Wolcott that Hammond delivered an intercepted dispatch from Fauchet to the French government, and after seeing this, Washington yielded to the pressure of Pickering and Wolcott and signed the treaty. Several days later he allowed them to confront Randolph with the dispatch unexpectedly and to charge the Secretary of State with what amounted to treason. Confused and outraged, Randolph immediately resigned.

The dispatch referred to "overtures" made by Randolph at the time of the "Whiskey Rebellion," when the federal government was being defied in western Pennsylvania because of the excise tax. It mentioned civil war in the United States and the possible use of French money, intimating that certain "pretended patriots" had their price. The construction placed by Pickering and Wolcott on this was that Randolph solicited a bribe from Fauchet to further "civil war" in the French interest. But Randolph got from Fauchet, who was then on the point of sailing for France, what amounted to a full exoneration. Though Randolph had suggested early payments to Americans who were selling flour to France, he had sought no bribe, and he really wanted to *prevent* the "civil war" which he believed the *British* were fomenting. But the circumstances were confused, and some of Randolph's comments on the pro-French and pro-British factions were indiscreet and lent themselves to misinterpretation.

His own "vindication," which was published with badly translated documents a few weeks later, served to confuse the situation further. The net result was that an unwarranted partisan charge was perpetuated not only through the lifetime of the victim, who suffered further persecution, but until our own time, when at last its falsity has been fully demonstrated. The immediate result was that the Hamiltonian Federalists now became wholly dominant in the government. Randolph's place was given to the bitterly partisan Timothy Pickering, and he was succeeded as Secretary of War by James McHenry of Maryland, who gave allegiance to Hamilton.

JAMES MONROE AND FRENCH RELATIONS

Monroe arrived in France in August 1794, several weeks after Jay got to England. The two missions provide a striking illustration of the division of American counsels and policies at a time when the Western World was the scene of a duel between the two chief powers. On the one hand, Jay, instructed by Hamilton, yielded too much to the British; and on the other, Monroe, instructed by Randolph, manifested American friendship for France too exuberantly. Monroe's appearance at the outset before the National Convention, the governing body of France after the fall of Robespierre, was well calculated to advertise the friendship between the two countries, and this was dramatically sealed when he was kissed on both cheeks by the presiding officer. His actions and his overenthusiastic speech were not in the tradition of diplomacy, and in due course he was rebuked by Edmund Randolph for his excess of zeal. In emphasizing American friendliness, however, and seeking to overcome the bad impression left by Gouverneur Morris, this inexperienced diplomat was following Randolph's instructions; and he performed his functions diligently during the months before he got news of Jay's Treaty. As he was instructed to do, he assured the French that Jay had been forbidden to do anything contrary to the American treaties with France and continued to minimize the significance of the negotiations.

He knew nothing about these negotiations except what he learned from Randolph, for Jay haughtily refused to inform him of the provisions of the treaty while it was still unratified. The American government seemed to be following the policy of not letting the left hand know what the right hand was doing. After he learned the terms that Jay had accepted, Monroe was deeply embarrassed, since he regarded the treaty as a slap in the face of the French and thought of himself as an unwitting instrument in deceiving them. His resentment was not unnatural but his comments in letters that he sent home lent color to the charge that his sympathies with the French had led him to oppose the policy of the administration. It would have been better for him personally if he had offered his resignation at this juncture.

After the text of the treaty got out and the French interpreted it as a betrayal, Monroe was in an impossible situation. Matters became critical early in 1796, after the Directory was established in France and, under more orderly domestic conditions, greater attention was paid to American affairs. The Directory decided to send a special envoy to the United States, who would recall Adet (Fauchet's successor), announce the end of the Franco-American treaties, and then withdraw. Such a severance of relations might have gratified Hamilton and Pickering, but it was not to be supposed that it would have pleased Washington, and in the eyes of Monroe and the Republican leaders as a group it would have been positively disastrous. Monroe successfully argued against this drastic action, which would naturally be interpreted as the prelude to war, but in his anxiety to forestall it he was guilty of grave impropriety. In a letter to the French Minister of Foreign Affairs he said: "Left to ourselves, everything will I think be satisfactorily arranged and perhaps in the course of the present year." The French interpreted this as a reference to the presidential election of 1796 and the probable victory of the Republican Party. Far from being dissuaded from interference in American domestic affairs, through Adet they actually worked against the Federalists in the election. We now know more about what was going on than George Washington did; but by the summer of 1796 he was dissatisfied with Monroe, and Pickering had already decided to replace him with a Federalist. That decision did not become effective until several months

later, and its results were part of the heritage that Washington transmitted to his own successor. Monroe became another casualty of the
international strife that imperiled the independence of his country and
beclouded its domestic problems. He was not ruined, as Edmund Randolph was, nor was he hung in effigy like John Jay, but as a public man
he was badly injured.

SPANISH RELATIONS AND PINCKNEY'S TREATY

The settlement with Spain was the most important diplomatic achievement of the Washington administration. Political partisanship did not
enter into it appreciably, and credit for it must be given to several men.
Jefferson was its architect, though he had been out of office nearly two
years when it was effected. In the spring of 1792, following his recommendation, William Short had been sent from The Hague to join the
American *chargé*, William Carmichael, in Madrid, and Jefferson had
briefed them well. The spread of the European war and the unexpected
alignment of Spain with Great Britain destroyed the hope of immediate
results, but success came in 1795, the year the Spanish broke away from
their temporary alliance, made peace with France, and got ready for
war with Britain. They were alarmed by Jay's negotiations and appre-
hensive of an Anglo-American alliance, specially fearing direct action
against Louisiana by American frontiersmen backed by British power.
So the situation now opened which Jefferson had hoped for. The United
States could, as he said, "drive in the nail," that is, demand a high price
from Spain for *not* joining Britain against her.

Short and Carmichael had been vainly arguing and kicking their heels
in the antechambers of the Spanish court. The credit for speeding the
negotiations into a decisive phase belongs to Edmund Randolph, who
found out that the Spanish were willing to expedite matters if a minister
of appropriate splendor were sent. Randolph tried to induce Jefferson
to assume this role, but the former Secretary of State had no intention of
leaving his new-found freedom in the country for thankless public service,
and he claimed that he was suffering from rheumatism anyway. In the
autumn of 1794 the appointment finally went to Thomas Pinckney, the
American minister in Great Britain, a moderate Federalist and a South
Carolina aristocrat, who had all the desired personal qualifications and
conducted himself with dignity and skill. Guiding himself by the original
instructions from Jefferson and refusing to agree to any alliance or
guarantee of Spanish territories, he was firm at the crucial moments and
achieved complete success. The agreement goes by the name of the
Treaty of San Lorenzo or Pinckney's Treaty (1795).

By this treaty Spain finally agreed to the southern boundary of the
United States at the thirty-first parallel of latitude, recognized the free

navigation of the Mississippi, and granted the right of deposit at New Orleans to American shippers for three years with the promise of renewal. In direct contrast to the treaty with Great Britain, both parties promised to restrain the Indians in their own territories. Furthermore, neutral rights were defined according to the historic American contention, which Jay had yielded to the British. The treaty was so favorable that it was unanimously approved by the Senate. Important territorial questions were left to the future, but since Spain was a declining power the growing republic could afford to be patient. The treaty marked a long step toward the attainment of full independence. Since the Republic had now established its claim to sovereign rights in the Southwest, and British garrisons in the Northwest were removed under Jay's Treaty, the prospect of retaining in the Union the western settlements was greatly brightened. Western discontent was stilled by diplomatic action that removed its causes.

The "Whiskey Rebellion"

The resistance of the farmers in the Monongahela country of Pennsylvania to the federal excise tax on whiskey was an expression of western discontent with eastern policy which assumed the form of a local conflict with national authority. The "Whiskey Rebellion" came to a head in the late summer of 1794, when Jay had been several months in England, Monroe had recently arrived in France, and Pinckney had not yet set out for Madrid, but its political reverberations lasted through the election of 1796, at least. The trouble rose in a region where the distillation of whiskey on farms was more important in the local economy than anywhere else in the United States. Roughly speaking, this was the settled part of Pennsylvania beyond the Alleghenies. Pittsburgh, then a village with about 1000 residents, was the metropolis of the region, but the disaffection was greatest to the southward, especially in Washington County. Not only was whiskey a product of relatively great value and small bulk which could be carried across the mountains to the East for sale; it was a medium of exchange among people who saw hardly any money from one end of the year to the other. The salaries of church ministers were often paid in Monongahela rye whiskey, and the use of it was virtually universal. Part of every farmer's crop was turned into whiskey at his or a neighbor's still, and the beverage flowed like water. This was scarcely an earthly Paradise, however, for these people were generally poor, and the ready flow of alcoholic spirits in this frontier society was a substitute for a good diet and warm shelter.

In Pennsylvania, previous taxes on spirituous liquors had generally been imposed only when these were sold, and the tax could be passed on to the purchaser. Hostility to any sort of tax on commodities was traditional in America, and these western farmers, who were generally at loggerheads with the easterners in their own state, held all excisemen in contempt and often treated them very roughly. The federal tax of 1791, which was somewhat reduced in 1792, fell on the product of all stills, even those that produced whiskey chiefly for barter or personal use. Almost to a man the farmers thought it unjust to be taxed on their grain when, instead of eating it, they drank it.

The tax was proposed by Hamilton in order to provide for the costs of assuming the state debts, in which these frontier farmers were not at all interested, and it was adopted because nobody could think of a good alternative. The various officials received a percentage of the collections, and this arrangement did not endear them to the taxpayers. The larger and more commercial stills were in a better position than the small ones to pass the tax on to the consumer, and the spirit of resistance was strongest among the poorer farmers. They resented the inquisitorial methods of the officials and took special exception to the requirement that excise cases should be tried in the federal court in far away Philadelphia. Popular sentiment against the law was so strong that only the boldest of men dared support it. The two Democratic societies in the region did not create the opposition, for it was already tremendous when they were established in 1794, but they served as centers of disaffection.

A conference of protesters against the tax was held in Pittsburgh in August 1792. Besides drawing up a remonstrance to Congress, these men set up Committees of Correspondence after the manner of the patriots in the American Revolution, and, what was more alarming, they adopted resolutions against excise officers that amounted to defiance. Albert Gallatin of Fayette County afterwards bemoaned the fact that he signed these. At this time Hamilton believed that the employment of military force by the government was warranted, but the President thought it sufficient to issue a strong proclamation. It was signed by Jefferson as Secretary of State, who persuaded Washington to omit a phrase implying that the excise law was necessary. Later in private he described the tax as "infernal," but he did not countenance defiance of public authority. Things quieted down for some months after the proclamation, but all the stills were not registered by June 1, 1793, as they were supposed to be, and the attempt to serve legal processes in the following summer brought on open conflict. By that time the law had been changed so as to make excise cases cognizable in state courts when parties to them lived at a distance, but writs were nevertheless issued under the old law. Certain critics of Hamilton in the West saw in this procedure clear proof that he welcomed a test of strength and really wanted to provoke a crisis.

A crisis came when the United States marshal, who was seeking to serve processes, and General John Neville, federal inspector of the trans-Allegheny counties of Pennsylvania, were fired on. Neville's country house near Pittsburgh was burned and both men were held captive, though both escaped. The effort of Hugh Henry Brackenridge, a Princeton graduate and wise and humane lawyer, to stay the tide of passion was unavailing, and in August, at Braddock's Field, there was a muster of armed men, variously estimated as from 1500 to 7000 in number. But they were divided in mind, and the tide of resistance soon began to ebb. Meanwhile, there was rioting elsewhere, in states as far away as South Carolina, and revenue officers were subjected to some manhandling.

Hamilton, more convinced than ever that force must be employed, wrote a series of newspaper essays under the *nom de plume* "Tully," and said that the question was whether there should be government or no government. Though more reluctant to employ coercion, Washington agreed that the situation endangered the government, and on August 7, 1794, he issued a proclamation to the governors of Pennsylvania, New Jersey, Maryland, and Virginia which caused them to call out the militia of those states. Meanwhile, he sent into the Monongahela country commissioners who tried to get pledges of submission in return for pardon for past offenses. They believed that the majority wanted to submit but were intimidated by a violent minority. Toward the end of September some 12,000 militiamen began to move. Washington visited them briefly and Hamilton accompanied them at his own request. Under the command of Governor "Light-Horse" Harry Lee of Virginia, the army proceeded to Pittsburgh without meeting any opposition. Hamilton was conspicuous throughout the operations, and his critics accused him of highhandedness in the investigations he conducted. A small detachment of soldiers remained in the region all winter, and in Philadelphia trials dragged on through the year 1795. A number of arrests had been made but evidence of treason was hard to get, and only two men, both of them unimportant, were convicted. Washington pardoned both of them.

Many poor men suffered hardship, but the bill of costs was smaller than Hamilton would have been willing to assume in order to uphold the majesty of the law and demonstrate the power of the federal government. Hardly a voice was raised in the eastern settlements in defense of the rebels, though some people thought that they should have been charged with riotous conduct rather than treason, and that this ostentatious display of force against them bordered on absurdity. In his address to Congress in November 1794, the President condemned the "self-created societies"— meaning the Democratic societies, which were now being blamed by the Hamiltonians for all this trouble. Seeking to identify themselves with the forces of law and order, the Federalists threw the Republicans on the defensive, just as they had done a year earlier in connection with Genêt. The Republicans continued to insist, however, on the constitutional right of free men to organize for political purposes and, if they should see fit, to criticize the government. There was no necessary choice between anarchy and tyranny, and most people wanted neither, but the lines of future political conflict were being drawn and, through force of circumstances, Washington was identified more than ever with the Hamiltonians.

WASHINGTON'S FAREWELL ADDRESS

The Constitution did not prescribe the number of terms a President might serve, but George Washington limited himself to two and thus started a tradition. In 1796, at the age of sixty-four he regarded himself as an old man and was pathetically eager to go home. He was surprised and deeply pained by the partisan spirit that had manifested itself during the last two or three years. He wrote Jefferson in 1796 that "truth and right decisions" had been his "sole objects" during the time they served together. "I was no party man myself," he said, "and the first wish of my heart was, if parties did exist, to reconcile them." He was always disturbed by any criticism of the government, but not until the time of Genêt was much criticism directed against him personally. Attacks on the President himself increased after that, especially in connection with Jay's Treaty. Washington, who was an exceedingly sensitive man and had naturally interpreted his unanimous re-election as proof that all groups were behind him, writhed under them. He wrote Jefferson that he had been described "in such exaggerated and indecent terms as could scarcely be applied to a Nero, a notorious defaulter, or even a common pickpocket."

The first President did not recognize that abuse is one of the perquisites of that office. Nor did he realize the inevitability of his becoming a target of the Republicans when they came to believe that his administration had become a Hamiltonian preserve. But personal attacks on the revered President often turned out to be boomerangs. In his own state the opponents of Jay's Treaty overreached themselves, and they were wisely admonished by Jefferson to avoid direct reference to the President. Even in the heat of partisan conflict Washington continued to be a cherished symbol of national unity, and he still had reason to think of himself as the President of all the people and all the states when he released his Farewell Address. The document was unique, just as his position was.

Washington, who had no more confidence in his ability as a writer than in his judgment of constitutional questions, had turned to James Madison in 1792, when he was contemplating retirement at the end of one term, and had asked this friend to prepare an address for him. He told Madison what to say, however, and Madison sought not only to present Washington's ideas faithfully but also to employ his customary language. In 1796, the President resurrected this document and, being now on much less intimate terms with Madison, he asked Hamilton to prepare a draft along the same lines. Hamilton drew a fresh paper, but Washington took this in hand, restored some things from Madison's draft and reworked others according to his own notion. This case presents no close parallel to modern ghost-writing, for the paper clearly reflects Washington and his philosophy, and in it one can hear his very accents. Though always referred to as an address, it was not spoken to any group of auditors. Washington published it in the *American Daily Advertiser* of Philadelphia (September 19, 1796). As news, the most important thing in it was the announcement that the President intended to retire, but time has proved that the passages dealing with foreign relations were most memorable.

Characteristically, Washington urged his countrymen to pursue a course of national independence. He deplored passionate attachment or antipathy to any foreign country and warned against foreign influences in American affairs. He may have been thinking at this time of the French minister Adet, who was intriguing against him, but his warning could have been directed equally well against the activities of the British minister, George Hammond. In regard to foreign nations, he recommended as a rule of conduct that the United States have as few *political* connections with them as possible. He recognized that existing engagements must be kept, and he did not recommend the repudiation of the French treaties. He did not want to extend these engagements, however, and he advised his countrymen to steer clear of permanent alliances. He urged that the United States keep out of European affairs, which were of only remote interest to Americans. This it could do because of the detached and distant situation of the country, and he urged that it avail itself of its unusual advantages.

The significance of these recommendations did not lie in their novelty, for they were a natural outgrowth of the neutrality policy of 1793. The importance of the pronouncement lay in the fact that it was made by such a man at such a time. Inevitably it came to be regarded as a classic statement of American policy, and it served as a guidepost for a century and more—until the situation of the United States ceased to be "detached and distant," and from being a weakling the nation had become a major power.

Washington's eulogy of the Union is less often referred to, and he could not speak with the eloquence of Webster or Lincoln, but a generation that recognized the supremely important part he had played in creating the Union must have been impressed by his sensible arguments and moved by his simple expression of devotion. No one saw more clearly than he the ease and the danger of appeal to local interests, and he spoke for a genuine nation that should comprehend and advance the interests of all. It is doubtful if he fully perceived the basis of economic conflict, but he clearly foresaw the danger of conflict between regions in a large country. The worst of all parties, in his opinion, were those based on geography, for they endangered the Union. His words of warning could have been read to advantage in the 1850's.

There is little of lasting value, however, in his other reflections on political organizations, even though some of these attracted great attention at the time. He again condemned the Democratic societies, without mentioning them by name, believing that their real design was to interfere with regular governmental procedure under the constituted authorities. "They serve to organize faction," he said, and to him "party" was just another name for faction. He feared that the public councils would be distracted and the public administration enfeebled by the spirit of party. He did not value the services of voluntary organizations in the political education of a people, and had no conception of the legitimate function of political opposition as subsequently recognized in the United States and Great Britain. Even under a system of popular elections, the sort of unitary government that Washington favored had greater dangers of tyranny than this broadly patriotic and genuinely untyrannical man perceived. He was unwittingly arguing the case for the Federalists, who were seeking to identify the government with themselves and to label opposition to their policies as factious if not positively subversive. But the fact that certain passages in his Farewell Address lent themselves to partisan interpretation does not destroy the appeal of that document as a whole to the entire American people. Few men have ever worn the mantle of authority more modestly or more conscientiously than the first American President, and after serving his country well he issued a noble valedictory which still moves the hearts of men.

The Election of 1796

In 1796, when for the first time there was a contest for the office of President, party presidential candidates were informally agreed upon by small groups of leaders. The Federalist group was dominated by Hamilton, while the Republican group consisted of Congressional leaders like Madison and Albert Gallatin of Pennsylvania, who had now admitted Senator Aaron Burr of New York to their councils. But the choice of the President and Vice-President lay with the electors, who were frequently chosen by the state legislatures, and nobody could be entirely sure how they would vote. Furthermore, the provision that each elector should vote for two men lent itself to intrigue in behalf of one or the other of the two men who had been informally designated as candidates of the party.

Washington expected Vice-President John Adams to be promoted to the first office, and the strength of Adams's claim could not be denied. Despite the unpopularity he had gained by his emphasis on ceremonies and his admitted distrust of the populace, he had a large following in New England and his distinguished services to the cause of American independence were by no means forgotten. Hamilton was idolized by a small and powerful group, but he had created too many enemies and had too little popular appeal to be seriously considered as a candidate. He was the major Federalist planner and organizer, however, and he had long had serious reservations about Adams. A man of notably independent spirit, the latter was not only fearful of popular rule but also of the rising financial group to whom Hamilton catered. He regarded certain policies of the Treasury as extravagant and detested the speculation to which they had given rise, and he was much more sympathetic than Hamilton with farmers. Furthermore, while extremely critical of the French Revolution, Adams was not disposed to support the British. He was often exceedingly indiscreet in public, but in reality he was a much more moderate Federalist than Hamilton and stood between the latter and Jefferson in both economic and political philosophy. Also, he still regarded Jefferson as a friend and he disliked Hamilton.

The former Secretary of the Treasury agreed that the Federalists must support Adams as a matter of political necessity, but he chose the other man who should be backed by the party. General Thomas Pinckney of South Carolina, who had distinguished himself in the Spanish negotiations, was himself less extreme than Hamilton, but this Southern aristocrat would balance the ticket from the geographical point of view and Hamilton really preferred him to Adams. The effort to gain a full vote for Pinckney from the northern electors was properly suspected by Adams as a scheme to enable the South Carolinian to run ahead of him, and the seeds of dissension within the party that were sown at this time bore bitter fruit before the next four years were over.

On the other side of the fence, the Republican leaders realized from the first that Jefferson was the only candidate with whom they could hope to succeed. His consent was not asked, through fear of refusal. In private he had expressed his strong disapproval of Jay's Treaty and he had been consulted regarding party policy in connection with it, but he was surprisingly indifferent to the outcome of this particular election and was criticized by his supporters for his inactivity. Burr was designated as his running-mate, but nobody seems to have expected the New Yorker to get many electoral votes. As things turned out, he got only one in Virginia to Jefferson's twenty, nearly all of the others going as a compliment to Samuel Adams.

While the principals were silent in the campaign, a battle of words was waged furiously in the newspapers, which descended to new depths of bad taste. Perhaps the lowest point was reached in the attacks on Washington by Benjamin Franklin Bache, grandson of the famous Franklin and editor of the Philadelphia *Aurora*, the most conspicuous Republican paper at the seat of government since the suspension of Freneau's *National Gazette*. He published an abusive open letter of Thomas Paine to Washington, in which the former described the latter as "treacherous in private friendship" and "a hypocrite in public life." On Washington's retirement, after the battle was really over, Bache expressed national rejoicing that the name of the first President had ceased to give "currency to political iniquity, and to legalize corruption." These words have gained an unenviable immortality in the literature of political abuse. The verbal assaults on John Adams are not so well remembered. He was attacked not only for his "monarchical" and "aristocratic" doctrines, but even for his legal defense of the British soldiers after the Boston Massacre, which was one of the bravest actions of his entire life. Scurrility was no monopoly of Republican editors, and in bulk the attacks on Jefferson probably outweighed those on anybody else. Not only did the Federalist press describe him as a disorganizer and a Francophile; the scandal-mongers probed the events of his governorship of Virginia during the Revolution and made charges of personal cowardice which were wholly without foundation but which haunted him throughout the rest of his public life. He was attacked, also, for his religious views and charged with being an infidel and atheist. The first presidential contest was one of the dirtiest on record.

The vote was very close: Adams got 71 electoral votes to Jefferson's 68; Pinckney received 59 and Burr 30. Adams got no votes in the West and practically none south of Maryland, while Jefferson got none north and east of Pennsylvania. The Republican victory in Pennsylvania was significant, though the margin was very small, and the political skill of Aaron Burr had not yet sufficed to carry the Hamiltonian citadel of New York. The Federalists bettered their situation in Congress, gaining a small majority in the House where they had been slightly in the minority.

The French minister, Adet, intrigued against the Federalists in this election—against Washington until Adet learned he would retire and then against Adams. No connection between Adet and the responsible Republican leaders has been established, but anti-Federalist arguments of his may have got into Republican papers and been bandied about in Democratic societies. He may have supposed that certain official actions of his would intimidate voters, though Genêt's experience should have shown him that their effect would be just the opposite. On October 27, 1796, he announced that the French would treat the commerce of all neutral powers as the latter permitted the British to do, and a couple of weeks later he announced the suspension of his functions. This breach in diplomatic relations did not really occur, however, until after Adams was inaugurated; and in the meantime Adet, in a letter to the authorities· at home, gave his mature impression of Jefferson, in whose interest, presumably, he had been intriguing. Jefferson feared France less than

England, Adet said, but he might change his opinion tomorrow. He admired much that the French had done in their revolution, but he was first of all an American and could not be a true friend of France. "An American is the born enemy of all the peoples of Europe," said the minister. He did not have it quite right, however, for the enmity of Jefferson was not to the people but the governments of Europe.

The incompatibility of the original electoral system with party government was now shown, since the vice-presidency fell to Jefferson as the second man. To his intimate friends the Virginian manifested great relief that he had escaped the first office and that his old friend Adams, his senior in years and in public life, had been preferred. It seemed to him that foreign affairs had not worn so gloomy an aspect since the conclusion of peace with the British in 1783. At a time when parties were still fluid and the office of President was not yet identified with party leadership, he wished his old comrade and recent rival well, but he correctly foresaw that honest John Adams would fall into a sea of troubles.

CHAPTER 4

The End of Federalist Control
1797-1801

JOHN ADAMS SERVED ONLY ONE TERM AS PRESIDENT
and almost the whole of it fell in a time of external danger. Diplomatic
relations were suspended with France, then the most terrifying power
in the world, and there were naval hostilities between the two countries
from 1798 until the very end of his administration. At home the close
division of political opinion was indicated by the narrowness of Adams's
victory—three electoral votes. Within the ranks of the Federalists themselves there was a division between the more moderate group, which
was practically unorganized, and the more extreme and closely knit group,
often designated as the High Federalists, of whom Hamilton was the undisputed leader. The High Federalists richly capitalized on the break
with France and the perfervid patriotism it aroused, but in the end
Adams defied them, returning to the policy of genuine neutrality and
splitting the party as a result.

Naval and military developments caused an increase in the national
debt and the imposition of fresh taxes. The High Federalists aroused fears
in many minds that they were promoting war at the expense of economic
groups, especially farmers, who stood to gain nothing from it. More
notorious were the actions against the foreign-born and the infringements
on individual liberties under the Alien and Sedition Acts. The essential
purpose of these was to crush the political opposition, and this repressive
policy has remained through the years a supreme American example
of the arrogance of power. Jefferson and Madison, in their reaction
against the tyranny of the central government, went so far in the assertion of the rights of states that they were charged by their foes with
the promotion of disunion.

Adams did not initiate the policy of repression, but he was identified with it by its victims; and his wise actions in the foreign field came too late to do him much good in the election of 1800. The Republicans were able to capitalize on the reaction against the extreme policy of the government. The American people had not become pro-French or disunionist, but a neutral foreign policy and moderate domestic policy were preferred in most parts of the country. Whereas the Federalists had identified themselves in policy with the interests of a relatively small economic group, the Republicans appealed to farmers everywhere, to most of the plantation interests of the South, and to the plain people in the cities—especially in New York and Philadelphia. This powerful combination was destined to endure and to make impossible the return of the Federalists to power.

The political conflict was reflected in the realm of thought and here, also, public opinion took a course between the two extremes. Ideas of political liberty persisted, despite the excesses and perversions of the French Revolution. The antireligious doctrines of the age had conspicuous American devotees, but, by and large, Americans viewed them with disfavor. Meanwhile, they clung to conventional modes in literature and turned to classic forms in the arts. Cultural independence of the Old World still lay in the distant future.

John Adams and His Political Surroundings

The second President, who was in his sixty-second year and still vigorous when inaugurated, was a man of strong mind and forceful personality. Yet he had about him until almost the end of his term a Cabinet that took orders from Hamilton and represented the extreme wing of the Federalist party when his own philosophy was more moderate. Timothy Pickering—harsh, humorless, and efficient in small things—remained as Secretary of State; Oliver Wolcott, Jr., continued to run the Treasury in loyalty to its first head; and James McHenry was in the Department of War, relying on Hamilton for the advice he sorely needed. Not until the Department of the Navy was created in 1798 and Benjamin Stoddert was appointed as its head did Adams have a Cabinet officer of his own choosing. He did not try to get rid of Wolcott, and not until his last year in office did he oust Pickering and McHenry, who had proved to be his secret enemies. The retention of such men by Adams now seems surprising, but when he took office no tradition had been established that would have led the department heads to present their resignations voluntarily, and he regarded his administration as a continuation of Washington's. There was a strong strain of suspiciousness in Adams's nature, but his personal vanity could be appealed to. This patently honest and deeply patriotic man was no kind of a politician and did not inspire the loyalty he deserved. He wanted to be an independent President, and eventually he became one, but when we look back on him the main impression he gives is that of extreme loneliness.

At the beginning he consulted Jefferson about foreign affairs and it is conceivable that between them some sort of bipartisan policy could have been worked out. But the Cabinet did not like these consultations, and circumstances soon made the Vice-President the target of fresh partisan attacks. A few weeks after the inauguration, a private letter that Jefferson wrote the previous year to Philip Mazzei, an Italian friend who had once been a neighbor of his in Virginia but had returned to Europe, was published in America. Describing the political scene in vivid but exaggerated language, Jefferson referred to men who were "Samsons in the field and Solomons in the council," but whose heads had been shorn by "the harlot England." This was interpreted as an allusion to Washington and aroused a tempest of indignation. Jefferson afterward said in private that he was actually referring to the Society of the Cincinnati, but no explanation was offered or would have been accepted at the time. He was regarded in Federalist circles as a maligner of the national Hero and an apologist for the despised French. He found presiding over the Senate a more painful task than he had expected. This was particularly the case from 1798 onward, and by that time the political indifference he had shown in the last election had given way to determination to encompass the defeat of an administration whose policies he disapproved.

Throughout his presidency, Adams was away from Philadelphia a great deal, partly because of his wife's health. He left routine affairs to his subordinates to a greater extent than Washington had done, and he made no particular effort to mobilize his own supporters. The relatively small commercial and financial groups that constituted Hamilton's clientele, along with a few great southern planters, would never have been sufficient to carry the country. Adams's appeal was broader but either he did not know how to realize on the strength of his position or did not think it incumbent on him to do so. He had no spokesman for the administration in Congress, while Hamilton maintained close contact with leading members and influenced the course of legislation considerably more than he did. He was not the author of the domestic policies that the opposition party most objected to, and he may not have realized how repressive and unrepresentative some of them were, even when he accepted them.

The domestic policy of the High Federalists was justified by them on grounds of foreign danger, and few administrations have been so dominated by foreign affairs as was that of Adams. He was widely experienced in his field, and in it the unpolitical President, after facing for long months perplexities which would have baffled the wisest of statesmen, performed his most signal services.

THE XYZ AFFAIR AND UNDECLARED WAR WITH FRANCE

The recall of James Monroe, who sympathized with the French in their resentment at Jay's Treaty, was decided on in the summer of 1796. He was informed of it in November by the man appointed to succeed him as minister, General Charles Cotesworth Pinckney of South Carolina, brother of Thomas Pinckney. But the French Directory, while praising Monroe, declined to receive Pinckney until there had been some "reparation" for their alleged injuries, and this refusal became known in America shortly after Adams's inauguration.

Adams decided to send a commission to treat with the French, and even thought of putting Jefferson on it, but both of them concluded that it would be improper for the Vice-President to leave the country. The Cabinet agreed to the commission after Hamilton had advised them that it would be a good political move. Pinckney had been forced to leave France but he was still abroad and an obvious choice. The other two members were John Marshall of Virginia, who was just coming into prominence as a Federalist in a state where they were scarce, and Elbridge Gerry of Massachusetts, a close friend of Adams who was not regarded as a party man though he was strongly anti-British. No valid objection to this commission could be raised by the friends of France.

Appointed in June 1797, Marshall and Gerry were in Paris with Pinckney in September, but the commissioners were never officially received. They had some talk with Talleyrand, the Minister for Foreign Affairs, and more with secret intermediaries who later became known in the United States as X, Y, and Z. The negotiations did not even get started and, in April 1798, Marshall embarked for America. Pinckney remained in France because of the illness of his daughter, while Gerry, with whom Talleyrand had offered to treat alone and who believed that his withdrawal would mean war, remained. Gerry was severely criticized at home for this action, but Adams defended him. Before Marshall returned, Adams had communicated to Congress a recent declaration of the Directory foreshadowing more severe treatment of American commerce and had announced that there was no reason to hope for the success of the commission. Therefore, he said, the country must put itself in a state of defense. He kept back the communications at first, but when the Republicans demanded them and were joined by the High Federalists, after the latter had gained an inkling of their contents, he revealed the "XYZ" dispatches and confounded the friends of France.

The most startling disclosure was that of a proposal by "X"' that the United States provide a *douceur* of some $250,000 as a preliminary to negotiations. Holdups of this sort by French officials were not uncommon in this period, and even the British government paid bribes for treaties, but Pinckney gained a place for himself in history by saying, "No! No! Not a sixpence." The chief popular hero, however, was Marshall, who got home after the dispatches had been published and was feted and toasted everywhere. This affair was a turning point in his career, for he had gained the strong approval of John Adams and become a national figure overnight. At a dinner to him in Philadelphia, which was attended by many dignitaries, one of the toasts was: "Millions for defense but not a cent for tribute." It was in this time of patriotic fervor that Joseph Hopkinson wrote the song, "Hail Columbia!"

The President assumed such a bellicose tone in his replies to various addresses to him that even Hamilton thought him indiscreet. The High Federalists as a group, however, were pleased with Adams. Meanwhile, the Republicans were discredited to an even greater degree than they had been at the height of the Genêt affair. If the French were trying to drive a wedge between the American people and the government, as the Federalists claimed, they had adopted the worst possible method. Actually, they had made friendship for France seem incompatible with American patriotism. The attitude of the Directory toward the American commissioners was one of contemptuous disregard, and its bullying tactics were those of men intoxicated with new-found power. But the French did not want war with the United States, and the stories in circulation about their intention to invade the country were fantastic.

Neither France nor the United States ever declared war, but Congress suspended commerce with France and French possessions, and by provisions for the armed protection of American shipping it authorized what amounted to defensive war on the seas. Furthermore, Congress declared the treaties with France abrogated, though these did not provide for such unilateral action. This was less than hot war and more than cold war, so perhaps it may be described as warm. In 1798, however, Congress was operating in a heated atmosphere and the High Federalists took control of the situation.

Navy and Army

Adams himself had been an advocate of preparedness from the beginning of his term, but the moderate Federalists and the Republicans had prevented effective action previous to the revelation of the XYZ dispatches. Meanwhile, Hamilton had formulated a full program of defense, and the actions that Congress now took were closer to his line than to that of Adams. That body made larger provision for an army than the President thought necessary and gave him fewer ships than he wanted. More than any other man he deserves credit for the creation of the Navy, though technically this began with the act of 1794, which authorized the construction of a few frigates at a time of trouble with the Barbary pirates. But work on these had been suspended, and it was in Adams's term that the *Constellation,* the *Constitution* ("Old Ironsides"), and the *President* were constructed. Also, the Department of War was divided in 1798 and the Department of the Navy created. It was well administered by Benjamin Stoddert and acquitted itself very creditably. While the British ships-of-the-line kept the heavily armed French ships off the seas, the American frigates with other smaller vessels made themselves very useful in protecting American commerce against French raiders, though the total of losses considerably exceeded American prizes. The frigates generally got the better of French warships of their own class in such actions as there were, and their successes were hailed with much enthusiasm.

In general the Republicans were small-navy men and, being fearful of a standing army, they would have relied on the militia. The High Federalists under the prompting of Hamilton emphasized the importance of an army and were less interested than Adams in the Navy—not because of indifference to commerce but because of their reliance on the British. Opposition to the Navy was strongest in the purely agricultural districts in the South and West, the costliness of it being specially objected to, and the increase in taxation because of the policy of naval and military preparedness lost to the Federalists in 1800 considerable support they had received four years earlier.

The naval policy of the government was wise, but the military emphasis of the High Federalists seems much less justifiable. The authorized strength of the regular Army (13,000) was never attained—whether this was because of the incompetence of Secretary McHenry or the indifference of Adams, who cared little for military preparation except for its diplomatic and political effect. But critics of the government could say that it was creating a standing army for purposes of domestic repression or for offensive actions of some sort in connection with the British. At this time Francisco de Miranda was trying to interest both British and Americans in his schemes for revolt in South America against Spain, and Hamilton was sympathetic, though that adventurous statesman was more interested in action against Florida and Louisiana to begin with, and, while he would have welcomed British connivance, he did not go so far as to favor an open British alliance. At all events, the military policy was suspect, and a character of high comedy was imparted to it by the controversy over rank in which Hamilton was the central figure.

Washington was nominated for the chief command, and a cry of exultation was raised at the news that the national hero would emerge from retirement in this time of emergency. Secretary McHenry bore him his commission, along with a list of possible appointees as major general or brigadier general. Hamilton's name was on it but did not stand first.

Washington drew up his own list on which Hamilton appeared as Inspector General and presumably second in rank to the Commander-in-
Chief. Other major generals, with Hamilton, were the former Secretary
of War, Henry Knox, and Charles Cotesworth Pinckney, and among the
brigadier generals was William S. Smith, son-in-law of Adams. Adams
submitted this list to the Senate for confirmation, but Secretary of State
Pickering by secret intrigue prevented the approval of Smith, and there
was a tempest in the teapot when Knox, who had outranked Hamilton
in the Continental Army and was considerably his senior in years, refused to serve below him. Adams supported Knox at first, but Washington himself refused to serve unless Hamilton were second in command,
and under the pressure of High-Federalist opinion the President yielded,
still smarting from the rejection of his son-in-law. In view of Washington's age, Hamilton would have been the actual commander in case of
war, and if he had been in position to make his dreams of southern
conquest come true he might perhaps have become an American Napoleon. But Adams had the last laugh, for there was no war and the
inspector general had very slight opportunity to exercise his unquestionable military talents and realize on his vaulting ambitions.

THE ALIEN AND SEDITION ACTS

The perfervid patriotism that was aroused by the XYZ dispatches and
the extreme partisanship of the group in power reached a climax in
the laws known collectively as the Alien and Sedition Acts. This restrictive and repressive legislation was similar to legislation in this decade
in England, which was faced with far greater and more immediate danger
from the French. The partisanship which sought to identify Federalism
with patriotism cannot be justified, but the psychological conditions under
which the effort was made can be understood by any generation that
has faced the fact or the terrifying threat of war. In 1798, James Madison
made this melancholy comment: "Perhaps it is a universal truth that the
loss of liberty at home is to be charged to provisions against danger real
or pretended from abroad."

The responsible public officials of that time are blameable for letting
their emotions obscure their judgment, but they must be blamed far
more for seizing this opportunity to translate their prejudices and partisan
purposes into restrictive and oppressive laws. The first of this set, the
Naturalization Law, was an expression of hostility to the foreign-born
and an incident in the long conflict between newcomers and old settlers.
Sentiment against recent immigrants was specially strong in New England,
and was generally characteristic of Federalists because the newcomers
tended to become Republicans. Congressman Albert Gallatin of Pennsylvania, who was Swiss by birth, had become the leader of the opposi-

tion in the House after the retirement of Madison from that body, and he was a special object of Federalist dislike. Some members of the ruling group favored the exclusion of the foreign-born from public office, and some went so far as to urge that they be excluded from citizenship. The law of 1798 extended the time required for naturalization from five to fourteen years and prescribed the registration of aliens. The latter provision was regarded by immigrants as insulting, and the law as a whole was obviously designed to decrease the Republican vote. It was repealed after that party came into power, but the New England Federalists clung to their antiforeign policy and thus made it practically inevitable that the immigrants should join the other political camp.

Two other laws dealt with foreigners. The Alien Enemies Act, calling for the removal of persons of that description in case of war, need not concern us since there was no war. The Alien Act authorized the President to order from the country all aliens judged by him to be "dangerous to the peace and safety of the United States." This law was objected to as a grant of arbitrary power to the Executive. Leading Republicans believed that it was directed against men of learning and radical political views like the eminent English chemist and Unitarian minister, Joseph Priestley, who had retired to the Pennsylvania countryside but was being hounded by the Federalist press, and the French philosopher Volney, who was then in the United States but soon sailed away. A good many people departed through fear, but Adams never availed himself of the authority granted him. Hamilton condemned him for his lack of energy and wanted him to deport certain Republican editors. By its own terms the law expired in two years.

Most notorious of all was the Sedition Act, which not only forbade conspiracy, but "false, scandalous and malicious" writing or utterances against the government, the President, or Congress tending to bring any of them into contempt or disrepute. The measure was justified by its advocates on the ground that the opposition press was scurrilous, as it unquestionably was. But the much more numerous Federalist papers were also ill-mannered toward their rivals, and the enforcement of the law showed beyond any doubt the purpose of the party in power to silence criticism of the policies of the government and muzzle the Republicans, at the expense of freedom of speech and the press. Hamilton objected to the bill in an earlier and even more extreme version as inexpedient but he was sympathetic with its purposes, and the only important Federalist with a clear record of opposition to it was John Marshall. Adams was not conspicuously active in connection with it, but uncomplimentary remarks about him wounded his vanity, while naturally incensing his wife Abigail, and he condoned a punitive policy. The major executive agent in the enforcement of the Sedition law was the bitterly vindictive Timothy Pickering, who was ever on the lookout for evil-doers.

Altogether, about fifteen persons were indicted, and ten were found guilty. All were Republicans and most of them were editors. The most cherished object of Federalist wrath was Benjamin Franklin Bache, editor of the *Aurora*, whose Republican partisanship was extreme and to whom neither the person of George Washington nor a confidential public document had any sanctity. He was indicted for libel by a federal court before the Sedition law went into effect, but death stopped his pen before the trial. One of the most conspicuous victims of the Act was Thomas Cooper, an intimate friend of Joseph Priestley, and a man of learning who delighted in controversy. He served a prison sentence for written remarks about John Adams that were highly uncomplimentary but certainly not subversive. Matthew Lyon of Vermont differed from the others in that he was a Congressman. This rough Democrat, who spat in the face of Roger Griswold of Connecticut after being insulted by that Federalist in the House and who afterwards repelled Griswold's cane with firetongs, was re-elected to Congress while serving his prison term. Least attractive of the victims was the unscrupulous journalist James Thomson Callender, the greatest scandalmonger of his day, whose venom was eventually felt by Jefferson as it had been by Hamilton. As a person he did not deserve much sympathy, but he commanded a great deal because of the political aspect of his trial and the bullying tactics of Justice Chase, who also hurled insults at counsel and alienated the bar. The high-handed conduct of federal judges in these trials, coupled with their practice of delivering political harangues in charges to grand juries, strengthened the impression that the entire machinery of the central government was being employed in the interest of a party and as an instrument to repress liberty. This effort to proscribe a major political group and destroy political opposition is without parallel in American national history, and no other period can be more fittingly described as a reign of terror.

THE KENTUCKY AND VIRGINIA RESOLUTIONS

At the session of Congress following the passage of the Alien and Sedition laws there was a Federalist proposal that they be printed for general distribution, but after a Republican amendment had been offered to print the Constitution of the United States with them the idea was abandoned. The most doubtful of them from the constitutional point of view was the Sedition Act. If the Supreme Court had formally ruled on this before its expiration on March 3, 1801, almost certainly that body would have upheld it; but if the law had been declared unconstitutional, the judiciary would have assumed the role of protector of basic individual liberties, as guaranteed by the Bill of Rights, and there would have been no occasion for Jefferson and Madison to appeal to the states as they did in the Kentucky and Virginia Resolutions.

Two sets of resolutions were adopted by the legislature of Kentucky, one in 1798 and the other in the next year. Jefferson was the author of the first set, though his name was not made public; and the second set followed his plan, though he did not write them. The somewhat milder resolutions of the General Assembly of Virginia in 1798 were the work of Madison, who also drew the little-noticed Virginia Report of 1800, the most carefully worded of them all and the best statement of the mature Republican position. The main purpose of the earlier and more famous resolutions was political: they were designed to arouse public sentiment against the Alien and Sedition Acts and to preserve a political party which the government was trying to extinguish. But Americans of a later generation, who were struggling over the issue between nationalism and state rights, viewed the Resolutions out of context and regarded their general constitutional arguments as the most significant thing about them. In a nutshell, these arguments were: that the government of the United States originated in a compact between one state and the others; that acts going beyond the delegated powers were void; and that an individual state had the right to judge of the infractions of its own powers and of the means of redress that it would employ. It will be recalled that the doctrine of judicial review was not yet firmly established, though leading Federalists hoped it would be.

Later commentators were to say that here were the seeds of nullification—the word, meaning the voiding of a federal law by a state, was actually used in the second set of Kentucky Resolutions—and that this was a formulation of the divisive philosophy of state rights. Never again did Jefferson go so far in the direction of state rights as he did in his correspondence with Madison at this time, and it is doubtful if ever again he felt more uncertain of the persistence of the Union. Yet the resolutions expressed devotion to the Union, and the mode of redress that was recommended fell far short of nullification. A single state was to protest to Congress, and to appeal to other states to do likewise.

The responses of other states to the appeal from Virginia and Kentucky were largely determined by the politics of the situation. The Resolutions were disapproved in Northern states where the Federalists were in the ascendant, and in the replies the federal judiciary, which was then thoroughly partisan, was usually pointed out as the proper authority for the judgment of constitutional questions. In Southern states where the Republicans were still in control or relatively strong there was no formal disapproval of the Resolutions but they alarmed and repelled a good many moderates. The Republicans as a group approved of the protest against the Alien and Sedition Acts, but except in two states they did not commit themselves to any specific procedure.

Historical judgment on the Kentucky and Virginia Resolutions, like the contemporary judgment, can be divided. They were in the state-rights tradition which the New Englanders took up divisively in the next decade and the South Carolinians carried to the last extreme in nullification and secession. But if the emphasis is laid on the specific evils that these resolutions protested against, they were in the tradition of human rights and civil liberties which has persisted since the Declaration of Independence.

THE SETTLEMENT WITH FRANCE

The man who stopped the High Federalists was not Jefferson but John Adams. He ordered a retreat from the extreme and untenable position they had taken in the foreign field. At the height of the excitement over the XYZ Affair he stated that no minister would be sent to France without assurances that he would be received as befitted the representative of "a great, free, powerful, and independent nation"; but, resisting later pressure from the Cabinet, he refused to say that he would not send one at all. By January 1799, he learned in a roundabout way that Talleyrand was willing to meet the conditions he had prescribed. William Vans Murray, the American minister at The Hague, transmitted a letter that the French Foreign Minister had written him, and Murray's judgment that Talleyrand meant what he said was supported by John Quincy Adams, son of the President and then American minister to Prussia. Meanwhile, word had come to America through informal channels that the French had undergone a change of heart. They had been impressed by the naval activities and military preparations of the United States, and were becoming fearful of an Anglo-American alliance such as Timothy Pickering favored. Already there was considerable naval cooperation between Great Britain and the United States, and the French did not want this to be formalized and extended. Their own naval defeat by Lord Nelson in the Battle of the Nile was sobering, as was the news of American opinion they had received from persons friendly to France —like the poet Joel Barlow and Dr. George Logan, who aroused the ire of the Federalists by engaging in a personal mission to France. This occasioned the "Logan Act" (1799), forbidding unauthorized activities of the sort. Talleyrand, who took a more realistic view of the situation in the New World than the Directors and who had his eye on Florida and Louisiana, had brought those indifferent officials around to a friendlier and wiser attitude.

Adams, on his part, was trying to be realistic. Believing that peace between the two countries was desirable, the President, without consulting Pickering and others in his own Cabinet who thought otherwise, nominated William Vans Murray to be minister to France and threw the High Federalists into consternation. Even those of them that had not advocated a declaration of war or a British alliance knew that, despite losses, commerce brought high profits under existing conditions and that they themselves had attained political dominance because of the war scare. They were not disposed to surrender these advantages and let the scepter of power slip from their hands. Furthermore, they could not admit good faith on the part of the French without eating their own words. Talleyrand was still a "shameless villian" to Pickering.

Most of the Eastern ultras were blind to the rising opposition to war policies outside of commercial circles, but some of them, including Hamilton, saw that they could not openly oppose Adams in his effort to remove the war threat, and they adopted the tactics of delay. On protests from the Senate, the President agreed to appoint a commission of three instead of a minister, and this eventually consisted of Murray, Chief Justice Oliver Ellsworth of Connecticut, and William R. Davie of North Carolina. Also, Adams agreed to seek more specific assurances from the French. These were received in the summer of 1799, but Pickering was in no hurry to draft the instructions for the commissioners, and by various pretexts he and his fellows prolonged the delay. After receiving a warning from Secretary Stoddert that there was a conspiracy to defeat his purposes, the President finally despatched the commissioners in November. They would have had an easier time if they had sailed sooner, for Napoleon had become First Consul before their arrival. His absence in Italy held things up, and he was a tough man to deal with anywhere.

From April 1800 through September the negotiations dragged on, and at length the commissioners concluded that they could not carry out their instructions—to secure indemnity for French spoliations of American commerce (from 1793 onward) and to gain formal release from treaty obligations. They made a temporary settlement, whereby commercial relations were restored and both the treaties and the claims of indemnity were suspended. The settlement which was finally ratified by both countries in 1801 was, in effect, a trade. The United States surrendered the claims for indemnity and France surrendered the treaties. Thus the Franco-American alliance was formally ended, peace was restored, and the United States returned to a policy of neutrality.

The wisdom of Adams in putting his country back on the road to true national independence now seems unquestionable, but the political results of his actions were not to his advantage. His own party split while the commissioners were still in France, and the High Federalists never forgave him. In an extravagant statement in later years he said that there would have been a unanimous vote against the Federalists in the Presidential election if he had not sent the commissioners, but the fact is that the opposing party won it anyway. His own motives were not partisan; they were in the fullest sense patriotic, and the settlement with France for which he was almost wholly responsible fittingly crowned his career as a statesman. Again the Atlas of the American Revolution was a great patriot and a great man.

THE ELECTION OF 1800-1801

The extreme Federalists could not afford to break openly with Adams at the time that he dispatched the commissioners. He was a fiercely independent character when aroused, and if his prerogatives as President in the conduct of foreign affairs were too much encroached upon, it was not unthinkable that he might resign the office, turn it over to Vice-President Jefferson, and denounce his opponents within his own party. The possibility of such a development was reported by the British minister. Furthermore, as the election year came around, it appeared that Adams had much more popular backing than any other Federalist. The Federalist leaders decided, therefore, to support him and Charles Cotesworth Pinckney for the two highest offices, and adopted the tactics of seeking equal electoral support for them, hoping that Pinckney (who was not a party to the scheme) would come in ahead.

Soon after this decision was reached in Congressional caucus in May 1800, Adams acted decisively to clear his cabinet of his enemies. Secretary of War McHenry tendered his resignation on request, and when Secretary of State Pickering refused to resign the President dismissed him. The purge stopped short of the Treasury, where Wolcott remained, but Adams secured a loyal and unusually able aide in the person of John Marshall, who resigned from Congress and took Pickering's place. This Virginian was strongly opposed to the disunionist tendencies that he perceived in the Kentucky and Virginia Resolutions and he was regarded as a Federalist of the school of Washington, who had strongly approved his candidacy for Congress.

Adams had strengthened his official family, but he had again defied the High Federalists, and he proceeded to inveigh against a "damned faction" and a "British faction" with characteristic brusqueness. Hamilton's actions in the late summer and autumn of 1800 provide a striking illustration of his proneness to overreach himself, but they can be explained, perhaps, as the result of his growing conviction that Adams was gaining ground within the party. Hamilton printed for circulation among Federalist leaders an exceedingly intemperate letter concerning the public conduct and character of Adams, and this inevitably fell into the hands of an eager Republican journalist who printed it again for all the world to see. The ostensible purpose of this extraordinary document was to explain the reasons for the equal support of Pinckney and Adams by the Federalists, but in stating these Hamilton admitted his preference for Thomas Pinckney in 1796 and Charles Cotesworth Pinckney in 1800 and framed an indictment of Adams which no irresponsible journalist of the opposition would have been likely to surpass. Hamilton described him as a man of eccentric and sublimated ambition, of unbounded vanity and a jealousy that was capable of discoloring every object. In a word, Adams was unfit to be President. To Thomas Cooper, emerging from the prison to which he had been committed because of less severe condemnation of Adams, it naturally seemed that Hamilton, more than anybody else, deserved to be tried under the Sedition Act. Even his warmest admirers deplored the imprudence of the most brilliant of all the Federalists, and some of them lamented that he had impaired his own usefulness.

During the presidential campaign the Republicans made the most of Federalist dissensions. There was little dissension in their own ranks, for their support of Jefferson was inevitable. Aaron Burr of New York was chosen as his running mate by the party Congressional caucus. He balanced the ticket from a geographical point of view, and there could be no possible doubt of his political skill. Republican success in the state election in New York, assuring control of the legislature and the choice of Republican electors, was a major reason for success in the nation.

Presidential nominations were made by Congressional caucuses in 1800, but there were no official party platforms. The constitutional provision that electors might be chosen in such ways as state legislatures should prescribe led to considerable maneuvering in these bodies, and the tendency was to adopt provisions favorable to the party in power in the state. Because of elements of irregularity in the choice of electors, the electoral vote was a far less accurate gauge of public opinion than it is today, and a much better index was provided by the Congressional elections. In these the Republicans won 65 seats to 41 for their opponents, showing beyond doubt that they had become the majority party.

Republican Party discipline had embarrassing results, for both Jefferson and Burr got 73 electoral votes. Surprisingly, discipline was almost as effective on the Federalist side: Adams got 65 votes and Pinckney 64, only an elector from Rhode Island declining to support them equally. The Federalists carried all of the New England states, along with New Jersey and Delaware. They divided the electoral vote of Pennsylvania and Maryland, and had a third of the electors from North Carolina, while all the rest of the country was Republican.

The Twelfth Amendment to the Constitution (1804), providing that the electors cast separate ballots for President and Vice-President, made impossible another such tie as the one between Thomas Jefferson and Aaron Burr. In 1801, the tie was resolved by the constitutional means already prescribed. The decision had to be made by the House of Representatives, voting by states, and a majority of all the states was necessary for an election—that is, 9 out of 16. The matter was necessarily referred to the old Congress, since the new one would not come in before March 4, when a new President was supposed to be inaugurated. The decision was not finally reached until February 17, 1801, and for a time it looked as though no one would be legally authorized to succeed John Adams.

The reason for the stalemate was that the Federalists supported Burr —partly because Jefferson had long been the most conspicuous object of their partisan hostility, and partly because some of them hoped that they could make a deal with the crafty New Yorker. For thirty-five ballots, Jefferson had 8 votes and Burr had 6, while two states cast no vote since their delegations were evenly divided. The jam was finally broken on the initiative of James A. Bayard of Delaware, who concluded that if there was to be a President it would have to be Jefferson. He could not persuade any of his fellow Federalists to vote for their arch-enemy, but the Federalist representatives from the two divided states (Vermont and Maryland) agreed not to vote at all, thus permitting the Republicans in these delegations to cast ballots for Jefferson. Other Federalists abstained except those from the four other New England states, who supported Burr to the bitter end.

Hamilton was frantic with fear, because he hated and distrusted Burr far more than he did Jefferson. Now he showed that he was more realistic than other leaders of the High Federalists. He still thought Jefferson "a contemptible hypocrite," but he regarded him as incorruptible, while he was convinced that Burr was both corrupt and unscrupulous. He did not view Jefferson as "an enemy of the power of the Executive," and believed that his zeal for France would cool. "To my mind," he wrote, "a true estimate of Mr. Jefferson's character warrants the expectation of a temporizing rather than a violent system." The arguments of Hamilton made no impression on the New England Federalists, and while they may have affected Bayard and other more moderate men, they were probably not the main factor in his case. It was claimed in later years that certain promises were made to Bayard on behalf of Jefferson, chiefly with respect to removals from office and fiscal policy. There is no reason to believe that Jefferson authorized any promises, but no one who really knew him would have expected him to follow a drastic policy in either case. At the end, there were wild charges on both sides about breaking up the Union, but Bayard concluded that the best way to avoid this was to let the majority party have the man of their choice. Thus the spirit of moderation triumphed over extreme partisanship.

Reasons for Federalist Defeat

Federalist dissension entered into their defeat in the election of 1800 —not in causing the Federalist electors to split their votes between Adams and Pinckney, but in raising doubts about the ability of a sharply divided party to conduct the government. The extreme policies of the Hamiltonian group had alienated many moderates. The repressive and nativistic policy that was symbolized by the Alien and Sedition Acts repelled many who persisted in thinking that America was a refuge for the oppressed and the home of personal freedom. These individuals could give ready allegiance to Jefferson, who stood as the antithesis to consolidation and tyranny.

In many places, especially in inland districts, reaction against the taxes that had been imposed because of naval and military preparations was an even more decisive factor. A direct tax of 1798 on lands and houses was a particular occasion of discontent, and in certain German counties of eastern Pennsylvania that had previously been Federalist (Northampton, Bucks, and Montgomery) it led, in the next year, to what is known as the Fries Rebellion. Raising the cry, "dämm de President, dämm de Congress, dämm de Aristokratz," the farmers threatened the tax officials until their resistance was put down by United States troops after a proclamation by the President. The leader, John Fries, was tried and sentenced to death. Adams pardoned him, over the protests of the High Federalists, but these counties went Republican afterward. On economic grounds the policy of the government offered little to back-country farmers, and the tobacco planters of the South suffered from the sharp decline of prices that followed the severance of trade with France.

Northern commercial districts, on the contrary, prospered greatly under the abnormalities of the times, and the high interest on new government loans was welcomed in financial circles. This was the policy of Wolcott and Hamilton, which Adams objected to, and the Republicans made a good deal of it in the campaign. The Federalist hold on New England can be considerably explained on the ground that governmental policy was specially favorable to commercial interests, but there were important religious reasons. The dominant Congregational clergy regarded Jefferson as their enemy and viewed the Republicans as the party of disorder and infidelity.

Near the end of 1799, George Washington died at Mount Vernon in his sixty-eighth year, and soon thereafter he was described by "Light-Horse" Harry Lee as "first in war, first in peace, and first in the hearts of his countrymen." The death of the nation's hero grieved an entire people but it cast a special pall over the spirits of the Federalists, and this was not lifted when, as one century ended and another began, the second President made his exit from public life. But to the enthusiastic supporters of the third President it seemed that the gloomy night had fled and the reign of terror ended. Soon they sang:

> Rejoice! Columbia's sons, rejoice!
> To tyrants never bend the knee,
> But join with heart, and soul, and voice,
> For JEFFERSON and LIBERTY.

THE CULTURE OF THE YOUNG REPUBLIC

The political struggle between Federalists and Republicans involved a struggle in the realm of the mind. The conflict of ideas that accompanied the French Revolution and the European war was reflected in the United States and served to intensify domestic political quarrels. The battle was also waged in other fields and it was specially bitter in religion.

Religion and Philosophy

The American response to Thomas Paine's book, *The Age of Reason* (1794), deserves particular consideration. In this the author of *The Rights of Man* made a frontal attack on all organized religion, denounced all forms of clerical tyranny, argued that reason alone should govern belief, and asserted that Deism was the only rational religion. Paine expressly stated that he believed in God, but he said, "My own mind is my own church." To the great body of church members he seemed a religious anarchist.

In the United States the various governments were crystallizing a unique relationship between Church and State in which government would not support or oppose any religion but would stand aside from all religious questions and institutions. The advocates of this system were not opponents of organized religion. Most of them were Protestant Christians who believed that true Christianity would best thrive if left to private initiative. In Europe, on the other hand, and especially in France, advocates of the separation of Church and State seemed intent on destroying organized Christianity. Paine's *Age of Reason* gave great impetus to Deism, not as a private faith tolerant of other faiths, but as a militant corollary of the fight for political liberty. Militant Deism had already been propounded in America by Ethan Allen, the Green Mountain rebel, in his *Reason the Only Oracle of Man* (1784), which was bitterly attacked by the orthodox clergy led by Timothy Dwight. The Frenchman Volney's *Ruins: Or A Survey of the Revolution of Empires* (1791) provided new ammunition for the Deists. But Paine's book reached more people. Blind Elihu Palmer, a graduate of Dartmouth and a former Baptist minister, John Fitch, and others proceeded to organize Deistic "churches" such as the Society of Ancient Druids, and to publish *The Temple of Reason* and other periodicals.

This movement reached its climax in the later 1790's and, while it influenced only a small minority, it frightened conservatives into such counterblasts that its net result was to discredit moderate as well as extreme versions of the philosophy of rationalism. Jefferson was a special sufferer from this reaction. The attitude toward him was reflected in the words of a Connecticut minister after the election of 1796. He prayed for President-elect Adams and then said: "O Lord! Wilt Thou bestow upon the Vice-President a double portion of Thy grace for *Thou knowest he needs it.*" In 1800, there was a widely-believed report in New England that Jefferson would confiscate all Bibles if elected, and the story is that many of these sacred books were hidden in wells. Actually, the only sort of religion he opposed was political religion, and what he believed in was complete religious freedom. It was in 1800, in a private letter to Dr. Benjamin Rush that he said: "I have sworn on the altar of God eternal hostility against every form of tyranny over the mind of man." His election did not stem the rising tide of religious conservatism, and his religious liberalism was a greater political liability in the nineteenth century than it had been in the eighteenth.

Another conflict of ideas centered in the doctrine of environmentalism, which had been advanced by English and French philosophers. In this view, not Divine decree or even physical heredity accounts for the differences among individuals, classes, and races, and between the sexes, so much as differences of environment and opportunity do. The political consequences of this philosophy were decisive. John Adams denied that attempts to improve the condition of less-favored portions of humanity could help them, while Thomas Jefferson affirmed the truth of environmentalism, particularly with respect to the virtuous influences of rural as compared with urban life. The environmental theory of human nature found in the works of John Locke, Helvétius, Rousseau, Condorcet, Godwin, and Mary Wollstonecraft was naturalized in America during this generation and provided philosophic foundations for new waves of social reformism in the next. The most significant reforms eventually occurred in education because it offered the readiest means of improving the condition of every individual. Detailed plans for the education of the whole people were proposed by Jefferson and Benjamin Rush among others, but cost and conservative opposition postponed action.

Books and Newspapers

In literature the spokesmen of optimism, democracy, and reform won the battle against pessimistic conservatism. The Hartford Wits lost their position of literary leadership except as the die-hard Timothy Dwight continued to fulminate against all forms of infidelity to the "standing order." One of their leading poets, Joel Barlow, who in 1786 had collaborated with John Trumbull and Lemuel Hopkins in *The Anarchiad,* a satire on the radicals, turned to enthusiasm for the French Revolution in his ominous *Advice to the Privileged Orders* (1792) and became an ardent Jeffersonian. The outstanding writer of the new generation, Charles Brockden Brown, was a forthright radical throughout his short life and used his novels as vehicles for reformist doctrine. He appealed to popular tastes for Gothic horrors and Richardsonian sentiment, while teaching liberation by reason from superstition in *Wieland* (1798) and democratic idealism in *Arthur Mervyn* (1799). His tract *Alcuin* (1798) struck a blow for women's rights with the environmentalist argument that subjection by men rather than innate inferiority prevented their development as the intellectual and moral equals of men. Royall Tyler in his novel *The Algerine Captive* (1797) satirized the shortcomings of the new republic, defending Federalism. An even balance between the present weaknesses of raw democracy and future hopes was achieved by Hugh Henry Brackenridge in his most popular novel, *Modern Chivalry* (1792).

Less important as literature but more important in popular influence were novels, plays, and histories which celebrated American experience in terms of simple patriotism. The most famous of such works was Mason L. Weems's *Life of Washington* (1800). "Parson" Weems had been a militant Deist, but in his book he pictured the Father of His Country as a sort of substitute deity—as a paragon of talents and virtues which, for all the imaginary incidents Weems used to bludgeon home his point, Washington very nearly was. The colossal sale of the book during the next generations fixed him permanently among the first of American folk heroes.

But book sales were trifling in comparison with the circulation of newspapers. The American, as an English visitor remarked, was "a newspaper-reading animal." The party battles between Federalists and Republicans gave new excitement to the press, and grandiose European events on which the fortunes of the American republic largely depended were thoroughly reported. The first American daily, *The Pennsylvania Packet and Daily Advertiser* had been founded in Philadelphia in 1784. By 1815, there were over thirty dailies. Chiefly political in subject matter, the newspapers were almost all party organs. Political leaders often took the initiative in founding or supporting papers to make sure that their views on all questions reached the public. Reference has already been made to such outstanding Philadelphia papers as the Federalist *Gazette of the United States,* edited by John Fenno, the Republican *National Gazette* of Philip Freneau, and the *Aurora* edited successively by Benjamin F. Bache and William Duane. Equally notorious with these men was the Federalist William Cobbett, publisher of *Porcupine's Gazette,* who returned to England in 1800 after Benjamin Rush won a libel suit against him growing out of his attacks on that doctor's treatment of yellow fever. After their defeat in the election, Alexander Hamilton and other Federalists in 1801 founded the *New York Evening Post,* most eminent of all newspapers of the time, which ultimately shed Federalism and turned to support the Democracy.

Architecture and Art

Jefferson had initiated a Roman revival in architecture when he found the Maison Carrée at Nîmes a perfect model for a republican temple and recommended it for the capitol of his state of Virginia. In 1791, President Washington asked Major Pierre Charles L'Enfant, who had served under him as an engineer in the Revolution, to submit a plan for the federal city. Although L'Enfant soon quarreled with Washington and Jefferson and was dismissed, and his plan was variously modified and violated, his conception still governs the city of Washington. Basically the plan combines the four-square grid of workaday streets with super-imposed diagonal avenues radiating from circles and squares, which provide grand vistas and invite ceremonial processions reminiscent of ancient Rome. The plan matched in splendor the vision of the Founders and, like the Constitution itself, it required the labor of many decades, involving many a setback and unforeseen alteration, before the reality lived up to the promise.

The story of the design and construction of the capitol typified the whole. William Thornton, an amateur in architecture, won the original competition with a design to which his successor, Stephen Hallet, added a Roman rotunda and dome flanked by wings for the Senate and House of Representatives. After much quarreling and less construction, President Jefferson in 1803 appointed his friend, Benjamin Henry Latrobe, a professional architect and innovator of the Greek Revival, to revise the plans. Latrobe believed that Greece had proved the compatibility of art and democracy and therefore provided more suitable models of architecture than the corrupted taste of the Roman Empire. He added Greek details and delighted Jefferson by substituting tobacco leaves and corn cobs for the Corinthian acanthus. The present dome—in some eyes disproportionately large—was completed only in the last days of the Civil War, an event which President Lincoln regarded as symbolic of the restoration of the Union.

Charles Bulfinch of Boston shared with Latrobe the honor of establishing architecture as a profession. His masterpiece was the Boston State House (completed in 1800) whose gilded dome dominates Beacon Hill. In the 1790's, he introduced the restrained elegance of Roman interior and exterior ornament which the Brothers Adam had made fashionable in England. This was the basis of the "Federal" style which expressed the aristocratic aspirations of the wealthiest Americans and was used for expensive residences.

American painting gradually freed itself from dependence on its original headquarters in the London studio of Benjamin West. Gilbert Stuart's innumerable portraits of Washington were British in inspiration, but the family of painting Peales in the new century drew increasingly upon American interests in nature and realistic portraiture. Sculpture was an art for which native traditions of woodcarving provided excellent beginnings. The ships' figureheads of William Rush, such as *The Genius of the United States* and *Nature,* both of which were installed on warships, fully displayed artistic intention and achievement. But Samuel McIntire, talented architect and decorator who rebuilt his native Salem, Massachusetts, in Federal style, tried to sculpture freestanding figures in wood without great success; and even the greater success of the Skillins family of Boston did not earn for them commissions in Washington. Jefferson was determined that the carvings and sculptures of the capitol should be in stone and believed that only Europeans had mastered that medium. He had already encouraged the French sculptor Houdon to create his masterly series of statues and busts of George Washington and other Americans; now for the capitol he organized the "Italian invasion" of sculptors and put them to work on American eagles and sundry classical allegories. The polished perfection of the Italian school dominated American sculpture for two generations, while the sturdy tradition of artisan-carvers in wood was all but lost.

The taste of the founding generation of Americans, whether Federalists or Republicans, was determined by European standards and haunted by ancient Greece and Rome. To modern tastes the work of the period is too subservient to its models and too pretentiously idealistic for high regard. It was as if the founders enlisted older cultures to sanction their experiment so long as its success remained problematical. The generation after 1815, no longer doubtful of success, took up more boldly the endless task of defining the cultural identity of the new society.

CHAPTER 5

Jeffersonian Liberalism
1801 - 1805

WHEN THOMAS JEFFERSON WAS INAUGURATED AS THE
third President of the United States in 1801, the population of the country,
which had risen considerably above the five million mark, was about a
third greater than it had been when he became Washington's Secretary
of State in 1790. Only one new state, Ohio, was admitted during his administration of eight years, but the most notable external fact about his
presidency was the doubling of the area of the republic by the purchase
of Louisiana. In political history he is also notable as the founder of
what came to be called the "Virginia Dynasty," for his lieutenants James
Madison and James Monroe succeeded him in the presidency and served
eight years each. His election has long been regarded as a turning point,
and he himself described it as a "revolution." It is proper to ask, therefore, what important changes his political victory really brought about.

The election of the leading opponent of the Federalists unquestionably
marked the resumption of the historic American trend toward political
democracy. But if this be measured in terms of universal suffrage and
the participation of the people in the operations of the government, the
movement assumed much greater momentum after Jefferson's day, reaching its climax in the presidency of Andrew Jackson. The Republican victory represented the triumph of the principle of majority rule, but Jeffersonian democracy was evolutionary rather than revolutionary; it was a
rising tide rather than a tidal wave.

Jefferson's election has often been interpreted as a victory for state
rights, but a more accurate statement is that it marked a reaction against
the consolidating tendencies historically associated with the name of
Hamilton. Actually, the strongest state-rights tendencies of the era now

dawning were to be manifested in New England, among foes of the administration. This is not surprising, for, as a rule, localism and separatism characterize minority groups. Also, there is a common tendency for the party in power to move in the direction of consolidation and centralization. It is a notable fact that among the Jeffersonians this tendency was resisted. As a result, the aggrandizement of national power was relatively slight during the early years of the Republican ascendancy. What there was came largely through the expansion of territory and the exigencies of international affairs.

The victory may be rightly regarded as one of agriculture over the Hamiltonian type of capitalism, though it was followed by no extreme actions. Jefferson did not overthrow the Federalist fiscal structure, and he was forced in the end to recognize the importance of industry, along with agriculture and commerce. But he did not grant industry and finance any favors, and his heart remained with the small farmers. To them he always tried to open the door of opportunity, and with them he would have filled the land. Furthermore, he and his successors created a political tie between the South and West (along with the urban masses in the East) which prevented the full triumph of business until after the Civil War.

The election marked the definite emergence of recognized political parties. The right of political opposition was vindicated by it, and Jefferson's victory was a landmark in the history of free speech. The downfall of the Federalists was owing to many causes besides their efforts to prevent criticism of the government by means of the Sedition Act, but there were important implications in the fact that the party responsible for that notorious measure was defeated. Furthermore, even though this need not be called a revolution, there was a change in the ruling group—the first since the establishment of the new government under the Constitution. This change was not so much to leaders of a different personal type, as to leaders and policies more representative of the people as a whole.

Finally, the accession of Jefferson had great significance in the world situation. In Europe the political trend had been and continued to be reactionary. Out of the chaos created by revolutionary developments in France, repressive governments, even despotisms, emerged in the Old World. This reaction was felt in the United States, and in the perspective of history the chief significance of Jefferson's career as a national political leader, perhaps, is that he checked it. He was the chief magistrate of the American Republic at a time that William Pitt governed Great Britain and Bonaparte ruled France. In an era of war and repression, he rededicated his own country to the sacred cause of freedom and gave the United States the most liberal government in the world. It was fortunate that such a leader appeared at such a time, but the outcome was not owing to him alone. A far higher degree of freedom was possible in remote

America than in war-infested Europe. Jefferson's task as President was to preserve his country and expand its liberties.

The Beginning of the Jeffersonian Regime

Jefferson was not the first President to serve in the new Federal City of Washington, which was really a straggling village, for John Adams spent several unhappy months in it. He was the first to be inaugurated there, and that was fitting, for as Secretary of State he had been the chief agent of the President in the planning and development of the new capital.

The executive mansion was unfinished when John and Abigail Adams arrived and remained unfinished during Jefferson's presidency. It was merely a big box and a rather cheerless place. The proportions of the house itself were good, but there were no porticoes as yet, no walls, no garden. After the widower President moved in, from Conrad's boarding house on Capitol Hill where he had been living unpretentiously, he rattled around in its emptiness. Only the north or Senate wing of the original capitol was ready, though the south wing was above ground. Temporarily, the House of Representatives sat in a brick building, called "the oven." Pennsylvania Avenue was a morass, and not until 1805 did an inaugural procession go down it. If Jefferson wanted a rural capital for his rural republic he unquestionably had one. There was plenty of opportunity here to vent his enthusiasm for the future, and he believed that he was embarking on an experiment.

He charted his course in the Inaugural Address he delivered in the crowded Senate chamber. He spoke in so low a tone that few people could hear him, but from that day till this, people have turned to this brief speech as the most convenient single expression of his political philosophy and public aims.

Since this was the first instance in American national history when the party of the opposition had been victorious in a presidential election, his immediate purpose was to reassure his recent opponents. But he spoke to all later Americans when he announced as a sacred principle that, "though the will of the majority is in all cases to prevail, that will, to be rightful, must be reasonable; that the minority possess their equal rights, which equal laws must protect, and to violate which would be oppression." To him the recent political conflict was a contest of opinion. Such contests are inevitable in a free society, and they lie at the base of the party system. "But every difference of opinion is not a difference of principle," he said. "We have called by different names brethren of the same principle. We are all republicans—we are all federalists." He was using the political terminology of the day, but in effect he said that when the real test comes "we are all Americans." Also, he spoke for the ages when he proclaimed that "error of opinion may be tolerated where reason is left free to combat it," and when he designated the free American system of self-government as "the world's best hope." These words were destined to live long. Abraham Lincoln echoed them in a time of grave civil conflict when he spoke of "the last best hope of earth."

The new President's more specific description of his policies and the functions of the government was directed to the conditions of his own time. There is enduring value in his claim that, in the end, a self-governing republic is stronger than any despotism, but much of his language sounds negative to any modern ear. The sum of good government, he said, is this: "a wise and frugal government, which shall restrain men from injuring one another, shall leave them otherwise free to regulate their own pursuits of industry and improvement, and shall not take from the mouth of labor the bread it has earned." There seems to be nothing here but the police power and laissez faire. Alexander Hamilton had a much more positive conception of the functions of the federal government. Jefferson spoke of the encouragement of agriculture and of commerce "as its handmaid," without mentioning industry; and he promised support of the state governments "in all their rights," as the most competent administrators of domestic matters.

In his eyes the major task of the federal government was to administer foreign affairs, and by announcing the policy of "no entangling alliances" he kept himself in the tradition of the Neutrality Proclamation and went even farther than Washington's warning in the Farewell Address against *permanent* alliances. In external relations he had never taken such a negative position as in the domestic field; and, when actually in authority, he had to disregard some of the theoretical limitations which he had set for the government during the years he was in opposition. The popularity of his rather negative political philosophy in his own time was chiefly owing to its suitability to existing conditions. After Hamilton's great work had been done there was no crying need for a forceful government in the domestic sphere. What most people wanted was freedom to take advantage of the vast opportunities of the country, without fear or favor, and this is what Jefferson sought to guarantee them. To him the strength and glory of the Republic would lie in the character and achievements of its citizens. The thought of fashioning an instrument of national power to achieve great social ends lay far in the future.

The Triumvirate

Next to the President himself, the most important members of the executive department were James Madison, the Secretary of State, and Albert Gallatin, the Secretary of the Treasury, who in conjunction with Jefferson constituted a triumvirate. Madison, now fifty-one, was a wizened little man who dressed soberly but was a good story-teller in private. Because of his long political and personal intimacy with Jefferson and his conspicuous past services to his country and party his appointment was inevitable; and because of the close attention which all the Presidents of this era gave to foreign affairs, their policy was in reality a joint policy. Dolley Payne Madison, who was friendly to everybody, was a great social asset to her husband and to the President, whom she generally served as official hostess.

Gallatin was now forty-one. His Swiss birth and French accent had been much ridiculed by the Federalists and he had never been one who cared greatly for conventional social life. From the time that he left behind him his aristocratic background in Geneva at the age of nineteen, he had lived mostly in the backwoods of Pennsylvania. Shortly before his marriage to Hannah Nicholson of New York, he had complained to her of his "anti-Chesterfieldian awkwardness in mixed companies" and told her she must polish his manners. He was a man of real personal distinction, however, and no one could question his grasp of finance.

Henry Adams has described these three men as the most aristocratic of democrats. Aristocratic they all were in origin, but as a friendly observer, Margaret Bayard Smith, said in this first year: "Never were there a plainer set of men, and I think I may add a more virtuous and enlightened one, than at present form our administration."

Jefferson was now fifty-eight. He was a gourmet and a connoisseur and he surrounded himself with books and pictures, but habits of sartorial indifference and social informality had settled upon him. Federalist newspapers never ceased ridiculing the "corduroy small-clothes, red-plush waistcoat, and sharp-toed boots with which he expressed his contempt for fashion"; and the yarn stockings and slippers down at the heel which a British envoy described have gained immortality in sober works of history. To hostile commentators these things seemed a sign of democratic affectation, the purpose of which was predominantly political. But if he looked like a tall, large-boned farmer, that was just what he was and wanted to be. As President he was just the sort of man that he was at Monticello and dispensed the same sort of hospitality. He had company for dinner—at 3:30 o'clock—every day; the food was plentiful and excellent, and the informal host put his guests at ease.

The President's style of living and entertaining was not unsuited to the rural capital of a rural republic. Yet, just as John Adams had rendered himself rather ridiculous when he urged that the President be surrounded with pomp and ceremony, Jefferson made himself a ready target when, as the presiding philosopher, he drew up democratic rules of etiquette and sought to solve the problems of precedence by the principle of "pell-mell." The carrying of this principle into effect almost created an international incident in the case of the British minister, Anthony Merry, whose wife was overlooked in the scramble at a dinner party. The Spanish minister, the Marques de Yrujo, who also had his grievance, joined with the Britisher in protestation without avail. Writing to his friend William Short, Jefferson said in 1804: "the principle of society with us, as well as of our political constitution, is the equal rights of all; . . . Nobody shall be above you, nor you above anybody, pêle-mêle is our law." He exaggerated equality to the point of making it rather absurd, but he served to establish a tradition of relative simplicity in official American society.

REPUBLICAN ADMINISTRATION

Jefferson fully shared George Washington's conviction that the government would gain respect and confidence by deserving it. No less than their Federalist predecessors the Jeffersonians emphasized good administration. Throughout his public career Jefferson himself found administrative detail boring, but by any standard he was an efficient man and he was appallingly systematic. Also, he was fortunate in having in his Secretary of the Treasury a man of genius comparable to that of Hamilton. Gallatin worked closely with Congress as Hamilton had done but was less high-handed toward the legislators, as his institution of the annual Treasury report clearly showed. In the House of Representatives when the Federalists were in power he had been chiefly responsible for the establishment of the famous Committee on Ways and Means, and he was not one to disregard Congressional prerogatives in financial matters.

Gallatin's most conspicuous early achievement was the reduction of the national debt, along with and in spite of the abolition in 1802 of the unpopular excise taxes—including that on whiskey. This reduction was accomplished in some part by economies in administration and, to a greater extent, by decreases in expenditures for the army and navy. One of the results of the latter policy was the unpreparedness of the country for war, but Jefferson believed that the United States could avoid entanglement in European conflict. During his first term his optimism was warranted, and his later foreign policies at least postponed the evil day of war. Meanwhile, despite the unexpected expenses of the Louisiana Purchase and the minor Barbary wars, and despite the loss of revenue occasioned by the Embargo of 1807, the policy of economy was conspicuously successful. By 1810, the national debt, which had been $80 million when Gallatin come into office, had been reduced by more than one-third, and during his first years the showing was a good deal better. This action was in accord with the philosophy of the President, who had long ago questioned the right of one generation to burden another by transmitting to it a vast load of public debt, and it fulfilled the promise of his inaugural.

The success of the economy program redounded to the popularity of the government. It also made possible the more positive program which was signalized by the Louisiana Purchase of 1803, and it led Jefferson himself to suggest in his second term that the surplus revenue might be applied, by constitutional amendment, to internal improvements and education within the states. He was flexible in his economic policy, while retaining his constitutional scruples. Gallatin had fewer of the latter and he was the most important early exponent of internal improvements at national expense. The program—dealing with roads, canals, and rivers—which he presented to the Senate in 1808 in a notable report, showed that he matched Hamilton in constructive imagination as in financial management.

The Republicans had inveighed against executive encroachments during their years in the opposition, and had emphasized the prerogatives of the legislative branch of the government. As Hamilton had perceived, however, Jefferson himself was no believer in a weak executive and an omnipotent legislature. At the very beginning of Washington's administration Madison had contributed signally to the creation of the executive departments and their subordination to the President, rather than to Congress, and Jefferson as Secretary of State had organized one of these. As President, he fully maintained the prestige and authority of his high office. Because of his constitutional scruples, however, and because of his temperament, he relied on indirect methods in dealing with Congress and sought to avoid any appearance of dictation. His abandonment of the practice of delivering Presidential messages in person was partly owing to his personal dislike for public speaking, but also it was in line with this policy. The chief institutional developments which marked his administration were the establishment of the floor leader in the House of Representatives as the recognized spokesman of the President, and the growth of the party caucus as a policy-making body. While Jefferson was charged by his foes with being a secret dictator, and was sometimes sharply opposed by dissenters among the Republicans themselves, he was more skillful than Hamilton, who angered many men by his imperiousness and officiousness. Jefferson was equalled in party leadership by few of his successors, and perhaps has never been surpassed.

As the first President whose advent marked a change in parties, he had to grapple with the question of the relation between political affiliation and appointment to public office. The Federalists had come to have a practical monopoly of the public service, and they aroused the indignation of the Republicans by creating new offices during their last months in office and filling these with Federalists. The most flagrant example was provided by the "midnight judges," whose commissions were signed at the last hour. Thus forty-two justices of the peace for the District of Columbia were appointed for five years—that is, they were protected until after another presidential election.

Jefferson cautiously worked out a policy of removal. This applied first to classes of officers the validity of whose appointment seemed doubtful —holders of offices created at the last moment or men appointed by Adams after his defeat was known. One of these cases—that of Chauncey Goodrich, collector at New Haven, whom Adams had appointed about two weeks before the end of his own term—aroused considerable talk and gave Jefferson the occasion to set forth his position and, unwittingly, to coin an epigram. He removed Goodrich and appointed a Republican, Samuel Bishop. Afterward he asked his critics: "If a due participation of office is a matter of right, how are vacancies to be obtained? Those by death are few; by resignation none." In shorter and more pointed form the saying is: "Few die; none resign."

Having restored the balance in a couple of years, he ceased making removals. In the course of time, Republicans came to dominate the public service just as the Federalists had done, but the policy was acceptable to the country and there was no lowering of standards. It has sometimes been said that Jefferson introduced the "spoils system," but the expression itself dates from the Age of Jackson, and it was not until then that the public service was really "politicized." There was more ground for the charge that Jefferson was hostile to the federal judiciary.

THE REPUBLICANS vs. THE JUDICIARY

The struggle between the victorious party and the judiciary, which ran through Jefferson's presidency, raised crucial questions about the relations of the co-ordinate branches—the executive, legislative, and judicial— and at several points it took on the form of a political duel between the President and his distant kinsman, the Federalist Chief Justice John Marshall. There was extreme partisanship on both sides which has served to discredit both parties at the bar of history, but the predominant judgment of the country then was essentially the same that it was more than a century later, when Franklin D. Roosevelt challenged the Supreme Court. Judges deserve rebuke when they play politics or arrogate to themselves unwarranted powers, but the executive and legislature deserve defeat when they make political attack on the independence of the judiciary.

The Federalists dominated the courts, as they had the civil service, and the judges had tended to identify opposition to the administration in power with opposition to the government itself and to the Constitution. The Sedition Act had been enforced by the federal courts in an extremely partisan manner. Also, the Federalist judges had shown little regard for the sovereignty of the state governments. Thus in the case of Chisholm vs. Georgia (1793), when the State of Georgia refused the summons of the United States Supreme Court to appear before it and defend itself against

Chisholm's claim to compensation under the Treaty of 1783 for property confiscated by the state during the Revolution, judgment was entered against the state government by default. State sovereignty is incompatible with such compulsion. The fears aroused by this decision led to the adoption of the Eleventh Amendment to the Constitution (1798), which forbids suits in the federal courts by citizens of other states or nations against state governments without the consent of the latter. This was a victory for state rights against consolidating tendencies, but the federal judiciary continued to be an agency for the establishment of national supremacy.

The Federalists gained more by a fortunate accident than by their deliberate action. The development of judicial power in the next generation is inseparable from the career of John Marshall, who was appointed Chief Justice by President Adams on January 20, 1801, following the resignation of Oliver Ellsworth and the declination of John Jay. He remained in office until 1835. The significance of Marshall's appointment was not fully realized at first, and the resentment of the Republicans was directed more strongly against the Judiciary Act of 1801, which has been aptly described as "the last word in the Federalist system." By means of it the defeated party had sought to maintain itself, irrespective of the popular will, in the least changeable branch of the government.

On practical grounds there were good reasons for a reorganization of the federal judiciary, and changes were suggested by Adams a good many months before he lost the election. The existing law (that of 1789, modified in 1793) provided for a Supreme Court, district courts, and circuit courts. The latter had no distinct set of judges, but consisted in each instance of a district court judge and a justice of the Supreme Court, who was thus required to ride the circuit—like a "traveling postboy," as one complained. In those days of slow and uncomfortable transportation this degree of travel imposed a hardship on elderly men. Furthermore, a justice might be required to consider on appeal cases on which he had already sat in a circuit.

The most important feature of the new act was the creation of sixteen circuit court judges. Adams named only Federalists to the new posts, and in some instances men who had been defeated for re-election to Congress were appointed to vacancies. Another provision of the law was that, beginning with the next vacancy, the Supreme Court itself should be reduced from six justices to five—thus depriving Jefferson of that potential appointment. Though the law had many merits it was inopportune and partisan. The Republicans, still smarting under the partisan administration of the Sedition Act, were determined to repeal it.

This they did, following Jefferson's suggestion, at the first session of the new Congress. In the course of the debate the Federalists said much about the "right" of the new judges to their offices, and charged that this Republican move was an attack on the independence of the judiciary and a preliminary to the overthrow of the Constitution. But the act of repeal (March 1802), restoring the old court system, accorded with dominant political opinion. It was carried by a strict party vote, and a supplementary measure provided that the Supreme Court should meet but once a year, beginning in February. The result was that the Supreme Court would be delayed at least nine months in passing on this particular piece of legislation. Actually, the justices signified their acceptance of the *fait accompli* by resuming their functions as circuit riders, and, a little later, they did so by formal action (in the case of Stuart *vs.* Laird, March 2, 1803). The first round in the struggle between the Jeffersonians and the judiciary had been won by the former, but the latter's turn came at the next session of the Supreme Court in the historic case of Marbury *vs.* Madison.

Marbury vs. Madison

One of the minor "midnight" commissions was that of William Marbury as a justice of peace of the District of Columbia. It was not delivered by Adams's acting Secretary of State, who was no other than John Marshall; and it was afterwards withheld on the new President's personal instructions, since Jefferson adjudged the appointment to be illegal or unwarranted. He reappointed most of these justices of the peace but Marbury was not one of them. This became a *cause célèbre* because Marbury applied to the Supreme Court under the Judiciary Act of 1789 for a writ of mandamus, that is, a writ commanding the Secretary of State to deliver the commission. The application involved the Chief Justice in a dilemma. A decision in favor of Madison would have strengthened the executive in its battle with the judiciary and given comfort to his detested political foes, whereas a decision in favor of Marbury would have been unenforceable, since the executive would ignore it and no force belongs to the judiciary. Marshall's decision has been described by a sympathetic biographer as a piece of "perfectly calculated audacity," and by more critical authority as a "partisan coup."

On the merits of the case he decided in effect for Marbury, holding that the latter had a right to his commission and that it was the duty of Madison to deliver it. Thus the Chief Justice lectured the executive branch about the performance of its duties. He then proceeded to declare that the Supreme Court could nevertheless do nothing, since a writ of mandamus could not issue from that body. Such a power had been conferred on it by act of Congress, to be sure, but Section 13 of the Act of 1789 was unconstitutional, he said, since the definition of the original jurisdiction of the Supreme Court in the Constitution did not extend that far. By denying to his Court a lesser power, which would have been useless to him under the circumstances, Marshall asserted the transcendent power of declaring an act of Congress unconstitutional.

The main objection to Marshall's decision at the time was not that the Supreme Court had invalidated a minor section of an act of Congress. It was that the Chief Justice had invaded the executive sphere by telling the President and Secretary of State what their duty was. Jefferson believed that he had the right to decide on questions of propriety and constitutionality in the exercise of his executive functions. Thus, believing the Sedition Act to be unconstitutional, he regarded himself as bound not to execute it. The co-ordinate branches of the government were meant to be checks on each other, he said, but he saw no warrant for making the judiciary a "despotic branch." What he feared was judicial supremacy, and there were times in the later history of his country when this became a real danger. But through the years the American ideal became clearer —a government of laws not men—and the independent judiciary has seemed the safest and most impartial interpreter of these laws and the Constitution.

Impeachments

Since federal judges were appointed for life, they could not be held accountable at the polls, and the only available weapon against bad behavior was impeachment. The Jeffersonians resorted to impeachment in the sad case of a district judge of New Hampshire, John Pickering, who was wholly incapacitated for office because of insanity and drunkenness. He was charged with high crimes and misdemeanors, so as to meet the constitutional requirements, and was removed by a partisan vote. The proceedings against Justice Samuel Chase of the Supreme Court were marked by ineptitude, but he himself arouses little sympathy. The grievances against Chase went back to his conduct of trials under the Sedition Act, but the immediate occasion for action against him was provided by a highly indiscreet charge he made to a grand jury in Baltimore in May 1803. In this he attacked constitutional proposals in Maryland and universal suffrage, saying that this pointed the way toward "mobocracy"; and it was said that he violently attacked the administration. His impeachment by the House of Representatives resulted from this, though the trial before the Senate did not actually occur until the beginning of the year 1805, after Jefferson's triumphant re-election, the vote on Chase being taken only a few days before his second inauguration.

This action was distinctly partisan, and the more extreme Republicans justified it on partisan grounds. One of them, William Branch Giles of Virginia, asserted that impeachment was no more than "an inquiry by the two houses of Congress, whether the office of any public man might not be better filled by another." In other words, the object of such maneuvers was to wreak venegance on political foes and give offices to good Republicans. More moderate and more philosophical Republicans were unwilling to go that far, however, and the division of opinion in the dominant group proved a fatal weakness. The charges comprised all the complaints against Chase, and there was a majority vote against him on some articles, but the constitutional requirement of two-thirds was met in no instance. The major weakness of the case lay in the fact that the genuine grievances against Chase did not amount to high crimes and misdemeanors. He deserved rebuke but not conviction.

This round in the fight went against the Republicans. Jefferson himself declared that impeachment was a farce which would not be tried again, and he kept on lamenting through the years that the independence of the judges was really independence from public opinion. They represented to him the stubborn changelessness of the Federalist Party. But the proceedings against Justice Chase, besides revealing the necessary limitations of impeachment in the American system, did have a sobering effect on the manners and utterances of politically-minded judges. They restrained their partisanship much more after this, though the conduct of Chief Justice Marshall in the Burr trial did not provide a good example. That trial constituted the final round in Marshall's open duel with the President.

FREEDOM AND SLANDER

In the philosophy of Jefferson, the freeing of the individual citizen to the fullest possible degree in all departments of life was fully as important as the attainment of popular rule, and to him freedom of the mind and freedom of speech were basic in human progress. It is in this sense that his philosophy can best be described as "liberal." He was still devoted to the ideals that he had inherited from the Enlightenment of the Eighteenth Century. There was irony, therefore, in his inability to check the rising tide of intellectual reaction and in his own grievous suffering from the freedom of the press.

In the sphere of religion certain tendencies that are commonly described as "liberal" continued in some quarters. At Harvard, the election of Henry Ware as Hollis Professor of Divinity (1805), after several years of controversy, signalized the defeat of the conservative Calvinists and the victory of the Unitarians in that historic seat of learning. But this period of religious revivalism throughout the country was marked by the rapid growth of the more evangelical Presbyterians, the Baptists, and the Methodists, all of whom tended toward religious orthodoxy. In the West and South these developments brought no political disadvantage to Jefferson as yet, since he was still remembered as the champion of freedom for dissenting sects against the old Church establishments. In New England, also, the dissenting religious groups who were warring against the privileged Church in such states as Massachusetts and Connecticut tended to be Jeffersonian, despite the growing conservatism of the public in religious matters. The latter was well exemplified at Yale College, where President Timothy Dwight had for some years been waging vigorous and successful warfare on "infidelity."

To the New England Congregational clergy, who were still closely allied with the civil rulers, Jefferson's religious views and attitudes provided an inviting target. He avoided all public reference to his own religious opinions, believing that these were wholly a private matter. Nominally he remained an Episcopalian, but he was essentially a Deist, though not at all militant, and in everything except name he was a Unitarian. During his first term he gave a handle to his critics by his public attitude toward Thomas Paine, who returned to America in 1802 and remained in the country until his death seven years later.

Paine had expressed the wish that if Jefferson should have occasion to send a frigate to France, he would give him the opportunity of returning by it. Jefferson offered him passage on the *Maryland,* expressing the hope that Paine would find the Americans "returned to sentiments worthy of former times" and that he might live long to continue his "useful labors" (March 18, 1801). This was a gracious offer, to which Paine's past services to the cause of American independence and universal human freedom may have entitled him, but he was now better known as the writer of an extremely abusive letter against George Washington and as the author of *The Age of Reason,* which was regarded by practically all the churches in the United States as a direct attack on them. He came by a private vessel, not in an American warship, but the President got the full discredit for the original invitation. Paine gave further fuel to partisan wrath when he published a series of letters *To the Citizens of the United States and Particularly to the Leaders of the Federalist Faction* (1802-1805). During his last years he lived in poverty as a social outcast, and in death he was denied burial in consecrated ground.

Jefferson's personal sufferings from abuses of the freedom of the press can best be illustrated by his experiences with James Thomson Callender, one of the conspicuous victims of the Sedition Act. Few sufferers under that law deserved less consideration, but President Jefferson pardoned him and remitted his fine. Impatient at the slight delay in the repayment of his fine and resentful because of his failure to receive any political reward, Callender turned on his distinguished patron. Dipping his pen in filth, he filled the columns of the *Richmond Recorder* (1802-1803) with charges against Jefferson of financial impropriety and gross personal immorality. The wholly unwarranted but lingering tradition that the master of Monticello had a slave mistress may be traced back to this vindictive scandalmonger, who so signally illustrated the abuses of freedom. The Federalist press gleefully took up his charges, coupling them with others that had already been aired in the campaign of 1800. Even after Jefferson's re-election the chorus of abuse continued. Early in 1805, in the House of Representatives of Massachusetts, a motion to dismiss the printers of the House for publishing libels on the President in the *New-England Palladium* was defeated. Neither of his predecessors had been subjected to such a campaign of hatred, and few if any of his successors were to be subjected to similar unwarranted attacks on moral grounds. Undeserved abuse is one of the perquisites of every President, but he got far more than a normal share of it.

The application of libel laws in *state* courts *after* the event of defamation, was not contrary to the philosophy of Jefferson; and followers of his actually instituted a few suits of this sort during his administration. In Connecticut, where state courts were under the rigid control of the bitterest of his political enemies and were engaged in penalizing his partisans, Republicans went so far as to start libel proceedings in federal courts, thus laying themselves open to the just charge of inconsistency. Nearly all of these cases were eventually dropped, however, and the total for his eight years in office was slight in comparison with the large number in the last two years of the Adams administration. Jefferson appeared to acquiesce in some of these actions of his own partisans, which is not to his credit, but his record is clear in declining to do anything whatever in defense of himself against personal charges.

During his presidency he went through a sharp revulsion of feeling toward the press. He had once said that if he had to choose between a government without newspapers, and newspapers without a government, he would prefer the latter—assuming that people were sufficiently educated to read and understand them. His private correspondence shows, however, that at this stage he was deeply conscious of the unreliability of the press and appalled by the public appetite for defamation. The doctrine of freedom greatly needed supplementation by that of responsibility. There was no revival of the Sedition Law, and, as Jefferson stated in his second inaugural, his re-election attested the success of the experiment "whether freedom of discussion, unaided by power, is not sufficient for the propagation and protection of truth." He believed that experience had proved that a pure and scrupulous government could not be written down by falsehood and defamation.

He never fully recovered his earlier enthusiasm for newspapers, and in his later life he reported that he had turned with relief from them to the ancient classical writers. Some years after his retirement, however, he said: "When the press is free, and every man able to read, all is safe." By and large, despite some failures, his entire career may be described as a successful experiment in freedom. But his triumph in 1804, when he got 162 electoral votes to 14 for Charles Cotesworth Pinckney of South Carolina, the Federalist candidate, gaining the votes of all the states except Connecticut and Delaware and two electors from Maryland, can also be attributed to other causes. The main one was the Louisiana Purchase.

CHAPTER 6

Expansion and Domestic Faction, 1803-1809

MOST OF JEFFERSON'S PRESIDENCY AND PRACTICALLY the whole of his successor's was set against the background of general European war, the reverberations of which were felt throughout the Atlantic world. The Treaty of Amiens, which brought a cessation of hostilities between Napoleon and the British, was signed in the autumn of 1801. For a couple of years there was a lull, but the titanic conflict was resumed in May 1803 and it continued practically without intermission until the final downfall of Napoleon toward the end of Madison's presidency.

From France, the chief warring country of Europe, President Jefferson gained a magnificent prize in the immense province of Louisiana. But in his second term, when the commerce of the young American Republic was caught in the cross fire, he suffered his greatest discomfiture in the ill fate of his embargo. In his conduct of foreign affairs he was motivated by the strong desire to keep his own country out of this world conflict in which, as he believed, it had no real concern, and to gain for it time to realize on its great potentialities. His greatest triumph, the Louisiana Purchase, redounded chiefly to the advantage of settlers in the West, which as he clearly foresaw was destined to become the heart of the American agricultural empire. By all rights he should be the patron saint of the Mississippi Valley. His foreign policy, though flexible in many ways, had one fixed point. As Secretary of State he was anxious to procure and as President he was determined to maintain the free navigation of the Mississippi, being convinced that this was necessary to retain the trans-Alleghany settlements in the Union.

His western policy could be properly described as nationalistic, but it was also infused with concern for the individual settlers and it turned out to be good politics. Nothing showed more clearly the blindness and un-teachableness of the Federalist leaders than their indifference and opposition to western development. The President, both as a politician and a national statesman, was looking to the future, while they were looking to the past. Writing to his successor shortly after his retirement, Jefferson described the expanded American nation of his dreams as such an "empire for liberty" as had not been seen since the creation. This was the transcendent American dream, and nobody did more than he to translate it into reality.

The Men of the Western Waters

When Jefferson was inaugurated in 1801 there were still only two states beyond the mountains, Kentucky and Tennessee, but the population of both of these had trebled since the census of 1790 and both were destined to double in the next decade. The reference to these people as "men of the western waters" was proper, since they were dependent on the waterways for their major transportation. The course of commerce in this growing inland empire was inevitably southward.

In the region above the Ohio in the old Northwest Territory, settlement had been slower than below that river, chiefly because of the presence of the Indians, but the tide really began to flow after the Treaty of Greenville (1795) opened up most of the present state of Ohio. By 1798, Ohio had been granted a territorial government of her own, and in 1800 Congress passed the Harrison Land Act, which served to encourage small settlers as compared with speculative companies, even if Federalist conservatism prevented its being as liberal as the frontiersmen wanted. The price of land remained at $2 an acre as it had been in 1796, but as small a tract as 320 acres could now be bought and only a fourth of the purchase money had to be paid in cash, four years' credit being allowed for the balance. The law was liberalized by the Republicans in 1804, when the minimum was reduced to 160 acres, the credit feature being retained. In 1800, Indiana became a separate territory under the governorship of William Henry Harrison; and in 1802 a convention in Ohio, authorized by Congress, voted almost unanimously for statehood.

The Jeffersonians supported and the Federalist leaders tended to obstruct these measures, but the net result was to facilitate settlement and add another state to the Union in 1803. One important early region of settlement was the Western Reserve centering on Cleveland, and here, as in the still earlier settlement at Marietta, New England influence was strong; but the leadership of the new territory and state was predominantly Southern and most of the settlements were contiguous to the Ohio and its tributaries. In politics, Ohio was Republican, just as Kentucky and Tennessee were; and her trade also had to flow southward with the currents of the rivers. To all these people it was vital that the gate at New Orleans should not be locked.

In the region south of Tennessee, settlement had been delayed by dangers from the Indians and by grave uncertainties about boundaries and land titles. The Treaty of San Lorenzo in 1795 had fixed the southern boundary of the United States at the 31st parallel of latitude, but the Spanish did not withdraw from the southern sector until 1798, and even then the Americans were cut off from the Gulf of Mexico by Spanish West Florida. The territory of Mississippi was established in 1800 in the region between the 31st parallel and the state of Tennessee, but the state of Georgia, which laid claim to it by virtue of its colonial charter, did not formally yield title to the federal government until 1802, and the story behind that cession suggests the turmoil and feverish speculation which accompanied the early development of the Old Southwest.

In the year 1795, by means of the infamous Yazoo Act, the state of Georgia sold to four companies the greater part of the land now comprised in the states of Alabama and Mississippi. The price, less than a cent and a half per acre, was absurdly low, and the act was passed under conditions of notorious corruption. The indignant citizenry rose up in protest, and the next legislature promptly rescinded the action. Sobered and ashamed, the officials of the state acquiesced in the action of Congress in creating the Mississippi Territory, while not yet surrendering the claims of Georgia, and then they negotiated with the federal government a settlement of the long-standing dispute. This was effected in 1802, the boundaries of Georgia being then drawn as they are today and the state being granted $1.25 million. One of the provisions of this settlement, by which the federal government agreed to extinguish as soon as possible the Indian titles within the state, was the occasion of much subsequent controversy. The Georgians afterward claimed that the process of abolishing Indian titles and opening the way to settlers proceeded more rapidly in the ceded territory than in Georgia itself. Not until the presidency of Andrew Jackson were the Indians expelled from Georgia, which, by accident of circumstances, retained certain frontier characteristics considerably longer than younger states like Kentucky and Tennessee.

The episode has significance in later constitutional history, for claimants to land titles in Mississippi Territory, on the basis of purchases from the defunct companies before the rescinding of the Yazoo Act, continued to besiege the federal courts. In the case of Fletcher vs. Peck (1810) Chief Justice Marshall upheld the sanctity of the contract, regardless of the corruption and the later rescinding action. In order to meet this legal situation, Congress (1814) voted $5 million to reimburse the purchasers. Marshall had taught a hard lesson in responsibility to voters and legislators while giving assurance to businessmen that henceforth a legislative grant would be deemed as binding as a contract between private parties.

THE LOUISIANA PURCHASE

The Spanish, who had received Louisiana from the French as a reward for their services in the Seven Years' War and had been in possession for a generation, found the province a financial burden and recognized that their own tenure was precarious. As American settlement continued to grow along the western waters, hardy frontiersmen might surge down the great river and take over the port of New Orleans. Also, in the changing pattern of international affairs there was always the possibility that the Americans would team up with the British, from whom the Spanish, in the settlement after the American Revolution, had repossessed themselves of the Floridas. Thus the Spanish Court was not averse to the suggestion that they return Louisiana to the French, who would be much better able to hold it. That was just the reason why the prospective transfer aroused alarm in the minds of American leaders. Far from being a declining power, France was the most powerful and aggressive nation in the world.

The Treaty of San Ildefonso, whereby Louisiana was retroceded by Spain to France, in return for a duchy on the banks of the Italian River Arno to be provided for the Duke of Parma, son-in-law of the Spanish King, was signed on October 1, 1800, but the transfer was delayed for several years and the agreement was not officially announced. In 1801, rumors of the retrocession became persistent. Robert R. Livingston, the new minister to France who sailed in October, was instructed to do his utmost to prevent the cession if it had not occurred and to preserve the free navigation of the Mississippi in any case. He was also to inquire into possibilities of the purchase of the Floridas.

It was the land east not west of the Mississippi that the administration was interested in, and Jefferson himself described the situation vividly and concisely in a letter to Livingston. He believed that the cession by Spain to France included Florida as well as Louisiana and that the crisis created by it would require a complete reversal of his own preferred foreign policy. Hitherto this had been guided by the conviction that France was the natural friend of the United States, whereas Great Britain was a natural rival and at times even an enemy.

There is on the globe one single spot, [he said] the possessor of which is our natural and habitual enemy. It is New Orleans, through which the produce of three-eighths of our territory must pass to market, and from its fertility it will ere long yield more than half of our whole produce and contain more than half of our inhabitants. France placing herself in that door assumes to us the attitude of defiance. . . . The day that France takes possession of N. Orleans fixes the sentence which is to restrain her forever within her low water mark. It seals the union of two nations who in conjunction can maintain exclusive possession of the ocean. From that moment we must marry ourselves to the British fleet and nation. (April 18, 1802)

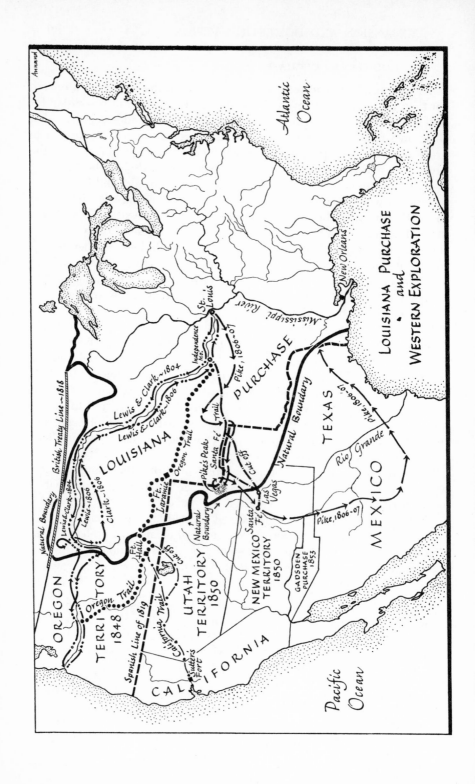

Louisiana Purchase and Western Exploration

Later in the same year (October 16, 1802) the Spanish Intendant, still in authority in Louisiana, announced the closure of the Mississippi. This action was not owing to the French, but most Americans thought it was and it seemed to mark the realization of their worst fears. Early in 1803 there was bellicose talk in Congress, and soon thereafter James Monroe was sent to France as a special minister to reinforce Livingston. He was authorized to offer $10 million for New Orleans and West Florida, but before he got to France Livingston had been offered the whole province of Louisiana. The famous bargain was concluded by him and Monroe. The cost went 50 per cent beyond instructions, since it came to $15 million including claims, and there was considerable uncertainty as to just what the Americans had purchased. But it was a noble bargain by any reckoning and the real question has always been, why Napoleon offered it, thus relieving President Jefferson of the necessity of "marrying the British fleet and nation."

Napoleon's larger plan to restore the French colonial empire had included the acquisition of Florida, but his blandishments were unavailing in this regard and the Spanish Court would not yield. In the meantime a disaster had befallen him in Santo Domingo. That highly profitable sugar island was central in the colonial scheme, and a major step in the Napoleonic program had been the putting down of the rebellion of the noted Negro leader, Toussaint Louverture. Toussaint was captured by Napoleon's brother-in-law, General Leclerc, but the latter and his army were destroyed by the rebellious Negroes and by yellow fever. The death of Leclerc was known in Paris in January 1803, and Napoleon is then reported to have said, "Damn sugar, damn coffee, damn colonies." By this time the conqueror of the continent of Europe had had enough of this distant overseas venture.

If he was to renew his duel with the British, he wanted no rupture with the United States, and American resentment at the closing of the Mississippi by the Spanish Intendant had given him fair warning. What, then, should he do with Louisiana? By selling it to the United States he could at least get some money out of it; and, what was more important, he could check the growing rapprochement between the Americans and the British, and create for his hated enemy a powerful future rival. This reversion to the earlier French foreign policy of Vergennes was not without important fruitage in his own time. When the United States finally became involved in the European struggle in the War of 1812 it was as an opponent of Great Britain. The immediate gain of Napoleon was slight. The money acquired by the transaction was actually spent in preparations for the abortive invasion of England. But he did something to restore the balance of power, and the United States was the major beneficiary of his action.

Questions and Consequences

The predominant contemporary opinion was that the acquisition of Louisiana, by treaty with France, was the most fortunate event in American history after the adoption of the Declaration of Independence and the Constitution. But the transaction aroused grave constitutional questions. In the Constitution there is no specific grant of power to acquire territory, and Jefferson, who much preferred a safe and precise construction to one that was dangerous and indefinite, suffered many qualms. While convinced that ratification of the treaty was imperative and that delay would be perilous in dealing with as shifty a ruler as Napoleon, he would have preferred that official sanction for this unexampled action should be given in the form of a constitutional amendment. His friends and advisers, Gallatin in particular, did not share his scruples and he yielded to them, trusting that the good sense of the country would correct the possible future ills resulting from this precedent. He may be praised for political realism even if blamed for theoretical inconsistency. Certain Federalist leaders, who now advanced arguments of strict construction against the treaty, were fully as inconsistent as he.

The chief argument was not so much over the power of the government to acquire territory as over the incorporation of new territory in the Union, and the speedy admission of the inhabitants to the rights of citizenship, as provided for in one article of the treaty. Opposition to this was based primarily on political and sectional grounds. A few went so far as to urge that the acquired territories of the United States be held in a dependent status and comprise a sort of colonial domain, but the New England Federalists were chiefly motivated by fear lest, in an expanding Union, their own position would become increasingly subordinate. Fisher Ames of Massachusetts, though he could not bring himself to accept extreme strict construction, was alarmed by this huge addition of territory, saying "we rush like a comet into infinite space." Jefferson himself was not disposed to hurry the peopling of the trans-Mississippi region. He would have been content to leave most of it as an Indian sanctuary for the present, transferring to it the tribes still east of the Mississippi. But the doubling of the size of the United States threatened an ultimate change in the character of the Union, and it is no wonder that some of the Easterners were frightened.

Despite all these forebodings, enthusiasm for the treaty was so great that its ratification was inevitable. The power of the federal government to acquire territory, either by conquest or treaty, was affirmed by Chief Justice Marshall in 1828 (American Insurance Company vs. Canter), thus setting to rest for all time that question. The incorporation of this territory assured the future material greatness of the United States, but the great controversy over the extension of slavery came to a head in this region. It is one of the ironies of history that, in the end, the greatest difficulties arising from the enlargement of the Union came not to New England but to the South. It would be an exaggeration to say that the new Empire for Liberty inflicted a death blow on the doctrine of strict construction, for that doctrine was by no means dead. It would be nearer the truth to say that it made inevitable the triumph of the nationalist spirit, the eventual victory of the North, and the abolition of slavery. All that lay in the future. At the time the brilliance of the diplomatic achievement silenced the voice of fear almost everywhere and brought the President to the height of his popularity.

Another set of problems arose from the uncertainties about the boundaries of the purchase. In the treaty the province of Louisiana was described as having "the extent that it now has in the hands of Spain, and that it had when France possessed it." Napoleon made the sale before the property was turned over to him, and it had actually been in the hands of the French only a few days when they transferred it to the United States. Most modern scholars interpret the wording of the treaty as meaning that the territory acquired by the United States east of the Mississippi included only the island of New Orleans and the swamps below it, agreeing with the Spanish contention that West Florida began at the Iberville River. The western boundary of Louisiana was not yet defined, and when eventually drawn (1819) it excluded Texas, but the province included the valley of the Missouri and extended westward to the Rockies.

In view of the original American purpose to get land east rather than west of the Mississippi, perhaps it is not surprising that the envoys, taking advantage of the vagueness of the description of the territory, persuaded themselves that it really included the part of West Florida that had been administered by the Spanish in conjunction with Louisiana. There was practical reason for this rationalization since this district cut off the Mississippi Territory from New Orleans, which the Americans could approach only by the river. Livingston soon claimed that the eastern boundary was really the Perdido River, where the present state of Florida begins, and his interpretation proved irresistible. It was elaborated by Monroe in a memoir, taken up by Jefferson, and accepted as the official position. Certain provisions of the Mobile Act of 1804 were based on these territorial assumptions, but under the force of Spanish protests the administration backed down, and then dispatched Monroe to Spain on what proved to be a futile mission. Despite cajoleries and threats, Jefferson was unable to convince or overawe the Spanish and the disputed region remained nominally in their hands until Madison's presidency, when it was seized. American settlers had overrun parts of it by that time. The present state of Florida was acquired by treaty a little later (1819).

EXPLORING THE INLAND EMPIRE, 1803-1807

The desire of the administration to possess the Gulf Coast arose from immediate considerations of commerce and national safety. The uses of the vast trans-Mississippi region north of the present state of Louisiana lay in a more distant future. Yet Jefferson had long been eager to learn more about this unknown country and, several months before it was ceded to the United States, he gained from Congress secret authority for a small expedition to explore the Missouri River "even to the Western Ocean." To head this he appointed his secretary, Captain Meriwether Lewis, a native of Jefferson's home county who had long panted to do this sort of thing. Lewis chose as his associate William Clark, recently a lieutenant in the army but called "captain" on this expedition. He was a younger brother of George Rogers Clark and was known among the Indians as "Red Head." By the time the expedition actually started up the Missouri in the spring of 1804, Louisiana was unquestionably American, hence the camouflage with which the President had originally obscured the project had become unnecessary.

Jefferson believed that the Missouri, with possibly a single portage to the headwaters of the Columbia, offered a better line of navigation from the Pacific Northwest than the one the British followed in the frozen North. He wanted to open up new routes for traffic with the Indians and hoped to tap the fur trade, but his specific instructions to the explorers show his great concern for the expansion of knowledge about his country and continent. He asked suggestions about scientific objects from leading members of the American Philosophical Society, and had Lewis visit some of them. The main object was to explore and chart the waterways, but the Indians, the soil and face of the country, the flora and fauna, the mineral resources and climate—all these were to be observed.

The story of the Lewis and Clark expedition comprises one of the most exciting, heroic, and significant episodes in the saga of western exploration. The leaders had been instructed to be friendly toward the natives, and the only serious skirmish was on the way back. This was peaceful penetration. After Lewis had spent the winter of 1803-1804 on the Illinois side of the Mississippi near St. Louis, he was joined by Clark at St. Charles, a little to the west. Then, proceeding up the river, they came to the Mandan region in what is now North Dakota in the fall and spent the winter in the fort they built there. In the spring of 1805, they were guided to the end of navigation by a French Canadian and his Indian wife, Sacagawea, carrying her infant strapped on her back. This woman of the Shoshones, who secured from relatives the horses on which the white men crossed the continental divide, rendered services which have been honored by more memorials, it is said, than have been erected to any other American of her sex. Coming at length into the Clearwater Valley, the explorers floated down the Columbia to the sea, which they reached in November 1805. They built Fort Clatsop near Astoria, spent the winter there, and started back for the East in the spring of 1806, arriving at St. Louis in September. The party divided on the return trip and thus explored additional tributaries of the Missouri.

Jefferson received "with unspeakable joy" the news of the arrival at St. Louis. The expedition had not shown that the line of the Missouri provided as easy access to the far Northwest as he had thought, and the details of geographical and other scientific information which the explorers had set down were not immediately available, since the history of the expedition was not published until 1814 and the journals remained in manuscript for generations. But time has heavily underlined the President's quiet statement that Lewis and Clark and their brave companions by their arduous service deserved well of their country.

Other expeditions of the time were less successful. A couple of attempts to explore the Red River to its source in what is now the Panhandle of Texas failed because of Spanish opposition. Lieutenant Zebulon M. Pike did not really get to the source of the Mississippi on his expedition of 1805-1806, though at the time both he and the President thought he did. He made a more famous expedition in 1806-1807, from St. Louis to the Colorado country, where his name survives in Pike's Peak. Besides exploring the upper reaches of the Arkansas, he descended the Rio Grande, became a captive of the Spanish at Santa Fé, and finally got back to the United States through northern Mexico and Texas. Jefferson fathered all these explorations, gaining Congressional support for them. Exploration died down after Pike's Colorado expedition, partly because of the absorption of the public mind in foreign questions.

FACTION AND CONSPIRACY, 1804-1807

The Louisiana Purchase served to check separatist tendencies among Westerners by giving them an assured outlet for their produce, but it seemed to many Federalist leaders that this immense accession of territory had upset the balance of power between the North and South, increased the "overbearing influence" of Virginia, and threatened to make the West dominant in the future. They were slow to perceive the import of the vast northern reaches of the new domain, which were destined to strengthen the position in the Union of the northern system of family farms, and they feared the political complexion of such new states as would be carved out of the northwestern wilderness and prairie

These fears continued to be most pronounced in New England. It seemed that Jefferson and his minions were creating a new national geography and politics to convert the land of the Puritans into a peninsula remote from the center of the country and excluded from the national councils. Thus the minds of the high priests of New England Federalism turned to the idea of a separate northern confederacy.

Toward the end of 1803, Senator Timothy Pickering of Massachusetts, writing privately, made a grave prediction: "There will be—and our children at farthest will see it—a separation." Early in 1804 he and other conspirators were seeking to hasten the day. Among these were Congressman Roger Griswold and Senator Uriah Tracy of Connecticut, and Senator William Plumer of New Hampshire. Disunionist spirit was weak among the rank and file, however, and the Sage of New England Federalism, George Cabot of Massachusetts, believed that separation would be impracticable until there was a stronger and more flagrant cause—such as a war with the British, "manifestly provoked by our masters." He believed that democracy would proceed from bad to worse, until intolerable ills would generate their own remedies. This was essentially the position of Hamilton, now in private life in New York, who grew even more alarmed when the conspirators turned to that "Mephistopheles of politics," Aaron Burr. They felt they had to, because of the centrality of his state in a future northern confederacy, and if he did not definitely agree to their plans they were disposed to rely on his vague assurances.

Burr and Hamilton

Vice-President Burr had become a man without a party. The attempt to defeat the will of the Republicans by electing him as President instead of Jefferson in 1801 had not been forgotten or forgiven; he had been ignored in the distribution of patronage in New York; and he was wholly out of favor with the dominant Clintons and Livingstons in his own state. Nonetheless, he aspired to the governorship and was put forward for it by a caucus of his friends in February 1804, just a week before he was dropped as a vice-presidential candidate in favor of Governor George Clinton. He got a great deal of Federalist support in the final voting, but Hamilton had prevented his formal endorsement by the leaders and he lost the election. Hamilton had no intention of letting Burr become the recognized leader of the northern Federalists. Besides personal motives there were public ones. He regarded Burr as a dangerous man, not fit to be entrusted with high office, and held "a still more despicable opinion of him." These comments got into a letter written by another, and this letter got into print. They were the occasion of the most famous duel in the history of the Republic.

Burr's not unnatural demand for a retraction was handled badly by Hamilton. His reply was evasive and its closing words practically invited the challenge which eventually came, despite a belated statement that his remarks were political not personal. There was a romantic streak in Hamilton and he was highly sensitive about his own honor. Also, he believed that his political hopes would be forever dashed if he now appeared before the public as a coward. He was intrepid in spirit and, at last, he had to pay the costs of recklessness. He stated that he intended to reserve his first fire and perhaps he had some thought that his antagonist might pause and reflect, but Burr was in dead earnest.

Early in the morning of July 11, 1804, Hamilton and Burr with their seconds and Dr. David Hosack crossed the Hudson from Manhattan to a spot under the Palisades at Weehawken in New Jersey. When the moment came, two shots rang out. Whether or not Hamilton's was unintentional, as he and his second claimed, it was harmless, while Burr's inflicted a mortal wound. Hamilton died after hours of agony. His funeral was accompanied by minute guns which were answered by foreign warships in New York harbor, and even followers of Aaron Burr now did him honor. The excesses which had marred his genius and hastened his end were forgotten. Friends rallied to the support of his impoverished family. He had gained no personal advantage from the huge financial operations he had carried on, and he died in virtual bankruptcy. It was power he had craved, not money.

Appalled by the fate of the most brilliant of the Federalists, though his counsel had been heeded little in recent years, the New England conspirators abandoned Burr. In effect they adopted Cabot's policy of waiting for a time of trouble before assailing the Union. This came in 1812 during "Mr. Madison's War." Burr meanwhile found New York and New Jersey too hot for him, but nothing ever came of his indictment for murder and he served out the remaining months of his term as Vice-President, presiding with notable impartiality over the impeachment trial of Justice Chase and delivering, on March 2, 1805, a moving valedictory. He had begun to weave a web of intrigue which confounded the administration and has never ceased to fascinate and baffle the historians. In the next two years he appeared more than ever as an adventurer, and he was looking to the great West as the orbit in which his star would yet rise to glory. Also, he looked to foreign powers, making proposals to the British and the Spanish and seeking money from both of them.

Burr's Expedition and Trial

Perhaps no one will ever know precisely what this brilliant and reckless man was planning during that last winter in Washington and during the two trips to the West that he made in 1805 and 1806-1807. Was he trying to promote the secession of the western states with British and Spanish aid? If so, he did not pick an appropriate time, since the worst fears of the Westerners had been calmed by the Louisiana Purchase. Was he planning an attack on Mexico, which might or might not have as its first step the seizure of New Orleans? There was plenty of anti-Spanish feeling in the West, but he could hardly have expected the Spanish themselves to aid him in his efforts to exploit it. Was he merely interested in establishing a settlement on the Washita River in Louisiana Territory, as he stated publicly? The project of a settlement appears to have been a blind to more ambitious plans, the precise development of which was contingent on circumstances. Burr seems to have dreamed, at least, of a new empire stretching from the Ohio to Panama, which he should rule as emperor; and his apparent intention was to do whatever he could get away with.

While he was still in office Burr contrived to make President Jefferson himself unwittingly serve his interests by extending the functions of his chief fellow conspirator, General James Wilkinson, to include the governorship of Louisiana. Jefferson was unsuspicious of Wilkinson, though we now know that for years that grand rascal had taken pay from the King of Spain while commanding the American army in the West. Adventurous frontiersmen like Andrew Jackson, whom Burr visited in Tennessee, were charmed by the elegant Eastern duelist. The vague prospects of conquest which Burr held out were alluring to many volatile Westerners, and he himself appears to have been deluded by the enthusiasm which he evoked. His wealthiest adherent was Herman Blennerhasset, an Irish exile who had set up a feudal domain on an island in the Ohio River near Marietta. There the expedition started which Burr himself joined at the mouth of the Cumberland and recruits were picked up as they went along. In the winter of 1806-1807, Burr and some sixty followers dropped down the Ohio and the Mississippi in flatboats on one of the wildest enterprises of the wild West's history.

Federal District Attorney Joseph Daveiss of Kentucky had tried to obtain an indictment against Burr for raising armed forces to break up the Union and wage war against Spain, but successive grand juries had cleared him. Though informed by Daveiss of Burr's highly sus-picious activities, President Jefferson was strangely quiescent until the traitorous Wilkinson double-crossed his fellow conspirator. On receipt of Wilkinson's message, charging that Burr designed a descent on Mexico and auxiliary revolt of the Orleans territory, Jefferson issued (November 27, 1806) a proclamation which led to the arrest of Burr. After clearing himself before another grand jury in Mississippi Territory, he fled toward Mobile but was apprehended. On March 30, 1807, he was brought before Chief Justice Marshall in Richmond, Virginia.

Burr's trial, which began in May 1807 and lasted into September, excited much attention at the time because of its political implications, and it also had great constitutional significance. In fact, it was the most important judicial proceeding against treason in American national history. The ironies of the situation were extreme. The Chief Justice of the United States presided over the Circuit Court in the Virginia state capitol. A couple of years earlier Vice-President Burr had himself presided over the impeachment trial of a Justice of the United States Supreme Court. Now the President publicly declared that Burr's guilt was beyond doubt and did everything in his power to procure the conviction of his former colleague. John Marshall, on the other hand, was a bitter political foe of Jefferson and eager to discredit him. The trial amounted to a political duel between the absent President and the adroit and persuasive Burr, who headed his own counsel; it also amounted to a duel between the Chief Executive and the Chief Justice.

The degree to which political partisanship entered into Marshall's rulings is a matter of opinion, but undoubtedly he made conviction impossible by his rigid interpretation of the constitutional definition of treason—"levying war against the United States or adhering to their enemies, giving them aid and comfort"—and of the constitutional requirement of "two witnesses to the same overt act." Rejecting the common-law doctrine which he seems to have accepted previously, Marshall ruled that the procurer of treason was not a traitor unless he had participated personally in the overt act—in this case the assemblage at Blennerhasset's Island. There seemed little doubt of Burr's responsibility for this assemblage, but even if it were shown to be treasonable he was not physically present at that place on the specified date. Hedged about with Marshall's strict instructions, the jury returned their verdict that Burr was not proved guilty by the evidence submitted to them. From the point of view of the prosecution and the President the trial was a fiasco, but it created a precedent against any loose interpretation of treason for political purposes and for the protection of the individual against any easy charge of this capital crime. This strict construction and emphasis on individual rights by Marshall was in the Jeffersonian tradition. His pronouncements in the Burr trial are a main reason why the United States government has so rarely brought charges of treason against citizens and has turned to the milder charge of sedition, even in wartime, to protect itself against subversion and internal enemies.

These events strengthened the position of the judiciary as the safeguard and recourse of persons subjected to possible executive persecution. Marshall issued a subpoena requiring President Jefferson to present certain documents bearing on the case; but this effort, which carried with it dangerous implications of judicial supremacy and executive subservience, was defeated. Jefferson ignored the subpoena, though he sent documents to the District Attorney. His action established a valuable precedent that the President is not subject to court proceedings short of the constitutional provision of impeachment.

Burr and his associates went scot free but he was disgraced. He fled in disguise from angry mobs to Europe and spent most of his remaining years in exile. Unfortunately, the spirit of separatism which he had thought to exploit did not wholly vanish from the country with him. Within a decade it showed itself again among the Federalists in New England.

The Navy and the Barbary Pirates

Part of the continuing grievance of influential New Englanders against the President arose from the belief that he was indifferent to their sea-going commerce and to the Navy which was supposed to protect it. The extent of the Navy, said Jefferson to John Adams long afterward, "must be governed by circumstances." Since he came into office as an advocate of economy and the European wars were approaching a lull, circumstances were unfavorable to a continued development of the Navy along the lines that John Adams and Secretary Benjamin Stoddert had laid down. The new policy was determined, not by the new Secretary, Robert Smith of Maryland, but by the President and the Secretary of the Treasury.

Gallatin had been a major critic of Federalist naval policy. In Congress he had said: "I had conceived it would have been our object to have become a happy and not a powerful nation, or at least noway powerful except for self-defence." He was not concerned to develop an instrument of national power and, like Jefferson, he had a passion for economy and peace. His protesting voice had been drowned by the clamor which the naval warfare with France had aroused in 1798, but now his influence was determinative. During the last year of the Adams administration more than $3 million had been appropriated for the Navy alone. Gallatin wanted to keep the entire expenditure of the government below that figure, leaving more than twice that sum for the reduction of the national debt. In the year 1802, expenditures for the Navy fell below a million dollars, but the economy policy had to be modified to some degree soon after that because of trouble with the Barbary powers in the Mediterranean.

These piratical states—Algeria, Tripoli, Tunis, and Morocco—had long been a scourge of commerce, and the young American government had fallen into the prevailing practice of buying them off. The Treaty of 1795 with Algeria not only called for the costly ransom of American prisoners, but even for the payment of annual tribute. The latter feature of this treaty made it unique in the history of American relations with other countries. The treaty with Tripoli about a year later was less costly but by means of it, also, the United States bought an uncertain peace. This cost about $107,000, whereas the one with Algeria cost $642,000, besides the provision for annual tribute in the form of naval stores. The Pasha of Tripoli, disgruntled that he had not gained more, repudiated the treaty in February 1801 and demanded a large flat payment and tribute. In May, he declared war, chopping down the flagstaff at the American consulate. The Pasha misunderstood the new American President, however, for Jefferson's pacific intentions had never extended to the Barbary pirates. Throughout his public career he had taken the position that payments to these brigands of the sea were futile, and that they understood no language but that of force. He ordered Commodore Richard Dale to the Mediterranean, and that officer proceeded to blockade Tripoli. These actions constituted an interference with Morocco also, and its Sultan declared war in the summer of 1802. This trouble was short-lived, however. Commodore Edward Preble was sent to the Mediterranean with another squadron and the Sultan decided to renew the Treaty of 1786 without change.

The Tripolitan War

The war with Tripoli continued. It was marked by sad mishaps, the chief of which was the grounding of the frigate *Philadelphia* and the capture of Captain Bainbridge and his crew (October 31, 1803). They were held prisoners for more than a year and a half, and were deeply chagrined when the Tripolitans salvaged the abandoned vessel. The later destruction of the *Philadelphia* by Americans under the leadership of Stephen Decatur (February 16, 1804) was the most spectacular feat of the war. Direct assaults on Tripoli failed, and the naval blockade was the most effective operation. It was directed at first by Preble and afterwards by Samuel Barron. Another spectacular American enterprise was carried out under the leadership of William Eaton, consul at Tunis, who got hold of Hamet, elder brother of the Pasha and a claimant to the throne, and marched across the Libyan desert and captured Derne (April 1805). Eaton was bitter when Tobias Lear, consul-general at Algiers, negotiated a treaty with the Pasha.

Agreed to on June 4, 1805, this was favorable, as treaties with the Barbary states went. The United States paid $60,000 on the exchange of prisoners and this amounted to ransom; tribute was not mentioned but in practice each new consul made a present according to ancient custom. The Pasha had granted better terms than to any other nation and had promised to protect American rights in the future. The Bey of Tunis made peace about the same time. Trouble with Algeria flared up in 1807 but simmered down, and it was clear that the United States had taken the lead among the nations against the practice of tribute and ransom and had succeeded in curtailing it. After the War of 1812 the United States finally settled matters. The treaty with Algeria that was concluded in the summer of 1815 completely abolished ransom and tribute, and in the following years of peace the practice ceased.

The story of the Barbary Wars contains rich materials for comic opera, but they served as a training school for the Navy. One of their bad immediate effects lay in the fact that, when they were over, Jefferson's enthusiasm turned to gunboats, which had proved useful in the shallow waters off North Africa. These would serve to defend American harbors, he believed. Through the years all manner of fun has been poked at Jefferson's gunboats. These were generally about 50 feet long, fitted with oars and sails, armed with one or two small cannon, and manned by crews of twenty or more. In the year 1807, the bulk of the naval appropriations went to gunboats, which could not possibly protect commerce on the high seas and had no purpose except that of protection against actual invasion. But this policy of the landlubber President, besides having the merit of relative inexpensiveness, was part of his larger policy of passive resistance coupled with economic coercion, and it must be judged as a phase of that. Naval force had to be used against the piratical Tripolitans, but in his opinion the struggle for naval power against the great warring nations of Europe was hopeless, and the ultimate salvation of American commerce lay in keeping it at home for a time. He sought to use it as a weapon of coercion by withholding it from countries which, he believed, could not do without it.

THE EMBARGO

The embargo of 1807-1809 may be described in modern terms as a unilateral attempt to secure redress of grievances, without recourse to war, by imposing "economic sanctions" on offending nations. It failed to its immediate purpose to force the fiercely contending European powers to respect American rights, and it brought Jefferson to a nadir of unpopularity at home. Given the circumstances of American weakness on the one hand and the strength and desperation of the British and French on the other, the chance of the success of this daring experiment in statecraft may seem to have been slight. Furthermore, the philosopher President failed to anticipate the unwillingness of many Americans, especially those dependent on foreign trade, to sacrifice short-term gains for the sake of a noble goal and a larger national purpose. Thus the embargo reveals Jefferson at the highest point of his idealism and the lowest point of his political realism.

As the responsible head of a neutral country in a time of international conflict he faced dread alternatives. Submission to the infringements on

American rights seemed intolerable; diplomacy had failed; and war, for which the country was unprepared, would have thrown the weight of the United States on the French side, since the British monarchs of the sea were the chief offenders against American rights and interests. Ostensibly, economic sanctions were directed against both the rival powers and fell within the historic pattern of American neutrality. Jefferson deserves credit for his attempt to find an alternative between war and submission, and if the course of events served to align the United States against the British in the world conflict this was not because he liked Napoleon.

That wily ruler had dropped Louisiana into the American lap in order to remove a motive for the United States to join Great Britain when France renewed her attack. Futhermore, he hoped to bring the United States as a friendly neutral into French service and thus revive the policy of Vergennes and Genêt. During the first stage of the Napoleonic Wars, from 1803 to 1805, American shipping and trade thrived and neither belligerent interfered with them. The United States owned the largest neutral merchant marine. This grew still larger as American owners took over the trade with many British markets and sold foodstuffs to the continent and to colonies at high prices. It was no favoritism towards France that led American businessmen to help Napoleon, but the British understandably came to regard the United States as a virtual ally of that tyrant.

Tribulations of a Neutral

The British Navy swept the French and Spanish merchant marines from the seas, therefore France and Spain permitted American ships to engage in the trade with their West Indian possessions which was ordinarily forbidden to foreigners. Britain invoked her "Rule of 1756," that trade forbidden in peace could not be legalized in war, but American shippers ingeniously evaded this by carrying West Indian cargoes to American ports where duties were paid and the cargoes put ashore, thus "Americanizing" them; then the cargoes were reloaded, most or all of the duties were repaid to the owners, and the cargoes were carried to Europe. At first the British Admiralty Courts consented to this device of the "broken voyage," but as the aggressive Yankee skippers threatened to nullify British naval supremacy by performing all the services of the vanquished French and Spanish merchant marines, British shippers bitterly complained that the broken-voyage farce amounted to economic warfare against Britain. In July 1805, a British Admiralty court in the famous *Essex* decision declared that only payment of a bona-fide duty, without rebates, could actually "break" a voyage and "Americanize" cargoes in an American port between the West Indies and Europe.

Under this decision the British Navy immediately seized and confiscated dozens of American vessels. British warships were stationed close off American ports. In exercising their unquestioned right to stop and their claimed right to search neutral ships to determine the nature, source, and destination of cargoes, the British acted with extreme contempt for American sensibilities and delayed many ships carrying innocent cargoes by sending them to Halifax under suspicion. Numerous incidents of insult and injury irritated American pride and raised a fearful popular clamor in addition to the wails of businessmen against the *Essex* decision.

Worst of all was the British practice of impressment. A basic reason for this practice was the superior living and working conditions of sailors on American ships as compared with the vicious cat-o'-nine-tails and rotten food meted out to sailors on British vessels. Naturally many British tars deserted and enlisted for service in Yankee ships. In the desperate war against Napoleon the British government continued the age-old practice of sending press gangs through the British Isles and to sea to force men into service. It did not claim the right to impress any but British subjects, but it followed the principle of *jus sanguinis,* that blood determined nationality: "Once an Englishman, always an Englishman!" The United States, on the other hand, with its greater respect for individual rights and its need for immigrants, supported the principle of *jus solis,* that place of residence might determine nationality, that anyone might become an American citizen by residence and desire. In practice a British sailor who deserted his "floating hell" in an American port could obtain citizenship papers in about five minutes and sign up on an American ship in five minutes more. Then the United States government was bound to defend him as entitled to all the protection of the stars and stripes.

At sea British impressment officers would stop any American ship, go aboard and require the crew to line up on deck for inspection. They paid no attention to papers but usually judged a man's nationality by his accent—a peculiarly misleading test. Sometimes, when the need for men was desperate, the British used no test whatever except health and strength. The Department of State argued that the American flag protected against impressment not only American citizens, including ex-Britons who had naturalization papers, but foreigners who did not even claim American citizenship. Thus the positions of the two governments were irreconcilable. Perhaps no foreign offense against the United States before or since has stirred American anger more deeply than impressment, which seemed to deny the very right of a man to be an American, and to claim the right to condemn to British slavery anyone at all who sailed under the American flag. This was an offense not against property but against persons.

Britain as well as France was dependent on American shipping and supplies for her war effort. In order to buy in the United States, the British had to sell their own products here. In April 1806, Jefferson signed a law that authorized him to forbid importation of certain British products. He did not invoke the law but held it as a threat while instructing James Monroe and William Pinkney of Maryland to negotiate a settlement with Great Britain. They were expressly forbidden to sign a treaty that did not include a British agreement to stop impressments. The British government bowed to the threat of non-importation to the extent of making some concessions regarding West Indian trade and offering to give an informal promise that no bona-fide American citizen would be impressed. Monroe and Pinkney violated their instructions and signed a treaty on the last day of 1806. Jefferson refused to send this treaty to the Senate. Using hindsight, some critics have argued that he should have accepted the Monroe-Pinkney Treaty and thus have avoided worse trouble that was in store. But we cannot ask of statesmen the gift of prophecy. Jefferson had sound reason to reject a treaty which would have amounted to American consent to the British practice of impressment.

The European war had now settled down to a titanic struggle between the sea, where Britain ruled unchallenged after Nelson destroyed the French and Spanish fleets at Trafalgar in October 1805, and the land, where Napoleon a month later at Austerlitz defeated the combined Russian and Austrian armies. Sea power and land power, like the whale and the elephant, could not meet for a decision, so the antagonists resorted to an economic war of attrition. Each side tried to cut off the other from outside trade and defeat its enemy by reducing it to beggary.

The United States, the leading neutral trader, was caught in the vise between the belligerents. In 1806 and 1807, Great Britain issued Orders in Council blockading the European coast and requiring neutral ships to pay English fees and licenses for the privilege of carrying a few non-contraband articles through the blockade, while Napoleon issued decrees imposing a "paper" blockade of the British Isles. Lacking a navy he enforced this by means of privateers, seizing any neutral ship that traded with Britain or even allowed itself to be searched by the British.

Meanwhile, His Majesty's frigate *Leopard* committed a grievous offense against the United States. The British government did not claim the right to board and search American naval vessels, only merchantmen in British waters and on the high seas. But when Vice-Admiral Berkeley, in command of the American station, heard that four British sailors had deserted and enlisted on the American frigate *Chesapeake,* he ordered on his own responsibility that they be taken off the American warship by force the moment that it put to sea. Suspecting nothing and unprepared for action, the *Chesapeake* stood out from Norfolk on June 22, 1807. The *Leopard* stopped the American frigate and asked to search. Commodore Barron refused. The British warship thereupon opened fire at point blank range, killing three and wounding eighteen American seamen. Barron was forced to strike his colors and submit to a boarding party that took off the four deserters.

This unparalleled attack aroused the American people to fury without distinction between Republicans and Federalists. Mobs assaulted Englishmen and called for war. But Jefferson decided merely to use the British offense, which put its government clearly in the wrong, to make Britain abandon impressment altogether. The British government was willing to make reparation for the injury to the *Chesapeake*, but refused at this time because Jefferson coupled reparation with the larger issue. The President, whose passion was peace and who wanted to side with neither of the warring powers, thereupon decided to try economic coercion against both of them. Harking back to the nonimportation, nonexportation, and nonconsumption agreements of the days before 1776, when such measures had won some concessions from the mother country, Jefferson hoped to show the world how a nation might secure its honor and interests without resort to war.

An Experiment that Failed

The noble experiment took the form of the Embargo Act of December 1807, which prohibited the export of almost all articles to any country whatever. Many American merchantmen were abroad when the law went into effect; they never returned home but continued to serve one or another of the warring powers. Other ships got away from American ports before federal agents arrived to detain them. Still others obtained papers permitting them to carry cargoes in American coastal trade and promptly sailed abroad. The ancient art of smuggling was revived, particularly along the land frontier with Canada, where drovers of wagon trains shot down federal agents. Enough American ships and supplies evaded the law to weaken its effects on the belligerents.

At the same time, the embargo was sufficiently effective to create an economic depression in the United States. Luckless ships were tied up, merchants went bankrupt, unemployment was widespread—while profits, prices of farm products, and wages fell to ruinous levels. The industrial revolution in the United States received its chief early impulse from the necessity to manufacture goods formerly imported from Britain, but this compensation for the economic ravages of the embargo was important only for the future.

What Jefferson did not understand was that American businessmen pre-

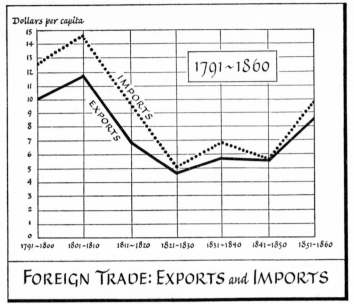

Dollars per capita

1791~1860

IMPORTS

EXPORTS

1791~1800   1801~1810   1811~1820   1821~1830   1831~1840   1841~1850   1851~1860

FOREIGN TRADE: EXPORTS and IMPORTS

SOURCE: Department of Commerce.

ferred the British and French injuries to American commerce to the
drastic Jeffersonian cure for them, which they likened to cutting one's
throat to cure a nosebleed. The agricultural President did not understand
that the weird manipulations of businessmen provided their own profitable cure for English and French depredations: losses by seizure of
American cargoes were more than compensated by the wartime rise in
prices for cargoes that evaded capture. Under these conditions sedate
commerce gave way to a wild speculative mania which was amply rewarded if one cargo in three reached a market. Federalists and merchants had been ready for strong measures following the *Chesapeake*
affair, but Jefferson's embargo measure seemed to them craven and
suicidal:

> Our ships all in motion,
> Once whiten'd the ocean;
>   They sail'd and return'd with a Cargo;
> Now doom'd to decay
>   They are fallen a prey,
> To Jefferson, worms, and EMBARGO.

In New England especially there was a revival of Federalism—bitter
and extremist, pro-British, anti-Southern, and anti-democratic. The South
and West, whose farmers suffered from the fall in prices, nevertheless
remained faithful to Jefferson and his experiment. The West Indies and

Newfoundland suffered for lack of American food, but these areas had small influence on British policy, and the working and manufacturing classes of Britain, which suffered for lack of American cotton, had no votes, while the powerful merchants and shipowners welcomed the opportunity to take over markets formerly controlled by Americans. Then the bumper crops of 1808 reduced British need for American food. Napoleon positively welcomed the embargo. It injured Britain more than France and besides, in April 1808, France seized all American ships and cargoes in French harbors on the pretense that they must be disguised British vessels!

Jefferson grimly held on to his policy until depression and the rising Federalist tide of resistance showed that the embargo was unenforceable and intolerable. Except in the loss of life it seemed as bad as war, without any of war's emotional compensations. It called for a negative heroism which proved galling. Jefferson had not expected such a crop of fraud and corruption, and had not foreseen that the successful operation of such a policy of control would require the exercise of arbitrary power by the government and grievous infringements on individual freedom. The "Force Act" of January 1809 was the logical result of the existing circumstances. As Gallatin saw and Jefferson had to admit, the embargo either had to be given up or be assisted by "means as strong as the measure itself." By this final supplementary measure federal collectors were authorized to seize without warrant any goods suspected of foreign destination in violation of the embargo, and these collectors were freed from legal responsibility for their actions.

Ironically, the administration invoked arbitrary powers which it itself recognized as dangerous and odious; and the New England opposition had recourse to arguments such as Jefferson and Madison had used in the Kentucky and Virginia Resolutions when protesting against the tyranny of the Alien and Sedition Acts. Timothy Pickering asked: "How are the powers reserved to the states respectively, or to the people, to be maintained, *but by the respective states judging for themselves and putting their negatives on the usurpations of the federal government?*" At this stage, also, certain New Englanders took a much longer step in the direction of nullification of a federal law than Jefferson and Madison had recommended. Early in 1809, when the Secretary of War asked the Governor of Connecticut to appoint officers of the militia with orders to aid the federal collector in enforcing the embargo, the Governor flatly refused on the ground that this measure was an unconstitutional infringement on the rights of the states, and he was strongly supported by the General Assembly.

On March 1, 1809, Congress repealed the embargo and Jefferson, with three days of his administration remaining, gave in. Thus an experiment which might have matched the Louisiana Purchase as a triumph of

Jeffersonian statecraft, seemed a disastrous failure. Yet war had been and would be avoided for five years; and the eventual repeal of the British Orders in Council, news of which came only a few days after the outbreak of the War of 1812, can be traced in part to Jefferson's policy of economic coercion.

When he left office, the failure of his campaign against the judiciary and of his attempt to find an economic substitute for war temporarily overshadowed his great success in adding an empire to the Union. But it is notable that these failures did not lead the country to return the Federalists to power in the elections of 1808. For sixteen more years the Virginian heirs of Jefferson, James Madison and James Monroe, occupied the first office and the generality of farmers and city folk clung loyally to the party organized by the Sage of Monticello. The majority of Americans recognized that he stood for human liberty and human rights. They forgave him his political failures, scorned his enemies, and revered him as the symbol of the American dream.

CHAPTER 7

The War of 1812

JAMES MADISON, THE FOURTH PRESIDENT OF THE
United States (1809-1817), had been groomed for the succession by his
friend Jefferson. He was a political scientist of great force and originality,
but his public personality was rather colorless. "Little Jemmy" was supported because the Virginians still controlled the loose alliance of southern
planters, western farmers, and northeastern city groups which comprised the Republican Party, and because he was obviously second
only to Jefferson in experience and in service to the party and the nation.
The other member of the triumvirate, Albert Gallatin, remained as Secretary of the Treasury. Madison easily met the challenge of James Monroe
in 1808, and toward the end of his first term (1811) he made his chief
Virginia rival his Secretary of State.

The eight years of this undramatic man in the presidency were more
dramatic than any previous administration. Madison was unfortunate and
seemed inept in his conduct of foreign relations and the second war
against Great Britain; but at least he delayed the outbreak of open conflict, and the failures of the war were characteristic of a young and
sprawling country which relied on crude strength without having achieved
effective military organization or developed habits of military discipline.
Despite blunders and disaffection, things turned out well in the end and
Madison closed his long and distinguished career in a glow of popular
approval. While the Federalist opposition, moving further in the direction of faction and provincialism, became impotent at last, the Republican Party emerged without loss of popular appeal as the nationalist
party. By continuing to identify the administration with expansionism
President Madison associated it with the West and with the future of a
fast-growing country; and, like President Jefferson before him, he thus
escaped from the paralysis of extreme state rights and strict construction.

DRIFTING INTO WAR AT SEA

The repeal of the embargo on March 1, 1809, was merely a sop to domestic discontent because the Nonintercourse Act was immediately substituted. This law re-established the embargo against all ports under British and French control, while freeing Americans to trade with any other ports of the world. Madison carried on the policy of economic coercion, and internal opposition to its modified form was hardly less than to the original embargo.

For a moment it seemed possible that Madison would launch his administration with a great diplomatic success. The friendly British minister, David Erskine, signed an agreement in April 1809 which made more concessions to the United States than his instructions authorized. This Erskine Agreement bound Great Britain to withdraw her Orders in Council against American shipping. As an executive agreement, the arrangement did not require approval by the Senate. Madison, unwisely taking it for granted that Canning would approve, issued a proclamation restoring intercourse with Great Britain, as he was authorized to do under the existing law. Americans were overjoyed. Hundreds of heavy-laden ships set sail for British ports. Then came the news that Canning had rejected the Agreement and recalled Erskine for violating his instructions. Overnight American joy turned to rage—against Britain for seeming perfidy, against the President for allowing himself to be duped. Madison was forced to restore nonintercourse against Britain in August 1809, but the great fleet that had got away relieved shortages in England and spoiled some of the hard-won effects of the embargo.

Anglo-American relations were further embittered by the violently anti-American conduct of Erskine's successor, Francis James ("Copenhagen") Jackson, a man notorious for his brutal treatment of the Danes. After Jackson accused the United States government of lying in the Erskine affair, Secretary of State Robert Smith refused to hold further communication with him. When Jackson's term was up, he went home and Canning refused at the time to appoint another minister.

The new Congress that met in December 1809 decided that nonintercourse, too, was a failure. On May 1, 1810, the Act was repealed by the enactment of what was known as Macon's Bill Number 2. The freeing of American commerce from legal restraint was really to the advantage of the British rather than to that of blockaded France, while the previous restrictive laws had drawn the United States unwittingly into Napoleon's continental system, which was designed to cut off trade with Great Britain. But Congress included in the new law an overly-clever fragment of the old coercive policy. France was promised that if she would withdraw her Decrees and Britain did not withdraw her Orders in Council within the three months following, the United States would restore non-intercourse with Britain. A similar promise, in reverse, was made to Britain.

This scheme to play the great powers against each other was out-witted by Napoleon, a more expert schemer. He had his Foreign Minister, the Duc de Cadore, write a letter to the American minister in France which seemed to withdraw Napoleon's Decrees against American com-merce but actually would not do so until the United States should *first* obtain withdrawal of the Orders of the British or alternatively restore nonintercourse against them. The tricky wording of the Cadore Letter trapped Madison. On November 2, 1810, he issued a proclamation that nonintercourse would be restored against Britain if she did not withdraw her Orders within three months. Since there were reports that France was continuing to enforce her Decrees and confiscating American ships, Canning concluded that Madison was determined to range the United States on the French side against Britain and refused to withdraw the Orders. The British bitterly and naturally resented it when Congress on March 2, 1811, restored nonintercourse against their country.

Ten weeks later the American frigate *President* hailed at sea a British corvette, the *Little Belt;* a shot was fired by someone and both ships opened fire. The *President* made short work of the smaller British vessel. Now, too late, the British government sent a conciliatory minister, Augustus Foster, who made proper reparation for the *Chesapeake* affair. Americans were not interested. They were content with the smashing of the *Little Belt* and excited over a western movement for the conquest of Canada and of Florida. They were talking war.

THE WESTERN EXPANSIONISTS

Maritime injuries at the hands of Great Britain probably were not sufficient to create a war fever in the United States. For one thing, the section that suffered most, the Northeast, was most inclined to submit to British rule of the sea, including impressment and abuse of neutral trade, for the sake of residual profits from trade and because sentiment in that section was strongly pro-British and anti-French. Furthermore, French injuries against American trade and, what is often forgotten, French impressment of American seamen, made war against France almost as reasonable as war against Britain, but no one imagined that the young republic could take on Goliath and Samson simultaneously.

Westerners had excellent reason in the Louisiana Purchase for friendli-ness toward France. They had equally good and traditional reasons for hatred of Great Britain. Even after the British had abandoned the mili-tary posts on American soil following Jay's Treaty, they had not given up ambitions to dominate the American Northwest and control the fur trade. By encouraging the Indians' natural opposition to the pioneers who deprived them of their land, Britain hoped to fix bounds beyond which American settlement and power should not expand. The leadership of two Shawnees, Tecumseh and his brother the Prophet, admirably served Britain's purposes. Tecumseh was an extremely intelligent leader who saw that the white men were destroying the Indians' physical and moral health by transmitting diseases, selling whiskey, and undermining tribal religion. At the same time the whites were defeating the Indians piece-meal, tribe by tribe. The Prophet, appealing to racial pride, urged separa-tion from the white man and revival of Indian religion and the Indian way of life. Tecumseh attempted to create a united front of all the tribes along the frontier against the encroaching pioneers. Their joint work was a remarkable effort to overcome the weaknesses and divisions of their people.

Jefferson believed that the Indians should be transformed by benevolent example into farmers who would not need as much land as they did as hunters. But during his administration federal agents speeded up the process of obtaining, by trade and treaty, more and more rights to the tribal lands which the deploying settlers coveted. By 1809, the message of Tecumseh and the Prophet destroyed whatever hope existed for Jeffer-son's agrarian vision of the Indian saved by the white man's civilization, and promised to save him by strengthening him in his own hunting civilization.

Frontiersmen generally believed that the only good Indian was a dead Indian. They were alarmed by the success of Tecumseh's revival which promised to put a stop to time-honored techniques of encroaching on Indian lands. Tecumseh and the Prophet organized a settlement in Indi-ana where the Tippecanoe River joins the Wabash. There redmen im-bibed stern virtues uncannily like those of the white Puritans and declared that no whiskey would seduce, no treaty would dislodge them. William Henry Harrison, governor of Indiana Territory and superintendent of the Northwest Indians, made a treaty with a few unconverted Indians who pretended to have the right to sign away Tecumseh's lands. Tecumseh countered by traveling south of the Ohio to add southern tribes to his confederacy. While he was gone, Harrison with a strong force invaded the Indian country and on November 7, 1811, wiped out the village at Tippecanoe. This "battle" excited the Northwest against the British, who were accused of backing Tecumseh's confederacy with gifts of arms. "On to Canada!" was the somewhat surprising response of the northern pioneers to the news of Tippecanoe.

Pioneers south of the Ohio River were equally alarmed by Tecumseh's plan to unite all the tribes for a stand, and they similarly saw the real enemy not as the Indian but as Spain, whose policy in the American Southwest more or less duplicated Britain's policy in the Northwest.

Spain was weaker than Great Britain, her territory was more loosely held, and by 1811 pieces of it were already falling into American hands. Southwesterners nevertheless clamored that the process of expansion at Spain's expense be speeded up. They hungered for West Florida, the strip of territory from the Apalachicola River to the Mississippi lying south of the 31st parallel. It spanned the mouths of the rivers that drain to the Gulf of Mexico and the present states of Georgia, Alabama, and Mississippi, giving Spain a throttle-hold on the trade of the region, and providing pirates, Indians, and desperadoes with hideouts from which settlements to the north and shipping in the Gulf of Mexico could be harassed.

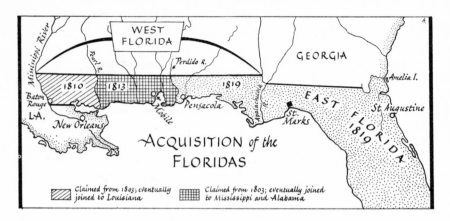

When he left office, Jefferson warned his friends that the United States must have the Floridas and Cuba. Napoleon's invasion of Spain in 1807 improved American chances. Under cover of loyalty to the displaced King Ferdinand, revolutionary juntas took charge of government in Spain's American colonies. The first and greatest of American empires was breaking up because of its inefficiency, corruption, and outmoded tyranny, as well as Napoleon's disruption of the mother country, and many Americans were determined to share in the spoils.

An advance party of American pioneers had already settled in West Florida. They were encouraged by the Madison administration to imitate the Spanish-Americans and revolt. In September 1810 they captured the Spanish fort in the colonial capital, Baton Rouge, tore down the Bourbon lily flag, and raised the flag of the Republic of West Florida containing a lone white star on a blue ground—ultraconvenient for incorporation in the flag of the United States. Then the revolutionaries applied for admission into the Union, offering the inalienable human right of revolution as expressed in the Declaration of 1776 as their legal passport. This part of West Florida was soon joined with Louisiana, which became a state in 1812. This was the first of many attempts to use revolution outside the national boundaries as a means of annexing territory to the Union.

Madison immediately proclaimed the extension of American authority over West Florida as far as the Perdido River, still basing the American claim on the Louisiana Purchase. Spain hung on to Mobile, but her weak forces were thrown out in April 1813. Lacking a force of American rebels in East Florida, Madison encouraged George Mathews, former governor of Georgia, to lead a band of invading American "insurgents" and supported them with gunboats and regular United States troops. Mathews got as far as Saint Augustine on the east coast early in 1812, then he failed and Madison repudiated him.

The Pensacola region of old West Florida and all of East Florida remained in precarious Spanish possession to inflame frontiersmen's longing. War was not declared against Spain, but that country had not, like Great Britain, given justification by maritime injuries. Furthermore, Great Britain was assiduously cultivating revolution in all Spanish America as a means of establishing for herself economic domination and political hegemony in the ancient empire of the Indies. Jefferson and many later American statesmen looked longingly at Cuba because they feared that Britain would get hold of this Gibraltar of the New World. Possession of Florida was the first step necessary to dispel such a nightmare.

In short, the magnificent meal which Jefferson had provided in Louisiana, far from satisfying the appetites of Americans, only whetted them. But if we are inclined to wonder at the gargantuan land hunger of our ancestors, we should reflect that the expansion of American liberty into empty or thinly held lands, in the face of predatory and tyrannical empires, may have been a necessary condition for its very existence.

The "War Hawks"

Expansionism, with its assertion of executive powers, cost the Jeffersonians the support of a faction which clung to the doctrine of a limited government that the Republicans had emphasized when they were in opposition to the dominant Federalists. Most bitter of these "Old Republicans" was John Randolph of Roanoke, a relative of Jefferson. Brilliant and irritating, Randolph as a member of the House refused to tolerate the devices by which his kinsman and Madison sought to gain West Florida, and extended his opposition to practically every administration measure in which he could detect a pro-French meaning, an imitation of Federalism, or a tendency towards nationalism. Stinging mockery of his fellow Virginians who compromised the old faith, as he understood it, was his chief weapon, but he and his dissident faction were powerless to move Congress. John Taylor of Caroline, chief keeper of the pure Republican doctrine, also went into opposition. But Jefferson and Madison gave the West pretty much what it wanted. Loss of the extreme state-rights faction was more than compensated by the growth of Republicanism in the West, and New England disaffection was considerably neutralized. Thus the Republican Party continued unbeatable as it sought to enlarge the country, gradually assuming the mantle of nationalism which the Federalists had discarded.

In the Congressional elections of 1810, the party won a landslide victory against the Federalists, and aggressive expansionists displaced legislators who had retreated from the costly economic warfare of the embargo to the futility of Macon's Bill No. 2. From the new states of the West and from western sections of eastern states there came to Washington in December 1811 a new generation of "buckskin statesmen," inexperienced but cocksure in their nationalism, their expansionism, and their hatred for "putrescent peace." Great Britain was their chief enemy and they gloried in the name of "War Hawks."

Men like Henry Clay of Kentucky and John C. Calhoun of South Carolina, who would dominate the political life of their sections for the next generation and grow conservative with age, were united in 1812 as belligerent nationalists. Although the War Hawks did not command a majority of the House, they managed to elect Henry Clay as Speaker, and he packed the committees with advocates of war. Fiery patriotism, revenge against Britain for outrages against the personal liberty and dignity of American citizens, contempt for the "decadent" brand of businessman's nationalism in the East, and Western brag about what mincemeat could be made of British power in Canada by a mere "frontiersmen's frolic": these were the themes of War Hawks' oratory and Western newspaper editorials.

The accusation that Clay exacted war as the price of support for Madison's renomination is false. Actually, the two, much as they differed in temperament and tone, were in close agreement on foreign policy by this time. In April 1812, Congress passed and the President signed a bill imposing a ninety-day embargo. This was not so much to renew economic coercion as to stop exports that would be useful to the prospective enemy. Late in May, the British minister conveyed to Madison and Secretary of State Monroe a message from his government which seemed to end all hope that the Orders in Council might be withdrawn. Unwilling to admit that Napoleon, too, had failed to end his restrictions of American trade, Madison on June 1 delivered a message to Congress virtually asking for a declaration of war against Great Britain.

Madison's formal accusations against Great Britain began with impressment, and the emphasis he always laid on this in negotiations shows that it was of prime importance in his own mind. His other main complaint related to the Orders in Council. Only by insinuation did he connect the British with Indian outrages against settlers in the West, and in a public statement he could not avow a desire for Canada and Florida. The House joyously responded to Madison's message by passing a resolution for war on June 4 by a vote of 79 to 49. The Senate, containing a larger Federalist contingent, delayed until June 17 and then passed a war resolution by the vote of 19 to 13. Members of the House and Senate from southern New England and the Middle States, except Pennsylvania, strongly opposed the war. Southern and Western representatives of agricultural interests voted for a war presumably fought to protect maritime interests. But the agricultural regions were the historic champions of personal liberty, their produce gave them a stake in foreign commerce, and they felt the injury of impressment more keenly than the shipowners who could easily hire other sailors to take the places of impressed men. It is impossible to separate out any one motive as *the* dominant factor, but exuberant Western nationalism undoubtedly played an important part in bringing on the war.

Although the President and Congress did not know it, a sudden turn in British policy had already eliminated a major American grievance. An Atlantic cable or radio would have almost certainly delayed and might have prevented war. The re-invocation of nonintercourse by the United States had seriously injured the business of British merchants and manufacturers. Furthermore, the government's decision to send a great expeditionary force to fight Napoleon in Spain had created a sudden need for American food and raw materials. But delays prevented Lord Castlereagh, the Foreign Secretary, from taking action until too late. On June 16, one day before the Senate passed the resolution for war, he announced that the Orders in Council would be immediately suspended in favor of the United States. Thus it may be claimed that the failure in 1812 lay not in the policy of economic coercion, but in impatience and imperfect communication. Castlereagh had removed only one main grievance, however. The problems of impressment and the Indians remained.

The American declaration of war seemed to the British a betrayal and to New England Federalists a crime. Napoleon's campaign to conquer Europe was at its climax: he invaded Russia a week later. The British were desperate and they believed that the cause of freedom in the Old World depended upon the defeat of Napoleon. For the United States to choose this moment to make war against the mother country seemed ignoble, no mere tweaking of John Bull's nose, but a stab in the back when he stood at bay. Many an American echoed the famous toast of Timothy Pickering: "The World's last hope—Britain's fast-anchored isle."

THE WAR ON LAND AND SEA, 1812-1813

British preoccupation with Napoleon made the Anglo-American war a sideshow in which military, naval, and diplomatic developments depended on the course of events in the big European tent. The boast of the

War Hawks that frontiersmen would take Canada and Florida turned out to be a dismal joke. Far from holding the offensive, the United States —on land, at sea, and in the negotiations for peace which began immediately—was thrown violently back on the defensive and had to struggle desperately to prevent utter disaster. In later years, Americans remembered the brilliant victories of their frigates in single-ship actions, although these did not prevent the overwhelmingly superior British Navy from virtually blockading the entire American coast. Also, they recalled the great victory of General Andrew Jackson against British veterans at New Orleans, although it came after peace had been signed at Ghent. But the only area where American victories affected the outcome of the war was on the northern lakes.

Military Failures

As in the Revolution the militia lacked discipline, training, and the will to fight outside their own states or districts. Jefferson, Madison, and Gallatin, fearing a standing army as a potential instrument of tyranny, had deliberately slowed the development of military power under their program of economy. Provision for additional regiments was made in 1808 and again in 1812, but when war broke out the regular army contained fewer than 7000 men, though it had an authorized strength of 35,000. Since young men preferred to serve with their local militia company or as sailors on lucrative voyages on privateers, the regular army could not obtain adequate enlistments. In 1802, President Jefferson had been authorized to establish a small corps of engineers, to be stationed at West Point and constitute a military academy. This was the beginning of the famous institution on the Hudson of which he is deemed the founder, but it was little more than a pioneer school of engineering until 1812. Then it was thoroughly reorganized but this was too late to help in the war. Military leadership in Washington was weak. President Madison had no talent for strategy; Secretary of War William Eustis inspired no confidence and resigned toward the end of 1812, to be followed by half a dozen successors. The ranking major-general, Henry Dearborn, who was placed in command of the Northeast sector, was old and soon showed himself to be incompetent.

General William Hull, the commander in the Northwest, was ordered to invade Upper Canada from Detroit without adequate forces and without regard for British troops and Indian allies in his rear. In July 1812, he entered Canada. The British General Isaac Brock was more competent than any American commander until Andrew Jackson took the field late in the war. In Canada there were about 4000 each of British regulars, Canadian regulars, Canadian militia, and Indian allies. Despite the great disparity of the populations of the United States and Canada, and the service of almost a half million American militiamen during the war, the British were able to defeat the United States on land with ease. They promptly captured Forts Michilimackinac and Dearborn (Chicago) and Brock marched westward from Niagara to Detroit, cutting off Hull, whom he summoned to surrender as an alternative to an Indian massacre. Deserted by some of his militia and cut off, Hull surrendered to Brock on August 16, 1812. The northwestern military frontier of the United States had been pushed back to the Wabash and Ohio rivers.

The crowning disgrace of the militia occurred at Niagara and at Lake Champlain. Captain John E. Wool gallantly led a few regulars across the river at Niagara and captured Queenstown Heights on October 13, 1812, but New York militia refused to follow them. Wool and his band were destroyed in sight of the mutinous New Yorkers. General Dearborn attempted in November to lead a militia force northward from Plattsburg on Lake Champlain towards Lower Canada, but after a few miles his troops also rebelled. Thus collapsed the War Hawks' plan to invade Canada in a frontiersmen's frolic.

In spite of these disasters Madison was re-elected in the fall of 1812. His victory came largely from the South and the West. He won only the frontier state of Vermont in New England, and among the Middle States only Pennsylvania by virtue of its western section. Farmer and artisan groups in New England and the Middle States whose votes Jefferson had won, abandoned Madison in 1812. Disaffection towards "Mr. Madison's War" drove New England Federalists to the edge of treason, and British collusion with them was suggested by failure to extend the blockade to the coast of Massachusetts until the war was almost ended.

Individual Victories at Sea

The gloom induced by military and political developments in the North was mitigated before the end of 1812 by events at sea. The United States possessed no ships-of-the-line (three decks of guns, the "battleships" of sailing navies), while the British had eleven in American waters. Thirty-four British frigates ("cruisers" with two decks of guns) far outnumbered American frigates. But the United States had three, the *Constitution*, the *United States*, and the *President*, which had more guns than the British frigates and more speed, by virtue of a cleaner design, than British ships-of-the-line. More important, the American crews were trained to aim their guns like sharpshooters at specific targets, whereas the British crews fired broadsides like buckshot without much aim. The American crews were volunteers, the officers were veterans of the naval wars against France and Tripoli, and all hands were determined to avenge the *Chesapeake*, while British crews were made up largely of impressed men and their officers were overconfident after the great victories of Nelson. The total

American Navy consisted of sixteen ships against ninety-seven British warships on American station, therefore the tactics of American commanders were to avoid fleet action and use their few ships as raiders in single-ship actions. They won astounding victories. The *Constitution* destroyed the *Guerrière* on August 19, 1812, and the *Java* on December 29. In November 1812, the *United States* forced the *Macedonian* to surrender. The sloop-of-war ("destroyer" with a single deck of guns) *Wasp* overcame the *Frolic,* and the *Hornet* sank the *Peacock* early in 1813.

These glorious victories enabled Americans to forget the disgraceful conduct of the militia, but they had no value beyond their effect upon morale. Most of the American warships, like hundreds of merchantmen, were tied up in port during most of the war. When the luckless *Chesapeake* accepted a British challenge to come out of Boston harbor for single-ship combat, the *Shannon* defeated her. The *President* grounded in trying to run the blockade at New York and was surrendered. The *Essex* after a gallant and successful raiding tour of the Pacific, was destroyed in Chilean waters. American privateers carried the war into European and Far-Eastern waters but their exploits served chiefly to enrich their crews. The United States had no weapons against the British blockade, which strangled American trade and enabled the enemy to invade the eastern seaboard wherever it chose.

Attempts at Negotiation

The War of 1812 might have ended in a few months but for the question of impressment. When the news of the suspension of the Orders in Council finally reached America, Secretary of State Monroe instructed the American *chargé d'affaires* in London to negotiate an armistice. The United States offered as a concession that it would prevent enlistment of British-born seamen in American ships if Britain would stop impressments. Foreign Secretary Castlereagh on August 29 rejected the offer. Next the British tried in Washington to secure an armistice without abandoning impressments, and the American government flatly refused. Britain insisted that impressment was an internal matter involving British subjects and not a question for international negotiation, while the American government insisted that it was a violation of the rights of the United States as a sovereign nation. These irreconcilable attitudes caused the war to drag on for two more years.

Meanwhile, Czar Alexander I of Russia had decided that it was to Russia's interest to end the Anglo-American conflict. The Russian "Holy City" of Moscow was captured by Napoleon in the late summer of 1812, and Alexander feared that the American war would divert the strength of his British ally from the European theaters. Also, Russia needed American trade. Therefore, the Czar proposed to the two governments that he should mediate between them in favor of peace. President Madison received the Russian proposal in March 1813 and welcomed it. By that time dreams of conquering Canada had gone glimmering; Great Britain controlled American territory in the Northwest; Napoleon's army had been destroyed in the winter retreat from Moscow; and if the French were defeated the British would be able to turn their whole weight against the United States. In his eagerness, Madison did not bother to learn whether Britain also would accept mediation. He sent Albert Gallatin and James A. Bayard, a moderate Delaware Federalist, to St. Petersburg to join John Quincy Adams, United States minister to Russia, for the purpose of negotiating there with British envoys.

Unfortunately Lord Castlereagh, suspicious of the Czar's friendliness towards the United States, refused his mediation. Castlereagh in November 1813 proposed, however, that the United States and Britain enter into direct negotiations, and Madison accepted. He ordered the three envoys in St. Petersburg to go to Ghent, Belgium, to meet British commissioners, and he sent Henry Clay and Jonathan Russell, American minister in Stockholm, to join them. Madison shrewdly named representatives of various points of view who could be relied upon to maintain particular interests and these men proved to be skillful diplomats, but they did not confront the British at Ghent until the summer of 1814.

Victory on Lake Erie

The American military situation improved in 1813, chiefly as a result of the remarkable performance of the little fresh-water navies on the Lakes. Captain Oliver Hazard Perry during the winter of 1812-1813 overcame enormous difficulties to construct a fleet of warships on Lake Erie. General Harrison attempted to retake Detroit but was beaten back. All depended on Perry's fir-built frigates and their crews of frontiersmen. On September 10, 1813, at Put-in-Bay, Perry attacked a British fleet that had been built with equal haste, and destroyed or captured all its ships. His exploit of transferring his flag, inscribed "Don't Give up the Ship," in a small boat from a shattered vessel to a sound one, and his simple report to Washington, "We have met the enemy, and they are ours," made him the hero of a classic naval tale.

Harrison then matched Perry's victory by taking Detroit and chasing General Proctor into Ontario, defeating him at the Battle of the Thames on October 5. Tecumseh was killed and his confederacy broke up. By the end of 1813, the United States controlled Lake Erie and had re-established its frontier in the Northwest. But during the same year the British retaliated against American raids across the Niagara River by capturing Fort Niagara on the American side. Undisciplined American militiamen had burned Canadian towns, including the provincial parliament buildings at York (now Toronto), and the British took revenge by inciting Indians against the American population around Niagara. A grandiose American plan to capture Montreal was easily defeated by the British.

This was the state of affairs when Madison accepted Castlereagh's proposal of direct negotiations, but it got much worse for the Americans before it got better.

The Crisis of 1814

Disaster threatened the United States in the summer and autumn of 1814, when the peace commissioners were meeting at Ghent and the abdication of Napoleon and his retiremenet to Elba had brought an end, as it seemed, to the fighting in Europe. American soldiers and officers were improving in the hard school of experience, but the British were now able to send powerful reenforcements to the New World. After the bitter but indecisive Battle of Lundy's Lane at Niagara on July 25, General Prevost got ready a force, including 10,000 of Wellington's veterans, to invade the United States by Burgoyne's old route of Lake Champlain and the Hudson River. That same year the British conquered Maine as far south as the Penobscot River and established a naval base on Cape Cod; a strong British raiding force sailed directly from France to Chesapeake Bay to strike at the national capital; another force landed at Pensacola, Florida, to join Creek Indians recently defeated by General Jackson; and the most formidable expedition of all set out for New Orleans. An observer in the late summer of 1814 might easily have despaired of the continued existence of the United States as it faced invasion from north, east, and south and seemed about to break asunder from internal strain.

To top all, the British negotiators at Ghent at this moment presented the Americans with peace terms which included Canadian annexations of American territory in Maine and New York and west of Lake Superior, and also, as an indispensable condition of peace, an independent Indian state south of the Great Lakes to prevent American expansion westward and provide a buffer-state between the United States and Canada. These terms called for the loss of one-third of the territory of the United States.

If they were rejected and the many-pronged invasion succeeded—as all signs indicated it would—worse terms might obviously be expected.

Disaffection in New England

New England disaffection now reached a climax in one of the darkest periods in the history of the Republic. The policies of economic coercion as an alternative to war that were pursued by Jefferson and Madison had the important political effect of giving new life to the moribund Federalist Party. Its turn towards extreme state rights and obstructionism had

caused that staunch son of Massachusetts, John Quincy Adams, to break
with his old Federalist associates at the time of the embargo, and he
had received his recent diplomatic appointments at the hands of grateful
Republicans. He was serving his country and his section well at Ghent,
but the Federalist leaders at home achieved no such happy combination
of national and local patriotism. They opposed the war and did everything
this side of treason to hinder it. The New England people as a whole
were not extreme, but by the summer of 1813 the Federalist leaders were
back in control of all the states in that region.

The best example of official obstruction was probably provided by the
state of Massachusetts. On June 26, 1812, Governor Caleb Strong, a
consistent though not as a rule a bitter Federalist, proclaimed a public
fast shortly after the declaration of war "against the nation from which
we are descended." At the same time the House of Representatives of
the Bay State condemned the war; and toward the end of the summer
the Governor refused to comply with the request of the Secretary of War
that he call the militia into the federal service. In this action he was supported by the judges of the Supreme Court of Massachusetts, who held
that the right to determine the existence of an exigency warranting the
placing of the militia in the national service lay with the governor. They
also held that the militia could not be lawfully commanded by an officer
not of the militia. In 1827, the Supreme Court of the United States ruled,
in the case of Martin vs. Mott, that the President had the right to determine the exigency, but during the War of 1812 this matter remained in
perilous dispute. Meanwhile, voluntary enlistments in the regular army
continued, and in this respect New England showed up well.

By the summer of 1814, the region itself was gravely imperiled, for
the British were now blockading these rocky coasts and had invested a
large part of the present state of Maine. Meanwhile, the federal government had refused to maintain the Massachusetts militia unless under
federal officers, and the movement for a New England convention, which
had been long talked about, was now well under way. The success of
Federalists in the Massachusetts election of 1814 was a sign of popular
approval, since they had gone to the electorate on this issue. The actual
call for a convention was made to the other states by the legislature of
Massachusetts in October 1814. Connecticut accepted the invitation
promptly, and Rhode Island did, though with less enthusiasm. New
Hampshire and Vermont did not accept, though a few districts of these
states were represented. Thus the convention which met at Hartford on
December 15, 1814, represented southern New England and the ruling
group there. The war situation had changed much for the better by that
time, and the clearing of the skies served to moderate the temper of the
gathering.

The secrecy of the sessions of the Hartford Convention lent color to the charge of treason, but the journal which was published some years later (1823) showed that there were no grounds for this. The extremist Pickering was not there, and George Cabot, who presided, had mellowed with the years and was more willing than he had been earlier to let the world ruin itself without Federalist interference. A report, probably written by Harrison Gray Otis, the leader of the Convention, was published after adjournment. This decried indiscriminate talk of disunion and proposed, as a solution of the militia question, that the states should assume their own defense, using part of the federal taxes for that purpose. It also proposed seven amendments to the Constitution: that direct taxes and representation be proportioned to the free population; that a two-thirds vote of both houses of Congress be required for the admission of new states, for nonintercourse acts, and for a declaration of war; that embargoes be limited to sixty days; that citizens hereafter naturalized should be incapable of holding federal office; that no President should serve more than one term; and that there be no successive Presidents from the same state.

These proposed amendments amounted to a list of long-standing grievances against the "Virginia Dynasty" and its policies. The procedure was legitimate, but Americans would not soon forget that these spokesmen of the old order had taken advantage of a time of war and national danger to press their special sectional claims. The course of later events made them look ridiculous and the Federalist Party never recovered.

Even before the Hartford Convention met, the tide had already turned from the dead low of the summer of 1814, and the British terms of peace themselves helped to turn it. President Madison undiplomatically revealed them to the American public and even Federalists were appalled. Unwilling to fight for western expansion, indifferent to a war against impressment, Federalists were finally recalled to a sense of duty by the spectacle of British imperialism. Perry's slogan was broadened into "Don't Give up the Soil!" Recruits flocked to the colors, state governments invigorated defense programs, and everywhere the sentiments of 1776 were revived for a last-ditch stand.

Faltering of the British Offensive

Only a few American gunboats and a hastily-gathered body of militia were available to hold off the British expeditionary force that headed up the Chesapeake in August towards Washington. The gunboat crews resisted but the militia ran away at Bladensburg, leaving the British free to parade into Washington. In retaliation for the sacking of York, Upper Canada, they burned the executive mansion, the capitol, and other public buildings, subjecting President and Dolly Madison to the indignity of flight. While this foray had its value from the British point of view as a "lesson" to the Americans, it had no military significance. The British tried to capture Baltimore but the Maryland militia held them off and Fort McHenry withstood a naval bombardment. It was then, "in the rockets' red glare," that Francis Scott Key saw the Star-Spangled Banner "so gallantly streaming"; and, in the patriotism of his hymn, he caught the renascent spirit of 1814. The British retreated down the Chesapeake and sailed away.

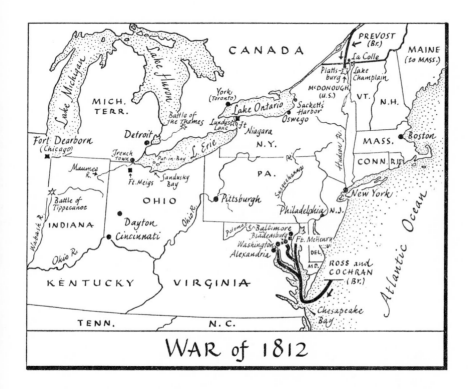

WAR of 1812

In the North, General Prevost reached Plattsburg early in September, but there a line of forts, even though undermanned, made him turn to flank them by gaining control of Lake Champlain. Commodore Thomas Macdonough had matched Perry's feat in building warships of green timbers. The British fleet attacked on September 11. Macdonough's crews laid their ships alongside the British, and by winding their anchors were able to fire broadsides from port or starboard at will. They destroyed the British fleet, and Prevost retreated to Canada. The Battle of Lake Champlain was the turning point of the war.

Now in the last days of the conflict the frontiersmen whose belligerence had done so much to initiate it finally produced in the South a victory to match their boasts. General Andrew Jackson of the Tenneseee militia was a man they would follow and one who knew how to use the harsh disciplinary methods frontier fighters respected. His crushing defeat of the Upper Creeks at Horseshoe Bend (March 27, 1814) accomplished one of the original objects of the war, and afterwards opened up vast Indian lands in the Southwest. This in itself was enough to make him a Western hero. Without orders from Washington, Jackson led a band into Florida and captured Pensacola from Indians and their British friends. Then he was ordered to New Orleans to defend it against the great expeditionary army of Sir Edward Pakenham. Inadvertently Jackson allowed the British to advance to within a few miles of the city, but Pakenham delayed his assault and gave Jackson his opportunity. He built earthworks across a strategic neck of land between the Mississippi and a swamp. On January 8, 1815, Pakenham ordered his troops to attack in close order. Laying their gun barrels between bales of cotton, the frontiersmen mowed the British down, losing only thirteen of their own number. Pakenham and more than 2000 officers and men were killed and the second and third generals in command were wounded before the victors of Europe retreated to their ships and sailed away.

Jackson's victory at New Orleans is one of the most celebrated in American military history. It had no effect on the peace treaty, which had been signed on Christmas Eve, but it indelibly impressed Americans with confidence that they were more than a match for any invaders and wiped out memories of unfortunate events on the northern frontier. Western brag was restored to prewar value and became a leading component in the ebullient nationalism of the following generation, whose greatest representative would be President Andrew Jackson.

THE TREATY OF GHENT

British territorial demands were increased over the original terms when news arrived in Europe, in October 1814, of the burning of Washington. The British commissioners at Ghent were instructed to demand more territory on the basis of *uti possidetis,* that is, Britain should receive all territory she actually occupied, and she expected to occupy a great deal. The American commissioners were ready to leave Ghent in despair when the news arrived of Macdonough's defeat of the northern invasion on September 11. Then the American diplomats complacently offered territorial terms on the basis of *status quo ante bellum.*

The British ministry now offered command to the Duke of Wellington in a new effort to invade the United States from Canada. But the wise hero of the war against Napoleon advised the ministry that British control of the Lakes was a necessary precondition of success. Since Britain lacked such control, Wellington bluntly told the government to make peace without territorial gains. Britain's greatest commander of land forces recognized the pre-eminence of sea power, and no more impressive tribute to Macdonough's victory can be imagined. The ministry decided that the war-weariness and tax-weariness of the British people forbade a new campaign on the Lakes preliminary to a new invasion of the United States. Therefore, they accepted Wellington's analysis of the situation and withdrew the demand for *uti possidetis*.

The European situation also helped the American cause. The powers which had defeated Napoleon were falling into disunity at the Congress of Vienna. Late in 1814, even before Napoleon returned from Elba to be finally defeated at Waterloo, the British government decided to liquidate the liability in America and make a quick peace. Once again dissensions in Europe strengthened the bargaining position of the United States.

The Madison administration itself had made an important contribution towards peace, in June 1814, by withdrawing its demand that Britain abandon impressment as a *sine qua non* condition. With the close of the Napoleonic wars at sea the British had stopped the hated practice and, actually, they never renewed it. Still His Majesty's government would not renounce impressment in a treaty, so the commissioners at Ghent agreed to ignore that issue and other questions of neutral rights.

The British government refused to renew without an equivalent the fishing privileges in British North American waters which had been granted the United States in the Treaty of 1783. John Quincy Adams was willing to concede renewal of the British right to navigate the Mississippi River from Canada to the Gulf, in return for renewal of New England's precious fishing privileges. But Henry Clay dreaded to face his Western constituents if he failed to push every vestige of British right out of the way of the advancing American frontier. He and Adams fought this sectional battle to a standstill. Then the astute Gallatin pointed out to the British that the American commission could not agree on the fisheries-Mississippi project and convinced them as well as his colleagues that it should be dropped from the treaty. This result was highly favorable to America because future negotiations secured the fisheries without conceding any British right south of the Canadian border. The treaty also provided for mixed arbitral commissions to settle boundary disputes in the Northeast and Northwest.

Otherwise the treaty provided simply for peace on the basis of *status quo ante bellum*. It was in the nature of an armistice, disputed questions being ignored or postponed for settlement in future treaties. Seldom has a nation recovered from disaster as swiftly as the United States between August and December of 1814, and events proved the wisdom of the commissioners. The full meaning of the Treaty of Ghent became visible only with the passage of many years. It inaugurated the era of un-challenged American security and expansion westward to the Pacific.

It marked the final acceptance of American independence by the only power in the world that was capable of destroying it.

Vocal sections of the British public were not prepared to accept the ministry's wise policy of accommodation to American long-range ambitions. The *London Times* said in an editorial: "We have retired from the combat with the stripes yet bleeding on our backs,—with the recent defeats, at Plattsburg, and on Lake Champlain, unavenged. To make peace at such a moment betrays a deadness to the feelings of honor, and shows a timidity of disposition, inviting further insult." But Napoleon's return from Elba soon justified the government's liquidation of the American war and diverted British attention back to the greater theater.

Hourly expecting news of disaster at New Orleans, the American public, early in the new year, received with unexampled joy the news of both Jackson's great victory and the signing of the Treaty of Ghent. Cities were illuminated by thousands of candles for all-night celebrations; there were parades and banquets, fireworks and endless toasts; and the pealing of bells went on for days. All this was in striking contrast to the sour public reception of the treaty in England and British North America, and it caused the "ambassadors" of the Hartford Convention—actually three men from Massachusetts—to look absurd. President Madison thankfully submitted the treaty to the Senate and it was unanimously approved. A century of world peace followed, a century that witnessed growth in American power and democracy unequalled by any people in human history.

Part II

NATIONALISM, SECTIONALISM,
AND DEMOCRACY, 1815-1841

CHAPTER 8

The Completion of
Independence, 1815-1823

FOR A FEW YEARS AFTER 1815, FOREIGN RELATIONS
continued to be a major preoccupation of the United States government.
The classical age of American diplomacy, when the very existence of the
young nation was at stake and foreign policy was necessarily dependent
on the European situation, was fittingly and brilliantly closed by the work
of President James Monroe (1817-1825) and his Secretary of State, John
Quincy Adams. With them a generation of insecurity ended, and a new
era of nationality began. In their knowledge of the ways of the Old World,
their skill in diplomatic maneuver, and their devotion to the ideal of an
independent republic, these two men equalled those great figures of the
classical age and founders of American foreign policy, Benjamin Franklin
and Thomas Jefferson. Their like was not to be seen in the land afterwards
until the world crises of the twentieth century would again create the
opportunity, and impose the necessity, for greatness in the conduct of
American foreign relations.

The dawn of the century of peace in Europe following the Battle of
Waterloo and the Congress of Vienna was the indispensable condition of
the success of American diplomacy after the war. The marvel of the settlement of 1815 is that the United States emerged unharmed after taking on
the most implacable of Napoleon's foes and thereby risking implication in
his defeat. Henceforth the Republic did not have to risk such hairs'-
breadth escapes. It could depend on peace in Europe while consolidating
its own independence, and on the relative indifference of European Powers
while devoting its abundant energies to the expansion of the nation.

Conventions and Agreements with the British

The Commercial Convention of 1815

No American was ever more devoted to independence and expansion than John Quincy Adams, and to him belongs the chief credit for the remarkable postwar triumphs of diplomacy which converted the "truce" of Ghent into a victorious peace. Immediately after the signing of the Treaty at Ghent, Adams, who was now Minister to the Court of St. James's, negotiated the first Anglo-American commercial treaty. Ever since the Revolution, the British had refused to make promises regarding reciprocal treatment of American trade and shipping. Perhaps the Embargo and Nonintercourse Acts won a delayed victory by teaching Britain that discriminations in tariff and tonnage duties only brought reprisals. Her policy during the new era was based on the importation of food and raw materials and the exportation of manufactured goods. A commercial treaty with the United States on the principle of reciprocity would be an essential safeguard and encouragement of increased Anglo-American trade.

Adams achieved an equitable arrangement under which each government agreed to apply to the other's goods and ships tariff and shipping rates no higher than it applied to the goods and ships of the "most-favored nation," that is, the third nation which enjoyed the most favorable terms granted to any. This Commercial Convention of June 1815 did not solve the problem of protecting American "infant industries" against British imports, but, by putting an end to the discriminations against United States trade and shipping arriving in the British Isles, it guaranteed that American merchants could sell food and raw materials there on a fair basis. The British government still refused to open the coveted West Indian trade. Consequently Adams shrewdly required that the term of the Commercial Convention be limited to four years.

The Rush-Bagot Agreement of 1817

The next step toward the achievement of permanent Anglo-American peace on the basis of mutual respect was marked by the establishment of mutual disarmament on the Great Lakes. When the war ended, Britain was building a great navy to secure supremacy along the water boundary between the United States and Canada. Congress in a postwar mood of economy refused to authorize a fleet that could match the British, and it was greatly to the advantage of both sides to avoid a naval-building race. In Parliament, however, much was heard of the necessity to prepare for another war. Minister Adams reported in 1816 that Lord

Castlereagh spoke ominously of "the great and growing military power of the United States."

President Madison and Secretary of State Monroe seized the initiative in favor of common sense and peace. They told Adams to propose mutual disarmament on the Lakes to Castlereagh. In April 1817, after Monroe had become President and before Adams had returned home to become Secretary of State, Charles Bagot, the able British minister to the United States, and Acting Secretary of State Richard Rush exchanged letters constituting an executive agreement that both governments would reduce their armed forces on the Lakes to a few revenue cutters that would be useless for war. At the British request, the Agreement was approved by the Senate so that it gained the status of a formal treaty. Later, from time to time, the principles of the Agreement were applied to the land frontier between the United States and Canada. In the end it covered the entire boundary of over 3000 miles, the longest undefended frontier in the world. With the growing Anglo-American practice of arbitration, the Rush-Bagot Agreement was far ahead of its time as a practical application of the ancient ideal that international disputes should be settled peaceably.

It is likely that without such a disarmament agreement the Canadian-American border incidents which occurred intermittently throughout the nineteenth century would have flamed into war. At the time, the Agreement signified that Great Britain, in good faith, had at last abandoned the policy of thwarting the westward expansion of the United States. Despite the recent threats of Westerners to conquer Canada, and despite the fears of the Canadians, who detected the beginning of a tendency to sacrifice their interests on the altar of Anglo-American friendship, Britain withdrew the menace of arms pointed at the American Northwest.

The Anglo-American Convention of 1818

The meaning of the Rush-Bagot Agreement was confirmed and greatly enlarged by the Convention of 1818. The British government was very anxious to renew the Commercial Convention of 1815 before it expired, and Adams exploited this anxiety after he became Secretary of State. He was unable to use the technique of exploiting divisions among the European powers to secure American bargaining advantage which had led to every previous major success in American diplomacy. But the old British contempt for "Yankee cowardice," "fir-built frigates," and "degenerate frontiersmen" had disappeared, and respect coupled with a healthy regard for the business profits of American friendship had taken its place. Only token applications of force and the threat of commercial retaliations were required to obtain a settlement of important matters on excellent terms in 1818.

A section of great importance in this treaty concerned Oregon. Just as the American negotiators of the Treaty of 1783 had reached out far beyond the frontier of settlement to secure the Old Northwest, so now the Monroe administration reached out to secure a new domain on the Pacific Coast for the future expansion of settlement.

In 1792, the crew of the Boston-owned ship *Columbia,* looking for furs, had discovered the great river which they named for their vessel and their country, thus establishing bases for the claim of the United States to the region. Thomas Jefferson had dispatched the Lewis and Clark expedition to find a virgin fur-trading area for Americans and to open up a water route to the Pacific. Other expeditions into the West found British fur traders in the North and Spanish forces in the South. In the vast region between them, American fur traders rapidly strengthened the territorial claims of the Republic.

New England ships first proved the wealth of Oregon by obtaining cargoes of furs from the local Indians, who called all white men "Bostons." One Yankee traded a rusty chisel for pelts worth $8000. The furs were carried to the Orient, to trade for tea, china, and silks, which were then sold in the United States for fantastic profits. John Jacob Astor, a German immigrant whose vision of profits matched Jefferson's continental vision of the Republic's boundaries, planned in 1810 to put the British Hudson's Bay and Northwest companies out of business by setting up a chain of fur-trading posts from the Great Lakes to the Pacific Ocean. By the summer of 1812, an expedition by sea had built a post at the mouth of the Columbia and named it Astoria, while an expedition by land discovered the best pass across the Rockies and the route later famous as the Oregon Trail. When news reached Astoria in January 1813 that war had begun and that a British warship was on the way to capture the post, Astor's partners sold out to the British Northwest Company. This was a private business exchange, but the captain of a British warship raised the Union Jack over the post and renamed it Fort George. The Madison administration, for its part, claimed in July 1815 that the provision in the peace treaty for territorial *status quo ante bellum* required that Astoria revert to the United States on the grounds that Britain held it as captured territory. The British government answered that the country around the Columbia River was part of His Majesty's dominions.

Early in Monroe's administration, Secretary of State Adams informed the British that the United States intended to retake Astoria by force, but the threat did not suffice. Therefore, in October 1817, President Monroe ordered the sloop-of-war *Ontario* to sail around the Horn with American commissioners and to expel the British from the mouth of the Columbia River. The British government then hastened to send orders that Fort George be peaceably turned over to the American commissioners. This was done in October 1818. The British thus gave up their claim to exclusive ownership of Oregon. In negotiations during 1818 the two governments agreed to postpone final settlement, meanwhile recognizing that both countries had claims to the whole area between Spanish and Russian territory. For ten years American citizens and British subjects should be free to enter, settle, and trade in the disputed region; and then the question of permanent boundaries beyond the Rocky Mountains would be reopened. The joint occupation was renewed periodically until the permanent division of 1846.

The Oregon provision was linked in the Convention of 1818 with a settlement of the boundary between the United States and Canada from the Great Lakes to the Rockies. Ignorance of geography had made earlier attempts at settlement of this boundary inoperable. Britain claimed the future bonanza wheat region of the Red River Valley in present-day Minnesota, and the United States claimed a slice of present-day Canada to the west as part of the drainage basin of the Mississippi River included in the Louisiana Purchase. These claims were evened out by agreement that the boundary should run from the Lake of the Woods along the 49th parallel to the watershed of the Rocky Mountains. In this way the Canadian border was kept above the headwaters of the Mississippi River, and Great Britain lost her right under the Treaty of 1783 to navigation of that stream. The epochal Convention of 1818 ended the story that began with the Proclamation of 1763, even as it opened a new story of consent by the Old World that the American pioneer should push on all the way to the Pacific Coast.

Settlement of the fisheries question was also obtained in the Convention of 1818. British subjects engaged in the Canadian fisheries petitioned their government to forbid the competition of Americans after the War of 1812. On the other hand, New Englanders regarded the freedom to fish inshore around the Canadian coast and to dry their catch on deserted shores as a vested interest established in colonial times and retained by revolutionary right. In spite of the failure to obtain recognition of the "right" in the Treaty of Ghent, New England fishermen returned to their accustomed grounds after the war. British warships chased them and, in the summer of 1817, an admiralty court claimed the right to confiscate any American fishing vessel caught in British North American waters. Adams found that his first job as Secretary of State was to win the codfish for Boston, as it had been the task of his father before him.

American warships were sent to protect fishing vessels entering their accustomed places. Holding out this threat of force with one hand, Adams with the other offered the British government an opportunity to negotiate. He astutely coupled the boundaries and fisheries questions with the renewal of the Commercial Convention of 1815. Britain had offered limited trade privileges in the West Indies, but in order to extort more, Congress passed the Navigation Act of 1818. This excluded British merchant ships from the trade between Britain and the United States just as the British Navigation Acts excluded American merchant ships from the British West Indian trade.

The despatch of the *Ontario* to Oregon and of other American warships to Canada and the passing of the American Navigation Act brought the British government to terms. Besides surrendering Astoria and agreeing to settlement of the northwestern boundary and joint occupation of Oregon, the British government granted Americans liberty forever to catch and dry fish along specified shores of Newfoundland, Quebec, and Labrador. In return the United States agreed to renew the Commercial Convention for ten years. Further retaliations were required before Britain in 1822 began to lower mercantilist barriers in the West Indies. Adams waged this fight throughout his eight years as Secretary of State and then for four more years as President, after which President Jackson in 1830 finally secured American privileges in the West Indies comparable to those of colonial times.

The Convention of 1818 was the first in which Great Britain treated the United States as an equal sovereign in fact as well as name. It was in reality the definitive peace settlement between the two countries. Unlike the Treaty of 1783, it was actually observed by Great Britain; unlike Jay's Treaty of 1794, it contained no terms humiliating to American sovereignty; and unlike the Treaty of Ghent it settled favorably to the United States the concrete issues in dispute. New disputes would arise between the two English-speaking nations during the next century, but without exception these would be settled peacefully according to the pattern established in 1818. True, the United States did not annex Canada and did not obtain an express disavowal of impressment. But if we remember that in the summer of 1814 it was British policy to annex northern areas of the United States to Canada and to throw an Indian state across the path of westward expansion, the territorial vista of 1818 which extended to the Pacific Coast seems a remarkable gain. As for impressment, the British abandoned the policy even though they made no promise on paper.

The Treaty of 1819 with Spain

In the Treaty of 1819 the United States matched with Spain in the South the settlement with Britain in the North and rounded out the permanent structure of peace. President Monroe and Secretary Adams successfully used with Spain the sort of strong methods they used against Britain. Spain was rapidly losing control over her revolted colonies in America and had already lost most of West Florida to the United States.

The proud Spaniards were faced with a choice of evils. They could refuse to settle issues and risk American intervention in behalf of the Spanish-American rebels; or they could beat a strategic retreat before the American advance into the Floridas in the hope of obtaining American abstention from aid to the rebels in the rest of the colonies.

Public sympathy for the Spanish-American revolutions was very strong in the United States. Sympathizers organized filibuster expeditions to aid the insurgents. Henry Clay led a movement in favor of open recognition of the new governments and public aid to them. Adams realized that if the United States were too slow in acting, the new republics would hasten to ally themselves economically and politically with Great Britain. But if the United States acted too soon, Spain would doubtless refuse to give way in the Floridas. Weighing these alternatives, Adams concocted the policy of postponing recognition of rebel governments until the chances of suppression by the mother country were "utterly desperate." A House resolution calling for immediate recognition of the new republics was defeated in March 1818, as a result of administration pressure.

Adams at the same time brought great pressure to bear on Spain to part with East Florida and the remainder of West Florida. An armed expedition was sent in 1817 to seize Amelia Island, near the Georgia coast, where the Spanish had lost control and pirates nested. In East Florida, the Seminole Indians, runaway slaves, and miscellaneous outlaws were accustomed to hide out between raids into the United States. Late in 1817, the Monroe administration commissioned General Andrew Jackson to punish the Seminoles and pursue them across the boundary if necessary. Jackson took on his job with gusto. Later he claimed that he received additional instructions from Monroe through Congressman Rhea that he should seize Spanish towns. He captured the military post at St. Marks in April 1818, and Pensacola a little later. He placed an American in office as Governor of East Florida and extended the revenue laws of the United States to the area. Besides punishing Indians, Jackson tried by court martial and executed two British subjects. Alexander Arbuthnot and Robert Ambrister, in order, as he wrote to the Secretary of War, to convince their government and its subjects that certain retribution awaited "those unchristian wretches who, by false promises, delude and excite an Indian tribe to all the horrid deeds of savage war." Lord Castlereagh refused to support English demands for redress because the two renegades, in his opinion, had placed themselves by their actions outside the protection of their government. Here was further evidence of Britain's new-found respect for the United States.

Henry Clay and other Congressmen castigated Jackson's bold procedures, but popular acclaim was such that resolutions condemning him were easily defeated. President Monroe and nearly all of his Cabinet members regarded Jackson's actions as unjustifiable acts of war against Spain, but Adams convinced them all that the government should support the impetuous General. Adams not only repelled Spanish demands for redress but demanded that Spain punish officials who had failed to prevent raids into the United States, and that Spain pay an indemnity for the expenses of Jackson's expedition. Otherwise, Adams hinted, American forces would have to go into Florida again, and the next time they would stay there.

Spanish officials in Florida confessed that they were unable to control the Seminoles. The home government decided, therefore, that it would be wise to sell Florida to the United States rather than risk losing it without compensation and chance a war which would range the United States on the side of the revolutionaries. Adams and Luis de Onís, the Spanish Minister, worked out treaty terms which solved problems all along the southern boundary. The United States received title to both of the Floridas and to Spain's claims to territory north of a stepped line from the Sabine River on the western border of the state of Louisiana to the 42nd parallel, and thence westward to the Pacific. In return the United States abandoned its claim to Texas based on the Louisiana Purchase and agreed to pay its own citizens claims amounting to $5 million which Spain owed them for depredations against American commerce.

This was the second United States treaty recognizing the right to expand to the Pacific Coast and the first treaty that established a transcontinental boundary. The Senate happily approved the excellent bargain in February 1819, but Spain, fearing that the United States would recognize and aid the Spanish-American rebels the moment the treaty was proclaimed in force, delayed ratification. She asked for a promise of nonrecognition, but Adams steadily refused. Finally Spain gave in and ratified, so that the treaty went into effect early in 1821.

By this time men like Henry Clay were bemoaning the loss of Texas and the "betrayal" of the Spanish Americans. After the decent interval of a year had elapsed and Spain's chances of reconquering the Spanish-American republics had become hopeless, the United States recognized them, being the first government in the world to welcome these new republics into the family of nations. As for Texas, Spanish officials in Mexico had already in 1821 granted a huge tract of land there to Moses Austin, and when the son of this American, Stephen F. Austin, began the work of settling American families, the independent government of Mexico confirmed the title. Frontiersmen thus created an American interest which would bring Texas into the Union later on.

The Adams-Onís Treaty of 1819 complemented the Convention of 1818 with Great Britain. Its substantial peaceful gains were basically a result of the determination to win security and ample boundaries which Westerners led by Andrew Jackson had proved in battle. After the Revolution, Spain had stood across the American path westward in the South just as Britain stood across it in the North. Now as a result of war and diplomacy, chiefly that of Thomas Jefferson and John Quincy Adams, both great powers had retreated. The United States had achieved security north, east, and south, and to the west there beckoned a territorial heritage for free men such as the sun had never shone upon in all man's previous history. Now Americans for the first time since 1776 could safely turn their eyes away from the Old World powers which had so persistently denied that the American experiment in liberty and self-government had a future. Now Americans could look to the West, and set about the business of building a nation whose extent and power should match the horizons of human hope. Little wonder that the new period of American history fixed the first article of American faith as simple optimism that every remaining economic, social, political, and spiritual evil could be abolished with just a little more effort on the part of the whole people and their government.

THE MONROE DOCTRINE

The Monroe Doctrine of 1823 is the symbolic capstone of the structure of security and expansion erected by the diplomatists of the classic period. The occasion for its announcement as the leading foreign policy of the United States was a final spasm in the death throes of the Old World policy of intervention in the New World. The unity of the powers, after the defeat of Napoleon and the restoration of the Bourbon government of Louis XVIII in France, contained a threat that the revolutions in America would be suppressed, just as the French Revolution had been. The Quadruple Alliance united the four victorious powers in a guarantee of the boundaries drawn by the Congress of Vienna (1815). France joined it, and the Holy Alliance united all of them except Great Britain with France in favor of monarchy and religion against republicanism and infidelity. From the point of view of American safety the disunity of the powers was desirable. Hence the refusal of Britain to join the Holy Alliance was promising, and her gradual withdrawal from the Quadruple Alliance during the years after 1815 was a boon to America. Britain controlled the seas, and she had a powerful trade interest in the independence of the American republics. These factors turned out to be fundamental reasons why the European threat against republicanism in America failed and why the United States and Great Britain slowly developed the most important friendship between two nations in modern times.

For a few years after 1815 co-operation among the European monarchs to put down rebellions succeeded. The fires of the French Revolution still smoldered among the oppressed peoples. They broke out in open rebellion after 1820 in Spain, Portugal, Naples, and Greece. The monarchs authorized Austria in 1821 to crush the Neapolitan rebels with armed force. They authorized France to invade Spain early in 1823 and place the brutal and perjured Ferdinand VII back on his throne. Then the monarchs planned a congress in Paris to authorize an expedition which would round out their victory in Spain by reconquering that country's former American colonies. Suddenly the hard-won security of the United States seemed again to be in danger. Would the monarchs stamp out the Spanish-American rebels and then hesitate to destroy the world's greatest breeding ground of republicanism?

Czar Alexander I of Russia, the leading spirit of the Holy Alliance, had shown in an imperial edict or ukase of 1821 a distinct ambition to expand Alaska. The ukase claimed that the southern boundary of Alaska lay deep in the Oregon country at the 51st parallel, and it forbade foreign ships to come closer to the Alaska shores than one hundred Italian miles, an unprecedented assertion of authority over the high seas. In July 1823, Adams, in opposition to this ukase, announced to the Russian Minister to the United States one of the great principles which was incorporated in the Monroe Doctrine a little later, namely, "that the American continents are no longer subjects for any new European colonial establishments." Britain joined the United States in opposing the Russian ukase, but the principle Adams had announced applied also to Britain, and therein is found the special character of the policy of Adams and Monroe: they were determined that the United States *alone* should repel *all* Old World interference *anywhere* in the American Hemisphere.

Britain had opposed the French invasion of Spain and was fearful lest the Bourbons would try to reconquer the former Spanish colonies. The new Foreign Secretary, George Canning, decided to make an ally of the United States. In August 1823, he proposed to Richard Rush, United States Minister in London, that the two governments join to prevent action by the European monarchs in America.

This was the offer that occasioned the announcement of the Monroe Doctrine. At first President Monroe was inclined to accept it. He asked the advice of the aged Jefferson, who replied favorably. Jefferson's advice was highly revealing. Here was the ancient leader of the anti-British party in American politics, the man who is usually considered the father of American isolationism as he was the spokesman of American independence, counseling an alliance with Great Britain such as he had been equally ready to enter into when Napoleon threatened to take over Louisiana. The seeming contradictions in Jefferson's policy can be resolved by the consideration that, while he preferred isolation, he wisely regarded both isolation and alliances as no more than alternative means to the one major goal: the security of the Republic. Therefore when a situation arose in which an isolated United States was menaced by one party of the perennially divided Old World, Jefferson was ready to embrace the opposing party even though he disliked it.

Nevertheless, Adams rejected Jefferson's advice and Canning's offer. He saw a possibility that the United States might secure all the advantages of British support while avoiding all the disadvantages. In the momentous Cabinet debates on Canning's proposed entente, the Secretary of State stood out for a unilateral announcement by the United States. For one thing, he did not want his country to "come in as a cock-boat in the wake of the British man-of-war." More important, Canning had proposed that the United States and Britain should formally promise not to annex any Spanish-American territory. The expansionist Adams refused to tie the hands of his country. If Cuba or Texas asked admission into the Union, why should the United States refuse? Adams furthermore calculated that the unity of the European allies was too shaky to support intervention in America. And even if they did intervene, Britain's interest would require the Mistress of the Seas to prevent their success.

Adams's brilliant argument convinced the President and Cabinet. Monroe decided to announce the policy in his presidential message to Congress on December 2, 1823. The "Monroe Doctrine," as the policy later came to be called, contained two warnings and two promises. The first warning stated to Britain and the Holy Allies the principle of non-colonization: that "the American continents, by the free and independent condition which they have assumed and maintain, are henceforth not to be considered as subjects for future colonization by any European powers." An important "corollary" of this principle which had already been announced by the United States in relation to Cuba was the no-transfer principle—that no existing colony of one European power might be transferred to the possession of another European power. The United States, however, was left free to acquire such territories by transfer. The second warning stated to the European allies the principle of nonintervention: that "we should consider any attempt on their part to extend their system to any portion of this hemisphere as dangerous to our peace and safety." In the manner of a *quid pro quo* for these warnings, Monroe promised first, that the United States would not interfere with the existing colonies in America of any Old World power; and second, that the United States would not intervene in the internal affairs of the European powers.

Reception of the Policy

British public opinion welcomed Monroe's announcement as evidence that the United States would support Britain against the allies in case of need. But Canning had learned that the allies would not carry out the plan to reconquer Spanish America and he had led the French Ambassador to sign the "Polignac Memorandum" denying any intention of France to intervene in America. Feeling free, therefore, to concentrate on the anti-British aspect of Monroe's message, he proudly announced to Rush that Britain had no intention of accepting the noncolonization principle. Nevertheless, in Parliament Canning indicated that he welcomed the other aspects of the message. Indeed, he claimed credit for them, saying: "I called the New World into existence to redress the balance of the Old" (1826). Thus the Monroe Doctrine established an Anglo-American entente against Europe even while it warned Britain against any further expansion in America.

The continental powers were contemptuous of Monroe's declarations. They found a ridiculous gap between the vast pretensions of the United States to guard the Hemisphere and the nation's slight armed power. Not the message but the jealousies of the allies prevented their intervention. The Czar was most anxious to restore monarchy and religion in Spanish America, but France by the Polignac Memorandum had left him in the lurch and the other powers refused to help. In the face of the British fleet, Russia could not possibly intervene alone.

The ever-current possibility of revolution in Russia and the vast extent of her unexploited territory in Asia also led the Czar to abandon his ukase of 1821. In 1824, Adams signed a Russian-American treaty which fixed the southern boundary of Alaska at its present location, 54°–40' north latitude. This success, though not so much a result of Monroe's warning as a fortunate coincidence, strengthened the claim of the United States to Oregon and repelled an Old World scheme for territorial aggrandizement in America. Since 1823, European powers have often retreated in the Western Hemisphere: they have never advanced, and only the United States has expanded its boundaries. Whether or not the Monroe Doctrine has been the "cause" of American advance and European retreat, these were certainly purposes of Monroe and Adams.

Latin Americans were inclined to believe that Canning, rather than Monroe, had saved America from the European allies. They also recognized that Monroe had left the way open for the expansion of his own country and that he was primarily concerned with its interests. When Mexico and Colombia planned an expedition to free Cuba from Spain and annex it to a mainland republic, the United States government opposed the move, and this indicated that Latin-American as well as European expansion in the Hemisphere was under the ban. Colombia and Brazil proposed an alliance with the United States against Europe, but this, too, the Monroe administration opposed. Many Latin Americans came to believe that "Monroeism" was nothing more than a cover for the imperialism of the "Yankee Colossus."

The Monroe Doctrine did not displace Great Britain as the most influential power in Latin America. Only during the last generation have the unilateral and expansionist aspects of the Doctrine been abolished. Under the "Good Neighbor Policy," instituted by President Franklin D. Roosevelt in the 1930's, the United States has agreed to multilateralization of the Doctrine, repudiated expansion and intervention in Latin America, and joined in a military alliance with all the republics against aggression by American as well as non-American Powers. These actions and the displacement of Britain by the United States as the greatest Atlantic power have finally made the United States the most influential nation in the Hemisphere.

Monroe's epochal message well expresses the national mood of unbounded confidence in Americans' ability to hew their own path towards a grand destiny in defiance of the predatory and corrupt monarchs of Europe. Americans have savored the Doctrine's opposition to British ambitions in the New World while scarcely appreciating that it long depended upon the British Navy for its effectiveness against Europe. Actually, for a quarter of a century following its pronouncement, the Monroe Doctrine was remembered by few Americans. Thereafter it was invoked and applied with increasing frequency by successive administrations, and gradually it acquired a sacrosanct character, as if it were a law of nature, and a cluster of interpretations and corollaries as if it were the Constitution or a text of Holy Writ. Yet the Monroe Doctrine was only a presidential statement, lacking any character of domestic or international law prior to its incorporation in the modern Good Neighbor treaties.

With the Monroe Doctrine the United States completed the formative stage of its foreign relations. Within a decade of the Treaty of Ghent, the Republic had achieved excellent treaty relations with the Great Powers and wide boundaries. France and Spain had disappeared as menacing neighbors in the South and weak republics had taken their place. Anglo-American relations pointed towards forbearance and even co-operation. The President had proclaimed the principles of the Monroe Doctrine as a summary of what had been achieved and a portent of freedom's future. Europe, not unmindful of the two unsuccessful attempts to destroy the independence of the United States in war, did not again attempt to snuff out the flame of American liberty.

CHAPTER 9

The "Era of Good Feelings":
Nation and Sections

THE PREDOMINANT MOOD OF THE AMERICAN PEOPLE after the conclusion of the War of 1812 was one of exuberant patriotism and political unity. This was reflected in nationalistic legislation at the end of Madison's administration, in the use of the expression, "Era of Good Feelings," early in the administration of James Monroe, and in the mortal defeat of the Federalist Party, which was deemed unpatriotic and particularistic. While gaining full political independence from the Old World, the Republic was emerging from a colonial into a national economy in which domestic commerce played an increasingly important part. It would be too much to say that the Americans now turned their backs on Europe, for foreign trade was of the utmost importance to a very large number of them, but more than ever they turned their eyes and their steps westward. Furthermore, as the country grew, its component geographical regions were assuming a more distinctive character. Besides being a union of states, it was now an empire of sections, comparable in size to European countries, though the sectional boundaries were shifting and loosely drawn. Behind the façade of political unity in a one-party period, there were sharp clashes of sectional and group economic interests. These were accentuated by the economic crisis which began in 1819; and, in the struggle over the admission of Missouri at the same time, slavery became a subject of hot debate. In an era of external peace the issues of the coming generation were taking form.

THE NATIONAL POLITICAL AND ECONOMIC SCENE, 1816-1824

The Tariff Act of 1816 and the establishment of the Second Bank of the United States that year, though Republican measures, would have

156

been fully approved by Alexander Hamilton. A few years later, when in retirement, Madison referred to the charge that the Republicans had deserted their cause and gone over to the policy of their old opponents. "But," he said, "they overlook the overbearing and vindictive spirit, the apocryphal doctrines, and rash projects, which stamped on Federalism its distinctive character; and which are so much in contrast with the unassuming and unvarying spirit which has marked the Republican Ascendancy." In the hands of Jefferson and Madison, Republicanism did escape the arrogance of High Federalism, and it was more flexible in both foreign and domestic policy. The "unvarying spirit" which Madison claimed for his party was that of devotion to the interests of the majority, not of small special classes. The actions of 1816 may have been afterwards regarded by opponents of the protective tariff and the Bank as victories for special interests, but at the time they seemed wise in view of the general economic situation.

National Legislation

The Tariff of 1816, the first in American history that was primarily designed for protection rather than revenue, was enacted in what was generally recognized as a time of emergency. The embargo and the British blockade during the war had created a sudden demand for domestic manufactures to replace formerly imported foreign articles. The result was the first burst of the American Industrial Revolution. Cotton mills multiplied so rapidly, chiefly in New England, that the number of spindles increased from 8000 in 1807 to 500,000 in 1815. Lesser advances were made in other lines of manufacturing. But immediately after the war ended, British imports began to flood the American market, threatening to overwhelm "infant industries" that ranged from the textile mills of New England to the iron foundries of Pittsburgh. It was believed that these required tariff protection. Also, it was believed that other important interests should be safeguarded. Agricultural products were not protected in this particular act to the same extent as in later ones, but hemp-growers of Kentucky and wool-growers from Vermont to Ohio were staunch and consistent supporters of the protective principle. At this time, Daniel Webster and other representatives of New England's commercial interests believed that low tariffs and a flourishing foreign trade would serve them best. On the other hand, John C. Calhoun of South Carolina favored this tariff, in view of the larger national interest. Most of the opposition to the bill came from the South, but not until the next decade did antitariff sentiment become general in that region. Sectional lines were not sharply drawn as yet on this historic issue.

The charter of the First Bank of the United States had expired in

1811, though the Secretary of the Treasury at the time, Albert Gallatin, had strongly urged that the institution be rechartered. Meanwhile, a large crop of state banks had sprung up, and in the absence of any central control the currency of the country had fallen into great disorder. During and after the war, the federal government had been embarrassed in its fiscal operations, and Madison joined with his Secretary of the Treasury, Alexander J. Dallas, in advocating a second Bank of the United States for the convenience of the government and the restoration of a sound currency. He was a hard-money man not an inflationist, and he regarded his earlier constitutional objections to such an institution as already overruled by public authority. The Supreme Court decisively affirmed the constitutionality of the Bank a little later (1819).

The new Bank was closer to the federal government than the old one had been, since five of the twenty-five directors were appointed by the President, but at the outset it was not so carefully or so conservatively administered. The liberal credit policy which its branches followed in the South and West showed that it was not unmindful of agricultural interests and the policy redounded to the Bank's popularity in those regions. But the reversal of this was one of the immediate causes of the Panic of 1819 and tended to alienate many Westerners and Southerners.

The Republican administration did not go along so readily with the policy of internal improvements, that is, the building of roads and canals at federal expense, which was especially urged by Westerners. Gallatin may be regarded as the father of the idea and Jefferson had approved it, on the understanding that an amendment to the Constitution should be passed to authorize federal action of this sort. Madison's objections were also constitutional, and he did not waive them in this case as he did in that of the Bank. In 1817, Westerners put through a bill for a large group of federal road projects but Madison vetoed it. President Monroe was rather more favorable, going so far as to sign the Survey Bill (1824), which looked toward a program of internal improvements without actually starting one. At this point the nationalism of the Virginia Dynasty became hesitant.

Leaders and Interests

The most articulate public spokesman of economic nationalism at this stage was Henry Clay of Kentucky, former leader of the War Hawks, whose program was known as the "American System." He linked together the protective tariff, the Bank, and internal improvements and continued to champion all of them vigorously for a generation. "Harry of the West" imbued his vision of the American System with an almost religious fervor, and his nationalistic spirit was most nearly matched, perhaps, by that of John C. Calhoun, who was afterwards most famous as a spokesman of the South.

These two men were Republicans, like John Quincy Adams and the other effective political leaders of the time, for the Federalist Party, though still strong in some localities, ceased to be a national institution not long after the War of 1812. The most important phase of the presidential campaign of 1816 was the struggle for the Republican nomination. It went to James Monroe, who well deserved it for past services but was objected to by many on the ground that the state of Virginia should not monopolize the presidency. Party nominees were chosen by Congressional caucus, and William H. Crawford of Georgia, Secretary of the Treasury at the very end of Madison's administration, was the most popular candidate with Congress. His failure to gain the prize may be attributed to his own vacillation and to the intrigues of Martin Van Buren of New York. Monroe received 183 electoral votes to 34 for Rufus King, who carried only the states of Massachusetts, Connecticut, and Delaware. In the next presidential election, in 1820, there was no form of opposition to Monroe, who received all the electoral votes but one that was cast for John Quincy Adams.

In the early years of the Republican Party, Monroe had seemed more partisan than either Jefferson or Madison but now, as the head of a one-party country, he sought to be conciliatory. Early in his first term (July 12, 1817) the *Columbian Centinel* of Boston, a paper which had been noted for its virulent Federalism, used the expression which has been generally attached to his administration, the "Era of Good Feelings." It was not that for long except upon the surface. Sharp clashes of economic interest appeared by the middle of his first term, and during his second term there was a scramble of personal factions out of which a new party alignment emerged.

Despite the nationalist trend of postwar legislation, constitutional arguments against the growth of national power continued and these naturally assumed a state-rights form, as they did in Monroe's own Virginia. From this time on, however, many political conflicts were in reality sectional; and the geographical regions which were assuming increased significance cut across state lines and were not recognized by the Constitution. These sections could not be definitely bounded as states can; their lines necessarily shifted in a rapidly growing country. They attained varying degrees of economic and political unity; and, having no legal existence, they garbed their claims and arguments in nationalistic or state-rights language. The great political problem of the era was to harmonize the various sectional and group interests when they were in conflict.

Prior to the commercial restrictions which accompanied the Napoleonic wars, the economy of the United States had continued to be essentially colonial. The country was still engaged primarily in the production of raw materials, shipping the excess to Europe, and receiving manufactured goods in return—much as the colonies had done under British rule. After the war the economy deserved to be called national. Raw materials (especially cotton and tobacco) continued to be shipped to Europe, and manufacturing, supported by protective tariffs, was maintained and developed, while internal commerce attained a new volume and importance. Self-sufficiency was not yet achieved and in the full sense it never was, but the movement was definitely in that direction. The United States was developing a better-rounded economy. In the Northeast, which was assuming the economic position once held by the mother country, industry and commerce were growing; the West emphasized food products and clamored for better transportation; while the South, continuing to produce staples primarily, was dependent on Northern and European manufactures, and to a considerable degree on Western food.

THE DIVIDED EAST

The East, comprising New England and the Middle States of New York, New Jersey, and Pennsylvania, was far from being a unified section. Just after the War of 1812, New England was the most homogeneous of American regions in population, but its economic interests were divided and to some extent antagonistic. Agriculture continued, especially in northern New England, but it was sharply declining while the richer lands of upstate New York and the West were being developed, and the first mill-workers were largely recruited from farmers' families. There was abundant water power which was relatively close to the sea, and the inventive and enterprising New Englanders took the initiative and gained the American pre-eminence in the textile industry. Manufacturing was gaining on commerce, which had hitherto been the major source of prosperity, but the interests of the two conflicted. The opposition of Daniel Webster to the protective tariff until 1824 and his espousal of it in 1828 was symbolic of the change in emphasis and political attitude. Also, the pessimism of that statesman at the beginning of this period was significant, and statistics of population reinforced his opinion that the region was declining in political importance. Both the West and the Middle States were growing much faster.

At the first census in 1790, Massachusetts had more people than New York. By 1820, the Bay State had been passed not only by New York but also by the young states of Ohio and Kentucky. By 1830, she had slipped behind Tennessee and was eighth in the Union. New England suffered greatly during this period from the migration of her children—chiefly to upstate New York until after the Erie Canal opened the way into the

Old Northwest—and immigrants from Europe had not yet come in sufficient number to compensate for the heavy loss. Not until after 1830 did newcomers pour through the open gates like a flood.

The Middle States had little economic unity, but by 1820 New York had gained the first rank in population and by 1830 Pennsylvania, which had always stood near the top, was firmly established in second place. New York City had gained on Philadelphia in shipping, and, even before the opening of the Erie Canal in 1825, it had become *the* American metropolis, not to be outdistanced. Upstate New York, into which New Englanders had been pouring for some time, was richly agricultural and eastern Pennsylvania was notably so. The Keystone State found compensation for relative commercial decline in the development of coal and iron. The economic interests of New York and Pennsylvania were diversified just as their people were various in origin, and these two great states were political prizes for which all groups contended. It was true until the Civil War, as indeed it was thereafter, that one or both of them was generally in the winning combination. Also, they were the breeding ground of many of the more unsavory political practices of the era. Urban machine politics were first perfected by Republicans of New York City and Philadelphia.

The South and the Rise of "King Cotton"

The South, which became within a generation a section apart and long remained one, had an unusually homogeneous white population but no geographical unity except such as was imparted by the climate. From 1820 onward, whenever the slavery question was in the forefront of political controversy, the South was understood to consist of those states where slavery was still legal. But otherwise, in the period now being considered, Kentucky and even Tennessee were more likely to be regarded as Western than Southern. The two new Gulf states which were admitted just after the War of 1812—Mississippi (1817) and Alabama (1819)—had a distinct Western flavor but they were specially dependent on slave labor. All of the South was predominantly agricultural, but on the basis of crops an important and continuing distinction can be made between the Upper South and the Lower.

In the Upper South, which began at the Mason and Dixon line (the boundary between Pennsylvania and Maryland), the major crop in colonial times had been tobacco. By the end of the War of 1812, grain crops had infringed on this, and in many respects the agriculture of Maryland, Delaware, and northern and western Virginia resembled that of Pennsylvania. Tobacco was still cultivated in southern Virginia and North Carolina, and its area was extended westward into Kentucky and Tennessee, where the soil was fresher and richer. Hemp was an important product in Henry Clay's Kentucky, and much grain was grown in Andrew Jackson's Tennessee. These two states, which were the oldest beyond the mountains and represented a special blend of West and South, were entering the most important period of their political leadership. Meanwhile, the older states of the Upper South were losing ground. This was specially true of Virginia. The first state in population until 1820, she was displaced by New York in the census of that year, and sank to third place in 1830. She was losing her population to newer regions, much as New England was.

The most important agricultural developments of the period occurred further southward. Rice was still cultivated along the coast in South Carolina and Georgia, as long-staple cotton was, and sugar was a major crop in Louisiana, but in the Lower South short-staple cotton had usurped the throne and begun a long and fateful reign. The success story of this plant is usually thought of as beginning with the invention of the gin (1793) by a Connecticut Yankee, Eli Whitney. This permitted the extraction of the seed rapidly by machine rather than tediously by hand and encouraged more extensive production. Equally important, however, were textile inventions and developments in England and the vastly increased demand there and in New England for raw materials. The story of the rise of cotton is a chapter in the history of the Industrial Revolution. The reasons for the spread of cotton culture in the southernmost parts of the United States were chiefly climatic. The plant grows in almost any soil but it requires a long growing season and an abundance of sunshine. In times of high prices there was a tendency to stretch cotton production northward beyond its normal limits, and some cotton was raised at one time or another in all the southern states. But its permanent home was in South Carolina, Georgia, and the Gulf states. They comprised the real land of cotton.

At the end of the War of 1812, only about 150,000 bales were produced in the United States, chiefly in South Carolina and Georgia, but within a decade this yield had quadrupled, as the new lands in the Old Southwest were put into cultivation. The speed of the development was affected by the ups and downs of prices, which did not again reach the postwar peak, but until the Civil War the trend of production was upward until the figure for 1815 had been multiplied by thirty. The South had gained a virtual monopoly of one of the most prized staples in the world.

Cotton and Slavery

The spectacular rise of cotton gave a new lease on life to the institution of Negro slavery. In the Upper South, after the virgin lands had been exploited and tobacco culture began to decline, slaves tended to become a burden on their owners. Whether or not slavery would have gradually disappeared in the old tobacco country if it had been left to itself there, is a question which no man can answer, but that was what many of the Fathers of American independence had expected. In the Lower South, Negro slave labor was regarded as indispensable in the rice and sugar districts, where crops were cultivated on a large-plantation system. Cotton thrived on small farms as well as great plantations, but this royal crop lent itself to large-scale production under the gang system even though it did not actually require it. When so much fresh land in a favorable climate became available after the War of 1812, the chief limitation on the culture of cotton was the supply of labor, and small independent farmers did not provide enough in the face of the demand.

The foreign slave trade had been abolished on January 1, 1808, by a federal law passed in the previous year. The trade had been forbidden by all the states by 1798, when Georgia legislated against it, but South Carolina reopened it in 1803 and about 40,000 slaves were imported into that state in the next five years. This action was connected with early developments in cotton culture, but among Southerners there was strong opposition to the continuance of the traffic. Besides such humanitarian motives as Jefferson expressed, there were economic and social considerations. Further importations would decrease the value of the slaves already held, and would increase the social problem and danger of revolt.

The British, who had played such an important part in the trade, abolished it in 1807, being followed in a few years by the Dutch (1814), the French (1818), the Spanish (1820), and finally the Portuguese (1830). The American law of 1807 was a mild one, imposing no severe penalties, but it was fairly effective until the high price of slaves after the War of 1812 led to an increase in smuggling. This in turn led to a strengthening of the law. In 1818, the reward to informers was increased, and in 1820 the maritime slave trade was designated as piracy and made punishable by death. So long as slavery continued as an institution in the Western World there were illicit importations, but in the United States these fell chiefly in the decade 1850-1860. A few years after the War of 1812, it seemed that the country had closed the foreign slave trade from which the maritime peoples of the Atlantic world had gained such great financial profit through almost four centuries.

Those who would procure more slaves for purposes of labor would have to draw, it seemed, on the existing American Negroes. Hence the call from the burgeoning cotton states on the old tobacco region for its surplus and the gradual weakening of resistance there. The heydey of the human traffic between the Upper and Lower South did not come until the middle of the 1830's, but not long after the Peace of Ghent, slavery, now the invaluable handmaiden of "King Cotton," began to cast an ominous shadow on the expanding American empire of freedom.

THE WEST AND THE WESTWARD MOVEMENT

The term "West" is a variable in American history, since settlement kept surging toward the sunset until it reached the Pacific and could go no farther. The West was migratory but what is meant by it here is the region beyond the Appalachian Mountains. The settlement of the lower Mississippi Valley was part of the larger westward movement. That part of the country is often called the Old Southwest. There is much stronger reason, however, to associate the oldest trans-Appalachian states, Kentucky and Tennessee, with the vigorous young society which was developing in the Old Northwest Territory, north of the Ohio River. After the War, Indiana (1816) and Illinois (1818) were admitted to the Union, and the organized territory of Michigan lay to the north of them. By 1820, Ohio, though less than twenty years old as a state, ranked fifth in population in the Union. In the whole of this vast inland region the country was growing with appalling speed.

After 1815, conditions favored the movement of settlers into the West as never before. No European power now blocked the advance of the frontiersman; and the Indian, shorn of his European allies, was helpless to halt the white invasion. Long-term mortgages and other land loans were financed by the western branches of the Bank of the United States at first, and state banks were even more eager to expand credit and the currency to meet the farmers' demands. The most crucial Western question was that of transportation.

Predominantly this was the problem of connecting the West with the East. Beyond the mountains there was no great difficulty about the southward movement of settlers and their products because of the course of the rivers; and when steamboats began to be used on western waters in 1811, four years after Robert Fulton's *Clermont* first appeared on the Hudson, it became relatively easy to go upstream. But the steamboat did not meet the problem of getting across the mountains. This occasioned the pressure for internal improvements. John C. Calhoun of South Carolina saw danger to the Republic unless it were bound together by roads and canals—the "most powerful cement" he called them. Before long it appeared that his state, blocked from the West by an unconquerable mountain barrier, could benefit little from federal internal improvements; but there was good reason for the cities of the Northeast to favor them. They would tie Western trade to their emporia and prevent it from moving exclusively down the rivers to the Gulf.

Roads and Canals

The greatest project of internal improvement in the period was the Cumberland and National Road. Private enterprise had built the first

improved roads in the United States. The Lancaster Turnpike from Philadelphia to Lancaster, Pennsylvania, was their prototype. The state government chartered a private corporation in 1792 and an Englishman who
was acquainted with the methods of the Scot, J. L. McAdam, directed
the construction of a smooth ("macadamized") surface of crushed stone
which was fairly impervious to weather and wagon wheels. Toll gates
every few miles collected fees which paid profits to the private owners.
Such roads were rapidly built between the main eastern centers, but
many of them aroused public opposition because of exorbitant tolls and
political chicanery. State governments sometimes subsidized roads into
western regions within their own boundaries, but long interstate roads
through difficult country were beyond the financial ability of single states.

In 1802, the federal government agreed to use some of the money
derived from sales of public lands in Ohio for a road to connect that state
with the Atlantic seaboard. The shortest route was one that Washington
had surveyed from Cumberland on the upper Potomac to Wheeling on the
Ohio River. State jealousies were temporarily overcome in 1811, and by
1818 the Cumberland Road was open to traffic. Baltimore built a turnpike
to connect with the terminus at Cumberland, and Pennsylvania countered
by extending the Lancaster Turnpike to Pittsburgh. New York in turn
began in 1817 to build the great Erie Canal and when completed in
1825 her "water-level" route from Albany to Buffalo was the best way
west.

Meanwhile, it seemed unfair that one seaboard state, Maryland, should
be favored by the federal government while other states had to build their
own roads. The Constitution did not specifically authorize the government to construct roads or canals, hence authority had to be found in
loose construction of the interstate commerce clause. In 1817, Westerners
put through Congress a bill for a large group of federal road projects,
but President Madison vetoed it on constitutional grounds. President
Monroe vetoed (1822) a bill authorizing tolls on the Cumberland Road
to be used for its upkeep. He signed the Survey Bill in 1824, but this
merely called for the preparation of a larger program of internal improvements and did not authorize any actual project. New Englanders and
Southerners were predominantly against the measure. By the presidency
of John Quincy Adams, who strongly favored internal improvements and
had no constitutional objections to federal action, the opposition of
Southerners and certain groups of Easterners had become so great that
the adoption of his great plan proved impossible.

Thus the movement for the building of roads and canals by the
federal government slowed down, and in the meantime individual states
like New York and Pennsylvania went on with their own projects to
facilitate traffic with the West. Proposals to extend the Cumberland
Road as the National Road across southern Ohio, Indiana, and Illinois to
Saint Louis occasioned endless wrangles in Congress. The upshot was a

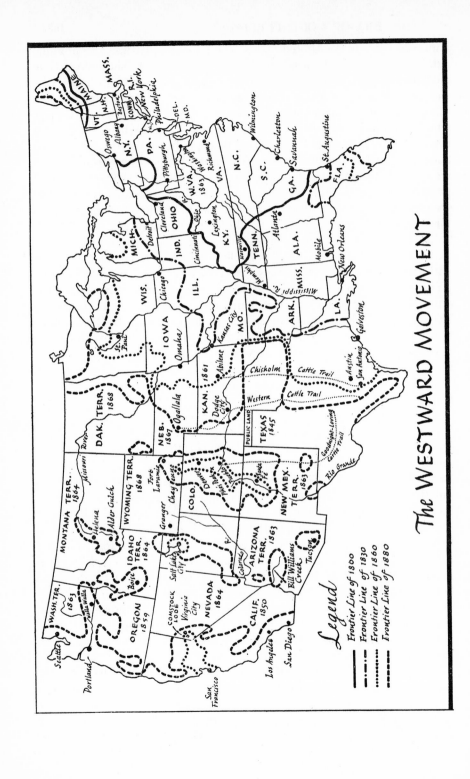

The WESTWARD MOVEMENT

Legend
——— Frontier Line of 1800
—·—·— Frontier Line of 1830
·········· Frontier Line of 1860
▬▬▬ Frontier Line of 1880

series of compromises whereby the federal government built stretches of this National Road in the 1830's, and then turned them over to the respective state governments, but the farthest it got was Vandalia, Illinois, at just about the time that Abraham Lincoln was doing odd jobs in the village of New Salem nearby. The great majority of roads and canals were built by state governments and private companies.

The Old Northwest

In the years immediately following the War of 1812 and through the 1820's, migrants to the West swarmed along the Cumberland Road, Pennsylvania's turnpike to Pittsburgh, and eventually the Erie Canal. Many from Kentucky and even from more distant Tennessee passed across the Ohio into the Old Northwest and across the Mississippi into Missouri. The general rule of settlement was that it roughly followed the parallels of latitude. The settlers in the lower halves of the states of Ohio, Indiana, and Illinois, and those in Missouri were largely of Southern origin. In the period before 1830, New Englanders were more numerous in Ohio than elsewhere in the West, but even in that state there were more people from the South and the Middle States, while Indiana and Illinois were still more strongly Southern. The greatest movement of New Englanders was after 1830, into the prairie districts which had seemed unattractive to the first settlers.

Corn to feed their families and their pigs, and pork and wheat for sale were the main crops of the farmers north of the Ohio. These crops did not invite gang labor as cotton did, and family farms were the typical units. While slave-owning planters followed and often displaced the pioneer farmers in the Old Southwest, the small farmers in the Old Northwest, and also in Kentucky and Tennessee, were soon followed by processors of various farm products. Energetic and enterprising men quickly capitalized on the advantages of processing hogs and cattle near the farms, shipping the meat to market in barrels, and of milling wheat into flour in local centers for shipment elsewhere. Cincinnati became a regional metropolis partly because of the steamboat business but chiefly because of the pork-packing industry. The "Queen of the West" was also called "Porkopolis." Progressively the West complemented diversified agriculture with diversified manufacturing, and thus tended to follow the model of the economy of the East, except for oceanic enterprises. But the flow of traffic was still chiefly southward down the rivers, and ties of kinship with the South were strong. The West was destined to become a crucial battleground in the economic and political conflicts of the generation, and the riddle of the future was whether it would ally itself with the East or South. Only when the Northwest and

Northeast were firmly tied together by railroads did the three sections of the country resolve themselves into two—North and South.

THE PANIC OF 1819

American exuberance had a rude shock in the financial crisis which began in 1818, reached its climax in 1819, and lasted for several years thereafter. This was the first of the economic depressions which occurred at fairly regular intervals in the United States until our own times. Though connected with the world situation, it was precipitated and accentuated by American actions and developments. It was a slump after a boom.

The restoration of trade with Europe had worked to the immediate disadvantage of the young manufacturers of the United States; and despite the Tariff of 1816 they had had difficulty in adjusting themselves to the situation. But there was a great boom in agriculture, resulting from an abnormal European demand for American staples which caused prices to soar. Cotton, the chief export, went to more than 30¢ a pound. Then, as a result of the great expansion of American production and the decline in European demand after supply caught up with it, agricultural prices dropped. In the year 1819, they were, in general, about half their previous maximum. There was a slump in all agricultural commodities but the heaviest blow fell on those most involved in the export trade—cotton and tobacco. Quite obviously the American economy was still dependent on the world market. Overexpansion in the United States, however, was a major factor and the panic was precipitated by actions within the chaotic banking system which amounted to a reaction against the reckless purchasing of land.

The federal government had encouraged westward migration by liberalizing the terms of sale of public lands. The law had not been changed since the Act of 1804. Under it, land could be bought at $2 per acre, the minimum quantity being 160 acres. The law was designed to facilitate purchase by actual farmers from the government land offices; and in the West and South after 1815 there was the proverbial "land-office business." The system also provided for auctions. Large purchases were made at these on a speculative basis; at the height of the boom as much as $78 per acre was bid in the Southwest. The government was a tolerant creditor, and in the year 1819 the arrears in payments on lands amounted to $22 million. Also, the government accepted the notes (paper money) of state banks in payment, though these were often not adequately backed by specie.

Western confidence in the future tended towards exaggeration. Farmers and speculators bought too much land from the government on credit and mortgaged it to the hilt to state banks, in return for paper money which had been issued in excessive quantity by those banks on the basis of assets that were difficult to liquidate. The western and southern branches of the Bank of the United States accepted the notes of state banks and loaned them money freely. State banks varied greatly in their soundness, but in general they were at their wildest in the trans-Appalachian country and in the Old Southwest, the one bank in the state of Mississippi being a notable exception. The situation in Kentucky and Alabama was particularly notorious, but throughout the newer country people were heavily in debt, while speculative mania pushed prosperity to dangerous heights of inflation.

The bubble of this western boom was pricked by the Bank of the United States, which had let itself become dangerously extended. It began in the latter months of 1818 to curtail its discounts and call on its branches for specie. Since a disproportionate part of the capital of the Bank had been drawn into the South and West, these regions were heavily involved in the process of curtailment. But the state banks could not readily pay their balances to the branches of the United States Bank and redeem their own notes in specie. They were forced to call in their own loans to farmers and speculators, often being forced to take over land which they could not sell, and soon they began to suspend specie payments. Nonetheless, many of them continued to issue their own notes, which inevitably shrank in value. Thus the finances of the country spun in a vicious circle, and the crisis soon affected all regions. Values declined even more in lands than in agricultural products, and there were foreclosures everywhere. The Bank of the United States came to own a large part of the city of Cincinnati. A common saying throughout the West and South was: "The Bank was saved and the people were ruined."

Political Effects

One of the most important consequences of this Depression was the arousing, in the West and newer parts of the South, of a spirit of hostility to banks in general and to the Bank of the United States in particular. This spirit tended to draw those regions together in common political cause. The Westerners and Southwesterners would not blame their sufferings on their own speculative fever; they blamed the Bank, now called the "Monster," whose heartless directors had transformed the institution into the servant of Eastern business, and they castigated the "Money Power." These sentiments, nourished by the long agony of the Depression, ramified into the whole complex of rebellious and reformist ideas which took shape in the movement called Jacksonian Democracy.

Losing neither their optimism nor their faith in nationalism, Westerners intensified their faith in democracy as the cure for all their woes. If the people could wrest the control of government from the hands of moneyed interests they could yet fulfill their dreams. Western state governments responded quickly to the demand for relief. Some of them defied the Supreme Court's decision in McCulloch vs. Maryland (1819) by taxing the branches of the Bank. Others evaded the constitutional provision forbidding them to issue bills of credit, an evasion which Marshall condemned in Craig vs. Missouri (1830). Westerners also turned to the federal government for relief. The Public Land Act of 1820 ended the credit system, which had resulted in the government's having to take back much of the land previously sold. The new law lowered the price of public land from $2 to $1.25 per acre and reduced the minimum size of a purchase from 160 to 80 acres. For $100 a farmer could now buy a small farm outright.

The West did not lose faith in the administration of President Monroe. He was not held responsible for the financial crisis with which his first term ended. During the next decade, however, there was increased demand for economic action on the part of the federal government. Besides the clamor for internal improvements, there was a strong movement for greater tariff protection, and this also aroused sharp political conflict. It was in connection with these clashes of interest that the new sectionalism showed itself most clearly, bringing to an end the Era of Good Feelings.

The Missouri Compromise

The Panic of 1819 sharpened the antagonism between the West and the East and tended to draw the agricultural West and South together in common hostility to the "Money Power." At just the same time a sudden eruption of the slavery question distracted the whole country and threatened a more serious antagonism between the North and the South. Then the successful solution, by compromise, of the immediate question of the expansion of slavery confirmed the hold of the Monroe administration on the voters of all sections.

Before this time slavery had not been the occasion of serious dispute between the northern and southern regions. The foreign slave trade was in process of being fully outlawed. The constitutional provision relating to slavery that bore most directly on the existing situation was the three-fifths ratio of representation, sometimes called the federal ratio. The representation of any state in the lower house of Congress was based on the number of its free inhabitants, plus three-fifths of its slaves. The free states were now forging ahead in total population and were gaining even faster in the House of Representatives, where they now had a definite majority. On the other hand, the delegation from the South was disproportionate to its free population, and the region actually had representation for its slave property. This situation vexed the Northerners, especially the New Englanders, who had suffered from political frustration since the Louisiana Purchase and who specially resented the rule of the Virginia Dynasty. Meanwhile, the admission of new free states and new slave states had been so timed that the balance between the North and South had been maintained in the United States Senate.

The tacit boundary between the two regions consisted of the Mason and Dixon Line and the Ohio River. But settlement had reached the point where Missouri, the next state to be carved out of the Louisiana Purchase, straddled the line between the free and slave states. After 1815, settlers had poured across the Mississippi and filled a wide belt along that river and also a belt westward on both sides of the Missouri River and of "Big Muddy's" tributaries—the Gasconade and the Osage. St. Louis became an important center of trade, migration, and manufacturing. Several thousand planters took their slaves into the area believing that Congress would do nothing to disturb the institution, which had enjoyed legal protection in the territory of the Louisiana Purchase under its former French and Spanish rulers. At the same time sentiment in the North was beginning to harden against slavery as a contradiction of American liberty.

In 1818, Congress received from the territory of Missouri a petition that statehood be granted. Early in the next year, during the discussion of a bill authorizing the Missourians to proceed with the drawing of a constitution, Representative James Tallmadge, Jr., of New York introduced an amendment prohibiting the further importation of slaves into the prospective state, and providing for the eventual freeing of those afterward born there. This proposal was similar to the moderate schemes of gradual emancipation which had been adopted in various northern states; but the amendment said, in effect, that Missouri could become a state only if it should present to Congress an antislavery constitution. The amendment as a whole was adopted by the House by a close vote, the representatives from the slave states being almost unanimous against it. In the Senate the two clauses were voted on separately and both were defeated, the latter overwhelmingly, sectional lines being drawn rather less sharply. During the next few months there occurred in the press and on the platform the first national popular debate on slavery. Then, at the next session of Congress, the debate was resumed in the capitol.

The Issues

Northerners did not at this time launch an attack on slaveholders, but they did publicly condemn slavery as an institution, raising the moral issue while not yet stressing it. Some of them expressed a frank hostility to Negroes as well as to slaves, and sought to preserve the interminable regions beyond the Mississippi not merely for free men but for white

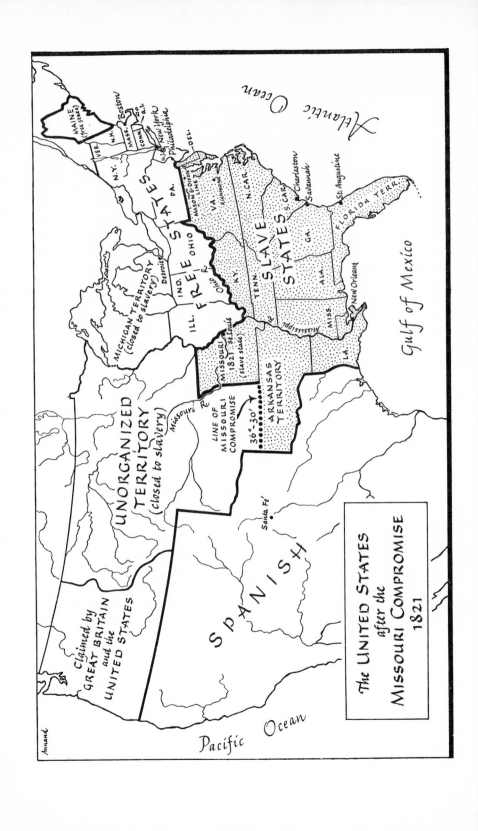

The UNITED STATES after the MISSOURI COMPROMISE 1821

men. In Congress this struggle was recognized as one for political power, as the references to the three-fifths ratio showed. Senator Rufus King of New York estimated that if this did not exist and representation were based solely on free population, the slave states would lose twenty representatives and Virginia would lose seven of her twenty-three. There was no chance to take this provision out of the Constitution, but Northerners did not want to add another state to the Southern interest, which they regarded as too great already. Federalists like King, who had New England antecedents, also saw in the Missouri dispute a particular opportunity to divorce the Southern Republicans from their Northern allies among farmers and city groups, to tie the latter to a wholly northern party, and unseat the Virginia Dynasty. Perhaps the effort to divide the Republicans was too transparent. Northern Republicans may have been lukewarm about slavery, but they were hot against "traitorous" Federalism.

In general, Southerners refused to debate the moral issues involved in slavery. Some of them, especially those from the Upper South, were ready to admit that the institution was an evil, but their major contention was that this question was irrelevant. They took their stand on the ground that Congress lacked power to impose conditions on the admission of a state. At this stage few of them denied that Congress had power over slavery in the territories. This was a question, rather, of the equality of a new state with the old ones.

One practical argument advanced by certain Southerners at this time is summed up by the pompous expression, "mitigation by diffusion"—in modern parlance, the "spread theory." Its advocates were men who clearly recognized that slavery was a problem which must eventually be solved, and who believed that it could be more easily solved if it were less concentrated. Speaking of slavery at this time, Jefferson said, "we have the wolf by the ears, and we can neither hold him, nor safely let him go."

The Southerners were aware of the struggle for political power. Already falling behind in the race for population, they wanted to attach another state to the Southern interest, and the desirability of maintaining a sectional balance in the Senate was henceforth axiomatic with them. The famous compromise with which this controversy was settled was worked out on that principle. Maine was also seeking admission to the Union, and she was coupled with Missouri. No restrictions were imposed on either, but one chose to be a free state while the other legalized slavery. It was agreed that slavery should be forever prohibited in the remainder of the Louisiana Purchase north of the parallel 36° 30'. As a political compromise this was from the Southern point of view a bad bargain, for the rest of the Louisiana Purchase above the line of 36° 30' was considerably larger than the territory below it.

The Missouri Compromise of 1820, which gained in the free states a sanctity comparable to that attaching to the Constitution, took the slavery question out of national politics until the struggle in Congress over the Gag Rule in the late 1830's and the rise of the Texas question. But, despite the confirmation of the Northern contention that Congress could prohibit slavery in the territories, that question was destined to arise again, and the moral question about slavery, once raised, would not down.

Jefferson was enjoying his peaceful retirement at Monticello when the "momentous question" that was raised in the Missouri debates, "like a fire bell in the night," awakened him and filled him with terror. "I considered it at once as the knell of the Union," he said. "It is hushed, indeed, for the moment. But this is a reprieve only, not a final sentence. *A geographical line, coinciding with a marked principle, moral and political, once conceived and held up to the angry passions of men, will never be obliterated; and every new irritation will mark it deeper and deeper.*" John Quincy Adams, who came from the other side of the line, was equally clairvoyant. "I take it for granted," he said, "that the present question is a mere preamble—a title-page to a great, tragic volume."

CHAPTER 10

John Marshall
and John Quincy Adams

AT JUST THE TIME THAT THE UNITED STATES WAS completing political independence by winning a series of brilliant diplomatic victories, the Supreme Court was setting up the constitutional framework of the future nation by means of a series of far-reaching decisions. Chief Justice Marshall remained in office for two decades after the War of 1812, but his most important services ended in 1824. Never again after the decision in the case of Marbury *vs.* Madison (1803) did he declare an act of Congress unconstitutional, but year by year he asserted federal authority against state legislatures and state courts, while also affirming the sanctity of contracts and the rights of private property. Doctrines of state rights were soon invoked against him, however, showing that a battle still lay ahead. Marshall was charged with indifference to the economic welfare of poor men, and he was unsympathetic with the trend of his times toward political democracy. Though a friend of individual liberty, he was a conservative man in the tradition of the Federalists.

From the chaos of personal factions into which the one-party system dissolved, Andrew Jackson was emerging as the central public figure of the era. But victory went to John Quincy Adams in the presidential election of 1824, consigning the stiff New Englander to an unhappy battle of four years with the large faction that swore allegiance to the General. The political history of Adams's presidential term is a tangled tale of individual leaders and their followings and their intrigues. The tariff emerged as the most controversial issue, and it was this, rather than slavery or the reaction against the judicial nationalism of Marshall, which gave sharpest point to state-rights doctrines at that time. Meanwhile, most Americans exulted in the rising political democracy which history has connected with the name of Jackson. In the long run this was to prove the most powerful unifying force within the country.

THE NATIONALISM OF THE SUPREME COURT, 1816-1824

Marshall dominated the Supreme Court during his entire thirty-four years as Chief Justice (1801-1835). Very rarely did his opinions fail to sway the majority of the Justices, and he personally wrote almost half of the more than 1100 decisions. Appointed by a Federalist, John Adams, Marshall saw the entire remaining personnel of the Court transformed by the appointments of five successive Presidents, nearly all of whom were politically unsympathetic toward him. Newcomers, like Joseph Story who was appointed by Madison as a Republican, fell under the influence of Marshall's brilliant logic, luminous analysis, and compelling nationalism. The bar of the Court, which included such men as William Pinkney, William Wirt, Daniel Webster, Joseph Nicholson, Luther Martin, and Jeremiah Mason, attained eminence in this period. Marshall drew upon the arguments of these noted lawyers when he liked them and was stimulated by them when he did not. His decisions are singularly free of the citations culled from dusty legal tomes which make most juristic prose unreadable to the layman. As the legend runs, he used to say to his colleague: "That, Story, is the law; now you find the precedents." He was less erudite than his contemporaries, John and John Quincy Adams, Jefferson and Madison, but his mind had been nourished in the eighteenth-century school of common-sense logic and he liked general principles. His written opinions were full of both and that made them lucid and convincing.

Proclaiming National Sovereignty

Probably the most famous of his decisions in this the most fruitful period of his service was rendered in the case of McCulloch *vs.* Maryland (1819). In it he set forth more fully than elsewhere his philosophy of national sovereignty, while saving the Second Bank of the United States from destruction at the hands of a state legislature. This was not an isolated incident, for the action of Maryland was paralleled by that of other states during this period, chiefly in the South and West. The facts were that the Maryland legislature had imposed a tax on the notes of all banks operating within the state and not chartered by it—which meant the Baltimore branch of the Bank of the United States—and that Treasurer McCulloch of that Branch refused to pay this tax. After the state government had hauled him into its own courts and won its case, McCulloch appealed to the federal Supreme Court.

Marshall saw in the situation, in the first place, a crucial question regarding the source of federal power and authority. Counsel for Maryland claimed that the powers of the general government were delegated by the sovereign states, and "must be exercised in subordination to the states, who alone possess supreme dominion." This was in the tradition of the Kentucky and Virginia Resolutions of 1798, and by this time it was the doctrine of Old Republicans. The Chief Justice, while recognizing that the people had necessarily acted by means of state conventions, declared that, nonetheless, the Constitution and federal government proceeded directly from the people, not from the state governments. This contention about the origins of the Constitution was to be challenged many times before the Civil War, but Marshall also voiced an ideal which was to be progressively realized and eventually accepted by everybody. He said: "The government of the Union, then, . . . is emphatically and truly a government of the people. In form and substance it emanates from them, its powers are granted by them, and are to be exercised directly on them, and for their benefit."

A second and more pertinent question was whether the power to charter a national bank had been delegated to the federal government. In answering this, Marshall went straight back to the opinion of Hamilton (1791) on the constitutionality of the First Bank of the United States which he himself had summed up, along with the opposing opinion of Jefferson, in his *Life of George Washington*. Hamilton had not glorified "the people," for he distrusted them, but his argument was superb and the Chief Justice repeated it. Jefferson, as one of George Washington's advisers, had defined the "necessary and proper" clause of the Constitution narrowly, but Marshall accepted the interpretation of Hamilton and used almost the same words: "Let the end be legitimate, let it be within the scope of the Constitution, and all means which are appropriate, which are plainly adapted to that end, which are not prohibited, but consist with the letter and the spirit of the Constitution, are constitutional." Thus "liberal construction" became official American doctrine, in so far as the Supreme Court could make it so. The doctrine is liable to abuse, but an effective federal government could hardly be attained without it.

The constitutionality of the Bank having thus been affirmed, the question remained whether the State of Maryland had the right to tax it. The answer to this was decisively in the negative. Marshall said that "the power to tax involves the power to destroy." The states, he declared, "have no power by taxation or otherwise, to retard, impede, burden, or in any manner control, the operations of the constitutional laws enacted by Congress to carry into execution the powers vested in the general government." Marshall did not distinguish between state taxes designed to destroy federal functions, which was the obvious intent of the Maryland levy on the Bank, and state taxes designed only for revenue. His dictum went too far, and it has had to be limited in our own time. But no organization or property of the federal government has been subjected to state taxes since Marshall's great decision.

In deciding for the Bank, Marshall had sided with a corporation which many people now called the "Monster," but his famous decision in Gibbons *vs.* Ogden (1824) brought no comfort to would-be monopolists. In this case he ruled against a New York steamboat monopoly and gave a far-reaching interpretation of the commerce clause of the Constitution. The main facts in the case were these. Robert Fulton, builder of the pioneer steamboat, the *Clermont* (1807), had entered into partnership with the politically-powerful Robert R. Livingston to exploit the commercial possibilities of the Hudson, and Livingston had obtained from the state a twenty-year monopoly of steam-navigation rights on that river. From these partners, exclusive right to steam navigation between New York and New Jersey was secured by Aaron Ogden, and the latter sought to restrain Thomas Gibbons from engaging in such navigation. Ogden was upheld by Chancellor James Kent of New York, but Gibbons appealed to the Supreme Court, which decided unanimously in his favor.

Speaking for the Court, Marshall defined "commerce" broadly—not as traffic or mere buying and selling but as intercourse. Furthermore, he declared that commerce among the states "cannot stop at the external boundary-line of each state, but may be introduced into the interior"; and he held that the power of Congress to regulate it under the Constitution may be exercised "to the utmost." Commerce that is wholly intrastate is under state control, but whenever interstate or foreign commerce is involved, federal power can pass the borders of any state and penetrate the interior.

Under this sweeping definition, the federal government has extended its control of interstate commerce into all the states and into many spheres which were unforeseen by Marshall—such as the regulation of railroad rates and the wages and hours of labor. His decision encouraged both the expansion of private business into the national market and the regulation of business by the federal government. The first effect was immediately apparent, and steamboat companies hastened to invade waters formerly reserved by states for favored monopolists. In New York the decision was celebrated with fireworks and a great tooting of whistles by "foreign" steamboats as they churned the emancipated waters of the Hudson. But the second effect of the decision did not become apparent for several generations and it was not entirely welcome to businessmen.

The Sanctity of Contracts

Yet the growth of American business enterprises from their small beginnings in Marshall's time to their colossal later stature was enormously facilitated by his work. Besides asserting the supremacy of the federal government over the states in its allotted sphere, Marshall in another great group of decisions asserted the supremacy of the business contract over any government or individual who would violate its sanctity. In Fletcher *vs.* Peck (1810), a case connected with the Yazoo Claims and the state of Georgia, he had denied the right of one state legislature to void a grant of land made by a previous one, even though in this particular instance the immense grant was obtained by fraud and was overwhelmingly condemned by public opinion. Marshall has been sharply criticized for this decision, but it gave assurance that financial agreements made with governments were contracts that could be relied on. This sense of security was an essential component in the advance of American business.

In the notable case of Dartmouth College *vs.* Woodward (1819), the Chief Justice expanded this doctrine under much more appealing circumstances. The legislature of New Hampshire had decided that Dartmouth, which had been chartered as a private institution and was governed by a self-perpetuating private board of trustees, might conveniently be transformed into a public institution governed by the state through trustees appointed by the legislature. The existing board appealed to the federal courts on the ground that the federal Constitution forbade a state to impair the obligation of contracts. Daniel Webster, Dartmouth's most famous alumnus, serving as counsel, winsomely said that his alma mater was a small college but that there were those who loved her well. Marshall agreed that the college charter was a contract which could not be violated by the state. Just as the decision in Fletcher *vs.* Peck encouraged business enterprises operated for private profit, so that in the Dartmouth case encouraged privately-endowed educational and charitable institutions.

Marshall's interpretation of the contract clause of the Constitution caused him to regard as unconstitutional various state laws designed to relieve debtors and meet the problems of insolvency. In the case of Sturgis *vs.* Crowninshield (1819) he ruled that a state law relieving insolvents from past contracts was invalid and his decision served to limit state actions in matters of bankruptcy. But in Ogden *vs.* Saunders (1827), one of those rare cases in which Marshall found himself in the minority, the Court later held that a state insolvency law did not impair the obligation of *future* contracts between its citizens. A more liberal tendency had appeared in the Court, and there was more disposition to leave some leeway to the states in these matters. But in his minority opinion Marshall strongly took the position that the Constitution protected all contracts, past or future, from state legislation which impaired them in any way. When it came to financial contracts, Marshall himself was a strict constructionist, and he has been described at this stage of

his life by his chief biographer as a "supreme conservative." The trend of
the times was against him in his last years.

Protests from Virginia

Ironically enough, the most formidable attack on him was made in his
own state. The grounds of this were partly personal. There was a long-
standing feud between him and Spencer Roane, the presiding judge of
the Supreme Court of Appeals of Virginia, who presumably would have
been appointed Chief Justice of the United States instead of Marshall
if Jefferson and not John Adams had made the appointment.

The case which occasioned the controversy arose from the lands of
Lord Fairfax, the ungranted part of which the state had tried to confiscate at the close of the American Revolution, in the absence of the
Loyalist proprietor; and the Supreme Court's decision long years later
was on the fundamental ground that the action of the state was contrary
to the terms of the peace treaty with Great Britain. The Marshall family
was personally interested in the Fairfax claims, and the Chief Justice
would not sit on the case when it finally came before the Supreme Court
in 1813, but he concurred in every word of Justice Story's opinion. He
was arrayed against a popular interest in Virginia, where the original
confiscation of Tory property was widely approved, while the interest of
his own family was on the other side, and he was held responsible for
the assertion of federal jurisdiction. Justice Story asked the Virginia
Supreme Court of Appeals to execute the decision, which was a tactical
mistake. Roane and his colleagues flatly refused, declaring that the
appellate jurisdiction of the United States Supreme Court was unconstitutional. This was in 1815. The next year, in the case of Martin vs.
Hunter's Lessee, Story upheld his previous position, saying that the case
not the court gave the jurisdiction. The case started in a state court but
it bore on the question of a treaty, which was a federal matter. He was
wise enough to order a federal official to serve the writ this time, and
Roane's court was not called upon to act one way or the other.

The question of jurisdiction was again involved in the case of Cohens
vs. The State of Virginia (1821), involving fines levied by Virginia courts
on the sellers of lottery tickets. The lottery had been organized in the
District of Columbia, which was under federal control. Taking the position that there was no intention of forcing the lottery business into the
state, the Supreme Court ordered that the fines be paid. It had, however,
asserted its jurisdiction, again on the ground that the nature of the case
not the court of its origin was the determining factor.

In Virginia, meanwhile, Roane wrote a series of vehement papers
against Marshall and his judicial works. The legislature passed a resolution denying federal jurisdiction over the state courts, and an amendment

to the Constitution expressing these sentiments was drafted. Also, in the period 1820-1823, John Taylor of Caroline published three notable works in which he expounded agrarian and state-rights doctrines. More than the belligerent Roane he symbolized the Virginia trend away from centralization and against the judicial nationalism of her famous son, John Marshall.

Tall, slender, and reddish-haired like Jefferson, pure-minded and unpretentious, Taylor was the ideal picture of a republican statesman. Rarely in federal office, he was a power in state affairs, but he was most interested in farming and was a pioneer in scientific agriculture. Though a defender of slavery, he was generally a reformer in the field of local political institutions, while Marshall supported the existing order. This prolific, diffuse, and difficult writer was a foe to special privilege of any sort, and his words of warning about the rising aristocracy of "privilege and paper" were strikingly prophetic. An old-fashioned country gentleman, he distrusted bankers while John Marshall was upholding the Bank of the United States and preparing the way for the future triumphs of business. While the Chief Justice was giving national sovereignty a legal framework, Taylor saw the individual state as the only sure bulwark of the individualism which had been the dream and was now the tradition of Americans. Time was to prove that the weapon of state rights which he chose was not sufficient, but he was the guardian of the enduring values which lie at the heart of Jeffersonian republicanism.

Jefferson could not reconcile himself to the trend of Marshall's decisions. "The great object of my fear," he said in his old age, "is the Federal Judiciary. That body, like gravity, ever acting with noiseless foot and unalarming advance, gaining ground step by step, and holding what it gains, is engulfing insidiously the special governments into the jaws of that which feeds them." To him as to John Taylor, and more in his declining years than during his own presidency, the "special governments" or states were a necessary bulwark against the potential tyranny of centralization.

Marshall may have been thinking of him or John Taylor when he said this in one of his famous decisions:

> Powerful and ingenious minds, taking as postulates that the powers expressly granted to the government of the Union are to be contracted by construction, into the narrowest possible compass, and that the original powers of the states are to be retained, . . . may, by a course of well-digested, but refined and metaphysical reasoning, founded on these premises, explain away the constitution of our country and leave it a magnificent structure indeed but totally unfit for use (Gibbons *vs.* Ogden, 1824.).

This was an excellent description of the Chief Justice himself in reverse. His immortal service was to breathe life and vigor into the Constitution. If, in his concern for effective means of government he at times overlooked the great human and popular ends to which the Republic had long ago been dedicated, his countrymen have found a necessary supplement in the thought of Jefferson. Lincoln was true in spirit to both men when he resolved, not merely that the Union should be preserved, but that "the government of the people, by the people, and for the people should not perish from the earth."

THE ELECTION OF 1824

Three members of the Cabinet of Monroe openly aspired to the high office which he had administered so moderately and on the whole so wisely, and as candidates they were joined by Speaker Henry Clay and, last but far from least, General Andrew Jackson. Never had there been such a presidential sweepstakes, and until the very end of the race the outcome was uncertain.

William H. Crawford, the Secretary of the Treasury, who came so near the Republican nomination eight years before, was a native of Virginia who had adopted the state of Georgia. He seemed the natural heir of the Virginia Dynasty and looked like a sure winner in the Congressional caucus of the party. But in 1823 Crawford, who was a giant of a man, suffered a paralytic stroke which probably would have completely wrecked his candidacy if his physical condition had been fully known. Furthermore, and this is an important item in the history of American political institutions, the caucus system was under fire from the other candidates, who could not in this instance expect much from it, and it was now charged with being undemocratic. More than any of the others, Crawford represented the existing political order. Through thick and thin he retained the loyal support of Virginia and Georgia, and he was backed by Martin Van Buren and the Albany Regency in New York. Van Buren, the most astute political organizer of the day, saw the light and made his important alliance with Jackson after the election.

John Quincy Adams, whose superb services as Secretary of State have already been described, was a man of the highest intellectual attainments and, in the best sense of the term, a trained public servant. In this respect, more than Crawford, he was a fitting heir of the Virginia Dynasty, and, notwithstanding the nationalistic trend of his constitutional views, he was not unacceptable to some of the Old Republicans. His sure support, however, was in the Northeast, especially in his own New England. Being his father's son, he was no sort of politician, and he was relatively inactive in the canvass.

His colleague John C. Calhoun, the able and ambitious Secretary of War, was exceedingly active; and the South Carolinian, still regarded as a nationalist, had political support throughout the country. He was at least second choice almost everywhere. Before voting time he concluded that he would have to content himself with the second place, and he gained the vice-presidency by default. He was still relatively young (forty-two) and he hitched his wagon to the rising star of Andrew Jackson, not realizing that eventually the General would unhitch him.

A fourth candidate, who was to gain the reputation of being a perennial one, was Henry Clay, eloquent spokesman for the West and the American System. But this convivial and extremely popular Kentuckian was blocked by Jackson, who in common opinion was the West incarnate.

Jackson, the most commanding personality among these strong men, eventually turned out to be the best politician. At this point, however, the most natural thing to say about him is that he was the first American after George Washington who gained the highest political eminence in consequence of a military reputation. The idea of capitalizing on his fame as an Indian fighter and the victor at New Orleans was not his, but was that of a group of his friends and neighbors who comprised what is known as the "Nashville Junto." Chief among these were Senator John H. Eaton, William B. Lewis, who had served as Jackson's quartermaster in some of his Indian campaigns, and John Overton, a large Tennessee landholder who had formerly been a judge. Jackson was in his mid-fifties by the middle of Monroe's second term and in bad health. According to his wife Rachel, he had not spent under his own roof a fourth of their thirty years of married life. He would have liked to rest at the Hermitage, where he had a hundred slaves and some very fine horses, though he had ceased training them for the racetrack by now. He was conservative in his economic views, and his political mentors executed a *tour de force* when they presented him to the electorate, not only as the "Nation's Hero" but also as the "People's Friend." The former designation was wholly accurate from 1815 onward, but he had only begun to win the latter.

At this stage the "democratic" emphasis in the candidacy which his friends had imposed upon the fiery but weary General lay chiefly in the criticism they directed against the Congressional caucus. As a device for nominating presidential candidates, the caucus had been distinctly successful up to this point, judging from the caliber of the men selected, but it had ceased to be responsive to popular opinion and was largely under the control of vested political interests. Jackson was quite as ready to attack these as he was Indians or British redcoats. It may be doubted if the system of national political conventions represented an improvement in nomination machinery, and actually this did not develop until the next decade. Jackson was first presented to the country as a presidential candidate by the legislature of his own state. Other state legislatures presented him or another candidate in the same way. His crucial pre-election victory came in his endorsement by a state convention in Pennsylvania in

1823. This action occasioned the withdrawal of Calhoun, who had actually been the first candidate to oppose the caucus. Crawford, slightly improved in health, persisted in the race and won a useless nomination at the hands of a rump caucus, from which nearly all of the supporters of his rivals had abstained.

Meanwhile, there were many indications of Jackson's great public popularity. As a political legend he was still in the making, but the difficulty of electioneering against the Hero of New Orleans was quickly perceived. In 1823, his friends caused him to be elected to the United States Senate, and there, besides voting for the Tariff of 1824, he favored internal improvements. He seemed as devoted as Clay to Western interests, and he gained support in the Middle States without losing much in the South, where Calhoun was now working for him. He spoke little in the Senate but made a dignified impression in social circles, in which he was considerably lionized, and he showed none of the violence of temper he had been charged with.

The net result of all the maneuvers was that the electoral vote was split four ways among the candidates, no one of whom had a majority. Jackson led with 99 votes, being followed by Adams with 84, Crawford with 41, and Clay with 37. According to the Twelfth Amendment to the Constitution, the election then devolved upon the House of Representatives, where the three top candidates were voted for, the vote being by states. Clay, who had carried three western states, was the lowest man and dropped out. Despite the undoubted preference of the West for Jackson, Clay did what he could to throw his strength to Adams, who was elected. He explained that Jackson was only a "military chieftain"— in which he was very much mistaken.

Other factors entered into the election, such as the swing of New York to Adams by a margin of one vote in the state delegation, but not unnaturally the defeat of Jackson was blamed on the "Judas of the West," as the General himself called the Kentuckian. When Adams appointed Clay Secretary of State, the cry of "corrupt bargain" would not down; and the austere New Englander could never overcome the handicap of seeming to be an accidental President, whose election had defied the popular will and defeated the people's choice. Meanwhile the "Military Chieftain" was defiantly renominated for President by the legislature of Tennessee, and resigned the seat he had briefly held in the United States Senate.

President Adams vs. the Jacksonians

Since the Monroe administration was the last for almost a century to be chiefly concerned with foreign relations, it would have been appropriate if a President principally interested in domestic affairs had been elected in 1824, as almost happened. Yet John Quincy Adams was by no

means devoid of a domestic program. He was as ambitious for the internal
as for the external welfare of his country, and he applied to the solution
of pressing domestic problems the same high intelligence and sense of
duty that he had to securing a safe, dignified, and enlarged position for
the nation in the world. But, like his famous father, he lacked popularity
and political sagacity. Regarded as a "President by mistake," he had no
party behind him and made no effort to create one. Scorning the use of
patronage to build up political support, he left opponents of his in ap-
pointive office to undermine him.

The Jacksonians spent the four years of Adams's administration making
sure that there would be no mistake in 1828, and the President himself
committed many tactical errors. In recommending a broad program of
internal improvements, he used such strong language of loose construction as to alarm former supporters of Crawford and impel them into the
Jackson camp, where Senator Van Buren was glad to welcome them; and
he neglected to appeal to those local interests which are of necessary con-
'cern to politicians in a representative government. The results were that
the people never understood what he wanted to do and that Congress,
ignoring his recommendations, planned his defeat. More money was
appropriated for roads and harbors in this administration than in any
preceding one, but this redounded little to Adams's political credit and
his full program never had a chance. With the mid-term election of 1826,
the Jacksonians won a majority in both houses of Congress and the President was hamstrung.

The New Democracy

The highly intellectual man in the White House, who recorded his
frustration in the most introspective of American political diaries, was
the victim of the surging political democracy which made Jackson its
beneficiary. Laws abolishing property qualifications for voting and establishing either a tax-paying qualification or manhood suffrage for white
males were adopted by nearly all of the northern states and most of the
southern by the next presidential election. By this continuing process the
United States became the first political democracy in the modern world.
Universal suffrage had been implicit in the earlier Jeffersonian movement,
but in 1800 low property qualifications for voting had not seemed inconsistent with the idea of popular sovereignty for no considerable
propertyless urban class existed. Now in the third decade of the century,
the new factories had created the small beginnings of an industrial working class, and there was great significance in the extension of the vote to
this landless group—a development which occurred in England only in
1867.

Conservatives were convinced that the result of giving the vote to citizens who had no stake in society would be demagogy and dictatorship. They believed that voters who lacked the sober stability of character presumably conferred by the ownership of property would follow the most blatant peddler of panaceas, the most reckless antagonist of wealth. A seeker for evidence that these dire prophecies were well-founded could find it in the crudity of the new generation of politicians who organized voters for Jackson, in the Jacksonian distrust of the able as well as of the rich and the well-born, and in the rough handling of delicate matters of government policy to make them yield votes—which was characteristic of most administrations during the next generation. But the Jacksonian movement also included a demand for universal education which ultimately brought dividends in intelligent use of the suffrage, and during the intervening years it was not so much the uneducated man who was glorified as the self-educated.

Jackson was the chief idol of the new democracy, and Calhoun was now ranged with him. Martin Van Buren in New York, James Buchanan in Pennsylvania, and lesser leaders in other states built up organizations pledged to the "People's Friend." For convenience we shall call these men Democrats, though the name did not become fixed until Jackson's presidency. Only "right-wing" fragments of the Republican Party remained loyal to Adams and Clay. Later they called themselves National Republicans, and in the next decade they became the Whigs. At first the two groupings were almost indistinguishable in their attitudes towards national policies. But, besides calling the Adams administration illegitimate and designating its projects as foul products of the "corrupt bargain," the Jacksonians charged it with trying to revive discredited and antidemocratic Federalism. This was a partisan exaggeration, but if the lines of descent must be drawn, the National Republicans and Whigs were the heirs of the Federalists, and the Democrats of the Jeffersonians.

The Panama Congress

Even in the field of foreign relations, where as Secretary of State he had won such acclaim, President Adams was frustrated by the vituperative partisanship of the Jackson men in Congress. His chief concern now was to counter British influence in Latin America. Canning's purpose there was to make the new republics into economic and political satellites of Great Britain. This is what Canning meant when he wrote in January 1825: "Spanish America is free, and if we do not mismanage our affairs sadly, she is English." Britain had the advantage of trade supremacy in Latin America and the prestige of having supported the revolutions more enthusiastically than the United States had. But Adams believed that his country might by a vigorous policy establish the hegemony of the United States in the Hemisphere.

When Simón de Bolívar, liberator of Spanish America, called the international Congress of Panama in 1826 to consider plans for a league to strengthen the commercial and legal positions of the new republics and to concert measures against Spain, he proposed that the British but not the United States government be asked to send representatives. Mexico and Colombia nevertheless invited the United States and Adams accepted. The prospect of the association of United States delegates with Haitian representatives or others who might not be "pure white" aroused an outcry from Southerners. In order to send delegates at all, the approval of the Congress of the United States and an appropriation were necessary. The Jackson men used the opportunity to lambast the President and Secretary of State with outlandish accusations. It was in the debate on this that John Randolph of Roanoke, who was a political eclectic, spoke of the coalition between "the Puritan and the Blackleg" with the result that he fought an absurd duel with Clay.

The mission was finally approved, but one American delegate died on the way to Panama and the other arrived only after the rather futile Congress had disbanded. The British delegation had carefully strengthened friendly ties with the Spanish-American governments; and, for a long time afterwards, diplomatic representatives of the United States cooled their heels in these courts, while all doors were open to British ministers.

The failure of Adams's plan to participate in the Panama Congress may not have altered the situation materially, but this was his first defeat in the field of foreign relations, and in bringing it about the opposition provided an unsavory example of playing domestic politics with foreign policy. The Jacksonians strengthened their hold on Southerners in this instance. Vice-President Calhoun was strongly opposed to the administration on the issue and he now drew closer to the Jackson partisans. Running with the General, he expected to be re-elected to the vice-presidency in 1828 and to succeed to the first office after the Hero should retire. He did not yet know how indestructible the Hero was.

Georgia and the Indians

Adams was also the political loser, and Jackson inevitably the gainer, from a heated controversy with respect to the Indians which had long been smoldering in Crawford's state of Georgia. Ever since Georgia ceded its western lands to the federal government in 1802, the people there had been restive because of the slow progress of the federal authorities in carrying out their promise to extinguish Indian titles in the state and thus permit land-hungry farmers to take up their lands. In their opinion the redskins were staying much too long. The controversy in Adams's administration related to the Creeks in the west of the state rather than the more civilized Cherokees. During Monroe's administration, by the Treaty of Indian Springs, which was made with a chief named William McIntosh, all the remaining Creek lands were ceded in return for lands west of the Mississippi and a considerable payment of money. This treaty was approved by the Senate, but afterwards McIntosh was shot and his actions were repudiated by other chiefs. Thereupon President Adams ordered that surveys of these lands, which were being speedily undertaken by the eager Georgians, be stopped and he had another treaty negotiated. His conduct was most honorable but this new treaty left some lands within the state to the Creeks, and the threat of Adams to use force to protect the Indians was matched by the defiance of Governor George M. Troup, a red-headed man who had for some time been aggressive in this business, gaining political strength thereby. In the end, further treaties fully extinguished the Creek titles (1826-1827), but the memory of the President's attitude remained vivid in the minds of Georgians and inevitably their thoughts and hopes turned toward the great Indian fighter, Andrew Jackson. He was just as much against the Indians as the Georgians were in the later and more famous case of the Cherokees.

THE TARIFF BECOMES A STORM CENTER

While political lines were being sharply drawn between the Adams administration and the Jacksonian opposition, sectional alignments on economic issues were assuming a more distinct pattern. The West, including Clay's Kentucky if not always Jackson's Tennessee, stood fast in support of a tariff to protect industry and agricultural products (especially wool and hemp), internal improvements at federal expense, and low prices for public lands. On the land question the Old Southwest took much the same position, but otherwise the South as a whole now tended to oppose all these policies.

As an exporting region which faced no domestic competition with its cotton and tobacco, the South needed no protection for its major staples, and it stood to lose when the tariff raised the prices of commodities that it had to buy. The Southerners could not sell all of their cotton in the United States. They had their best market in the British mills, and they saw their best interest in free trade. As for internal improvements, very few of these were being made in the South and hardly any in the South Atlantic states—largely for topographical reasons. It would have been a waste of money to try to build roads and quite impossible to dig canals through the towering mountains which blocked these states from the West. Maryland and the Potomac and western regions of Virginia were in a different case, but along the South Atlantic seaboard men argued not unnaturally that the states benefiting from internal improvements should pay for them.

On only one major economic issue, the Bank of the United States, were the South and West in basic agreement. Since the Panic of 1819 both of them opposed a Bank with credit policies that were unfavorable to farmers and favorable to Eastern business. But the Bank did not become the subject of major controversy until the 1830's. Before then the South had assumed a negative attitude on all the great economic questions of the day, and doctrines of state rights were revivified as a defense mechanism. The protection of slavery, like other Southern interests, could be best entrusted to the states, and this question loomed in the background from the Missouri debates onward.

In the East, the growth of industry was weakening the dominant position of merchants among businessmen, except in such commercial centers as New York City, and it swung votes to protective tariffs. The value of internal improvements in developing the Western market for Eastern manufactures and the Eastern market for Western food was recognized, whether these were financed by the federal government or by states. Because of the needs of the labor market, however, Eastern businessmen wanted to check the westward migration of potential mill hands, whether native-born or immigrant, and even more than Southerners they tended to oppose free-and-easy terms for the sale of public lands. The new lending policy of the national Bank perfectly suited Eastern businessmen. The newly-enfranchised factory workers were disposed to favor a generous public-land policy and they were afterward rallied against the Bank. On the great issue of the tariff, however, they stood with their employers in favoring the protection which, at least during the "infant" period of industrial development, meant jobs and high wages.

Battles of the Twenties

The clash of sectional interests became clearly visible during the tariff battles of the 1820's. Manufacturers regarded as insufficient the protective rates established in 1816, and their dissatisfaction was increased by the Depression that began in 1819. In 1820, a bill to raise the rates failed in the Senate by one vote, but an act was passed in 1824, raising the rates on cotton textiles, raw wool, hemp, iron, and other commodities. The New Englanders in Congress were fairly evenly divided. Daniel Webster opposed the bill. But the Middle States and the West strongly favored it, and they overcame the almost complete opposition of the South. Most Northern interests were satisfied by this Act, with the important exception of woolen textile manufacturers, who found the rates on raw wool increased without compensating advances in the rates on finished products. They failed in their efforts to extend to woolen cloth the "minimum principle" of valuation which had caused the duties on cheap cotton cloth to be virtually prohibitive. Cheap woolen cloth was chiefly imported for the clothing of slaves. To Southerners, this proposal was a danger signal: North and West could unite to defeat their section.

During the next few years, interested groups of manufacturers formed organizations and held conventions; and the protection argument was set forth in articles, books, and addresses. The chief nonpolitical spokesman of these views was Matthew Carey, a prominent publisher of Philadelphia, and the cause was constantly aided and abetted by Hezekiah Niles, publisher of *Niles' Weekly Register* in Washington, with whom Henry Clay was intimate.

The Tariff of 1824 was most bitterly resented in South Carolina. Dr. Thomas Cooper, president of South Carolina College, who has been termed the "schoolmaster of state rights," proclaimed free-trade doctrines in the classroom and in pamphlets at a time when Calhoun was either equivocal or silent on the subject. The local state-rights movement got under way without the Vice-President. In the legislature of 1825 strong resolutions were adopted, condemning the Tariff, the Bank, and internal improvements; and in 1827, Dr. Cooper boldly declared that it was time to "calculate the value of the Union." This fiery man of learning was in advance of local opinion and was roundly condemned by many, but in the course of the same year resolutions of the legislature asserted that internal improvements at federal expense and tariff acts for the protection of domestic manufacturing were unconstitutional. The right of a state to remonstrate against violations of the fundamental "compact" was asserted at the same time, and the idea of nullification by a state had been voiced by Robert J. Turnbull, though it was not emphasized by public men as yet.

Earlier in the same year a woolens bill had been defeated in the Senate by the vote of Vice-President Calhoun, who thus came out openly on the anti-tariff side now that the interests of his state and section so manifestly required it. In the summer a protectionist convention with a hundred delegates from thirteen states met in Harrisburg, Pennsylvania, and this recommended increases in the duties on both raw wool and woolen goods—the latter to be applied on the principle of minimum valuation, which would have the practical result of making them much greater. Such changes would serve only to increase the cost of clothing in regions that produced neither wool nor woolens.

Thus the issue was sharply joined and it put the Jacksonians in a quandary. Maintenance of the alliance between the South and West, which had been symbolized by the understanding between Calhoun and Jackson, seemed essential to victory in the presidential elction of 1828. On the other hand, while New England was conceded to Adams, the Middle States certainly were not. Pennsylvania had played a crucial role in the 1824 campaign; and Senator Martin Van Buren of New York had swung the powerful Albany Regency behind the General. Perhaps the best single explanation of the complicated political maneuvering which was carried on in Jackson's behalf in 1828 is that the bid for the Middle States and the West—especially the former—was the crux of it. It undoubtedly was in the astute mind of Van Buren, who already had the old Crawford states pretty well lined up behind his man. New England could be written off, and Jackson's popularity in the South as a slaveowning planter and Indian fighter could be relied on to keep that section sufficiently in line against the highly unpopular Adams. Jackson was being presented as all things to all men and all sections, but it seemed much more important to cater to New York and Pennsylvania than to South Carolina.

The Tariff of Abominations

According to vitriolic John Randolph of Roanoke, the main purpose of the Tariff Bill of 1828 was to manufacture a President of the United States, and the traditional opinion has been that the inner coterie of Jackson men in Congress artfully loaded it down with provisions which would in the end defeat it. That does not seem to have been the purpose of Silas Wright, a lieutenant of Van Buren's who played a major part in getting it through the House. But the Act was filled with so many contradictions and absurdities that it has been known ever since as the Tariff of Abominations. Duties on raw materials—including wool, hemp, and molasses— were high and some of them incompatible with a rational protectionist philosophy. Thus the duties were raised on coarse wool, which was much used in factories but little produced in the country. Meanwhile, the woolens schedule afforded little protection to the quality of goods produced in New England. By any interpretation the scheme was clever. If this distasteful bill were defeated by New England votes (combined with Southern), blame could be laid on the Adams group; and whether passed or not it would gain credit for the Jackson cause among Northern farmers and Middle-States manufacturers. If the plan was that it should fail, the plotters overreached themselves. The growing appetite of New Englanders for protection caused most of them to swallow the un-palatable measure as a matter of principle. Commercial interests in Massachusetts still objected, as they did in New York City, but Daniel Webster, now a convert to the protective principle, delivered the chief supporting speech in the Senate. Enough New Englanders voted for the bill, in combination with representatives of the Middle States and West, to carry it by a close vote in both houses.

The action inflamed the South Carolinians. One of them, William Drayton, moved in Congress to amend the title of the bill to read: "An act to increase the duties on certain imports, for the purpose of increasing the profits of certain manufacturers." Disunionist talk was still generally deplored, however, and the doctrine of nullification was not brought forward conspicuously until fall. The legislature did not meet until after the election, in which South Carolina and all the other southern states registered their distinct preference for Jackson over Adams. But at this time the Assembly ordered the South Carolina *Exposition and Protest* to be printed. This document was destined to historic fame as the classic statement of the doctrine of nullification—that is, that a state could annul an act of Congress deemed by it to be unconstitutional. The paper was not formally adopted and the authorship of Vice-President Calhoun was not yet make known. Behind the scenes he had taken his stand with his state—against the nation if need be—but upon the surface he was still allied with Jackson, whose views on the tariff and state rights were ambiguous.

CHAPTER 11

Jackson and Democratic Nationalism, 1828-1833

THE ELECTION OF ANDREW JACKSON IN 1828 AS PRESI-
dent has always been associated with the growth of political democracy
in the United States, and rightly so. His accession was marked by the
invasion of the White House by the populace, and of public office by
political spoilsmen. These events represented the triumph of a man, a
party, and the popular will, but for a good many months men must have
wondered if they meant anything more. The "Nation's Hero" did not
enter on his distinctive course of presidential leadership with full vigor
until he had reorganized his Cabinet, about the middle of his first term;
and not until the last year of it did the meaning of Jacksonian democracy
begin to be revealed in its fullness.

In the name of the whole people the indomitable old commander in
the White House defeated the most powerful financial institution of his
day, the Bank of the United States, which he regarded as a special and
privileged interest, inimical to the general good. Also, before this first
term was over, he checked the centrifugal localism which appeared in
South Carolina in the form of nullification, threatening to paralyze the
federal government and imperiling the Union. Democracy was his sword
in one case, his shield and buckler in the other; he could do what he did
because the people as a whole, the regnant people, were with him. His
enemies spoke of the "reign" of "King Andrew," and he was a sort of
People's King, but it seems fairer to describe his regime as one of democratic nationalism.

This was not nationalism such as had been aimed at by Alexander
Hamilton, who despised the plain people: in spirit it was distinctly Jeffersonian. It was not the judicial nationalism of John Marshall, who never
missed a chance to strike down a state; for Jackson was far from accepting
the full doctrine of judicial review and sharply challenged the Chief

Justice in behalf of a state upon occasion. It was not consolidation, for he retained much of state-rights philosophy in which he had grown up and tended to be a strict constructionist of the Constitution. He showed slight concern for political theory in itself, however. He met crises as he perceived them, relying on his own robust common sense. The vibrant national patriotism of his day was assuming the distinctively American form of unity in diversity, whether or not he fully realized it; and in his hands the powers of the presidency were wielded with unexampled vigor in behalf of what he regarded as the public good.

Personal and partisan motives can be discerned by the critic in Jackson's actions, and at times he sounded like a demagogue, but he responded to deep instincts, represented broad interests, and had the courage of his convictions. The tactics of the grim old warrior were often ruthless, but his over-all strategy was superb. His enemies were implacable in their hatred of him, but the vast majority of his countrymen rejoiced that he won his major battles.

Jackson Takes Over

The campaign of 1828 was much the dirtiest since that of 1800, and for this the Adams men were quite as responsible as the Jacksonians. The General, in retirement at the Hermitage, let his partisans battle for him. One of the most gruesome documents ever circulated in an American campaign was used against him. This was the *Coffin Handbill*, referring to six militiamen who had been shot at his command during the fighting in Alabama, and it bore the heading: "Some Account of the Bloody Deeds of General Jackson." Also, old slanders on the reputation of his wife Rachel, relating to the circumstances of her marriage to him, were revived. Jackson, who was prone to personalize his politics, put the blame on Clay and even on the remote Adams. He had already killed one man and threatened others in Rachel's sacred name and he was entirely capable of doing so again, but soon there was no need for him to be her champion. She died in January 1829, taking all the joy out of his political victory.

Very little was said in the campaign about the problems of the day, including the tariff. The position of Jackson was purposely left vague by his partisans, and the main issue that got before the public was that of personalities. In a contest of that sort Jackson had no rival in his time, and he was triumphantly elected over Adams, as no doubt he would have been over anybody else. His popular majority was not overwhelming but his support was so widely distributed that he gained the electoral vote of all the states except for New England, New Jersey, Delaware, and half of Maryland. He even got one electoral vote in Maine. Calhoun was reelected Vice-President.

When Jackson was inaugurated as the seventh President of the United States on March 4, 1829, he was sixty-one years old and a sick man. A consumptive cough often racked his tall, thin body, and splitting headaches made miserable his days and nights. But his iron will so dominated his ailments that vigor, firmness, determination, and remarkable swiftness of decision were all that even his intimate associates saw in him. Those who did not know him, especially the stiffer kind of Eastern conservative, thought of Jackson as a frontier barbarian given to savage rages—brutal, dictatorial, and vulgar. That was essentially the opinion of John Quincy Adams and, at an earlier time, of Thomas Jefferson. Yet those who knew him, even political enemies, gladly denied the legend. Though by no means a learned man, he was a very shrewd one and also a natural gentleman. His courtesy and respect for others were most notably directed towards women; and, for all his determination to down an adversary, he rarely lost his self-control. Often when he seemed to be furious he was simply putting on an act for some purpose of his own.

His friends believed that the chief source of the greatness they saw in him was his ability to grasp a situation correctly and to reach an accurate judgment at the same moment, seemingly by intuition. Action followed judgment, and then an unbreakable determination to make his action succeed. He aroused a strange combination of awe and affection in others in rough proportion to their intimacy. The word "noble" occurs with significant frequency in impressions recorded by persons who only glimpsed him in a parade as well as by those whom he admitted to closest friendship; but he was also loved by these and by millions who never saw him. Somewhere in the make-up of this white-haired veteran there persisted the magical, inexplicable gift of leadership that had made him the choice of frontier fighters for their captain and would make him the guide of the Democracy for years after he left the presidency.

Democracy Triumphant

"Frontier barbarism" was not entirely missing from the ceremonies of Jackson's inauguration. His political opponents were certain that a Jacobin revolution by savages in coonskin caps and buckskin shirts was at hand when hordes of his followers invaded Washington and made a frolic of the installation of the first President from west of the mountains. He himself was a dignified and impressive figure at his inauguration in the Senate chamber, and afterwards on the balcony, where he delivered a brief speech which satisfied the vast crowd even though they did not hear it. He had walked bareheaded to the Capitol and returned gallantly on horseback. Then the real fun began.

The picture was elaborated in great detail by grim opposition editors: the mob rushing the White House for the hero's reception; the muddy moccasins on the damask-covered chairs to give their wearers a glimpse of him; and Jackson, too courteous by far, ordering that tubs of punch be hauled out to the lawn to accommodate the overflow of thirsty guests. From this hilarious people's party the exhausted old man was glad to slip away.

The frontiersmen had not made the trip merely to get drunk on the taxpayers' punch; they were there to make sure that Democracy triumphant should yield plenty of government jobs for deserving Democrats. William L. Marcy, a leader of the New York Democracy, defending Van Buren a little later, coined the slogan of political warfare: "To the victors belong the spoils!" Jackson's victory in his first political war did result in a division of the spoils of office unparalleled since the founding of the government.

Previous Presidents had not appointed political opponents to high office, but in the lower reaches of the federal service it had been generally understood that ability and experience safeguarded tenure without regard for the way a jobholder acted at the polls. This system had the virtue of providing continuity on levels of routine administration. But from the Jacksonian point of view it was vicious because it created a caste of bureaucrats pretending to knowledge of hidden matters, panoplied by power and inaccessible to the people's will. In short, the system embodied aristocratic, Federalist principles, and it must go. Running the people's government, the Jacksonians argued, required no more than the common sense with which the common people, especially those who had voted for Jackson, were so richly endowed. Throw the aristocratic rascals out and put in plain men to do plain jobs, and government responsive to the plain people would follow. So it was done, and later administrations found the spoils system so convenient an instrument for rewarding political service and winning elections that it was applied in time to the lowliest janitors of government buildings and scrubwomen until, in the 1880's, the small beginnings of civil service reform began to correct its phenomenal abuses.

During most of Jackson's first year in office—until Congress met in December—he seemed to be occupied chiefly by matters of appointment and with a tempest in the social teapot which was occasioned by the wife of one member of his original Cabinet. The President's first official family was so unimpressive that one observer dubbed the new regime the "millenium of minnows." Secretary of State Van Buren, the "Little Magician," was no political minnow. A fastidiously dressed New Yorker, he brought sartorial splendor to a homespun administration, but he had no such intellectuality or personal distinction as Vice-President Calhoun, his rival for Jackson's favor. Most of the appointees to the first Cabinet appeared to be from the Calhoun camp.

The Secretary of War, John H. Eaton, was a Jackson man pure and simple. A few weeks before the inauguration, this old friend of the General had married with his encouragement Peggy O'Neale Timberlake, daughter of a Washington tavern keeper and widow of a Navy purser not long since deceased at sea. Eaton's relations with the lovely Peggy, at whose father's tavern he long stayed, had occasioned much talk and this did not die down with his marriage. His appointment seemed questionable to many people but not to the loyal Jackson. An extremely chivalrous man toward women, he drew an unwarranted parallel between the scandalmongers who were attacking Peggy and those who had slurred the name of his own beloved Rachel. But the Cabinet ladies and Mrs. Calhoun disdained Mrs. Eaton, as did Emily Donelson, niece of the President's dead wife who was living at the White House as its only mistress until Jackson sent her home for discipline. Jackson's determination that the tavern-keeper's daughter, now the wife of his old friend, should be accepted socially arose from the deepest emotional springs, but not even he could command the stubborn women.

The blame for the outcry against Mrs. Eaton was originally laid by Jackson on Clay and his crew. That it fell ultimately on Vice-President Calhoun, who had the misfortune to be a conspicuous figure, was largely owing to the skill with which the Secretary of State exploited the delicate situation. Van Buren, a widower without daughters, found it convenient to please his chief by befriending Mrs. Eaton. Furthermore, he convinced Jackson that the "Eaton malaria" was actually bred not on the feminine social heights of Washington but in political swamps of the South. Calhoun, so "Little Van" suggested, was determined to rule the administration or ruin it and had organized the phalanx of women to hide behind until their work would permit him to consolidate his victory. If Van Buren could destroy the alliance between Jackson and Calhoun, he had good reason to think that he would become the heir apparent.

Besides this social war and the war of intrigue for the succession there were other conflicts in Washington during the presidential novitiate of Andrew Jackson. The most important of these took the form of a constitutional debate on the relations between an individual state and the federal government. Into this Calhoun had already entered; Hayne and Webster took it up; and behind it lay conflicts of interest and struggles for power among the sections.

DEBATING THE NATURE OF THE UNION

The South Carolina *Exposition* of 1828 had appeared too late to affect the election and Calhoun's authorship was not avowed until the summer of 1831, but the widely circulated work was generally recognized as his. In this important treatise Calhoun set forth doctrines of state rights which were more extreme than those which Jefferson and Madison had expressed in the Kentucky and Virginia Resolutions. They had termed the Alien and Sedition Acts unconstitutional, as violations of the First Amendment, while Calhoun asserted the unconstitutionality of tariffs that were deliberately designed to promote particular industries rather than to produce revenue. While many people in later years denied the wisdom and the fairness of the protective system, few in our day would support Calhoun's position on constitutional grounds. A much larger number would support that of Jefferson and Madison with respect to the Sedition Act. Furthermore, Calhoun's purposes seemed more particularistic. He sought to guard the special interests of a geographical region, whereas they were trying to guard local interests everywhere and the freedom of all Americans, North and South.

There were also important differences between him and his supposed prototypes with respect to the remedies proposed in case of unwarranted federal actions. The earlier leaders were most concerned with the right of protest. The right of states to judge for themselves the mode of redress was claimed in Jefferson's Kentucky Resolutions of 1798, and the word "nullification" was used in the Resolutions of that state in the next year. But, as Madison pointed out in the 1830's, Jefferson regarded the right to revolt against intolerable oppression as a natural not a constitutional right; it had been invoked in the Declaration of Independence before there was a Constitution. Furthermore, these earlier protestors against supposed infringements of human and state rights had worked out no mechanism of defense and Madison definitely disapproved of Calhoun's.

The Doctrine of Nullification

Rejecting the doctrine of Marshall that the Union originated with the people and was their agent, Calhoun declared that it originated with the states, which retained sovereignty even though they had delegated specific powers to the federal government; and that a single state, acting through a convention specially chosen for the purpose, could annul an act of the federal government which it deemed unconstitutional. Recognizing, however, that the other sovereign states had some check on the actions of one of them, he conceded that nullifications of a federal act could be overruled by the vote of three-fourths of the states. That is, he would have reversed the process of amending the Constitution and thrown the burden of proof on the federal government. Finally, he declared that nullification was not secession, that is, a dissolution of partnership, but an instrument to prevent secession. In his hands it was that, but the doctrine of secession afterward flourished in the country of the nullifiers.

Calhoun's safeguards never got beyond the realm of theory and the dominant leaders in South Carolina were less reasonable than he. Since he did not originate the doctrine of nullification, it would be a fair description of his role to say that he elaborated and refined it and sought to guard it against abuse. Furthermore, his record shows that he did not want to use it and that in fact he was a moderating influence in the local scene. What he had sought to do with his powerful mind was to create a mechanism for the protection of a minority interest. But, as Madison pointed out, the process which Calhoun recommended could and probably would result in the ascendancy of a minority over a large majority. This was certainly not in the spirit of Jefferson, who declared that acquiescence in the will of the majority was the most vital principle of republican government. In his own thinking Calhoun had taken a lonely path; and it was a fair question then and often afterwards whether he did the cause of his beloved state more harm than good by defining her "rights" so sharply. This emphasis on action by a single state worked to the disadvantage of anyone who was trying to gain the co-operation of others on the larger stage.

Debating in the Senate

Of all the major questions of the day the one of greatest concern to South Carolina, and on which opinion was most inflamed, was that of the tariff. The issue of public lands in the West was less important, hence it seemed that a political alliance between South and West might be cemented if Southerners should support a more liberal western land policy in return for Western support of Southern tariff policy. Senator Thomas H. Benton of Missouri advocated a plan calling for a gradual reduction in the price of unsold lands that would lead finally to the free gift of those for which there were no bidders. This was known as the policy of "Graduation and Donation." On the other hand, the favored Eastern scheme for maintaining a policy of tariff protection with Western support, without endangering the labor market by lowering the price of western lands, was to distribute among the states the federal money from their sale. This policy was known as "Distribution," and it was advocated by Henry Clay, a Westerner who was always conscious of the opinions of Eastern businessmen. But Westerners like Benton were chiefly interested in lowering land prices and in December 1829 they joined with Southerners to defeat a Distribution bill.

It was at this juncture that Senator Samuel A. Foot of Connecticut stepped into the delicate web of sectional diplomacy. He offered a resolution that called for stopping surveys and limiting sales of western lands. In January 1830, this provoked a hot debate. Benton bitterly attacked Foot's resolution and the Northeastern manufacturers, charging the latter with intent to oppress and hold back the West in order to keep labor cheap, and criticizing the tariff policy which he himself had recently supported. Robert Y. Hayne, an eloquent and popular Senator from South Carolina, leaped to accept Benton's virtual invitation to a fresh alliance. He accused the Northeasterners of trying to rob the West of settlers just as they had robbed the South of its wealth through tariffs. Unity of the South and West, he declared, was necessary against their common enemy.

This was the occasion of the famous Hayne-Webster debate. Webster, who had been indifferent to his Senatorial duties of late, rushed into the breach and saved his section from the consequences of Foot's ineptitude by adroitly changing the subject. While defending New England he baited Hayne by attacking the state-rights philosophy of South Carolina, which Hayne thereupon defended, and Webster then answered him by powerful logic garbed in sonorous prose. Thus the debate was shifted to the highest level of constitutional theory. In reality Webster was speaking for New England as truly as Hayne was for South Carolina. His region had been a seat of state rights during and previous to the War of 1812, while its interests now called for a federal government that was armed with power. But his Second Reply to Hayne deserved to become a classic since events proved, and were already proving, that he spoke for the future nation. He voiced John Marshall's nationalistic philosophy with an eloquence which the Chief Justice could not muster, and his closing words were to be echoed in the speeches of thousands of schoolboys through the generations: "Liberty *and* Union, now and forever, one and inseparable." Webster was expressing an ideal, not describing an accomplishment, but ideals mold men and societies and this one has endured.

Webster had transformed the issue, so that it was no longer one between sections but between Unionism and Nullification. Foot's resolution was lost, but so was a bill offered a little later by Benton calling for Graduation and Donation. The alliance between South and West was too incomplete to offset powerful Eastern opposition. About the same time, in May 1830, Jackson vetoed a bill providing for federal participation in the building of the Maysville Road in Kentucky by a private company, on the ground that the road lay wholly within a state and that the federal government could not afford a part in it. This was the first of the vetoes of a President who used more of them than all of his predecessors together. It slanted in the direction of state rights and strict construction, marked a check in the policy of internal improvements at federal expense, and anticipated opposition to federal aid to private enterprise. But there was still the question of the tariff.

Jackson Breaks with Calhoun

In terms of sectional politics Jackson had made a concession to the South, though for some time now his mentor had been Van Buren, not

Calhoun. His constitutional views were predominantly pragmatic but there could be no possible question of his whole-hearted devotion to the Union, and his suspicions of Calhoun had been fanned by the sedulous Van Buren. By December 1829, he was fully convinced that the Vice-President was chiefly responsible for the petticoat warfare against Mrs. Eaton, and by that time the infirm old man was looking toward the useful Secretary of State as his eventual successor in the presidency. But the incident which has been most often pointed to as a public sign of a breach with the Vice-President occurred on April 13, 1830, at a dinner in celebration of the birthday of Jefferson.

The dinner was designed to associate Jeffersonian orthodoxy, as understood by the Calhoun group, with the party in power—which through the passing years was to go by the name of Democratic. The celebration was expected to have a state-rights flavor, and in general it did, but attention was afterwards directed chiefly to the "volunteer" toasts of the President and Vice-President after the innumerable prepared ones. That of Jackson has become, perhaps, his best-known saying: "Our Federal Union —It must be preserved." The words of Calhoun have become almost as famous: "The Union—next to our liberty most dear. May we always remember that it can only be preserved by distributing equally the benefits and burdens of the Union." Van Buren, who followed, drank to "mutual forbearance and reciprocal concession," thus sounding a note of conciliation.

The circumstances of this occasion were afterwards embroidered by partisan journalists and exaggerated by some of the participants themselves, but the reasons for this soon appeared upon the record. In May, Jackson sent Calhoun a letter from William H. Crawford, who had been in Monroe's Cabinet at the time of Jackson's expedition into Florida, alleging that Calhoun as Secretary of War had urged in 1818 a reprimand or punishment of the General for his conduct. Except for Adams, the Cabinet members as a group had thought Jackson's action high-handed, and Calhoun rightly suspected Crawford of a political trick. Indeed, Jackson himself had long known about Calhoun's earlier position, and the demand for an explanation at this time must have been made because the President had now decided that he did not need him. Calhoun's elaborate explanation, which would have been better left unmade, could not possibly be satisfactory, and Jackson now described him without hesitation as a traitor.

The *coup de grâce* to the Calhoun-Jackson alliance was delivered the following spring, after Van Buren had offered the President means to cure the social warfare within his Cabinet, get rid of the last trace of Calhoun influence, and reorient his administration. The Secretary of State and Eaton resigned simultaneously, in order that Jackson might call for the resignation of the remaining Cabinet members—all identified more or less with Calhoun. When Lewis Cass of Michigan succeeded Eaton as

Secretary of War, Jackson's friend and Peggy escaped from the social vendetta and the President heaved a sigh of relief. Of the new appointees, those who rendered him most signal service in later crises were Edward Livingston of Louisiana, formerly of New York, and the cadaverous-looking Roger B. Taney of Maryland, who took over the office of Attorney General. But from day to day the President relied on the counsel and help of a small informal group, known as the "Kitchen Cabinet" and much ridiculed by his political foes. The most important members of this were two unpretentious men recently come from the West: Amos Kendall, a former newspaper man who then had a minor post in the Treasury, and Francis Preston Blair, editor of the Jackson paper, the *Washington Globe*. Meanwhile, Van Buren was rewarded with the post of minister to Great Britain—on a recess appointment, since the Senate would not confirm him. It was understood that in due course he would succeed to the presidency.

The internecine war was liquidated and the administration reorganized at the cost of an irreparable breach with Calhoun and the sure loss of the political support of South Carolina. But circumstances served to isolate that state, as they had to isolate Calhoun in Washington; and Jackson actually lost little support in the South. Among the reasons for his continued appeal there were his policies with respect to the Indians and internal improvements and his attitude on the revived issue of the Bank. The latter appealed even more strongly to the plain people of the North, and their votes more than made up for losses elsewhere.

First Phase of the Bank War

The Second Bank of the United States was a private institution, though a fifth of its capital was owned by the government. By right of its charter it had certain great privileges, and in return for these it performed important public services. Besides having the deposits of the United States, generally made in the notes (paper money) of other banks which were presentable to them for payment, it had the power of issuing its own notes. Thus it could bring pressure on other banks to restrict their notes and credit policies and could regulate the currency. A major objection to it in the West and South was that it restricted credit and controlled the currency too well; state banks were much more responsive to the inflationary tendencies of new regions and the credit needs of farmers. The objections of Jackson to it, however, were chiefly based on other grounds. He was old-fashioned in his financial ideas, being suspicious of all banks and in favor of coin not paper as the basis of the circulating medium. He feared the Bank for its power. The government elected five of the twenty-five directors but did not control the institution, and in his opinion there was real danger it would control the government.

Under Nicholas Biddle, a cultivated Philadelphian who had been president since 1822, the Bank had followed a conservative policy which did not commend it to Western and Southern farmers but had gained the approval of Eastern businessmen, while Biddle had been careful to satisfy the needs and meet the convenience of the federal Treasury. Also, he performed favors for leading politicians, newspapermen, and other influential persons; and at the outset he was conciliatory towards Jackson.

In his first message to Congress, the President, probably at the instigation of Van Buren, had questioned both the expediency and the constitutionality of the Bank. Its affairs were afterwards inquired into by committees of the two houses of Congress, both of which made favorable reports. Opposition to the institution came chiefly from men who spoke for state banks and a more liberal currency and credit policy. Senator Thomas Hart Benton of Missouri, a hard-money man who had won the name "Old Bullion," was a vigorous exception. Jackson seemed more kindly toward the Bank as his first term wore on, and his battle with it was precipitated by an unnecessary challenge to him by its friends, the motives of which were predominantly political.

Not until 1836 was the charter to expire. But Henry Clay, who was now in the Senate and looking for an issue in the approaching presidential campaign, obtained Biddle's consent to the presentation of a rechartering bill early in 1832. Congress passed the bill early in the summer as Clay had been sure it would, and Jackson, who was no man to decline a challenge, was presented with one. The General, sick in bed, told his political lieutenant who was just back from England: "The bank, Mr. Van Buren, is trying to kill me, *but I will kill it!*" He returned the bill to Congress with a powerful veto message which Amos Kendall, Attorney General Taney, and others helped prepare. In this he skillfully avoided the issue between the soft-money and hard-money critics of the Bank and directly appealed to the plain people of the country to help him put an end to governmental favors to the rich.

Jackson's Veto Message

This appeal was not in conflict with the philosophy of free economic enterprise with which Americans had been so long imbued, for he recognized the right of men of superior ability and industry to the full enjoyment of the property they had gained thereby.

> But [he said] when the laws undertake to add to these natural and just advantages artificial distinctions, . . . to make the rich richer and the potent more powerful, the humble members of society, the farmers, mechanics, and laborers, who have neither the time nor the means of securing like favors to themselves, have a right to complain of the injustice of their government.

According to Jackson, the Bank was a monopoly enjoying governmental favors which amounted to gifts of many millions of dollars to the private stockholders. The government was making a bad bargain, in his opinion, and the cost must come at last from the earnings of the American people. He reminded Congress of Biddle's remark, which was truthful though indiscreet, that most of the state banks existed by the forbearance of the Bank of the United States; and, bringing all his batteries into play, he denied to that institution the constitutionality which the Supreme Court had affirmed. Repudiating Marshall and Hamilton, he reverted to the position of Jefferson, denying judicial review in so far as it related to the executive and legislative departments and identifying himself with the school of strict construction. Many features of the recharter bill, he said, were not "necessary and proper" in the ordinary meaning of those words. This part of one of the most famous of all veto messages amounted to a judicial opinion handed down by the Executive.

The historic message ended with the most radical appeal to the class feeling of the poor against the rich which had yet appeared in an American public paper:

> There are no necessary evils in government. Its evils exist only in its abuses. If it would confine itself to equal protection, and, as Heaven does its rains, shower its favors alike on the high and the low, the rich and the poor, it would be an unqualified blessing. In the act before me there seems to be a wide and unnecessary departure from these just principles. . . .
>
> Many of our rich men have not been content with equal protection and equal benefits, but have besought us to make them richer by act of Congress. By attempting to gratify their desires we have in the results of our legislation arrayed section against section, interest against interest, and man against man, in a fearful commotion which threatens to shake the foundations of our Union. It is time to pause in our career to review our principles. . . .

Jackson's assertion of the competence of the Executive to judge questions of constitutionality within its own sphere did not become a significant precedent, but as a campaign manifesto the message was a sweeping success. Congress did not override the veto, the Bank became the chief specific issue in the election of 1832, and the newly-enfranchised groups of the North, led by a sprouting crop of reformers and organizers, moved towards Jackson.

Inevitably he aroused the fierce resentment of interested parties and frightened many of the conservative and well-to-do. Nicholas Biddle saw in the veto message all "the fury of a chained panther, biting the bars of his cage." To his friend Henry Clay he said: "It is really a manifesto of anarchy, such as Marat or Robespierre might have issued to the mob of the Faubourg St. Antoine." In the Senate, Webster said:

"It manifestly seeks to influence the poor against the rich. It wantonly attacks whole classes of the people for the purpose of turning against them the prejudices and resentment of other classes."

Beyond a doubt Jackson was seeking to arouse the many against the special beneficiaries of a particular institution. In actual number the latter were very few, but in the Northeast he revived and accentuated an older alignment. The cleavage between the party of Jefferson and the more prosperous economic groups in that region had seemed almost closed during the Monroe administration, but Jackson widened it into a chasm which was destined to endure long. By the same token, he strengthened his hold and that of the Democratic Party after him on the "farmers, mechanics, and laborers," to whom he specifically referred, and if they were mobilized they could easily outvote the groups he had offended.

THE NULLIFICATION CRISIS

The first phase of the Bank war ended when Jackson vetoed the recharter bill in the summer of 1832, and the sovereign people did not speak decisively until fall. Meanwhile, federal authority was being challenged not only in South Carolina, but also in the neighboring state of Georgia, where there was less emphasis on constitutional philosophy.

Jackson did not accept the latter challenge, which grew out of the efforts of the Georgians to extend their political authority over the Cherokee Indians and acquire their lands. With these purposes the old fighter was thoroughly sympathetic. In March 1832, Chief Justice Marshall, in the case of Worcester vs. Georgia, denied the right of the state to impose its will upon the Cherokees still within its borders, since these people were protected by treaties made with them by the United States. The President tacitly supported the state in its self-assertion and defiance. As the story runs, he said: "John Marshall has made his decision; now let him enforce it." His nationalism was pragmatic and lacked theoretical consistency. He was not disposed to press it against what he deemed to be the will of the people. He is often blamed for his indifference to the nullifying policies of Georgia, but he has generally been praised by historians for his stand against the brand of nullification which emanated from South Carolina. The latter, in his opinion, presented a much greater threat against the Union.

The national event which occasioned nullification in Calhoun's state was the passage of the Tariff of 1832. This was a more rational measure than the Tariff of Abominations and, for that reason, it was more acceptable to the groups and districts that were seeking protection. In general, high duties were imposed on goods produced in America and lower duties were now placed on noncompetitive foreign products. But the bill represented no real improvement from the Southern point of view, and when Jackson signed it in July the South Carolinians claimed that he had betrayed them. For several years they had been divided into the State Rights and Union Parties, but nobody defended the tariff and by this time the former party, which proclaimed nullificaton doctrines, was in full control, having a clear two-thirds majority in the legislature. The leaders were now poised for action, but they awaited the outcome of the presidential election.

Vice-President Calhoun sought to restrain them from precipitate action. In theory he was with them and by this time his constitutional position was generally known. President Jackson had not yet had occasion to make his position public, and the South Carolinians found encouragement in his attitude toward the Georgians, but he had already given informal warning. The nullifiers might pass resolutions to their heart's content, but if they should shed any blood in defiance of United States law, he would not hesitate to do some hanging. In view of his record, his words were in no sense humorous. In the election, South Carolina was the only southern state that did not support him. The electors there threw their votes to Governor John Floyd of Virginia, with no effect whatever on the outcome.

Challenge and Response

After the election the South Carolina legislature called a convention for the special purpose of considering the tariff, and this body adopted on November 24, 1832, the Ordinance of Nullification—a precursor of the more famous Ordinance of Secession. This declared the tariff acts of 1828 and 1832 null and void, forbade the collection of customs within the state, prohibited appeal to the United States Supreme Court in any cases arising under the Ordinance, and required a test oath of the civil and military officers of the state. Finally, it declared that any attempt to coerce the state would absolve it from all further obligations to the Union and be followed by the organization of a separate government. Nullification carried with it a direct threat of secession, which was just what Calhoun had said it was designed to prevent. Furthermore, the Ordinance contained no reference to any possibility that this action could be overruled by three-fourths of the other states—a provision which Calhoun had included in his South Carolina *Exposition*. His fellows had assumed a more intransigeant attitude than his and they were more impatient. They set February 1, 1833, as the effective date, which was earlier than he liked.

If the reckless South Carolinians counted on the support of the other southern states they were doomed to disappointment. In Virginia there was general disapproval of the tariff but practically no approval of this method of combating it. The legislature of the Old Dominion formally declared that the historic Virginia Resolutions of 1798-1799 did not support the South Carolina doctrine, as had been claimed, and James Madison took the same ground. In Alabama, where the federal government was being practically defied on the Indian question at just this time, the doctrine of nullification was described as unconstitutional and revolutionary, and similar disapproval was expressed elsewhere. In constitutional philosophy South Carolina seemed to stand alone. Also, President Jackson, who had been born in that state, took positive and immediate steps to neutralize its actions. Unionists recalled these in 1860 and longed for him in place of irresolute James Buchanan—who faced, however, a more difficult situation. Jackson reinforced Forts Moultrie and Sumter in Charleston harbor, ordered federal officials to collect the customs in South Carolina as elsewhere, and deployed revenue cutters to do this off the coast if the officials on land were resisted. On December 10, 1832, the President issued a Proclamation to the people of South Carolina. With its ringing nationalism this complemented the democracy of his Bank veto message.

The President admitted the right to resist acts of the government which were "plainly unconstitutional and too oppressive to be endured." But South Carolina was claiming a different right, namely, that any one state might remain in the Union and yet be bound by no other laws than those it might "choose to consider as constitutional." Furthermore, Jackson's Proclamation declared, the Constitution expressly requires the judges in every state to be bound by that Constitution, the treaties, and the laws of the United States—"anything in the constitution or laws of any State to the contrary notwithstanding." By denying the possibility of appeal from its own Ordinance to the federal courts, South Carolina was clearly destroying the federal compact.

Under the South Carolina doctrine, said Jackson, the Union could not have survived infancy. Pennsylvania would have defied the whiskey tax, Virginia the carriage tax, the eastern states the Embargo and Nonintercourse Acts. In practice, the doctrine of a state veto would be an absurdity. The President repudiated it completely, describing it emphatically as *incompatible with the existence of the Union, contradicted expressly by the letter of the Constitution, unauthorized by its spirit, inconsistent with every principle on which it was founded, and destructive of the great object for which it was formed.* As for secession, this might be morally justified as a revolutionary act against extreme oppression, he said, but to call it a constitutional right was to confound the meaning of terms and to declare that the United States was not a nation.

Jackson believed that those who argued that nullification might be achieved peaceably had deceived the people. They knew that only force could prevent the execution of the laws and that force would be repelled by force. Their object was disunion, he said, adding that disunion by armed force is *treason*. The fate of free government was in the balance, the world was looking on, and the Chief Magistrate could not and would not avoid the performance of his duty. Yet he would not allow any offensive act by the United States to bring down on man the primeval curse for the shedding of a brother's blood. He would, if possible, by moderate and firm measures prevent the necessity of force.

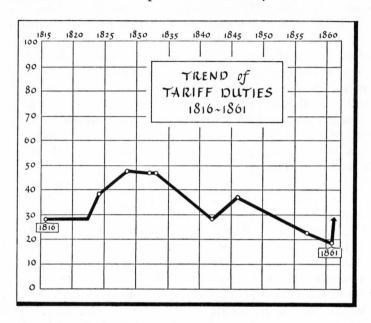

South Carolina's legislature met the challenge by raising armed forces for defense against "invasion." The Virginians did not like the threats against a sovereign state, but they sent commissioners to the rebellious commonwealth to urge moderation. Jackson talked of leading an army into South Carolina and asked Congress for a Force Act, but he also supported the attempt to compromise the tariff conflict, even though Henry Clay got a lion's share of the credit. An administration tariff bill was shelved and a proposal of Clay's was given right of way. This bill provided for a gradual reduction of all duties during the next ten years so that none would be higher than 20 per cent on July 1, 1842. The South Carolinians found that most Southern legislators were willing to support Clay's bill and, being isolated, they postponed the nullification threat and finally abandoned it. In this time of peril Senator Hayne resigned his seat to go home and become Governor, while Calhoun, resigning his position as Vice-President, succeeded to Hayne's place. He supported the compromise.

The federal government and the South Carolina Convention both reasserted their doctrinal positions while accepting the compromise Tariff Act of 1833. On March 2, Jackson signed the Tariff Act and also a Force Act authorizing him to use the Army and the Navy to collect duties if judicial process were obstructed. The South Carolina Convention repealed the Nullification Ordinance and then declared the Force Act null and void. If statesmanship consists in avoiding a fight to the finish on theoretical grounds for the sake of mutual accommodation on substance, then statesmanship had won the day.

Both sides claimed a victory, and certainly there was no acknowledgement of defeat by the nullifiers. They had proved that a single state could by threats of secession extort from the federal government the modification of a law; and, regardless of the merit of their objections to the existing tariff, this success encouraged the idea that a minority could challenge the majority. The spirit of localism continued to flourish in South Carolina, and the belief became even more firmly fixed there that loyalty to the state came before loyalty to the Union. While the nullification doctrine itself was not revived, the doctrine that secession is a constitutional right remained and grew. But most of the leaders in the state had learned that they needed support from outside their own borders, and they did not again take extreme action until convinced that other states would follow.

On the nationalist side, Jackson's Proclamation and his manifest readiness to preserve the Union by force if necessary became an unforgettable part of the historic record. His attitude aroused the enthusiasm of the vast majority of Northerners and Westerners, regardless of party, and of large groups of Southerners. Conservatives supported his nationalism, while approving radicals knew, from the Bank war if from nothing else, that his nationalism was profoundly democratic. Jackson provided average Americans with a nationalism that they liked better than that of Marshall and Webster and could more easily understand. He brought this into focus as the creed they lived by and the cause for which they would fight. South Carolina had won a compromise of the tariff, but Jackson had won the more crucial battle for national opinion.

CHAPTER 12

The Flood and Ebb of the Jacksonian Tide, 1832-1840

THE ELECTION OF 1832 REPRESENTED AN EVEN GREATER triumph for Jackson than that of 1828. It strengthened his hand against the nullifiers, and he naturally interpreted it as a full vindication of his hostility to the Bank of the United States. In the history of American political institutions it is also significant, for in the campaign presidential candidates were nominated by national party conventions for the first time. In contrast to the party caucus, which was viewed as oligarchic, the convention represented an effort to democratize party machinery. In this election and in Jackson's second term, when the opposition took on the name of Whigs, political parties and political alignments assumed a form they long maintained. There was no major regrouping until the 1850's, when sectional issues dwarfed all others.

The main controversies of the term centered on financial questions. Under the soothing operation of the compromise Tariff of 1833, nullification disappeared as an immediate issue, but the Bank war was resumed and it did not yet end, since Whig leaders continued to favor such an institution through several additional administrations. The impossibility of rechartering this particular Bank soon became apparent, however, and the more immediate problems toward the close of Jackson's presidency arose from an excess of inflated prosperity. In his own old-fashioned way the President sought to check the boom, and there is still dispute whether he did more good or harm. Recession was inevitable and Jackson's successor, Van Buren, bore the brunt of it. His unhappy administration ended with his defeat in 1840 at the hands of the Whigs, who were the rabble-rousing party in this instance. The tide of Jacksonian popularity reached its highest point early in the General's second term and it ebbed somewhat before he retired to The Hermitage, but not enough to endanger Van Buren's succession. The low point was reached in the latter's defeat.

THE ELECTION OF 1832: SOCIAL UNREST AND POLITICAL PARTIES

Henry Clay, the presidential nominee of the National Republicans, had seized upon the Bank issue. His partisans printed 30,000 copies of the veto message for campaign purposes, thus revealing their colossal ignorance of the trend of the people's thinking. There was a third party in the race, the Anti-Masonic Party which nominated William Wirt, a former Attorney General of the United States. Fortunately he had no real hankering for the highest office. He got 7 electoral votes to Clay's 49 and Jackson's 217, while South Carolina's 11 went to John Floyd. The figures on the popular vote are unreliable, but the General got most of it. After the election Wirt expressed the opinion that Jackson could be President for life if he wanted to.

"Old Hickory" had lost none of his appeal as the Nation's Hero, and personal loyalty probably attached very many voters to him without much reference to specific policies of his administration. He fulfilled an often-forgotten premise of the American system of government: that the general trustworthiness of a candidate's character and the broad outlines of his political philosophy should determine the voter's choice, after which the successful candidate must exercise his own judgment as the *representative,* not merely the echo, of the electorate. In Jackson's hands the presidency attained unexampled popularity and was notably a representative institution—in the full meaning of the term. He sensed and reflected public opinion far better than his political opponents, and at the same time he aggressively exercised his executive functions and assumed leadership. The plain people rejoiced that they had found a champion and they trusted him.

By now the Jacksonians gladly called themselves Democrats. Hickory Clubs were created by enthusiasts over the country to celebrate their hero's fame and organize the vote. Beneath the manifestations upon the surface deep new currents of social unrest were flowing in national political life. These were chiefly the product of the Industrial Revolution, which seemed to challenge the adequacy of existing political arrangements and call for new ideas. A remarkable feature of Jackson's leadership was his ability to command the loyalty of clamorous new elements in spite of the fact that he did little that was specifically designed to satisfy their demands. His war against the Bank rallied the support of a bewildering variety of dissidents from the status quo. Jackson was the symbol but only to a slight extent the instrument of the rich assortment of new popular movements that are called Jacksonian Democracy. Important social and intellectual movements will be described in another chapter, while we limit ourselves here to those entering more directly into politics.

Workingmen and Politics

The granting of the vote to propertyless males differentiated the position of the American workmen from that of the Europeans of their class during the early stages of the Industrial Revolution. It is not surprising, therefore, that the first political party in the world devoted to the interests of labor appeared in the United States. This was the Workingmen's Party, which was organized in Philadelphia, New York, and other cities shortly before and during Jackson's first term. In these cities and in mill towns the growth of factories had created the first American slums. Cheap immigrant labor, which was now coming in though not yet in torrential volume, permitted employers to stretch out hours and reduce wages. Handicraft unions of skilled artisans were helpless to improve conditions, while under the factory system the ranks of the unskilled were growing.

The platforms of the Workingmen's Party show that the chief object of laborers was to achieve recognition of themselves as human beings. Mechanics' lien laws were demanded to establish the priority of laborers' claims to wages when an employer went bankrupt, the implication being that the rights of labor are human rights and are, therefore, superior to the rights of property. Abolition of imprisonment for debt was demanded on the same principle: it merely meant granting to poor men comparable consideration to that given corporate debtors by means of bankruptcy laws. The Workingmen's Party bitterly opposed the laissez-faire philosophy of employers—that labor was a commodity which must be subject to the law of supply and demand, that any form of governmental intervention in favor of the laboring class would invite economic disaster, and that the only remedy for its ills was harder work and more frugality. Terming this "irrational, antirepublican, and unchristian," the laborers blamed the poverty of the workers on the new techniques of exploitation which machinery placed in the hands of employers.

The workmen could not hope to create a national party because they were too narrowly localized in the Northeast, but by showing strength in state elections they made themselves interesting to leaders of the national parties. These could add the workingmen to their regular following by adopting specific demands of labor. In 1829, the party in New York City polled 30 per cent of the vote in local elections. After that, factions of the party heeded offers of the Democratic leaders to carry out labor reforms in return for support of Democratic candidates in state and national elections. Under this arrangement, New York passed a mechanics' lien law in 1830 and abolished imprisonment for debt. Similar developments elsewhere resulted in a nation-wide wave of prolabor reform laws in states during the following decade.

Jackson strongly appealed to workingmen by his veto message against the Bank. Labor was interested in hard money as the medium for wage payments which was least subject to depreciation in buying power, and was opposed to the paper money of both the state banks and the Bank of the United States. Jackson had not yet pressed the hard-money issue as much as he did later, but in 1832 the Workingmen's Party virtually dissolved in favor of him and the Democrats.

During his second term, Jackson ordered (1836) that the daily hours of labor in the United States Navy yards should be limited to ten. This may be regarded as the first instance of federal support of labor's demands. On the other hand, when a strike occurred among laborers building the Chesapeake and Ohio Canal, he did not hesitate to use federal troops to break it. To Jackson a strike was rebellion against proper authority. This, too, was a Jacksonian precedent in labor relations.

Anti-Masons

Another "third-party" movement appeared in the early 1830's and this was of the "crackpot" type. In 1826, a man named William Morgan had disappeared after revealing the secrets of his Freemasons' lodge. A widespread agitation against all secret societies, which were generally regarded as undemocratic, followed unproved accusations that the Masons had done away with Morgan, and it was proposed that they be outlawed. Anti-Masons saw this reform as a cure for all public ills and organized a political party to secure the remedy.

After winning victories in New York elections, the Anti-Masons devised an instrument which became an important American political institution. This was the party nominating convention, which assumed the place formerly filled by the Congressional caucus. Criticism had been leveled at the caucus because it denied the rank and file of the party a voice in the choice of candidates. The Anti-Masons saw an opportunity to stir up enthusiasm by holding a convention of delegates chosen by local groups, and arriving at the party's choices by public debate and ballot. Besides satisfying the democratic impulses of party members, such a convention would launch the party's campaign on a high tide of oratory and unity. The Anti-Masons held a national convention late in 1831, nominating William Wirt as their candidate for President. A little later in the same year the National Republicans nominated Clay in a convention. In 1832, the Democrats followed suit, and, to no one's surprise, nominated Jackson for President and Martin Van Buren for Vice-President. This Democratic Convention adopted the famous two-thirds rule in the choice of candidates, a rule suggestive of Calhoun's later theory of concurrent majorities, as in effect it gave a veto to any section commanding one-third of the delegates. In many a later Democratic Convention the majority was checked by Southern delegates, until the two-thirds rule was abandoned in 1936. After 1832, both major parties gradually institutionalized the party convention on the various electoral levels and evolved techniques of exciting the voters by colorful shenanigans.

The Whigs and "King Andrew"

The opposition party dubbed Jackson "King Andrew I," and during his second term called themselves Whigs—seeking to identify themselves with the political group, in Britain and America, historically opposed to royal power and pretensions. In reality they constituted the more conservative party, and under the leadership of Clay they were in the tradition of Hamilton except for their interest in the West. In the East, where Webster was their best-known leader, they maintained the allegiance of business interests, but they lagged behind the Democrats practically everywhere in their popular appeal and did not perfect their campaign machinery until the election of 1840, when they "out-Jacksoned" the Jacksonians.

The President himself seemed almost to have created a new "era of good feelings" when, shortly after his second inauguration, he toured New England much as Monroe had done and was greeted with vast acclaim. Even Harvard College overcame its doubts about the backwoods hero and awarded him an honorary degree, to the considerable chagrin of that learned Harvardian, John Quincy Adams. For his part, Jackson charmed those of his enemies who were brave enough to come beneath his gaze, inspiring such warm words as these written by an elderly Massachusetts Federalist, Elijah H. Mills:

> He was considered extremely rash and inconsiderate, tyrannical and despotic, in his principles. A personal acquaintance with him has convinced many who held these opinions that they were unfounded. He is very mild and amiable in his disposition, of great benevolence, and his manners, though formed in the wilds of the West, exceedingly polished and polite. Everybody that knows him loves him.

Few conservatives, however, allowed personal admiration to color their political hatred for the man who wedded nationalism to democracy, and interpreted his re-election as a command to make war against that sacred institution, the Bank of the United States.

The Bank, the Boom, and Hard Money

The charter of the Bank of the United States would run out in 1836 if the law were left to take its course, but the old fighter in the White House, armed with what he regarded as a mandate from the people, assumed the offensive against the "Monster" shortly after his re-election in order to consolidate his victory. He feared there might be another move to re-charter the Bank, and by now he was convinced of its unsoundness as a financial institution. Most competent observers thought him wrong on the latter point, but he had not overestimated the Bank's political power—which was his fundamental reason for opposing it.

The method he devised for weakening and decisively defeating Nicholas Biddle's establishment was to withdraw the government deposits from it. By law the Secretary of the Treasury was authorized to do this, but Jackson had to overcome stubborn resistance in his own official family. Within a period of a few months in 1833, he got rid of one Secretary of the Treasury (Louis L. McLane) by promoting him to the Secretaryship of State when Edward Livingston became Minister to France; and he quickly removed another (William J. Duane), putting in the vacant place Roger B. Taney, who as Attorney General had supported him against the Bank from the beginning. A significant aspect of these developments was the assertion and full assumption by Jackson of presidential responsibility for the actions of the department heads. Early in the fall of 1833 (September 26), Taney issued an order that henceforth the public funds should be deposited in certain state banks. These were designated by critics as the "pet banks." Meanwhile, former deposits in the United States Bank were gradually withdrawn in the course of ordinary operations.

When Congress met in December, these actions and the reasons for them were reported to that body, as the law required; and the debate that was engendered there continued through this session and the next one, as it did intermittently till the end of Jackson's term. Meanwhile, Biddle had brought his financial batteries into play. Beginning in the summer of 1833, the Bank contracted its loans, thus arousing fear of a recession and bringing pressure to bear on the business community, which eventually complained. During the winter he granted personal favors to legislators. At this time Webster wrote him: "I believe my retainer has not been renewed or *refreshed* as usual. If it be wished that my relation to the Bank should be continued, it may be well to send me the usual retainers."

But it was obvious by the spring of 1834 that the Bank was waging a losing fight against the implacable President. In the Senate, it is true, Clay carried through resolutions censuring the latter for his conduct, and these remained on the record until the last weeks of the administration, when Senator Benton finally got them expunged; but the House supported Jackson, and no effective means to stay his hand could be devised by anybody. In the fall of 1834, Biddle, giving up the fight to all practical purposes, began to expand his loans in what soon developed into a boom period. When the federal charter of the Bank ran out in 1836, it got a state charter and continued to operate as a private institution in Pennsylvania.

The Flood of Speculation

The speculative mania which marked the remainder of Jackson's administration cannot be blamed primarily on the "pet banks." They were selected with considerable care and subjected to fairly stringent conditions, which were formalized by Congressional action in 1836, though inevitably there were evasions. Nor can it be blamed on any inflationary policies of the President, who was still a hard-money man. The change in the coinage ratio between silver and gold in 1834, to 16 to 1 (from 15 to 1), was designed to favor gold and increase the circulation of the soundest of all monetary mediums. This measure, which owed its success chiefly to Senator Benton, or "Old Bullion," was thoroughly approved by Jackson. But no effective agency was devised in place of the "Monster" to control the host of state banks and their loans and their myriad issues of paper money.

One traveler of the time described his experience as follows:

At Wheeling exchanged $5.00 note, Kentucky money, for notes of the Northwest Bank of Virginia; reached Fredericktown; there neither Virginia nor Kentucky money current; paid a $5.00 Wheeling note for breakfast and dinner; received in change two $1.00 notes on some Pennsylvania bank, $1.00 Baltimore and Ohio Railroad, and balance in Good Intent shinplasters; 100 yards from the tavern door all notes refused except the Baltimore and Ohio Railroad.

This chaos created a happy hunting-ground for speculators and sharp operators as prosperity developed into a runaway inflationary boom. By January 1, 1835, the whole national debt was paid off, to Jackson's great satisfaction, but the government now faced an embarrassing problem in the growing surplus in the Treasury. The tariff, which was the chief source of the surplus, could not be touched before 1842, when the compromise provisions of 1833 would have been carried out. At this stage Westerners cared little about further reductions of the price of public lands because inflation made the price of $1.25 per acre easy to pay and aroused vast hopes of increased values. Federal internal improvements as a means of spending money were ruled out by continued Eastern opposition and Jackson's veto of the Maysville Road Bill.

The plan that Congress adopted was much closer to Henry Clay's distribution scheme than to Jackson's more conservative policy. This was a program to "deposit" the federal surplus with the state governments, under the tacit understanding that the money would never be repaid. Calling the gifts "deposits" had the advantage of avoiding delicate constitutional problems, and Jackson signed the Deposit Act in June 1836 though he had not recommended it. Senator Benton of Missouri called the procedure: "in name a deposit; in form a loan; in essential design a distribution." All surplus funds in the Treasury above $5 million on January 1, 1837, were to be divided among the states in proportion to their representation in Congress. Three out of four quarterly installments went to the states in 1837, before a turn in the economic tide caused the policy to be abandoned.

This device relieved the Treasury from the embarrassment of riches, but it stimulated the national boom by encouraging the state governments to embark on fantastic spending sprees. Imaginations already overheated by visions of canals and paved roads were crowded by dreams of railroads which should bring enormous advantages to everybody. A few states used their money wisely, but others borrowed huge sums of money on the strength of the Deposit Act and launched grandiose programs of internal improvements. State governments issued bonds and for a time speculators bid up their price wildly. The state authorities were lulled into thinking their dreams would come true and offered new issues.

The great London bank of Baring Brothers bought bonds in the United States and resold them to British investors who hardly knew the difference between federal bonds, which were as good as gold, and dubious state bonds. British investment throughout the nineteenth century substantially speeded up American industrialization and formed an important British interest on the side of peaceful relations. But the scale of investment during the middle thirties was out of all proportion to the actual progress and needs of the American economy. While borrowing increased, prices went up on both sides of the Atlantic and a mounting intoxication of prosperity seized both peoples. Wildcat banks multiplied in the South and West as state governments chartered new ones in order to sell them bonds. The banks issued paper money on the security of the state bonds and loaned the paper money back to the states as well as to land speculators. Businessmen believed that the increase in land values and the profits of transportation routes would pay huge dividends to all holders of paper securities. The federal government was sucked into the paper hurricane, since payments for public lands could be made with paper money. On this basis, land sales increased from less than $3 million in 1832 to almost $25 million in 1836.

The Specie Circular

The spiral could not move forever upwards. Since the Collapse of 1819, the business cycle had come full circle again. Bust was certain to follow boom, and the whole episode was a startling lesson in the irresponsibility of state governments and the need for some central authority to regulate the excesses of the business cycle. The eventual Crash was owing to business failures in England as well as to crop failures and other developments in America. When Jackson tried to stem the flood of speculation, his action was so rude that it accelerated the inevitable catastrophe. As a hard-money man he saw in the speculative mania proof that any kind of "paper" finance—whether federal, state or private borrowing—whether paper money of the United States Bank or state banks—was wrong, and injurious chiefly to the poorest classes. Jackson personally had been a victim of debt and had struggled for years with great probity to pay his creditors and recover solvency. He had also put the federal house in order by paying off all its debts. Now he saw the nation imprisoning itself in a colossal structure of state and private and international debt. With his usual decisiveness, he seized the handiest axe available and delivered a fearful stroke at the base of the structure. He had previously sought to restrict somewhat the receipt of state bank notes by the public-land offices; and on July 11, 1836, he issued the Specie Circular.

This was a Treasury Order instructing public land offices to accept only gold or silver in payment for public lands after August 15. Jackson tried to aim the blow chiefly at speculators and soften it for actual settlers by providing that paper money would be accepted for four more months in payment for small purchases. His broad purpose was made clear in the last paragraph of the Circular:

> The principal objects of the President in adopting this measure being to repress alleged frauds, and to withhold any countenance or facilities in the power of the Government from the monopoly of the public lands in the hands of speculators and capitalists, to the injury of the actual settlers in the new States, and of emigrants in search of new homes, as well as to discourage the ruinous extension of bank issues, and bank credits, by which those results are generally supposed to be promoted. . . .

The essence of Jacksonian Democracy was in the Specie Circular: aggressive exercise of national Executive authority in the interest of the plain people. Businessmen of the more speculative sort called Jackson a tyrant; and even Western farmers were aggrieved by his dislike for their inflationary proclivities; but most people recognized the purity of his motives.

The full effects of the Specie Circular were not felt until after Jackson had turned over the presidency to his chosen successor, Martin Van

Buren, who found in 1837 that he had acquired a panic along with Jackson's mantle. In Jackson's time people often said that his popularity would withstand anything. It had receded somewhat before he left office, but he escaped the test whether it could survive a depression while he was still in the seat of responsibility.

JACKSONIAN FOREIGN RELATIONS AND THE ADVANCING FRONTIER

The Jackson administration was far more notable in domestic than in foreign affairs, though the President's national patriotism was manifest in both spheres. He succeeded where John Quincy Adams had failed in reaching a settlement with Great Britain that fully opened the British West Indies to United States trade and shipping. In his annual message of 1830, he assured the country that the British government had shown "a sincere desire to cultivate the best relations with the United States." Smaller men in both countries continued to whip up hatred, as though they regretted Anglo-American peace, but the hero of New Orleans kept that hatchet buried.

In dealing with France, Jackson had much less reason to be conciliatory. He gained a diplomatic victory when the government of King Louis-Philippe in 1831 signed a treaty with the United States agreeing to pay 25 million francs to discharge American claims for injuries to shipping during the Napoleonic Wars. In consideration of this, duties were reduced on French wines. But the French Chamber of Deputies refused to appropriate the money, and the French Treasury defaulted on the first payment. To Jackson this was deliberate bad faith. He waited until the Deputies again met, and when they refused to act he ordered the United States Navy to prepare for action. Jackson asked Congress to authorize reprisals on French property if payment were not forthcoming, and the French Minister requested and received his passports early in 1835. Jackson's partisans enjoyed a bit of excitement over the prospect of war, but the French quickly appropriated the money with the proviso that Jackson's language to Congress be explained. In his next message to that body the President denied that he had intended to "menace or insult" France, but declared at the same time that he would never stain his country's honor by any apology. A "war of etiquette" was averted, for the French eventually accepted this statement and paid what they owed with interest.

The President engaged in a more peaceable diplomatic adventure in the Orient. In 1832, he sent Edmund Roberts, a seagoing merchant of New Hampshire, on a secret mission to negotiate treaties with the fabled kingdoms of the Far East. Roberts was unsuccessful in Cochin China because, being a good republican, he refused to kowtow to the Emperor in token of subservience. In Siam and Muscat, however, he obtained treaties which authorized American trade on favorable terms and the Senate ratified these. On a later visit Roberts died of the plague in China while on his way to open negotiations with Japan. His mission was the first chapter in the story of the diplomatic relations of the United States with the Far East, and he was a forerunner of American expansion into the Pacific.

Moving the Indians Westward

Far more important in Jackson's time was the expansion of settlement in the vast reaches of the North American continent, and this was greatly expedited by the large-scale removals of Indians from the white men's path. Statesmanship found no place for the aborigine in freedom's rapidly growing empire except on its extreme outskirts, and Jackson's concern for the "plain people" did not extend to redmen. In spirit he was one with the frontiersmen, who regarded treaties with Indians merely as successive devices for removing them, rather than with his predecessor John Quincy Adams and Chief Justice Marshall, who tried vainly to impart some sanctity to these agreements.

The policy of removing the Indians across the Mississippi River had been started, actually, in Monroe's administration, but it was implemented and vigorously carried out in that of Jackson. The Removal Act of 1830, which was occasioned by the struggle between the Georgians and the Cherokees, definitely legalized this policy, and in 1834 Indian Territory (now Oklahoma) was formally established. Jackson sought to employ methods of persuasion and thus avoid both legal appeals and recourse to force. He sent emissaries among the Indians, especially in the Old Southwest where he had won his fame as a fighter, and they negotiated nearly a hundred "evacuation treaties" by the well-known means of cajolery, bribery, and threat. The removal of the Creeks, Choctaws, and Chickasaws was effected without very great difficulty, and as a result rich new cotton lands were opened up beyond the Mississippi as well as east of it. During this time, however, the ruthless Black Hawk War was fought in the Northwest and the Seminole War began in Florida, while the Cherokees were speeded out of Georgia under distressing circumstances.

Part of the fame of the Black Hawk War (1832) came from the fact that Abraham Lincoln served in it as a volunteer and gained one of the most gratifying honors of his life when he was elected captain of his company of Illinois militiamen. Black Hawk, a chief of the Sauk tribe, technically violated a treaty whose validity he denied when he sought to repossess his fertile ancestral lands near the mouth of the Rock River. He led from Iowa a band that included women and children, claiming that his intentions were peaceful, and the fighting began when militiamen fired on a flag of truce. But he had previously been planning a confederacy against the encroaching white men and his move struck terror in Illinois. In the end he was pursued into Wisconsin, and in the Bad Axe Massacre women and children were slain along with the braves. Black Hawk himself survived and dictated an autobiography which became a classic. Following the massacre, many of the Northwestern Indians were induced to move to the Far West, and very few were east of the Mississippi at the end of Jackson's term. Settlers rushed into the undeveloped upper stretches of the Old Northwest, and in 1837 Michigan was added to the states—balancing Arkansas, which was admitted to the Union the year before. Coming out of the region covered by the Northwest Ordinance of 1787, the former was necessarily a free state; while the latter was from the Louisiana Purchase and below the line of 36° 30' drawn by the Missouri Compromise.

In the South the Seminoles of Florida, protected by the swamps, resisted removal longer than any other tribe. War with them began late in Jackson's administration and did not end until 1842, though Chief Osceola was taken earlier, while bearing a flag of truce. The trouble with the Cherokees provided the most important Indian episode of the administration. It was peculiarly embarrassing because these people showed a special aptitude for the white man's civilization, and they appealed not to arms but to the law.

The Cherokees

The Cherokees in northern Georgia were engaged in diversified farming, cattle-raising, and such industries as spinning and weaving cotton, gristmills and sawmills. They built good houses and roads, reduced their language to an alphabet created by Chief Sequoya, published a newspaper, the *Cherokee Phoenix*, and established schools. They imitated the white man even to the extent of owning some Negro slaves. Americans had long argued that their harsh ways of dealing with the Indians were justified by the redman's refusal to abandon barbarism. The case of the Cherokees provided a test, and neither the American people nor President Jackson could meet it on high ground.

These peaceful Indians framed a constitution of the Cherokee Republic. The Georgians, who had as little forbearance and as great landhunger as the generality of Americans and had been frustrated longer than the white men in other states, did not want this island of redmen to remain in their midst under any conditions, and the Indians had now committed the constitutional offense of erecting a government within the boundaries of a state without its consent. The discovery of gold within the "republic" brought mobs of unruly frontiersmen into the rugged Cherokee country; and the Georgia legislature extended the laws of the commonwealth to the Cherokees while denying them legal rights in cases involving white men. This action made encroachment by white men so safe that it was inevitable.

The Cherokees did not take to the warpath but used such peaceful means of redress as American civilization provided. They appealed to Congress, where they were answered by the Removal Act of 1830, and they turned to the Supreme Court, asking recognition of their rights under treaties with the federal government. But that body decided in the case of Cherokee Nation *vs.* Georgia (1831) that Indian tribes did not constitute foreign nations and therefore had no right to bring suit in a federal court. The case of Worcester *vs.* Georgia (1832) arose from the appeal of a missionary who had been imprisoned because of his failure to secure the license now required by state law for any white man residing among the Cherokees. In this instance Marshall ruled that the Cherokees were a "domestic dependent nation" enjoying the protection of the federal government, and that the state of Georgia had no right to extend its jurisdiction over them, in violation of United States treaties and federal laws. This decision was unenforceable by the Court and was virtually repudiated by the President.

Federal agents among the Cherokees exploited quarrels, practiced bribery, and persuaded a faction to sign away all the Georgia land in return for land in Indian Territory and a payment of $5.6 million. The majority rejected the agreement (the Treaty of New Echota of 1835), but gradually these Indians moved westward until finally United States troops forced the last of them to go. In far-away Concord, Ralph Waldo Emerson spoke with horror of this transaction: "Such a dereliction of all faith and virtue, such a denial of justice, and such deafness to screams for mercy were never heard of in times of peace and in the dealing of a nation with its own allies and wards since the earth was made." In Indian Territory with remarkable fortitude the Cherokees restored their uprooted civilization, little dreaming that, by a strange turn of fortune, their remote descendants would one day come into sudden riches when oil was found beneath their lands.

The human tide of frontiersmen, pioneers, and settlers surged into new river bottoms and plains of opportunity, overwhelming the redmen who dared oppose it. This tide even lapped over the international boundary line and moved into the Mexican province of Texas where some 30,000 persons of Anglo-American stock were living before the Jackson administration came to an end. President John Quincy Adams, regretting that in the Treaty of 1819 with Spain he had abandoned claim to this imperial domain, had vainly tried to persuade the government of Mexico to sell it. Jackson repeated the effort, but the question of the sale of Texas became a test of Mexican patriotism, and no Mexican administration dared attempt a deal. In 1836, the Texans, who had taken matters into their own ready hands, achieved independence under the leadership of Jackson's former comrade at arms and old friend, Sam Houston. Jackson recognized the Republic of Texas in one of his last official acts. Perhaps he would have done a good deal more if the time had been more propitious. But his main concern at the end of his term was to secure for his protegé, Martin Van Buren, succession to the presidency under favorable circumstances. He did not want to provoke a controversy over slavery or bequeath to him a foreign war.

THE END OF THE JACKSON ERA

A Democratic National Convention registered the wish of the party chief by unanimously nominating Van Buren for the presidency. The Whigs had no similar gathering, despite the precedent of the last campaign, and in the election their vote was split between three candidates: Hugh Lawson White of Tennessee and William Henry Harrison of Ohio, both of whom claimed to represent pioneer democracy just as well as Jackson had; and Daniel Webster, whose ability as a vote-getter did not match his eloquence. Van Buren won the election handily, by an electoral vote of 170 to 57, though he lost ground in both the West and the South Atlantic states.

At the age of seventy Jackson returned to The Hermitage, where he could smoke his pipe in peace during the eight years that were left to him. Unlike Jefferson, he founded no dynasty. Economic difficulties diverted attention from all other questions during Van Buren's four unhappy years in the White House and were a sufficient reason for his failure to be re-elected. Jackson's disciple Polk succeeded after another four-year interval and was distinctly in his tradition, though he lacked the public appeal which had made "Old Hickory" invincible. The Democratic Presidents after that until 1861 bore him no resemblance. By any reckoning Jackson was a strong President, but none of his successsors was, with the possible exception of Polk, until Lincoln. His record remained as an example which could be invoked and heeded, as it has been in our time, but the truth seems to be that he brought great personal power to the presidency, rather than that he greatly strengthened the office itself.

His political philosophy was so pragmatic that many have been unable to recognize it as a philosophy, and no thinker of his time ever reduced it to anything that could be called a system. Like Jeffersonianism, which had deeper intellectual roots, Jacksonianism was essentially an attitude. Jackson himself was the strong friend and dauntless champion of the plain people and the Union. Because of particular circumstances, his vigorous personality expressed itself chiefly in defensive actions—such as those against nullification and the Bank and the madness of speculation.

He fought valiantly for freedom but he was no architect of a free society like Jefferson; he was no builder of institutions like Hamilton or Marshall. But, like Washington and Jefferson before him and Lincoln after him, he has remained until this day a legend.

Jackson's Heir

After "Old Hickory's" administration, that of anybody else would have seemed an anticlimax, as Van Buren's surely did. Jackson, a Tennessee planter, had always sought to reduce the antagonism between North and South, and in his Farewell Address he warned, as Washington had, against the danger of basing party divisions on geographical distinctions. This danger grew during the term of his successor. Soon after his retirement, he spoke privately of another and more immediate conflict which he had shown no disposition to avoid. He foresaw a continued effort to make of honest laborers "hewers of wood and drawers of water to the monied aristocracy of the country through the credit and paper system." The Van Buren administration was in the democratic spirit of Jackson, and it fought the same sort of fight in the financial sphere.

Neither the new President nor his advisers believed that the federal government should act positively to alleviate bankruptcies and unemployment, or to cushion collapsing prices and markets. A policy of strict laissez-faire and nonintervention was still assumed to be the correct one in bad times as well as good. Governmental policy in the fields of banking and money did affect the private economy, but this was not as well understood then as it became in the twentieth century. Van Buren's most important domestic achievement showed no more understanding of economics than was common in his day, yet it revealed a very clear social and political orientation.

This was the Independent Treasury Act of 1840. Jackson, in his haste to destroy the second Bank of the United States, had not allowed for the possibility that the "pet" state banks in which he deposited the federal funds might turn out to be merely smaller versions of the big "Monster." The favored banks were privately controlled for private profit, after all. Some of their officers used public funds for gambling and a number of the banks defaulted in the Panic of 1837 with losses of millions of dollars to the federal Treasury. The radical wing of the Democracy in the North, particularly the "Loco-Focos" of New York, successors of the Workingmen's Party, blamed banks in general for the Depression and demanded that the government should entirely deny them the use of federal funds. Only thus, they believed, could the credit monopoly of private bankers be curbed. Van Buren called a special session of Congress in 1837 to consider his proposal that branches of the Treasury itself be established in the most important cities to receive, hold, and disburse all government money. Hamilton's and Marshall's argument, that a Bank was a "necessary and proper" means of carrying out the government's financial powers, was answered by this simple alternative.

Numerous Democrats, including the bankers who had profited by Jackson's deposits in their institutions and various advocates of "soft money," strongly opposed the Independent or Sub-Treasury Bill. Several times it was defeated in Congress before the persistence of depression and rising clamor for it secured its passage. Actually, whatever may be thought of governmental patronage of private banks, the withdrawal of federal funds from use as a basis of credit, and their "sterilization" in the public treasury, would be considered today a mistaken way to meet a depression. Banks are easy targets of unthinking anger whenever they are forced to collect loans in order to satisfy depositors' demands or go bankrupt; and the Loco-Focos were out to punish banks.

The bankers had certainly done much to excite popular hatred, and Van Buren by acting against them strengthened his hold on the plain people of the North, while offending conservative Democrats. Many of the latter abandoned his party and joined the Whigs, who proceeded after their campaign victory in 1840 to repeal the Independent Treasury Act in 1841, only to see the Democrats re-enact it in 1846. Van Buren's extension of Jackson's anti-Bank policy crystallized opposition in such a state as New York, where conservative groups elected William H. Seward as governor.

The Log Cabin and Hard Cider Campaign

The Democratic party lost the presidential election of 1840, however, not so much on issues as because of its failure to match the Whigs in "buncombe." By 1840, it seemed that the Democrats had maintained the support of the plain people in the North without losing that of Southern planters. This powerful coalition came very close to winning the election. The Whigs correctly assumed that their policies were unpopular among the masses of the people and that businessmen and conservatives generally would vote against Van Buren no matter what campaign nonsense was uttered by candidates. Therefore the Whig leaders decided to make a rousing demagogic appeal.

The Whig campaign of 1840 was something new in American national politics and, for all its wonderful jollity, it boded ill for the great experiment in democracy. Jackson and Van Buren had won the masses by organization around policies which served their interests; the Whigs would outdo the Democrats by organizing enthusiasm to distract attention from their own policies. The Federalists had gone down to defeat with anti-democratic flags flying, and had lost largely because they publicly professed their faith. The Whigs would not make that mistake.

A national Whig Convention met at Harrisburg, Pennsylvania, but could not agree on a platform, so none was offered to the voters. Nor did the Whigs dare to nominate either of their outstanding leaders, Clay or Webster, because the political principles of these men were too well known. They hit upon the hero of Tippecanoe, General William Henry Harrison, who had carried a few western states four years before. As a candidate he might win the plain people as Jackson had, without much danger that he would match Jackson's strong leadership in their favor. John Tyler of Virginia was named for Vice-President as a concession to Clay and the South. The Whig strategy in the campaign had been laid down as long ago as 1835 by the astute Nicholas Biddle:

> If General Harrison is taken up as the candidate, it will be on account of the past. Let him say not one single word about his principles, or his creed —let him say nothing—promise nothing. Let no committee, no convention, no town meeting ever extract from him a single word about what he thinks now or will do hereafter. Let the use of pen and ink be wholly forbidden.

The Democrats nominated Van Buren and adopted an elaborate platform of Jacksonian principles. But the Whigs quickly forestalled a debate on issues. Van Buren and Democratic policies were blamed for the Depression, while promises were made that the Whigs would waft away the dark clouds. In the North, they charged that the Seminole War proved the administration to be proslavery; in the South they made the refusal to annex Texas the basis of the charge that the administration was anti-slavery. But it was also necessary to prove that Harrison was a man of the people. A sarcastic Democrat's remark that if he were provided with a pension and a barrel of hard cider he would gladly retire to a log cabin for the rest of his days, was seized upon. The Whig orators shouted that Van Buren was a champagne-drinking aristocrat, while Harrison was a hard-cider, log-cabin Cincinnatus:

> Let Van from his coolers of silver drink wine,
>   And lounge on his cushioned settee.
> Our man on his buckeye bench can recline,
>   Content with hard cider is he!
>   The iron-armed soldier, the true-hearted soldier,
>   The gallant old soldier of Tippecanoe!

The Whig campaign became a ritualized picnic. Log cabins with cider barrels and coonskins were rolled from town to town. Even Daniel Webster found it expedient to apologize for not having been born in a log cabin. Genuine hard cider put voters in an appreciative frame of mind for Whig oratory and in good voice for song. Clay denounced the Independent Treasury as the "union of the purse and sword" which the Revolutionary Fathers had fought to sunder; and the Democrats were forced to deny that Van Buren used cologne to scent his whiskers.

"Tippecanoe and Tyler too" won a sweeping victory in the electoral college without large popular majorities. Clay and Webster were soon to be sadly surprised, for Harrison died a month after his inauguration and they could not control his successor. Nonetheless, Whig tactics had finally defeated the Jacksonians and brought an era to a close.

CHAPTER 13

Slavery Is Attacked and Defended

During the debate on the admission of Missouri, Northerners in Congress had attacked slavery on moral grounds, but Southerners as a group did not then take up the moral challenge, preferring to make an issue of the equality of new states with the old. The main concern of Southerners then was to maintain the balance of political power. During the 1820's there was some philosophical defense of slavery in the Lower South, especially in South Carolina, but the great ideological controversy did not reach a climax until the 1830's, and not until then did abolitionism become an exclusively Northern movement. Before that time antislavery agitators and organizers like Benjamin Lundy and James G. Birney carried on most of their activities in the slave states; and the American Colonization Society, a moderate organization in which men from the Upper South and the Middle States were the chief participants, was in operation.

The great turning point in the history of American attitudes toward Negro slavery came in the years 1831 and 1832. In 1831, William Lloyd Garrison started the *Liberator,* proclaiming militant and uncompromising abolitionism; and the following winter, the Virginia legislature ended its greatest debate of the slavery question by doing nothing. This negative outcome amounted to the failure of the last best hope of voluntary emancipation in this important and generally moderate state, and proslavery sentiment grew there in the next decade. Meanwhile, the fear of slave revolt and of incitation from the North caused the slave states to adopt repressive measures and to limit freedom of speech. And, in response to moral censure, Southern thinkers worked out a formal philosophy in which slavery was represented as a positive good.

The struggle in the realm of ideas was reflected in Congressional debates over the right of petition, but slavery did not dominate the national stage until the question of its extension into the West again arose. Here we are concerned chiefly with the conflict of opinion.

THE TURNING POINT IN THE DISCUSSION OF SLAVERY

In the decade after the adoption of the Missouri Compromise there were distinct signs of more positive public support of the "peculiar institution" in the Lower South. Since that region was the seat of cotton culture, which developed so rapidly after the War of 1812 with the aid of slave labor, this attitude can be attributed in part to economic reasons which did not apply to the Upper South to the same degree. At this stage, the slavery system was condemned by some Virginians because of its unprofitableness in their agriculture. But owners were not disposed to sacrifice their property, and there were other factors which affected all the southern states in rough proportion to their slave population. A major obstacle to emancipation was the social uncertainty. What should be done with the slaves if they should be freed? It was a tragedy of the antebellum period that neither in the North nor the South was a convincing answer given to that crucial question.

Free Negroes and the Colonization Movement

In the year 1830, along with about 2,000,000 slaves, there were in the United States some 300,000 free Negroes who were divided in almost equal parts between the North and South. The growth of this group had been rapid in the first two decades of the new government, 1790-1810, but the rate of increase afterward slowed down. The legal status of the free Negroes was deteriorating instead of improving. By 1830, state laws had made manumission more difficult than it was at the end of the Revolution, and privileges that had been granted freedmen had been curtailed, so that their condition was little better than that of slaves. They were obligated to no individual master, but their movements and opportunities were sharply restricted. Until the time of the Civil War their presence was unwelcome in most parts of the country and their status was considerably below that of white men, though an exception must be made in behalf of New England.

The main reason why free Negroes were not wanted in the southern states was that they were believed to constitute a danger to the slave system. But many liberal and high-minded men who favored emancipation also regarded them as undesirable members of society and were thus confronted with a dilemma. The inability of the statesmanship of the age to resolve this is well illustrated by the opinions of Jefferson, who always regarded slavery as a contradiction of the doctrine that all men have a natural right to liberty and as a denial of the dignity and sanctity of human nature. Speaking of the slaves, he said: "Nothing is more certainly written in the book of fate, than that these people are to be free." But he continued: "Nor is it less certain that the two races, equally free, cannot live in the same government. Nature, habit, opinion have drawn indelible lines of distinction between them." This melancholy judgment was echoed by Alexis de Tocqueville, the most famous foreign writer of the day on the subject of American democracy, who doubted if the white and black races would ever live together in any country on an equal footing. In the light of later events, these noted and generally liberal observers may be condemned for lack of faith, but the importance of building up the free Negroes as a transitional group was not then perceived. Most Southern and many Northern emancipationists advocated their removal from the country.

The symbol of this policy was the American Colonization Society, established on January 1, 1817, under distinguished leadership and patronage. Justice Bushrod Washington, nephew of George Washington, was the first president; and among the vice-presidents were Henry Clay, William H. Crawford, and Andrew Jackson. This was a moderate movement in which the largest part was played by the Middle States and the Upper South. In its lifetime greatest opposition to it was expressed in New England on the one hand and in South Carolina and Georgia on the other.

It operated until 1832 or 1833 in a generally favorable climate of opinion. The Colony of Liberia was established in Africa (1822) and several thousand settlers were sent there, a large number of whom died. The peak year was 1832 when there were about 800 emigrants. Emphasis was laid on the expatriation of free Negroes, but the Society also hoped to encourage emancipation and some of the settlers had been freed with a view to transportation to Africa. Soon the underlying assumption of racial inferiority was bitterly assailed by the abolitionists. The shipment of any considerable number of Negroes to the land of their forefathers would have been ruinously expensive, and by this time the slaves and freedmen as a group regarded America as their homeland and wanted to remain there. Also, in the Lower South at least, the white men believed that they could not do without them. But the colonization policy had not been discredited in the Upper South by the time of the great slavery debate in Virginia, and the proposals of emancipation which were made there were coupled with it. Also, they were made at a time of acute fear of insurrection.

Slave Revolts

Throughout the South people were aware of what had happened on the West Indian island of Santo Domingo during and after the French

Revolution. The whites and mulattoes had been massacred or expelled and the former slaves had taken over. To be sure, there was no parallel between conditions in any American state and those in the French part of Santo Domingo (Haiti), where on the eve of the French Revolution the whites and free Negroes together comprised little more than 10 per cent of the total population, but developments there continued to be held up as a terrible warning. In the American states slave revolts had been and continued to be very few. In 1822, the discovery of a projected revolt in Charleston under the leadership of a free Negro, Denmark Vesey, resulted in the deportation or hanging of about seventy conspirators. In 1829, David Walker, a free Negro from North Carolina now living in Boston and engaged in the old-clothes business, issued an appeal to the slaves who, as he believed, could and should gain their freedom by destroying their masters. Copies of *Walker's Appeal* were discovered in the hands of Negroes in Savannah in the late autumn of 1829 and were found soon afterward in several other southern states. These events created for a time a panic of fear and led to repressive legal actions. Northern whites strongly disapproved of Walker's method of solving the problem of slavery. The first number of Garrison's *Liberator* appeared on January 1, 1831. Though he claimed that his own appeal was to the conscience, not to physical force, his language was so extreme that it seemed to Southerners a call to violence. Nat Turner's Rebellion occurred in Southampton County, Virginia, in August of the same year.

This was the bloodiest of all the insurrections. Taking advantage of the absence of many of the whites, who had gone across the border into North Carolina to attend camp-meeting, Turner, hitherto a faithful slave who had come to regard himself as a prophet, led an uprising which resulted in the killing of about sixty whites, mostly women and children. Turner himself was not captured for two months, though the revolt was broken by the second day. Most of the insurgents were shot down and the rest were tried and executed, along with others who were innocent. Panic gripped the entire South, and it was weeks before the Virginians in slavery districts ceased to sleep with fear. Garrison described this as the "hour of vengeance," and declared that the insurrection was a "prelude to the deluge," but the *Liberator* had no subscribers in Virginia and did not reflect Northern sentiment. This was very sympathetic toward the Virginians, and the affair tended to solidify the whites everywhere, showing that violence of this sort served to defeat its own ends. The uprising led to further restrictive legislation throughout the South, but many Virginians were determined to do something about the disease of which it was a symptom. In the legislative session of 1831-1832 occurred the most extensive and famous of all Virginian debates of slavery, and the last one that was held in public. The state that had given to the world George

Mason's Declaration of Rights and Jefferson's Bill for Religious Freedom was erecting its last great monument to liberty of discussion.

The Virginia Debate of 1832

Much of the concern over the ills of slavery in Virginia arose from economic and social causes. Times were hard, slavery did not appear to be profitable, and there was deep anxiety over the growing preponderance of the slave population in the region east of the Blue Ridge. The whites had exceeded the blacks there in 1790, but in every decade thereafter through 1830 the latter had been in a growing majority. After Nat Turner's Rebellion, even the liberals favored temporary repressive measures for the public safety. There was talk of getting rid of the free Negroes, and of getting rid of enough, free and slave, to guarantee a white majority in the eastern as well as the western part of the state. There was also talk of general emancipation, but practically everybody believed that this would have to be coupled with a scheme of deportation.

The proposal of this sort which commanded strongest support was made by Thomas Jefferson Randolph, grandson of the late President. He proposed the submission to the voters of a plan by which all the slaves born after a specified date (July 4, 1840) should become the property of the state when they came of age; they were then to be hired out until sufficient funds had been accumulated for their removal from the United States. The impracticality of the deportation feature was recognized at the time, and neither the state treasury nor public opinion would have sustained it. For these reasons, the legislators contented themselves with declaring the existing situation an evil one and deferring further action until there could be further development of favorable public opinion.

Thus, at last, the chief significance of the debate, which lasted for two weeks in January 1832, lay in the arraignment which the Virginians themselves made of slavery. Some defended it as a positive good, while some still asserted that freedom was a natural right; but chief emphasis was laid on the injury which slavery brought to the character of the whites themselves and on the ineffectiveness of the existing economic system. In the negativeness of the outcome, this debate was typical of the more violent one which raged through the country in the next generation: evils were recognized but no acceptable solution was discovered, and victory went by default to the forces of inaction, which were afterwards solidified into reaction.

Unfortunately, the most important immediate effect of the debate was the stirring of conservatives to formulate stronger defensive arguments than the mere absence of a feasible remedy. Later in the same year, President Thomas R. Dew of the College of William and Mary made a highly significant contribution to the proslavery argument, entitled *Review of the Debate in the Virginia Legislature of 1831 and 1832.* The reform spirit, which had failed to bring about constructive action, declined thereafter. In the next few years, especially 1832-1836, the increase in the sales of slaves to the cotton region lessened the fears of Negro dominance in the East and at the same time brought money into depleted purses. Thus the Virginians, gradually overcoming their repugnance to the domestic slave trade, eased both their economic and social problem. A further reason for the quiescence of the liberals was that they were embarrassed by the abolitionist propaganda and were unwilling to be associated with it.

The Abolitionist Crusade, 1830-1840

Abolitionism as an organized national movement was directly inspired by the British Anti-Slavery Society, which began in 1823 and reached a climax of success ten years later when Parliament abolished slavery in the British West Indies. In certain respects American antislavery leaders availed themselves too little of the British example. They might well have given more thought and emphasis to the provisions for compensation and a temporary apprentice system which were a part of the British settlement of the slavery question. Parliament arrived at a more realistic solution of the problem than any that was ever pressed by American abolitionists.

The immediate stimulus to American abolitionism was provided by the debates on West Indian slavery in Parliament in 1830, which were much read in the United States. Among those greatly impressed by them was William Lloyd Garrison, who was then assisting Benjamin Lundy on the *Genius of Universal Emancipation* in Baltimore but who soon broke with his elder and started his own *Liberator*. Also, these debates occasioned apostles of benevolence in New York, especially the brothers Tappan, Arthur and Lewis, to move prematurely for a national organization. The American Anti-Slavery Society was established under their patronage a little later (1833); and Garrison, recently returned from a visit to England as a self-appointed representative of American abolitionism, had a conspicuous part in this. But Garrison was essentially a free-lance at all times, and he was largely responsible for the split in the Society in 1840, when the Tappans withdrew, leaving the original organization as little but a name. In that year, the Liberty Party emerged and the slavery question was henceforth enmeshed with politics, though Garrison and many others were opposed to direct political action. His own period of most significant agitation, and that of the most important activity of the national Society, fell within the 1830's.

The American roots of abolitionism, and particularly of the parts and phases of the movement that were not connected with Garrison, lay in the religious revival associated with the name of the Presbyterian evangelist, Charles G. Finney, which reached its climax in 1830. The converts of Finney went forth charged with a spirit of active benevolence which manifested itself conspicuously in abolitionism. Though sympathetic with abolition, Finney himself never made it his major business. His spirit was reflected in the crusading zeal of other men, such as the Tappans in New York and Theodore Dwight Weld, who was probably his most important convert.

Garrison and Weld

Garrison, who issued the first number of the *Liberator* in Boston on January 1, 1831, was a native of Newburyport, Massachusetts. He had emerged from poverty and had gained practically all his schooling at the printer's bench. A man of strong will and intense emotions, he identified himself utterly with the cause he championed and did not at all mind if people identified it completely with him. He was a brave man who suffered for the sake of conscience, and he showed himself to be unconquerable. Always a highly controversial figure in his own time, he is still one; but he may be regarded as a classic American example of fanaticism, which William James has described as "loyalty carried to a convulsive extreme." There was impatience, intolerance, and even cruelty in him because of his excess of devotion to his cause. The fame of the *Liberator* was less owing to its Northern supporters than to its Southern enemies. Garrison carried on a continuous campaign of denunciation against the slaveholders; and not unnaturally hatred bred hatred, while violent agitation accentuated fear.

Garrison strongly opposed the colonization policy, as the abolitionists as a group did from this time on, but he was most distinctive in his extreme emphasis on "immediatism." In the first number of his paper he said: "I shall strenuously contend for the immediate enfranchisement of our slave population." That sounded as though he believed that the slaves could all be turned into voting citizens overnight. He also said that he would not equivocate, nor excuse, nor retreat a single inch, and that he *would* be heard. He had no constructive program for the slaves who should be freed, and actually he was a philosophical anarchist, being opposed to political action. Always an independent agitator, he was personally unco-operative even within the abolitionist ranks. In the end he denounced everybody who would not echo his words of immoderation. He described the northern clergy as a "Brotherhood of Thieves" and termed the Constitution "a covenant with death and an agreement with Hell," because it left slavery as a state question. On July 4, 1854, he publicly burned a copy of that document. The chief historic significance of Garrison, besides the opposition and fear he aroused, lay in his emphasis on slavery as a moral issue. With what he regarded as a moral wrong this dauntless and implacable man could tolerate no compromise whatever. But even in the North few believed that, in a national government based upon consent, statesmanlike policies could be compounded of such untractable materials as he provided.

Among the New England abolitionists, Wendell Phillips of Massachusetts was most like Garrison in his complete identification with the cause. This high-minded man of wealth, who imperiled his superior social position by his unpopular moral crusade, was a more attractive personal figure than the editor of the *Liberator*. A younger man than Garrison, he got into the crusade later, and he gained his chief fame as an orator. He also attacked the slaveowners violently, denounced the Constitution, and valued abolition more than Union.

Theodore Dwight Weld (1803-1895) now seems the greatest of the abolitionists, though he was less widely known than Garrison since he worked behind the scenes. Moral reform can have no purer symbol than this self-effacing organizer to whom the cause was everything and personal glory nothing. He was one of Finney's converts in whom religion manifested itself in the effort for social betterment; and, far from breaking with the churches, he used the methods of personal evangelism. He himself was "converted" to abolitionism, and in turn he "converted" some of the most important leaders in the movement—such as James G. Birney, hitherto a supporter of colonization.

Commissioned by the Tappans to find a site for a seminary for Finney's converts, he selected Lane Seminary in Cincinnati. Among the students he afterwards organized a debate on slavery, destined to become famous. He aroused the ire of President Lyman Beecher and the trustees but left an indelible impress on Henry Ward Beecher and the latter's sister, Harriet Beecher Stowe. He trained a group from Lane Seminary and sent them forth as agents to win new converts to abolitionism. The regions evangelized by them became important seats of antislavery strength in later years. Later, Weld served as a power behind the legislative scenes in Washington, supplying ammunition to John Quincy Adams and others, and *Uncle Tom's Cabin* was based in part on his tract, *American Slavery As It Is*. More than any other single man, Weld was the heart and the brains of the effective abolitionist movement. He was an evangelist of reform, seeking to win hearts, and the great service that he and his converts rendered the cause was to give it a religious sanction. He sought to make abolitionism synonymous with religion, and among the evangelical sects in the North he very considerably succeeded, though he won no converts in the South.

The abolitionists designated slavery as a sin rather than a social evil, and they addressed themselves primarily to nonslaveholders. They fired inhabitants of the free states with zeal to extirpate sin from the lives of others, who lived under very different conditions and would have to face the painful task of reconstruction if the slaves should be freed. Southerners regarded them as unbearably self-righteous and Abraham Lincoln, who never lost sight of the immense practical difficulties that would be associated with emancipation, would never permit himself to be coupled with the abolitionists. Even in the North they were generally regarded as fanatics. But they gave an immoral stigma to slavery and imparted a religious sanction to Northernism. Also, they served to solidify Southern sentiment; and, since they would recognize no middle ground, they had a discouraging effect on the emancipation cause in the border states. Few have ever believed more fervently in the American dream of freedom and equality than they, but they had no part in the American tradition of political compromise and they played into the hands of the Southern extremists. Fear of abolitionism was the excuse for a great variety of repressive actions.

THE SOUTH ACTS AGAINST AGITATORS

After the outspoken debate on slavery in the Virginia Assembly in 1832 and the rise of aggressive abolitionism, the prevailing Southern policy became one of preventing all agitation of the subject. Practically all the southern states passed laws for this purpose. This was no mere matter of protecting slave property, though that motive was always present. Fears of slave revolt and consequent social revolution tended to unite the white men, whether slaveholders or not, in all regions where Negroes were numerous. At times the legislators operated in an atmosphere of hysteria, and when the tide of terror receded the states were left with a residue of laws restricting their own freedom of discussion.

A tide of terror had followed the appearance of *Walker's Appeal* in 1829. This violent pamphlet occasioned several state legislatures to forbid the introduction of literature inciting to revolt and the teaching of slaves to read and write. After Nat Turner's rebellion in 1831, new restrictions were imposed in some states on the freedom of Negroes to preach and assemble. The most intolerant period of all followed the abolitionist pamphlet campaign of 1835-1836. This literature was sent to whites, not Negroes, but it was nevertheless regarded as incendiary. In Charleston a mob took a sack of pamphlets from the post office and burned them. The federal authorities were by no means outraged by this. On the contrary, President Andrew Jackson was horrified by the "wicked procedure" of the abolitionists and believed that all good men should frown upon the circulation of their writings. Postmaster General Amos Kendall countenanced the policy of the postmaster in New York in declining to send abolitionist literature to the South. This pamphlet warfare proved generally unsuccessful even in the North, and it was at this juncture that

Theodore Dwight Weld turned back to personal evangelism and sent forth an enlarged band of missionaries to win converts in the free states.

The Southern laws which resulted from this scare were directed chiefly against persons who denied the right to own slaves or advised abolition or circulated literature urging slave revolt. They were severe in the Upper South, except in Kentucky, and even more severe in the Lower South. In practice these laws were rarely invoked, and there are indications that they were interpreted liberally in the case of Southerners, whose fundamental loyalty to their own society could be assumed. But they were a constant threat against any sort of criticism of the existing social order, and they effectively closed the South to Northern critics. "Foreign emissaries" would have been harshly treated if they had entered the region, and very wisely they stayed out.

So far as discussion of the "peculiar institution" was concerned, the freedom of the press declined after 1835 until it practically disappeared. Abolitionist editors had their troubles in the North also, the murder of Elijah Lovejoy by an Illinois mob in 1837 being a tragic illustration. The term "abolitionist" was unpopular almost everywhere and in the South it became a fighting word. A courageous Virginia editor, John Hampden Pleasants, felt compelled to issue a challenge to a younger rival when the latter applied it to him a decade later. Actually Pleasants had done little more than protest against what he regarded as hysteria, but he would not accept this epithet and died in the ensuing duel.

The fear of slave insurrection and social revolution, which hung like a cloud over Southern society in this generation, goes by the name of the "Black Terror." There was hysteria in the air at times which distorted reality, and wisdom is hard to come by when the minds of men are dominated by fear. The worst effects of these repressive measures fell upon Southerners themselves, who in their effort to assure safety lost part of their own heritage of freedom.

They gained much sympathy from other parts of the country when seeking to block the extremes of abolitionism within their own borders, but they fared worse when the fight was shifted to the national arena. A great struggle in Congress, reaching its height in the years 1836-1840, centered on the right of petition. Thousands of petitions, resulting from abolitionist zeal and relating most often to the questions of slavery in the District of Columbia and the domestic slave trade, were introduced. These were often couched in denunciatory language which aroused Southern resentment. The proslavery group secured the adoption of the so-called "Gag Rule" (1836) in the House of Representatives, requiring that all petitions and other papers on the subject of slavery or its abolition should be laid on the table automatically without further action. John Quincy Adams, who served in the House after his retirement from the presidency, gained the title "Old Man Eloquent" for his opposition to a measure which he regarded as unconstitutional; and the abolitionists saw that petitions, constantly reiterating the same themes, should continue to appear. In one period of three or four months there were enough of them to fill a large room from floor to ceiling. The Gag Rule in some form remained on the books until 1844, and Southern support of it did the section great harm. The defensive tactics of Southerners had thrown them into opposition not merely to the emancipation of the slaves and freedom of discussion in their own states, but to the liberties of their Northern countrymen.

THE PROSLAVERY PHILOSOPHY AND THE CHURCHES

Just as the efforts of Southerners to prevent agitation were directly related to their fears of slave revolt, their philosophical defense of the existing system was a response to the charges of immorality and sinfulness that had been directed against it. These charges rankled in the minds of Southerners, who were notably religious people. The desire to arrive at a philosophical and ethical justification of a system which, for a variety of reasons, they had now concluded that they could not give up, was stimulated by the Missouri debates. In the next decade the Southerners took up the moral challenge to some extent, especially in South Carolina; and in the 1830's the defense movement made strong headway in Virginia. Until the abolitionist pamphlet campaign of 1835-1836 this was largely directed to local opinion; the Southerners were trying to convince themselves. Thereafter, goaded by the abolitionists, they would have convinced the country of their rightness if they could have; but in this respect their failure was comparable to that of the abolitionists in trying to convince them of their wrongfulness.

Though the names of Thomas R. Dew, William Harper, William Gilmore Simms, James H. Hammond, and George Fitzhugh are specially associated with the proslavery philosophy, which was elaborately formulated in the generation before secession, this should not be regarded as the work of a small group. It was the fruitage of the intellect of the entire section. Statesmen developed and proclaimed it on the political front; clergymen, educators, and literary men on the social, moral, and religious fronts—at just the time that the reform spirit was burgeoning and blossoming in the North. The philosophical defense of the South in the political realm centered on an emphasis on the historic Constitution and the rights of the states that were supposed to be safeguarded by it. The classic figure here was John C. Calhoun but he was aided and abetted by a host of others. This conservative attitude toward the basic law was paralleled by a social philosophy which looked backward even farther and found its arguments in much more ancient writings. It was more than conservative; it was reactionary.

From the expressions of some of the writers who proclaimed it, it may be regarded as a repudiation of the philosophy of the Declaration of Independence; but as generally understood it represented a limitation rather than a repudiation of the historic faith and doctrine. It denied rights and opportunities to Negroes on the ground that they were distinct and inferior by nature, while affirming the political equality of white men. Thus it was fundamentally racial in its basis, though it represented an attempt to rationalize a system which was now deemed essential to Southern economic life. Negro labor was regarded as indispensable, but the free Negroes were thought to be untrustworthy and degraded. Therefore, so the white men said, there was in the South no feasible alternative to slavery.

Furthermore, the claim was made that the merits of the system were shown by its fruits. By means of slavery, savages had been lifted from barbarism to Christian civilization and they enjoyed a better situation than the free Negroes. In view of the status of the latter in nearly all parts of the country, there was point in this argument, and the Southern apologists did not fail to call attention to the plight of white industrial workers in the East and in England. As for the Southern whites, there was now a repudiation of the charges previously made in Virginia that slavery had an ill effect on their character and effectiveness. It was claimed that, far from degenerating, the white race in the southern United States had developed a unique civilization and a high degree of culture. There was more boastfulness now, and that in itself was a sign of weakness.

In their effort to find support for this social philosophy, the Southern clergymen, writers, and teachers found their greatest literary arsenal in the Sacred Scriptures. The abolitionists had turned to the Bible for texts, and the Southerners naturally did so in a time when church membership was rapidly increasing. Passages in the Old Testament sanctioning the practice of slavery in distant centuries would have been wholly unconvincing to men like Jefferson and Franklin, but the South had turned away from their religious liberalism and was little affected by that of William Ellery Channing and Emerson in New England. Southern religion had passed into what we would now call a fundamentalist phase. A biblical text was a biblical text, whether it came from Genesis or Leviticus or one of the Gospels. Southern divines pointed out that slavery was not condemned by Christ, and that the Apostle Paul actually enjoined obedience on slaves, going so far in one instance as to return a runaway slave to his master.

The Christian attitude toward slavery should have been arrived at on consideration of the spirit of Christian teachings as a whole; and the Northern divines tended to emphasize the spirit of brotherhood. The Southerners tended to be strict constructionists with respect to both the

Bible and the Constitution. But they became increasingly aware of their religious duties in human relations. Toward the end of the antebellum period, far more than at the beginning, religious leaders instructed masters in their duties and sought to carry the Gospel to the slaves.

More basic, actually, than the biblical argument was the ethnological. This was an attempt to justify on scientific grounds the concept of the natural inferiority of the Negroes which was practically universal among Southern whites and was widespread throughout the United States and the world. Inevitably the Negroes, both free and slave, were backward at that time of extremely limited opportunity; and the physical differences between them and the whites were visible to any eye. Yet, as modern anthropologists and sociologists have pointed out, it is illogical to attribute this backwardness to race and to regard color as a sign of intrinsic inferiority. The abolitionists were unrealistic in underestimating the social problems arising from the presence, side by side, of races as different in history and in external appearance as the whites and Negroes, but some of the Southern apologists went to an unbearable extreme when they denied the unity of mankind. That was too much for the Southern religious leaders. They continued to believe that God "hath made of one blood all nations of men, for to dwell on the face of the earth." The ethnological argument was the most powerful of all, and up to a point it coincided with the predominant popular opinion, but beyond that point very many would not go. There were contradictions and inconsistencies and anomalies in this racist philosophy.

Among these was miscegenation. Tocqueville is authority for the statement that there was less admixture of whites and blacks in the southern United States than in the colonies of the continental European countries, but intermixture there unquestionably was, and, as Lincoln afterward remarked, this was greater under a system of slavery than under freedom.

Division in the Churches

Nothing shows more clearly how, in this age of controversy, the union of hearts among the best of men was broken than the split in certain important churches on a North-South line. The period, 1820-1850, was one of notable increase in church membership in the South, especially among the evangelical sects—the Methodists and Baptists and certain groups of Presbyterians. In this period in Virginia, the Carolinas, and Georgia, the Baptists and Methodists increased in number at a much faster rate than the population; and the dominance of the evangelicals was as great or greater in the newer states in the interior. These sects were warmer and more democratic than the older churches, though they were less intellectual and more fundamentalist in doctrine. It was under their influence that more attention was paid to the religious life of the slaves, but a chasm opened between them and their Northern brethren. This led to a split in the largest groups, the Baptists and the Methodists. Owing to the fact that the organization of the Baptists was predominantly congregational, the split in their ranks was rather less painful and less significant. The trouble among them arose from alleged discrimination against slaveholders in connection with missionary activities, and this led to the formal withdrawal of the Southern churches and the establishment in 1845 of the Southern Baptist Convention. This is still in existence, the split never having been healed.

The Methodists were more highly organized, with bishops serving in different parts of the country, and national meetings in General Conferences. Prior to 1832, there had been a weakening of opposition to slavery within this denomination. Slavery was still regarded as an evil, but members were permitted to hold slaves. Ministers were forbidden to hold them except where the laws forbade emancipation, as they did increasingly in the southern states. With the growth of abolitionism in the North after 1832 the temper changed, but in general the church frowned on controversy and left matters to the states. As a result, some opponents of slavery in the North withdrew from membership. The controversy became acute at the General Conference of 1844, centering on Bishop James O. Andrew of Georgia, who had come into the possession of a few domestic slaves by bequest and marriage and could not emancipate them readily under existing Georgia law. The question that was raised was whether as a slaveholder he could effectively perform his episcopal functions in the free states. A motion was made that he desist from these, so long as the impediment remained, and it was carried by a vote that followed sectional lines. The Bishop himself would have been glad either to desist or to try to rid himself of the impediment, but Southern opinion would permit no action which threw upon the institution of slavery a stigma of immorality and irreligion. As a result, the Southern conferences withdrew and the Methodist Episcopal Church, South, was set up in 1846. Nearly a century was to pass before this split was healed; and in the meantime each of the sectional branches flourished the more after its separation from the other.

In a famous speech in the Senate in 1850, John C. Calhoun referred to these church affairs, pointing out that important ties of spiritual union had already been snapped because of the slavery question. He blamed it on agitation, but the situation was ominous under any interpretation. Men in the North and South could no longer understand each other, even when they used the same language of devotion.

CHAPTER 14

Jacksonian Reform Movements

A MERE CATALOGUE OF SECULAR REFORM MOVEMENTS during the Jackson era would fill many pages. They were all expressive of the expectation that humanity and society could be perfected in the United States in a prodigious hurry. In earlier decades, faith in limitless human and social improvement had been confined to a rather small class of highly educated men, of whom Benjamin Franklin and Thomas Jefferson were the archetypes, most of them rationalists in philosophy and indifferent to orthodox religion. They had accepted the responsibilities of public office in a spirit akin to *noblesse oblige*. Free political institutions were their great achievement. They hoped that within such a framework the mass of men would be encouraged to improve society and themselves, and thus bring human life closer to rational perfection.

Their faith was justified by developments in the decades following 1815. A multitude of reformers emerged, both women and men, who usually held no public office, often lacked advanced education, and were spiritually closer to evangelical religion than to rationalist philosophy. The reformer became as distinctive a type of American as the frontiersman. Democratic evangelism, the faith that a world-shaking mission beckoned America, is evident in the following passage from a manifesto written by Lyman Beecher, member of a notable family of reformers:

> ... If it had been the design of Heaven to establish a powerful nation in the full enjoyment of civil and religious liberty, where all the energies of man might find full scope and excitement, on purpose to show the world by one great successful experiment of what man is capable, where should such an experiment have been made but in this country! The light of such a Hemisphere shall go up to Heaven,. it will throw its beams beyond the

waves; it will shine into the darkness there, and be comprehended—it will awaken desire, and hope, and effort, and produce revolutions and over-turnings until the world is free. Then will the trumpet of jubilee sound, and earth's debased millions will leap from the dust, and shake off their chains, and cry, "Hosanna to the Son of David!"

So religion turned to social reform and democracy acquired religious fervor in a stupendous effort to make America, and then, by virtue of its example, the world into a paradise.

EDUCATION

If the reformers agreed on any one route to the secular paradise, it was that of education. They promptly disagreed on what should take the place of aristocratic models after these should be overthrown, but one thing they all believed: that *more* people should be educated.

This faith had been projected by the Revolutionary generation, but before 1800 little had been actually done beyond providing plans and such tools as Noah Webster's great series of textbooks. The latter enjoyed enormous popularity for almost a century. Both Americanization and secularization were apparent in the first line of his *New England Primer*, which substituted "A was an Apple Pie made by the Cook," for the tra-ditional "In Adam's Fall We Sinned All." In the twenties and thirties, the most urgent problem was to get Webster's books into the hands of every child under competent teachers. Probably a majority of Americans were illiterate. Even in New England, the compulsory common schools had been grossly neglected by the towns. Elsewhere, as a rule, charity schools offered the only chances for poor children.

Horace Mann and Educational Reform

Horace Mann of Massachusetts was the greatest spokesman of educational reform. He agitated for the appointment of a state superin-tendent of education, and occupied the office himself for eleven years after it was established in 1837. He published annual reports which were the Bible of public-school reform in all the states. Declaring that in a republic ignorance was a civic crime for which the government was re-sponsible, he and his followers proceeded to renovate every phase of educational theory and practice. Children began to be treated as human beings rather than as "limbs of Satan"; reason made headway against the rod in obtaining discipline; teachers' explanations superseded pupils' memory work; and practical knowledge of nature, technology, and so-ciety gradually displaced preceptorial dogmas. Mann warned the public in his eloquent eighth report that improved education was not only a means to the improvement of society but the only certain bulwark against the failure of the American experiment:

If we do not prepare children to become good citizens—if we do not develop their capacities, if we do not enrich their minds with knowledge, imbue their hearts with the love of truth and duty, and a reverence for all things sacred and holy, then our republic must go down to destruction, as others have gone before it.

Partly owing to Mann's efforts, the first state normal school was founded at Lexington, Massachusetts, in 1839. Samuel Read Hall had opened a private normal school in Concord, Vermont, sixteen years earlier, and its fame led to imitation in many states. A host of reformers joined the pioneers and fought in the states to improve the elementary schools and to bring every child inside their doors without distinction between rich and poor. Laborers and their unions supported the crusade, although the poor did not always favor it, while some property owners bitterly protested that their taxes should not be squandered on other people's children. To such opponents of reform the most effective answer was that the propertyless who were now entrusted with the vote must be educated or they would fall prey to demagogues who would tear down private property as well as republicanism.

The Eastern states, especially New England, produced the generative ideas of the campaign for educational reform; the Western states, lacking extremes of wealth and poverty, were quickest to adopt them; and the Southern states remained least touched by the movement until after the Civil War. By that time, all the Northern states had systems of free, compulsory, tax-supported elementary schools. In the South, planters paid for private education for their own children and had little interest in the fate of the poorer youngsters; but in the Southern cities municipal public schools became available to most white children. Free Negroes as well as slaves remained mostly illiterate. Education for them was considered dangerous to white supremacy in the South, and they suffered from discrimination in most parts of the North.

Private academies, usually religious in sponsorship, dominated secondary education and concentrated on preparation of boys for college. The idea that the states should support secondary schools was slow in winning adoption. Massachusetts once more led the way with the first high school in Boston in 1821 and a law in 1827 requiring towns with more than 500 families to provide for high schools. A high mortality rate among private academies encouraged the various state governments to take over individual institutions, but education for all qualified persons on the high school level was not provided for the whole country until the twentieth century.

During the Jackson era, a variety of experiments in what is now called progressive education were conducted by radicals, most of whose ideas came from abroad. The fountainhead of educational progressivism was Pestalozzi, a Swiss who applied the principles set forth in Rousseau's

Émile. The key to the Pestalozzian method was "naturalism." According to this view, children were naturally good and naturally talented, but their goodness and talent were frustrated by traditional education, which reflected the corruption of traditional society. If the happiness of the child could be brought about, virtue and creativity would thrive; and when enough graduates of Pestalozzian schools had filled the world, they would recreate society.

Reformers from all Europe and from America flocked to study Pestalozzi's schools in Switzerland. Robert Owen was one of them and, in the course of organizing his socialist colony of New Harmony in Indiana, he invited educational utopians to establish ideal schools there. The journey of Owen in his "boatload of knowledge" down the Ohio River in 1826 has been called the greatest cultural event of the midwestern frontier. Pestalozzism failed at New Harmony along with the whole experiment, but modifications of the Swiss system were widely adopted in the region largely through the influence of Owen's son, Robert Dale Owen.

A more consistent application of the Pestalozzian doctrine occurred in the Boston Temple School of Bronson Alcott. He surrounded pupils with works of art and beautiful furnishings. Problems of discipline were turned over to the student body for social solution, corporal punishment being forbidden. Alcott's Transcendentalist faith that evil is an illusion and his own innocent spirituality made him a model progressive teacher. In his Conversations on the Gospels, conducted by the Socratic method, he assured the children that they would find truth in their own souls and dared even to violate taboos by encouraging discussion of the mystery of the birth of Jesus. Cultivated Boston was willing to sample almost any variety of unorthodoxy except one involving sex. The Temple School closed in 1838 after two years of shocked public controversy.

Very different from Pestalozzian naturalism were the Prussian ideas which became influential in American higher education during the same period. Prussia combined exalted standards of objective scholarship and academic freedom on the university level with almost military discipline and heavy doses of nationalist propaganda on the lower levels. The regimentation of the Prussian student was firmly rejected in America, but graduates of American colleges who were ambitious to become professional scholars frequently studied in the German states, whence they brought back invigorating devotion to pure learning. Harvard was the first to benefit when George Ticknor, Edward Everett, and George Bancroft made the pioneer pilgrimages to Germany shortly after 1815 and returned to their alma mater to teach and write. Pure scholarship and academic freedom had found homes in America by the time that German militaristic nationalism destroyed them in their birthplace.

Selection and adaptation of foreign influences in education produced in America a new amalgam derived from the European extremes represented by Pestalozzism and Prussianism. "Pluralism" is the best description for the net product. Expansion of practical subjects and training in citizenship did not destroy classical learning or inhibit the growth of pure scholarship. Disciplinary methods were humanized without enthroning the child. The spread of free public education did not put an end to existing private and religious institutions or prevent the founding of many new ones. The Jeffersonian ideal of education to train an intellectual aristocracy was not abandoned in the face of the Jacksonian ideal of opening the halls of learning, like the offices of government, to all without distinction. The average quality of American education was definitely inferior to the best European standards; but in America the decisive steps were taken during the Jackson era in an unprecedented experiment to democratize education, and optimists hoped that the sacrifice of quality would be temporary.

State Universities

The highest expression of the Jeffersonian-Jacksonian amalgam was the state university, publicly controlled and financed, and open with little or no charge to all citizens of the state. The first state university to be chartered was that of Georgia, in 1785, though it was not opened until after the beginning of the next century. The University of North Carolina, though chartered a little later, began to give instruction sooner (1795). Other early state institutions of higher learning were the University of Vermont and South Carolina College, out of which the present University of South Carolina developed after the Civil War.

It was left to Jefferson to launch a broader experiment in the University of Virginia, chartered in 1819. The students had to pay fees, but the University was public in its purposes and more than a college. Jefferson himself designed the buildings as models of correct classical taste and left in this "academical village" a superb architectural monument. His purpose was to combine the traditional education of a gentleman with a love for republican institutions and a capacity to serve them. The classical curriculum was enriched by scientific and political studies under an elective system, professors were brought from abroad, and the students were granted an unusual degree of freedom. The results were not encouraging at first, for liberty became license when the high-spirited sons of planters descended on Charlottesville with Negro servants and horses. Eventually a notable honor system was developed, but the University acquired an aristocratic flavor that its Father had not intended. It could not serve as the capstone of a state system, since the state made inadequate provision for supporting schools on lower levels, so the public purposes which Jefferson had in mind and stated so prophetically were carried out more logically in the West than in his own commonwealth. The University of Michigan, authorized by the legislature of the new state in 1837 and anticipated a score of years before that, provided an admirable early example.

The Education of Women

At the beginning of the Jackson era, most parents looked upon advanced education for girls, and many even on literacy, as certain to destroy their innocence and their capacity for domestic careers. The first example of college co-education in the world occurred in Western institutions. In the East, prejudice against feminine literacy had been weakest in New England, but even there many persons believed women incapable of such studies as higher mathematics and physics, while biological and social sciences were considered injurious to feminine refinement.

Emma Hart Willard, who had educated herself in "masculine" subjects by solitary study after marriage, founded Troy Female Seminary in New York in 1821. Other women, believing it a mistake to compete with men for careers, furthered higher education in the domestic arts and sciences. Catherine Beecher founded such colleges in Hartford, Connecticut, and Cincinnati, Ohio. For the brilliant Mary Lyon this smacked too much of the despised "finishing" school for girls. She founded Mount Holyoke Female Seminary (later Mount Holyoke College) at South Hadley, Massachusetts, in 1837, modeling the curriculum on that of nearby Amherst College. The first American institution for women to bear the name college was chartered a year earlier. This was Georgia Female College at Macon (afterwards Wesleyan College). But the West nourished the most advanced experiment in higher education. Oberlin College in Ohio (1833), planned by New England reformers, opened its classes not only to women as well as men, but to Negroes as well as whites.

WOMEN'S RIGHTS

The laws inherited from England and maintained by the states after the Revolution made women minors for life. If unmarried, they were legal wards of their male relatives; if married, they were chattels of their husbands. A single woman or widow was allowed to hold property and earn a living as concessions to her abnormal position, but upon marriage the husband, while assuming responsibility for violations of law committed by his wife, acquired title to her property and earnings, and authority over her person like that of a parent over his child. A Massachusetts judge, in a fit of liberality, limited the instrument with which a husband might beat his wife to a "stick no thicker than my thumb," but other judges countenanced periodic beatings with a horsewhip.

Regardless of the law, the shortage of women in early America placed a premium on good treatment of them. Foreign visitors were astonished by the chivalry towards women. Especially among the well-to-do and in the South, women were placed on a pedestal for admiration as moral paragons whose honor must be defended against the slightest question. They were deemed superior to men in their devotion to religion, charity, and domestic glory, and too refined for the coarse masculine worlds of business, politics, social reality, and sin. Young girls were carefully trained to attract husbands by affecting weakness, ignorance, and coyness, while "strong-minded women" were travestied as freaks.

Strong-Minded Women

The Jackson era nevertheless produced a remarkable crop of strong-minded women who fought their way to improvements in the position of their sex. The spirit of the times favored them as the implications of the American Revolution were now being worked out in all areas of life. They were further stimulated by a number of English women writers who visited the United States and expressed in lectures and books disillusionment with the status of women in the land of the free. Most of all, the working equality of the sexes at the frontier, and in the new factories of the East, pointed the way to legal recognition. Among countertendencies the contemporary victory of romanticism in literature was important. The women's rights movement in America was least successful in the southern states, where the romantic novels of Sir Walter Scott were specially popular. Besides the widening of opportunities for education, the chief gain made by women was in property rights. By 1850, New York, Pennsylvania, Indiana, Wisconsin, Mississippi, and California had recognized women's right to own property after marriage. Gradually codes were altered to make women joint guardians with their husbands of their children and able to sue and be sued. Men were horrified by the demand of reformers that the drunkenness of a husband be allowed as reason for his wife to divorce him, but Indiana gave in and was followed by other states.

Lydia Maria Child in 1832 published an early comprehensive manifesto of the women's movement, entitled *History of the Condition of Women in All Ages*. Margaret Fuller, queen of all strong-minded women, published in 1845 the definitive book, *Woman in the Nineteenth Century*. In this she not only demanded complete economic, social, and political equality but shifted the blame from her own sex to men for such evils as prostitution. Embodying all that advanced women aspired to, she succeeded in making strong-mindedness seem glamorous. She had been educated by her father as a son would have been, she conducted a brilliant school-salon in Boston for aspiring and accomplished philosophers, and she won the friendship of the inner circle of New England Transcendentalists, for a time editing their rarified journal, *The Dial*. She made a happy marriage to the Italian Count Ossoli, and presented for the contemplation of women and men a career more "romantic" than that of any ethereal heroine. Her program of liberation for the sake of individual self-realization placed the women's movement on the highest plane.

Many clergymen who were liberal on other subjects used the Bible to prove that woman, created belatedly by God from Adam's rib, was ordained by Him to be a man's subordinate. On one occasion clergymen who were disrupting a women's rights convention in Akron, Ohio, were silenced by the noted Negro abolitionist, Sojourner Truth, an old woman who had been born a slave in New York. She said:

> . . . I have ploughed, and planted and gathered into barns, and no man could head me. And ain't I a woman? I have borne thirteen children, and seen them most all sold off to slavery, and when I cried out with my mother's grief, none but Jesus heard me! And ain't I a woman? Then that little man in black there, he says women don't have as much rights as men, because Christ wan't a woman. Where did your Christ come from? From God and a woman. Man had nothing to do with him!

Organizers and Reformers

While a Margaret Fuller and a Sojourner Truth from their diverse backgrounds provided arguments, other leaders proceeded in the thirties and forties to organize thousands of women and a fair sprinkling of men into strong pressure groups. The outstanding organizers were Elizabeth Cady Stanton, Susan B. Anthony, and Lucretia Mott. By the mid-forties, local women's rights societies were active, especially in the Northeast and the West. Most of the New England intellectuals, led by Emerson and William Ellery Channing, supported the women's movement, and some editors, notably Horace Greeley, aided its campaign.

In 1848, Mrs. Stanton and Mrs. Mott called a national convention at Seneca Falls, New York. The delegates adopted a Declaration of Women's Independence modeled with devastating logic on the great document of 1776: "We hold these truths to be self-evident: that all men and women are created equal. . . ." For King George as tyrant, the women substituted "Man." Besides demanding "the institution of a new government" by means of the repeal of all discriminatory laws, and the end of masculine monopoly of trades, professions, and business, the Convention asserted that it was the duty of the women of the country "to secure to themselves their sacred right to the elective franchise." This demand for the vote aroused serious opposition in the Convention and caused some delegates to repudiate the Declaration as too radical. Outside, it stirred up a gale of ridicule, but still the radicals persisted. National conventions were held annually except during the Civil War, when the women suspended their own demands in favor of abolition of slavery, and the historical descent of the Woman Suffrage Amendment to the Constitution (1919) from the Seneca Falls Convention is direct.

The long delay is partly explained by the special effectiveness of ridicule in this area of reform. It was easily directed against Amelia Bloomer, who found the feminine dress of the period—all whaleboned, flounced, and upholstered—a hindrance to her work as postmistress in a New York village. She invented a costume featuring a loose-fitting coat over "Turkish" trousers neatly gathered into shoe tops. The Bloomer costume and short-cut hair were affected by leading feminists until they surrendered to imputation of harem-like morals and such doggerel as this:

> Gibbey, gibbey gab,
> The women had a confab
> And demanded the rights
> To wear the tights
> Gibbey, gibbey gab.

As Miss Anthony remarked, it was impossible to win a man's attention to her argument when he was preoccupied with gazing at her clothes.

Another much-ridiculed movement was launched by Lucy Stone. A graduate of Oberlin and lecturer on abolitionism and women's rights, she and her husband signed a "Protest" immediately after their marriage. This document renounced all the laws giving the husband "injurious and unnatural superiority, investing him with legal powers which no honorable man would exercise, and which no man should possess." To symbolize her legal equality with her husband, the bride kept her maiden name, and she founded the Lucy Stoners' League to encourage other brides to follow her example. Conventional minds could not imagine a successful marriage on this basis, but Mrs. Stone combined a notable career as a reformer with a happy marriage and children.

Professional Women

It was fairly easy for women to break into the teaching profession, and by 1860 women outnumbered men in the elementary schools. The reformers made equal pay with men an important item on their agenda. School boards nevertheless continued to take advantage of the greater readiness of young women and older single women without family obligations to accept jobs at low salary. The women who invaded medicine, the law, and the pulpit had to be endowed with the pioneer's spirit and more talent than the average male competitor. One of the earliest woman graduates of an American medical college, Dr. Elizabeth Blackwell, was allowed to enter Geneva College in New York on the vote of the male students who took it as a joke. She graduated at the head of her class, founded the New York Infirmary for Women and Children in 1857 and staffed it entirely with women, headed a contingent of field nurses during the Civil War, and afterwards was the first woman to be admitted to medical practice in England. The first woman to preside in a pulpit as an ordained clergywoman was Antoinette Brown, who had found even the radical leaders of Oberlin College hard to convince that theology should not be a masculine monopoly.

By a curious paradox, the most successful women authors glorified a sentimentalized version of the romantic heroine who achieved her highest destiny in suffering self-sacrifice for her menfolk and her children. By the fifties the "Starry Sisterhood" of authors dominated the market for popular magazine verse and fiction. Mrs. Lydia Huntley Sigourney, the "Sweet Singer of Hartford," reigned supreme among them. One of them was Sara Willis Parton, who wrote as "Fanny Fern." She was the sister of Nathaniel P. Willis, editor of the profeminist *Home Journal,* and married as her third husband the eminent biographer James Parton. Her writings achieved enormous popularity, but although herself a person of notably independent spirit, she fed her readers models of retiring womanhood.

Sara Josepha Hale, editor of *Godey's Lady's Book,* combined appeals to traditional femininity—especially interest in the latest fashions—with indirect propaganda for women's rights, and was rewarded with the largest subscription list of any magazine of the period. Her brother, while studying at Dartmouth, had instructed her in every lesson as he learned it. For nearly fifty years she subtly conveyed to the readers of *Godey's* that strong-mindedness in women was fashionable, and that the right of women to equality with men was taken for granted by intelligent people. Probably in the long run she was more effective than the unconventional come-outers in converting women themselves to the cause.

LABOR REFORM AND UTOPIAN SOCIALISM

The formation of an industrial working class made Jacksonian America the laboratory of early attempts to solve the problem of the social position of labor in an industrial society. Reformist proposals were nowhere more bewildering in variety, ranging from mild economic unionism to programs for voluntary or forced social revolution. The labor problem is usually treated as a purely economic one involving material standards of living, but there is much reason for believing that the question of social status was equally or more important to the American workman.

Formerly the small scale of business enterprise had made possible personal relations between employers and employees, and there was little caste feeling on either side. No sooner had these relations begun to break down in the face of large-scale factory production, than self-appointed leaders of the working class began to advocate panaceas. The partial successes of labor groups in winning political influence have been noted in connection with the Jackson administration. The leaders were not satisfied, however, with slow gains. They championed various anticapitalist schemes which they firmly believed would bring in the millenium. Meetings evoked endless debates among doctrinaires, including the British crusaders, Robert Dale Owen and Frances Wright. Working-men lost interest in the labor parties and they all died of factionalism by 1834.

Observing this failure, some leaders of the trade unions determined to avoid politics and panaceas and concentrate on strengthening the economic power of labor. They conducted strikes for the ten-hour day with some success. A convention of delegates of city centrals organized in 1834 the first national labor body, the National Trades Union with Ely Moore at its head. This body memorialized Congress and obtained the federal government's concession of a ten-hour day for labor, first in the Philadelphia Navy Yard in 1836, and in 1840 on all federal works.

Strikes continued to be held illegal by the courts until, in 1842, Chief Justice Lemuel Shaw of Massachusetts ruled in Commonwealth vs. Hunt that unions and strikes were not conspiracies but legitimate means to improvement of laboring conditions. This rule was gradually accepted in other states. State governments were also led to enact reforms desired by labor. The leaders of a major party, usually the Democrats, adopted one or another of labor's demands as a means of appealing for votes. The majority of American laborers were not organized in unions, much less in a labor party.

Utopian Communities

In the Jackson period impatient reformers experimented with Socialist alternatives to the capitalist system. Formerly utopian communities in America had been exclusively religious in inspiration. In the 1820's, secular utopianism based on radical social and economic philosophies came to the fore. The greatest utopian Socialist was Robert Owen, owner of textile mills in New Lanark, Scotland, who built for his workers a model com-munity and became convinced that he had found the way to release mankind from the chains of poverty and all other evils. Failing to con-vert British capitalists to his views, he determined to establish in hos-pitable America a community which should provide a model for universal imitation. Membership would be voluntary and existing governments and capitalism would not be overthrown but, so to speak, superseded as the millions would organize new communities and make old institutions empty shells. In its voluntarism and avoidance of direct action against existing institutions, utopian socialism significantly differed from the socialism of Karl Marx.

Owen bought the estate of a German Rappite, religious-communist colony at New Harmony, Indiana, in 1825, and advertised for members. The experiment got under way in an atmosphere of public good will. Daniel Webster said a good word for it. A mixture of farmers, laborers, and middle-class reformers flocked to New Harmony. But the contradiction soon appeared which dogs all socialist communities, voluntary or not. Economic success required centralized control, and the directors sacrificed for the sake of unity the democracy which they claimed would be perfected by economic co-operation. Owen found it distasteful to face the factionalism of his members and turned over management to his son, Robert Dale Owen. Workers left in disgust at the ineffectuality of the reformers and the petty tyranny of the leaders. After two years the Owens abandoned the colony and the colonists abandoned co-operation.

Frances Wright, a wealthy protegée of Lafayette, established in 1825 at Nashoba, Tennessee, a variation of Owenism designed to solve the problem of Negro slavery. Slaves were purchased and set to work on a great plantation to earn their purchase price, after which they were to be freed and the money used to buy another group. But the slaves found that petty tyranny at Nashoba was as bad as on an ordinary plantation, and that the management was worse. Fanny Wright gave up and made herself a leading trumpeter of radicalism to the American people. For a woman to mount the lecture platform, edit newspapers, and found schools was remarkable enough, but Miss Wright, short-haired, statuesquely beautiful and possessed of genuine talents, taught free thought in religion, free love, birth control, and freedom of children from parental control.

Others adopted a new variety of socialism originated by the Frenchman, Charles Fourier. He recommended that people should band together in "phalanxes" to supersede family life, build model communities rather resembling army barracks, institute a complicated system of government for themselves, and share the products of their labor. He worked out his plan in the utmost detail. It was widely propagated in the United States by Albert Brisbane in a book, *Social Destiny of Man* (1840). Some forty "phalancteries" were founded in the northern states. The most famous convert was Horace Greeley, who for a time promoted Fourierism in his *New York Tribune* along with all manner of other reformist ideas. He liked to spend his Saturday afternoons sampling socialism by pitching hay for a Fourierist community near Red Bank, New Jersey.

The most famous utopian community was Brook Farm near Boston. It was founded in 1841 by George Ripley, a Unitarian minister, and numbered Nathaniel Hawthorne, Charles A. Dana, and George William Curtis among its members. Margaret Fuller was a tempestuous visitor. It began in an arcadian atmosphere of devotion to the arts and conversation, with brief sessions of manual farm labor according to personal tastes to provide necessities. For several years the Brook Farmers represented the high noon of New England social idealism, although Emerson and Thoreau remained skeptical. Then members drifted away and an attempt to organize more strictly as a Fourierist community was cut short when a fire burned the phalanctery. Hawthorne gently satirized the experiment in a novel, *The Blithedale Romance*. Along with Brook Farm, all the Fourier communities died out by 1860. Icarian communities in Texas and Illinois on the plan set forth in Etienne Cabet's *Voyage en Icarie* fared no better. Only socialist communities with a religious basis, like the Shakers and the Mormons, not to mention Roman Catholic and Episcopalian monastic groups, enjoyed lengthy histories of success. The conclusion was inescapable that secular Americans preferred an economy salted with individualism and the stimulating mixture of rewards and risks provided by the competitive system.

Lesser forms of noncapitalist economic organization were tried, particularly by labor groups during depressions. Josiah Warren developed out of his anarchistic view of the evils of government and private ownership a program of economic co-operatives whereby labor should abolish both. Labor unions, frustrated in attempts to make gains during the Depression of 1837, turned to Warren's scheme for consumers' and producers' co-operatives. The New England Protective Union was established in 1845 to centralize purchases for retail co-operatives. Most of the co-operatives foundered for lack of capital and managerial talent; and with the revival of prosperity laborers lost interest. The Scandinavian immigrants of the Northwest turned out to be the first successful conductors of co-operatives.

The Homestead Movement

The reformist cause that won the most ardent support of American laborers during the Jackson era was the homestead movement. George H. Evans was the chief prophet of free land as the solution of laboring men's problems. An Englishman who came to the United States during the twenties, he edited a labor newspaper and emerged from the failure of the Workingmen's Party with the conviction that western land provided the means for workers to escape from the evils of industrialism. "Our refuge is upon the soil, in all its freshness and fertility—our heritage is on the Public Domain, in all its boundless wealth and infinite variety." Man, Evans argued, has a natural and unalienable right to land just as he has a right to air, water, and sunlight. The public lands should be given in family plots to the landless, who were mostly laborers, and they should be forbidden to sell or mortgage their farms. This would transform the propertyless of the next thousand years into prosperous, independent farmers.

This program elaborated Jefferson's vision of how best to build happiness in a free republic, and its popularity marked a revulsion against the first raw impact of the Industrial Revolution. Evans alone among the radical Jacksonian intellectuals found wide support among workers. Loosely organized by him as Agrarians, they formed a disruptive left wing of both major political parties and, from 1848 to 1856, the separate Free Soil Party which held the balance of power in many eastern cities.

The first Homestead Bill was introduced in Congress in 1846 by Andrew Johnson, a tailor of Tennessee who would suceed Abraham Lincoln as President, and annually thereafter the proposal was pushed in Congress. Southern opposition to the homestead movement led Northern labor to turn to abolitionism. The idea of Evans was expanded into the final slogan of the Free Soil Party: "Free Soil, Free Land, Free Labor, Free Men." Only after the Homestead Act was passed by the Republican Party of Lincoln did laborers learn that for a laborer to turn farmer more was required than free land. He needed capital for transportation, farm implements, and livestock, besides food for his family and seed for a year or more until he could bring in a good crop. Furthermore, once urbanized, people rarely wished to revert to farm life. Few natives or immigrants who took jobs in the new factories ever turned pioneers. The power of the homestead idea over the imagination of workingmen during the decades before the Civil War nevertheless helped to hold the West for free farmers against the threat of slave labor, and the homestead movement was an effective expression of labor's reformist idealism.

Temperance, Humanitarianism, World Peace

Drinking in early America was probably no more common than in the countries from which Americans had migrated, with the exception that at the frontier hard liquor was a staple of diet compensating for deficiencies of food and of heat and clothing in winter. Foreign authors of travel books stressed American drunkenness as one more evidence that emigration meant degeneration. For sheer variety American intoxicants were more impressive than those of any European nation, precisely because each immigrant group added its favorite beverages to the resources of the American grog shop, and Americans developed their own varieties of whiskey. Pennsylvania rye figured in the Whiskey Rebellion of Washington's time, and the most famous corn whiskey was "bourbon" —named for a county in Kentucky. Rum never regained the position it held in colonial times, but imported wines continued in favor, while English ales gave way to German lager beer, apple cider, and domestic wines. Cheapness, however, made whiskey the almost universal drink. Some kind of alcoholic beverage was kept in supply by most families; shops and taverns in the cities and inns in the country served alcoholic drinks with or without meals; and they were an obligatory sign of domestic hospitality and of good fellowship on such occasions as ordinations, barn-raisings, and election campaigns.

American drinking increased in the early nineteenth century. The overt attack on it began in New England among preachers and reformers; it quickly extended to western areas to which New England migration was heavy, and was supported by many in the South. At first drunkenness rather than drinking was condemned. Hundreds of local temperance societies sent delegates to Philadelphia for a national convention in 1833. Out of this grew the federated American Temperance Union. Temperance publications soon outnumbered those devoted to any other reform. This cause first brought women to the lecture platform because their sufferings at the hands of drunken husbands were thought to give them a peculiar right to be heard. Children were enlisted as in the medieval crusades, the "Cold Water Army" of children staging great processions.

One group of reformers insisted on total abstinence, while conservatives held out for a campaign against distilled liquors alone, but the "teetotalers" won control of the movement by 1840. During the next decade the most sensational agitation was conducted by the Washingtonians, who were reformed drunkards. Their lurid autobiographies sometimes made drink and vice more fascinating than repulsive, but it was found that harrowing published narratives, pictures, and public interviews won larger audiences than theoretical arguments. Such eminent authors as Oliver Wendell Holmes and John Greenleaf Whittier contributed to the propaganda, but the most popular writings were heart-wringing stories by Lydia Sigourney and *Ten Nights in a Bar-Room* (1854) by Timothy Shay Arthur.

Voluntary abstinence won many converts but barrooms continued to flourish, and the majority of thirsts were not slaked by cold water, fruit and root juices, or even the synthetic fizz of carbonated beverages which were invented at this time. Those who would not abstain voluntarily were clearly enslaved by the "Demon" and must be liberated by force. Neal Dow of Maine was the greatest spokesman of the early prohibition movement. In 1851, his state passed a prohibition law. Other New England states followed suit, and the western centers of New England influence became in time the chief bases of the national prohibition movement. Thus the old Puritan passion for publicly enforced righteousness found new expression.

If the wisdom of moving beyond temperance to teetotalism and beyond that to prohibition by law now seems dubious, the agitation of the Jacksonian era must be credited with a beneficial change in American attitudes towards intoxication. Formerly drunkenness had been looked upon as laughable; now it was looked upon as ill-mannered and shameful. Social disapproval turned out to be a powerful corrective. Drinking by women and children virtually ceased and in this respect Americans were well in advance of Europeans. At the same time, improved diet and heating facilities in the home reduced the need for liquor; and there was a suspicious increase in the alcohol content and popularity of "patent medi-cines."

Relieving the Unfortunate

Attitudes toward the insane and other unfortunates also radically changed. Formerly persons afflicted by mental illness were either thrown into prisons indiscriminately with normal persons or segregated in asylums where wardens treated them barbarously or, what was most often the case, they were left as hopeless burdens on their families. Dorothea L. Dix made herself the special champion of the insane. Her Quaker train-ing made her sensitive to the sufferings of every class of unfortunates, and her work in the prison of Charlestown, Massachusetts, filled her with pity and indignation. She forced the public and legislators to listen to her message, and the awakening of the humanitarian conscience favored her cause. Private and public bodies reorganized existing asylums and established new ones on better principles. Such an institution as "The Retreat" in Brattleboro, Vermont, signified the new attitude in its name, and it was one of the first in the world to be founded on the principle that insanity is a disease which may be alleviated if not cured by kind-ness and therapy.

Ordinary prisoners and paupers also commanded the attention of Dorothea Dix and many other reformers. Such elementary improvements were won as separation of men and women prisoners, privacy in cells, abolition of the worst forms of physical punishment, and the use of constructive work as a means of rehabilitation rather than hard labor as punishment. The greatest achievement in public opinion was the popu-larization of the principle that a prison should be operated not merely to punish criminals but to reform them. Experiments were carried out at model prisons like that of New York at Auburn, which was studied by reformers of other states and of Europe.

Pauperism had formerly been negligible in the United States, but it grew with urbanization and, as indentured servitude fell into disuse, with the increase of penniless immigrants who became public charges. The custom of letting-out paupers to a contractor who could make a profit by neglecting his charges yielded slowly to public demands for humane treatment.

Samuel Gridley Howe, a wealthy Boston doctor, made the problems of the blind his special province. He devised means of communication for the deaf, dumb, and blind Laura Bridgman, and in 1832 founded the great Perkins Institution for the Blind. There were other expressions of the new sensitivity to suffering, but so long as most Americans lived on farms, the aged and unfortunate were mostly cared for by their families. The whole array of modern problems associated with social wel-fare came only dimly into view during this period.

Crusaders for Peace

Humanitarianism, like most new faiths, was subject to fanaticism. Few today would call fanatical the movements that got under way at this time to abolish capital punishment, to prevent dueling and eye-gouging matches, to prohibit cruelty to animals, cock-fighting, and animal-baiting. But hypersensitive spirits moved onwards from vegetarianism based on pity for animals to agitation against killing insects and chopping down trees because they, too, had lives and destinies to fulfill. The sentimentality that marred so much of the literature of this period had its counterpart in reformist thought. Enormous energies were poured into experiments to improve man and society, and numerous visionaries roamed the land castigating old habits and calling upon the people to march forthwith into the new Jerusalem. Surprisingly few of their programs proved to be dangerous or merely absurd, and so many were usable that the history of social reform in subsequent decades amounts to little more than the effectuation of principles first pronounced in Jacksonian times.

The movement to abolish slavery, whose importance merits treatment in separate chapters, combined admirable and fanatical tendencies in a mixture more portentous for the immediate fate of the nation than any other. The movement for world peace which got under way at the same time was wholly free of fanaticism but equally portentous for the long future of the nation. Formerly action against war had been limited to individual pacifism on religious grounds among such groups as the Quakers, to the schemes of philosophers, and to the diplomacy of statesmen who did not enlist the support of the people themselves. The peace movement that originated in the United States shortly after the War of 1812 was new in that it enlisted the ideas and methods of democracy. The logic was simple and compelling: the ravages of war bear hardest on the mass of plain people, therefore a society organized by and for them must abolish war; and democratic institutions provide the technique for the just and peaceful settlement of disputes within a nation, therefore similar international institutions will serve the same function among the nations. An implied premise was that all nations must be democracies. Failing this, the democratic program for world peace has foundered time and again.

When nearly a quarter-century of world war ended in 1815, men everywhere longed to avoid a recurrence. David Low Dodge was one of many religious pacifists who saw that private protest was not enough. In August 1815, he organized the first peace society on lines suggested by Noah Worcester of New England in his book of December 1814, entitled, *The Solemn Review of the Custom of War, Showing That War*

Is the Effect of Popular Delusion, and Proposing a Remedy. The book quickly ran through five editions as people eagerly read this indictment of the wars of history and proposal for a confederation of nations and a high court of international justice. The significance of Worcester's proposal is that he saw the American compromise between state and national sovereignties as a model for relations between national governments and a new international government. The latter should enforce peace and co-operation among the nations as the American federal government did among the states; and similarly he proposed to imitate in an international government the American division of legislative, judicial, and executive powers as a safeguard against tyranny. This work continued to be influential for a century until the League of Nations and the United Nations attempted to realize his dream.

William Ellery Channing in 1815 organized the Massachusetts Peace Society. Under Worcester's editorship, this group published a periodical, the *Friend of Peace*, which urged the formation of peace societies everywhere. The technique of popular propaganda and pressure groups to secure governmental action for peace was a new thing in the world and expressed the democratic faith of the new generation.

William Ladd, a wealthy graduate of Harvard, was inspired by Worcester's writings to dedicate his life and fortune to the peace crusade. In 1828, he organized in the home of David Low Dodge the American Peace Society as a national federation of the local groups. Ladd avoided doctrinal quarrels between those who would condemn all wars and those who would make exceptions in favor of defensive wars. He invited all friends of peace to work to eliminate offensive wars first. The propaganda of the Society spread far and wide, and during the thirties peace became the passion of numerous Americans.

The Learned Blacksmith

Extremists captured control of the American Peace Society in 1837. William Lloyd Garrison and other abolitionists came out for absolute condemnation of all war; they preached moral pacifism and political anarchism. During the next years the peace crusade was saved from impotence by Elihu Burritt, Ladd's successor, and the most attractive reformer of the period. Combining a Christ-like purity of purpose with a genius for practical affairs, "The Learned Blacksmith" was a counterpart among private leaders of Abraham Lincoln among statesmen. Born to poverty in Connecticut, he apprenticed himself to the forge and educated himself in languages and history by propping his books alongside his anvil. Burritt remained all his life a workman, teaching laborers the dignity of their calling while showing how it could be combined with mental culture and civic pursuits.

His extraordinary knowledge of foreign languages and cultures led him to gain a lofty conception of the brotherhood and interdependence of all peoples. He schooled himself in practical propaganda during the Anglo-American crisis over Oregon. Burritt organized "people's diplomacy," a concert of agitation against war by crusaders in the United States and England. Leaflets called "Olive Leaves" were exchanged between the two peoples, English and American cities exchanged "Friendly Addresses," business and labor groups on both sides joined in expressions·of common desire to avoid war, and mass meetings sent resolutions to the two governments demanding a peaceful settlement. Burritt edited the *Advocate of Peace and Universal Brotherhood,* acted as middleman in the international exchanges, and personally distributed propagandist literature on railroads, canals, and street corners.

It would be too much to say that the peaceful compromise of the Oregon dispute in 1846 was caused by Burritt's "people's diplomacy," but this had some effect, and it was a significant expression of the connection between democracy and peace. Burritt thereafter worked to strengthen popular international ties. He was received with enthusiasm in England and organized there the League of Universal Brotherhood. The revolutions of 1848 in their early stages manifested radical attitudes against war. Burritt quickly moved to capitalize the favorable situation by calling international peace conferences which he hoped would become instruments for the peaceful settlement of international disputes. Four international conferences of the League of Universal Brotherhood were held from 1848 to 1852 with such personages as Victor Hugo and John Bright as speakers. An American blacksmith leading the international movement which promised so much for humanity is symbolical of Jacksonian democracy.

The peace crusade temporarily failed in the general failure of the revolutions of 1848. Reaction set in when monarchs and upper classes recovered power by whipping up hatred of foreigners. Liberal nationalism went down to defeat in a new cycle of wars. The problem of slavery produced a comparable defeat in the United States. The crusaders were torn between their hatred of war and their hatred of slavery. Most of them, including Burritt, supported the Union when the war came. Theodore Parker wrote to a friend: "I think we should agree about war. I hate it, deplore it, but yet see its necessity. All the great charters of humanity have been writ in blood, and must continue to be for some centuries."

So the Civil War swallowed up another of the great Jacksonian reform movements. It would be a long day before Americans would recover the visions of Dodge, Worcester, Ladd, and Burritt and again go to work to build peace on earth,

CHAPTER 15

Cultural Achievements in a Democratic Era, 1820-1850

NO SOONER HAD EUROPEAN CONSERVATIVES GIVEN UP predicting the imminent collapse of the American Republic than they turned to equally confident predictions that it would make no notable contributions to human culture. The keynote was struck at the opening of the period by an Englishman, the Reverend Sidney Smith, in his contemptuous query of 1820: "In the four quarters of the globe, who reads an American book? or goes to an American play? or looks at an American picture or statue?" Americans eagerly accepted this challenge. Economic independence was rapidly following upon political independence. Now they set out on a still more difficult enterprise: to establish their cultural independence.

RELIGIOUS FERMENT

Until after the Civil War, religion continued to provide the dominant spiritual, intellectual, and emotional experience of most Americans. The eighteenth-century drift away from Christianity ceased. Their individualism and democracy did not lead the people away from religion; rather, the mass of them turned with intensified fervor to evangelicalism, which asserted that salvation was available for all. While the cool Unitarian of Boston shrank from the camp-meeting spirit, he agreed with the evangelicals that man and his life on earth are good, or at least may become so. The most extreme form of the old idea, the Calvinist doctrine of total depravity, gave way to extreme forms of faith in progress, human and social perfectibility, and the overwhelming supremacy of goodness. The spark of divinity in man to which every great creed has borne witness was proclaimed to be a triumphant flame.

261

Unitarianism and Universalism

It has been said that after the upper-class Federalists of New England had rejected the democracy of Jefferson and the French Revolution as a political faith, they accepted it as a religious faith. Unitarianism asserted that God is all love and no wrath, that man is all virtue and no sin, and that human reason is sufficient to distinguish truth from error. If revelation, miracles, and atonement were not rejected by the Unitarians, they were politely ignored. William Ellery Channing, Boston's great prophet of the new dispensation, preached that religion is no more or less than "the adoration of goodness." Whole congregations of the Episcopalian, Congregational, and Presbyterian churches went over to Unitarianism until by 1830 most of the wealthy and educated classes of New England had abandoned the old orthodoxy.

Still the moral earnestness of Puritanism persisted among the New England élite as their famous conscience continued to require untiring good works. The typical Boston capitalist was a Unitarian and a philanthropist; the typical Boston intellectual was a Unitarian and a reformer. Chilly respectability and rationality made Unitarianism unattractive to most people, but the philanthropists and reformers of Boston and its environs were accepted East and West as models of civic responsibility, personal integrity, and lofty vision. Furthermore, it was this sector of American society that produced the first great literary and cultural flowering in the Republic. The Boston influence was rejected only in the South, where it was considered synonymous with self-righteous hypocrisy.

Similar to Unitarianism in theology was Universalism, whose central dogmas were literal denial of hell and assurance of universal salvation. This genial faith spread to some extent among the farmers of New England and the West but never displaced the evangelical faiths of the majority.

Transcendentalism

The most brilliant and ardent young intellectuals of New England found Unitarianism cold to their taste. In rejecting instinct, emotion, and mysticism, Unitarianism seemed better suited to businessmen than to poets. Without reviving orthodoxy or even rejecting the basic doctrines of Unitarianism, a group of enthusiasts revolted against its prosaic attitudes and attempted to create a faith which should satisfy man's imaginative as well as his rational and ethical faculties. Led by Ralph Waldo Emerson, they asserted the transcendent reality of the supernatural and its existence in the natural. They were so far from wishing to create an organized religion that their only "church" was the short-lived Transcendental Club which met occasionally for conversational communion. The membership never numbered more than a dozen, but among those present at one or another symposium were Emerson, William Ellery Channing and his nephew William Henry Channing, Bronson Alcott, Theodore Parker, Henry David Thoreau, Nathaniel Hawthorne, Margaret Fuller, James Freeman Clarke, and George Bancroft. By their writings the influence of the Transcendentalists became nationally and internationally important. Their magazine, the *Dial*, lasted only from 1840 to 1844. Organization was not the forte of these individualists.

Transcendentalism drew upon Plato's ancient Greek and Kant's modern German philosophic idealism, the Oriental mysticism of the *Baghavad Gita*, Christian medieval mysticism, the French revolutionary thought of Rousseau, and the contemporary English literary romanticism of Wordsworth and Carlyle. The waters of all these streams were, however, mixed into a peculiarly American draught. Mystical experience had formerly been regarded as reserved for the spiritual élite, but the Transcendentalists declared that Everyman is endowed with spiritual power, and is in fact divine. By trusting his instinct he can know truth, and by acting on inspiration he can express truth, as surely as any saint. Formerly saints had been expected to purify themselves of evil and worldly dross by means of spiritual exercises; the Transcendentalists declared that evil is an illusion, that Everyman can purify himself and the world of dross by listening to and acting upon his divine inner voice. Thus these extraordinary descendants of the Puritans provided the sanction of Old-World philosophy and mysticism for the American dream of democracy.

Emerson defined the Transcendentalist as follows:

He believes in miracles, in the perpetual openness of the human mind to the new influx of light and power; he believes in inspiration and ecstasy. He wishes that the spiritual principle should be suffered to demonstrate itself to the end, in all possible applications to the state of man.

Emerson himself did not undertake direct action for social reform, believing his mission to be that of the scholar and teacher. In his essay, "Self-Reliance," and dozens of other popular sermons which he delivered from the lecture platforms of the North, he taught the new gospel that individualism and holiness, democracy and spiritual greatness, social reform and the divine plan, were all identical. The public became deeply reverent of the Concord philosopher as its greatest teacher. If his conception of the "Over-Soul" was too Oriental for prosaic American minds, if his charge of self-reliance was distorted by some into a sanction for materialistic ruthlessness, and if his refusal to admit the reality of evil encouraged the tendency of Americans to shallow optimism, nevertheless Emerson's great influence on his countrymen was on the whole a fruitful one. His was the noblest formulation of the meaning and promise of the American experiment. Its fundamental paradox, which is so baffling to foreign observers, the juxtaposition of material preoccupations and idealism, he resolved in a synthesis of practical spirituality.

Evangelicalism

Although the New England intellectuals and the preachers of evangelical Protestantism seem at first glance to have had nothing in common, both expressed the crusading optimism of the times. Following the Great Awakening of the eighteenth century, revivalism was endemic until it became epidemic in the Great Revival of the first decade of the new century and periodically thereafter. The Baptists and the Methodists became the largest organized religions in America, expanding with the frontier. The Baptists were more given to theological controversy, insisting on adult baptism by total immersion, while the Methodists stressed the "creedless religion of the heart." Both held that any individual might find salvation by renouncing sin and submitting to Jesus. Violently emotional preaching induced the crisis of conversion, and only that kind of preaching held much meaning for frontiersmen.

The Congregational and Presbyterian churches were leaders in the effort to bring higher education and general culture to the West, but their emphasis on an educated clergy put them at a disadvantage in new districts. The Westerner was inured to a rough, lonely life of physical dangers and privations, he was highly susceptible to oratory and crowd emotions, and he responded violently to preaching of hell-fire and salvation by men like himself. Pious people who had been left behind in the East were aroused by accounts of the godless state of the West and poured out money for missionary work. Many preachers were sent from New England to follow migrants into western New York. Religious excitement became almost universal there, producing an amazing crop of new prophets, revelations, and sects and causing the district to merit the name of "The Burnt-Over Region."

The camp meeting became the most striking feature of Western religion. In a forest clearing, for days and nights without a stop, preachers spelled each other crying defiance at Satan and pleading with sinners to yield to Jesus. Whole families from miles around joined in frenzied longing for the lightning of conversion to strike them. The most popular preachers presided over scenes of mass hysteria, of weeping, screaming, writhing on the ground, and—highest sign of grace—pentecostal "speaking in tongues." Certain preachers became famous for their ability to elicit "the jerks," the "barking exercise," and "holy laughter." These were regarded as the final throes of Satan evicted from the sinner's soul.

Revivalism encouraged the subdivision of older sects and the sprouting of many new ones. Factions split away from conservative churches in favor of livelier experience. The episcopal organization of the Methodists and their reluctance to quarrel over fine points of theology preserved them from schisms better than the Baptists, whose love of theology and extreme individualism produced the bewildering variety of Hard-Shell Baptists, Soft-Shell Baptists, Particular Baptists, General Baptists, United Baptists, Primitive Baptists, Free-Will Baptists, Disciples of Christ, and others. America became the home of more different Christian sects than any other country in the world.

Millenialism and Spiritualism

Some of them were quite original, almost meriting the name of American religions. Vermont was a breeding ground of prophets and cults, but most of them moved west. The Green Mountains seemed to encourage more eccentricity than ordinary Vermonters would tolerate. William Miller, a farmer of Poultney, Vermont, calculated on the basis of hints in prophetic books of the Bible that the Second Coming of Christ would occur in 1843. His followers spread the message through the frontier country of northern New England and western New York; they even attracted great crowds in cities and built the Millenial Tabernacle in Boston. The burden of Millerite preaching was that only believers would ascend to heaven on the last day of time. When 1843 passed, the leaders confessed a slight miscalculation and named October 22, 1844, as the actual date. Excitement led in some cases to insanity and suicide. Adventists gave away all their property except white ascension robes and gathered on hilltops on the evening of October 21. Disbelievers jeered and riots occurred in several cities. The dawn of October 23 ended Millerism, but a few Adventists, while denying that the exact date could be predicted, continued to preach that the Second Coming was very near. They settled down as the Seventh Day Adventist Church.

For those who wished to penetrate the spiritual world beyond time, Spiritualism offered a technique that enthralled many Americans in the years following the Millerite disappointment. Interest in the mystical teachings of Emmanuel Swedenborg culminated in the establishment of many small churches and the conversion of educated persons as notable as the elder Henry James. More palpable communion with the other world was provided by mediums. Most famous of these were the Fox sisters, Maggie and Katie, daughters of an upstate New York farmer, who convinced many that they could communicate with sundry spirits by means of table rappings. Horace Greeley's love of new ideas overcame his skepticism; he took the Fox sisters into his home and only objected that it was boring to wait in a dark room for hours on the chance that someone's dead grandfather would make "dull music." The type of message that came from the other world ("Tell Tabitha that her dear dead Aunt Sue misses her gooseberry jell") did not disillusion believers with the glories of spiritual revelation. Nor did the admission by the Fox sisters, following a family spat, that the rappings had been produced by their double-jointed toes, make many apostates. For decades Spiritualist mediums could be found in almost every town. On a somewhat lower plane of pretension, science and pseudo-science gave birth to cults of mesmerism or hypnotism, animal magnetism, and phrenology. These raveled edges of the fabric of Jacksonian democracy suggested that optimism could conquer reason.

The Mormons

Most impressive of the new faiths was that of the Mormon Church of Latter-Day Saints. Its founder, Joseph Smith, was a homespun prophet, the movement was saturated with millenialism, and it supported the most exotic social institution imaginable—polygamy. Born in Vermont in 1808, Smith at an early age moved to Palmyra, New York, in the heart of the Burnt-Over Region. His father was indigent and his mother imbued her children with dreams of holy visions and miracles. Young Joseph became engrossed with the possibility of finding buried treasure by means of the diviner's traditional forked switch. He found a "magic peek stone" which he believed bestowed special powers on its owner. He attended revival meetings but one day Jesus and God the Father appeared to him and denounced all existing religions as false. His magic stone led him to the hiding place of "golden plates" on which were written in a strange language—translatable with the aid of two stones used as spectacles, Urim and Thummin—a tale which Smith published in 1830 as a new revelation, *The Book of Mormon*. Containing a mixture of Indian legends, religious dogma, and current economic, social, and political ideas in "biblical" language, it won converts very slowly. Joseph organized a few persons into a new church but his neighbors could not believe he was divinely chosen.

The Smith family moved to the Western Reserve in Ohio, and there the receptivity of Westerners and skilled work by several practical men, including Brigham Young, brought success. Joseph Smith was pictured as the prophet of a revived apostolic group. He ended disputes among his lieutenants by producing new revelations, decreed that converts must turn over their goods to him in favor of communism, promised that the imminent millenium would bring a division of the world's riches among the faithful, and hinted that, like the patriarchs of Israel, the elders of the new Church were entitled to a plurality of wives. Polygamy and sharp financial practices caused antagonism against the "saints," but persecution merely strengthened the faith of a hard core of followers. Smith removed his scattered bands from settled areas and organized a state of his own at Nauvoo, under charter from the government of Illinois. Prosperity and thousands of converts followed. Recruits came from as far away as England. The prophet ruled as dictator, authorized polygamy for himself and his closest associates, and proposed himself in 1844 for President of the United States.

Smith overreached himself when he attempted to acquire for himself the wife of one of his associates and violently suppressed as schismatics some who resisted him. Rumors of strange goings-on in the "City of the Saints" led to action by the Illinois authorities, but before Smith could be tried he and his brother were murdered in jail by a mob. Brigham Young made himself successor of the prophet and proved to be one of the greatest leaders of Western history. He organized the epic trek to the region of the Great Salt Lake where, despite incredible hardship, the semicommunist theocracy called the "State of Deseret" became the prosperous Zion of a hundred thousand Mormons.

After the United States acquired title to the Mormon territory in the Treaty with Mexico, Congress organized it as the Territory of Utah (1850). There followed a struggle between Young and the federal authorities which culminated in the bloodless "Mormon War" of 1858. A compromise left Young in charge of the Church, which controlled virtually all secular as well as religious affairs, while the Church recognized the authority of the federal Constitution and laws. A federal enactment against polygamy was eventually obeyed by the elders, and communism gradually gave way to private ownership of property. The Mormons remain to this day the distinctive element in the population of Utah. The extraordinary sturdiness of character of the pioneers and their descendants and their achievements in building a great state have overcome prejudices and made their checkered history a romantic memory.

The Shakers

Mormonism was the most successful of numerous Western experiments in religious communism, while the Shakers were the most prosperous and longest-lived Eastern group. Their movement was hardly distinguishable from the Society of Friends but for "agitations of the body." These induced prophetic trances and were ritualized in a sacred dance whereby worship was expressed by the body as well as the soul and sin was shaken out of both. "Mother Ann" Lee, the illiterate daughter of an

English blacksmith, after an unhappy experience of marriage joined the Shaking Quakers in 1758, experienced revelations, and made herself leader of a small group who in 1774 sought refuge from persecution by coming to the New World. The little band settled near Albany, New York, and presently made Mount Lebanon their headquarters. From there branch settlements were organized in almost every state from Maine to Kentucky. Mother Ann taught that Christ had represented only the masculine aspect of Divinity; she herself, the Second Incarnation, represented the feminine aspect. Celibacy was required of all her followers. As the sect grew, members were gathered into new "families" of ten to fifty men and women who shared ownership of worldly goods and worshipped and labored together with great devotion.

The Shakers believed that their families were the first islands of heaven on earth. Although Charles Dickens remarked that Shaker life was fearfully drab, no observer of their communities denied that they lived up to their conception of paradise as a bee-hive ruled by faith, honesty, charity, simplicity, and hard work. Competent leaders succeeded Mother Ann upon her death in 1784, many converts were won during the religious excitements of the Great Revival, and by 1830 more than a dozen prosperous communities under the benevolent dictatorship of the elders and eldresses of Mount Lebanon represented the highest achievement of Protestant monasticism in America. Their slogan, "Hands to work and hearts to God," found expression in agricultural and handicraft products, especially seeds and furniture, which were probably never matched for quality in the country. The designs of their houses, furniture, and tools were a triumph of esthetic simplicity. The virtue of their lives and the respect of their neighbors were such that a suspicious legislative committee of New York state made a report which was a vindication.

For a few years in the late thirties, the Shakers' formalized dance dissolved in a revival of pentecostal hysteria, spiritualist mediumship, gifts of song in gibberish, the climbing of real mountains to receive spiritual gifts of jewels, and exercises such as the "Midnight Cry" to worship. In later decades the Shakers became more sedate and conversions fell off. In our own time the last members of the few remaining communities are too aged to maintain the family dwellings and vast barns or to worship in the assembly halls, which, like medieval monastics, they had built for the ages.

SCIENCE AND PHILOSOPHY

While Emerson bade Americans to "hitch their wagons to the star" of idealism, President John Quincy Adams bade them to build observatories and contribute to knowledge of astronomy. "We have neither observatory nor observer upon our half of the globe and the earth revolves in perpetual darkness to our unsearching eyes," he said. Adams mourned that Americans received new discoveries "second-hand from Europe" and demanded that they return "light for light." But they did not begin to do so until the expansion of maritime commerce created a utilitarian need for accurate astronomical knowledge as an aid to navigation. Many governmental contributions to scientific knowledge resulted from the United States Exploring Expedition of 1838-1842, commanded by Lieutenant Charles Wilkes, which studied the coasts of the American hemisphere and South Atlantic and Pacific islands. Civilian geologists, biologists, ethnologists, and botanists attached to the Expedition collected materials so valuable that Congress provided for them the United States National Museum and the United States Botanical Garden. The Naval Observatory was founded in 1844 to conduct astronomical studies in aid of navigation. Perhaps the most eminent scientist in government employ during the period was a naval officer, Matthew Fontaine Maury of Virginia, a brilliant oceanographer whose studies of winds and currents pointed to more advantageous sailing routes. After the success of the Wilkes Expedition, lesser expeditions engaged in similar work, and even Matthew C. Perry's commercial-political expedition to Japan in 1852-1853 included a talented corps of scientists.

Pure Science

Federal sponsorship of pure research came about somewhat accidentally. James Smithson, an English aristocrat and scientist, decided that the rising republic of the West should become the home of scientific learning. He bequeathed in his will the princely sum of £100,000 to the federal government to be used for the advancement and diffusion of knowledge. Science seemed the best means of using the bequest, because it paid the most practical dividends. Accordingly, Congress in 1846 established the Smithsonian Institution to conduct original research and to spread knowledge by means of a library and museum. Soon the foundation became a world center of work in physics, archeology, and ethnology, and a clearing-house for knowledge in all fields. Its Early Victorian Gothic building in Washington also became a mecca of museum-goers.

Most scientists attached themselves to colleges and universities, which were rapidly expanding their instruction in the physical and biological fields. Benjamin Silliman was the greatest pioneer of scientific studies in American colleges. Early in the century he created an important place for them in the curriculum of Yale, which took leadership in supporting a faculty of scientific researchers as well as teachers. There Willard Gibbs worked as a virtual recluse, making the great discoveries in pure mathematics that lie at the basis of modern theoretical physics. Harvard and other colleges were not far behind Yale in supporting science, and new institutions like Rensselaer Polytechnic Institute and the Franklin Institute were exclusively devoted to scientific and technological studies. The *American Journal of Science,* founded in 1818 by Silliman as an organ for "original American contributions," was actually devoted to co-operation with European scientists. In 1846, the organizing work of the period was climaxed by the founding of the American Association for the Advancement of Science as the professional agency for all fields.

A strong spirit of nationalism inspired the thinking of many scientists, and more so the interest of the public. In the spirit and tradition of Jefferson's *Notes on Virginia,* American geology, flora, and fauna were glorified to refute the sneer of the Frenchman, Buffon, that nature degenerated in America. Textbooks presenting New- rather than Old-World data were enthusiastically received. By 1850, it was proclaimed with some justification that the dependence of American scientists on European teachers had ended. The work of a galaxy of American scientists was admiringly studied abroad. But the career of one of the most eminent of them, Louis Agassiz, a Swiss who came to Harvard in 1846, transcended national boundaries. He revolutionized the study of zoology from arid concern with classification to laboratory study of comparative anatomy. In geology he concentrated on the midwestern prairies and proposed the fruitful glacial hypothesis. Although his religious faith in repeated creations by God was proof against Darwin's evolutionary theory, Agassiz's researches in several respects anticipated the great Englishman's.

Medicine

Striking advances in medical science, education, and practice during this period reflected the new humanitarian concern to relieve human suffering. Public prejudice which had opposed vaccination and produced riots against lecturers on anatomy died out. Twenty-seven new medical colleges were founded between 1810 and 1840, as well as many medical journals, and in 1847 the leading professional body, the American Medical Association, was founded. Quackery was reduced by systems of state licenses for doctors and dentists, though enforcement remained lax for several generations. The *United States Pharmacopoeia,* prepared in 1802 by state medical societies, was accepted as the national authority. American technical ingenuity brought about that boon to humanity, anesthesia. Dr. Crawford W. Long of Georgia performed eight operations under ether between 1842 and 1846, though he did not publish any account of them until 1849. Dr. William T. Morton, who removed a vascular tumor in Massachusetts General Hospital in 1846 under anesthetic, was the first to publicize his discovery. The French Academy of Medicine awarded a prize for this American development.

Epidemics of cholera, typhoid fever, typhus, and smallpox grew more severe with the spread of city slums. Public-health services were quite inadequate until after the Civil War. A beginning in the knowledge of contagion was made by the eminent poet and doctor, Oliver Wendell Holmes, in his report of 1843 entitled, *Contagiousness of Puerperal Fever*. Dramatic pioneer studies of digestion were made by an alert Army doctor, William Beaumont. He induced a Canadian, Alexis St. Martin, who had suffered a wound in the wall of his stomach that healed without closing, to accompany him on duty in Michigan and Wisconsin and allow him to make prolonged observations. On these he based a revolutionary publication in 1833 on the chemistry and physiology of digestion. For every Holmes or Beaumont, however, dozens of poorly educated and occasionally unscrupulous doctors and quacks continued to practice. The public furthermore demanded panaceas, absorbed untold gallons of dubious patent medicines, which no pure-drug laws as yet prohibited, and followed fads, the most harmless of which was Dr. Graham's cure-all cracker and the most preposterous "hydropathy," the water cure for all diseases.

Science aimed to release man's mind from ignorance and his body from material want and suffering; the romantic movement in philosophy and the arts, on the contrary, aimed to free man's spirit from the limitations of rationalism and the chains of materialism. During the Jackson era both of these conflicting currents exerted profound influence on American thinking. Insofar as the conflict was resolved, it found a common denominator in the social purpose of both the scientist and the romanticist to elevate the lives of the people.

Romanticism and Utilitarianism

The philosophy of romanticism in the North superseded eighteenth-century rationalism as a source of democratic faith and inspired opposition to both Northern industrialism and Southern aristocracy, because both wage and chattel slavery frustrated the exaltation of man. The Transcendentalists erected a quasi-religion on the attitudes of romanticism. Less ecstatic were the students of philosophy who brought to America the ideas of Kant, Schelling, Fichte, and their English interpreters, particularly Samuel Taylor Coleridge. Asserting the primacy of the idea over material reality and the superiority of intuition to the rational faculty, these philosophic idealists concluded that man was supremely valuable as man without regard for class or other external circumstances. Such thinking found a ready response in America because it provided a justification of the doctrine of human equality much broader than the natural-rights philosophy of the rationalists. Its influence was felt by the people at large, however, not so much in philosophic terms as in the literature of romanticism.

A more popular formal philosophy was that of Utilitarianism, which came chiefly from England in the writings of Jeremy Bentham. In 1817, John Quincy Adams brought back from England bundles of Bentham's works which he distributed to libraries, and by 1840 an American journal, *The Diamond,* edited by Gilbert Vale in New York, was entirely devoted to the spread of Bentham's ideas. His thought was summed up in the famous slogan, "the greatest happiness of the greatest number," signifying that all human behavior, laws, and institutions should be evaluated objectively for their usefulness to the majority, granting nothing to habit, tradition, or privilege. Whatever could not meet the test should be abolished and utilitarian practices substituted. Most Americans had long been Utilitarians without knowing it, wherefore Bentham described himself to President Andrew Jackson as more of an American than an Englishman. Bentham placed greater emphasis on majority rule than on the minority rights with which the American Fathers, fearing the tyranny of majorities, had strived to reconcile it. Still Bentham's test of majority interest became a standard ingredient of American thinking. It expressed the increasingly democratic tendency of American life, and even those who spoke for minority interests were constrained to argue that they actually served the majority, if not immediately, then in the long run.

A Benthamite of this ambiguous sort was Henry C. Carey, the most eminent political economist of the period. A wealthy Philadelphia businessman and son of the distinguished publisher, Mathew Carey, he modified the systems of the English classical economists to prove that the Bank of the United States, unlimited freedom for business corporations, and protective tariffs actually served the interests of the majority of the people. In fact, they served "free trade" more effectively than the policies of laissez faire, because for Carey free trade meant freedom for businessmen to operate successfully. He presented government encouragement to private business corporations as a more effective means to group enterprise than socialism. On the other hand, Carey opposed legislation to protect labor because the profits of employers were the best guarantee that labor's status would be raised by means of higher wages. Similarly, he held that slaveowners' property in human beings should not be interfered with by government or criticized by agitators because the security of the institution would increase its profitability, and this would cause the price of slaves to rise so high that planters could no longer afford to buy them. Women, also, would achieve equality if they stopped agitating for legal protection and went to work in factories. Theoretical problems of population, wages, prices, and rents Carey solved in a way that overcame the pessimism of the English economists and pointed to hopeful consequences for the mass of humanity—always provided that government protected and encouraged property-owners while leaving others to benefit from the owners' prosperity.

His *magnum opus* was the three-volume *Principles of Political Economy,* published in 1840 and revised in 1858 as *Principles of Social Science.* He was the chief theorist of the Whig Party and later supported the Republicans. His work signified the adoption by businessmen of the goals of democracy which Hamilton had scorned. Many disciples of Carey continued his work during the next generations.

The most prevalent single idea in America during the pre-Civil War decades was that of progress. Its inevitability was accepted as an axiom. This idea had roots in the Enlightenment philosophy of natural rights. It was confirmed by Romanticism, received common-sense formulation in Utilitarianism, and was paid court by Carey. Nevertheless it was also agreed, as Albert Brisbane wrote, that nature reserved for the intelligence of human beings the noble prerogative of hastening progress. A society which was united on basic philosophic principle could nevertheless produce a babel of conflict over specific programs. Even slavery was advocated as a means to human progress and when this view met its opposite, that progress required the abolition of slavery, the conflict spread far beyond the words of philosophers.

LITERATURE

Some of the conditions necessary for the creation of a great literature were present in the United States following the War of 1812. A mood of self-confidence overcame lingering colonialism. The day when politics was the crucial interest of the nation's best minds had passed in the North, if not yet in the South. Prosperity made possible leisure and higher education for widening classes, while improvement of public education created mass hunger for stimulation by the printed word. Critical appreciation, social prestige, and fair financial rewards were accorded some of the best writers as a result of the most significant condition of all: the identity of interests and ideals between the society as a whole and some of its most talented individuals.

The Knickerbocker School

The "Knickerbocker School" of writers were the first to give evidence of the readiness of America for a mature literature. They took their name from *A History of New York by Diedrich Knickerbocker* (1809), in which Washington Irving delighted readers with urbane satire at the expense of the Dutch founders and set the tone for New York as the nation's capital of secular culture. Traveling in England and on the Continent after 1815, Irving continued to mine the vein of local lore with notable success in "Rip Van Winkle" and "The Legend of Sleepy Hollow," contained in *The Sketch Book* (1820). Irving also demonstrated in *A Chronicle of the Conquest of Granada* (1829) and *The Alhambra* (1832) that an American could use to excellent effect the materials of Europe's past. When he returned to the United States in 1832 he was greeted as the first American writer to win an international reputation. He settled down at "Sunnyside," his country house in the new romantic-Gothic style on the bank of the Hudson near Tarrytown, New York. Travels in the West resulted in books which revealed the colorful possibilities of the frontier for literature. The chief work of his later years was the *Life of George Washington,* the fifth and last volume of which was published in 1859. Irving's career as the first American professional man of letters was important evidence that the young Republic could produce and support an original artist.

William Cullen Bryant was born in Massachusetts but moved to New York in 1825, already famous for his lyric nature poems "Thanatopsis" and "To a Waterfowl." For two decades he continued to write poetry while serving as editor of the *Evening Post*. His fifty years in the latter capacity made that newspaper a leading organ of democratic influence as he abandoned the Federalism of his New England days and successively championed Jackson, the Free Soil Party, and the Republicans. "Thanatopsis" suggested the possibility of discovering in nature a better understanding of life and death than any religion offered and of achieving serenity by accepting the inviolability of every man's individual faith. When he read this poem, Richard Henry Dana, Sr., refused to believe that anyone "on this side of the Atlantic" could have written it. Bryant himself complained that Americans did not praise a thing until they saw the "transatlantic seal of approval" on it, and his own reputation verified this. His recognition as America's leading poet came only after an English edition of his poems in 1832 had been admired. Contemporary American readers found his poetry difficult; today it is read for its pleasant simplicity.

James Fenimore Cooper was not strictly a Knickerbocker; he spent most of his life in his father's village of Cooperstown, New York, and his greatest work celebrated the frontier of the Old West which had already passed. In thirty years from 1820 to his death, he wrote thirty books, including novels of the sea and of the Revolution besides his forest masterpieces, *The Last of the Mohicans, The Pathfinder,* and *The Deerslayer*. His fame was sudden and world-wide; in England he was called second only to Walter Scott. Primitivism overcome by civilization was his master-theme, treated not entirely to the advantage of the white man as compared with the Indian, and to the clear disadvantage of settled ways compared with the frontiersman's virtues, immortalized in Leatherstocking. But it was superior skill in the art of adventurous narrative that accounts for Cooper's popularity more than any philosophy. His later years were marred by angry revulsions against the new democracy, expressed in fretful attacks and bootless libel suits. He had decided that mankind needs authority more than liberty and was particularly horrified by the antirent riots of the Hudson Valley tenant farmers. Still his patriotism was passionate and his animadversions are now forgotten while his portrayals of the American struggle for civilization continue to be read, although more in foreign translation than in English.

William Gilmore Simms of South Carolina has been called the Southern Cooper; in the best-known of his many novels, *The Yemassee* (1835), he chronicled an Indian war and he depicted frontier scenes and characters with skill and power. But this prolific writer, instead of following his bent for robust realism, spent most of his vast energies glorifying the institutions and history of his native state, especially in the series of novels beginning with *The Partisan* (1835), and he never gained much of a hearing in the nation. There was no shadow of aristocratic romanticism in Augustus B. Longstreet's *Georgia Scenes* (1840), which anticipated to some degree the rollicking frontier humor of Mark Twain, but Longstreet was only incidentally a literary man and the Southern "school" of writers became increasingly sectional. Not until after the Civil War did Southern writers as a group command the attention and support of the country as a whole.

Emerson and Thoreau

Meanwhile, by 1840, Boston with Cambridge and Concord had clearly superseded New York as the literary capital of the nation. True to the Puritan inheritance, the New England Renaissance glorified moral earnestness even while it overthrew the ancestral theology; and, while both the English and the Americans found entertainment in the Knickerbockers, they found uplift in the New Englanders.

Ralph Waldo Emerson turned the gnarled sermons of his clerical forefathers into luminous essays of free, organic artistry. He knew poverty as a boy, was educated for the Unitarian ministry at Harvard, and accepted a pulpit in Boston. But, following his own prescription of self-reliance, he resigned from the ministry and, beginning with *Nature*, published in 1836, set out to deliver to a larger parish a new declaration of spiritual independence. This compound of common sense and idealism was expressed in the doctrine that the physical laws of nature and the moral law apprehended by human conscience were parallel expressions of divine unity. Emerson himself was a rare combination of shrewd Yankee and world seer; his language brought the salty New England speech into fruitful company with the vocabulary of scholarship; and his essays held all these dualities in tense suspension.

In "The American Scholar," delivered as the Phi Beta Kappa Address at Harvard in 1837, Emerson called for revolt against American intellectual and literary colonialism with such effect that James Russell Lowell called it "an event without any former parallel in our literary annals." His own career was the best answer to his call. His profound Americanism synthesized materialism and spirituality in absolute faith that the sovereign individual exercizing economic, political, and spiritual liberty would justify all hopes not only by his works but as the greatest of creations—a whole man. This did not mean that Emerson did not criticize his countrymen; his faith was in their potentialities. He made himself their chief lay evangelist on the lecture platform, for forty years exhorting them to envision and fulfill their destiny. Nor was he an ordinary nationalist: following travels abroad, where he formed a notable friendship with Carlyle, Emerson wrote in *English Traits* (1856) a brilliant appreciation of British civilization. His single example did much to allay the mutual antagonism of the two peoples that lingered on after the War of 1812.

Living in Concord from 1835 until his death in 1882, Emerson the world sage was at home in the gracefully time-worn village and first among its remarkable group of literary citizens. A significant criticism of his outlook is that he was blind to the reality of evil, but this charge could not be leveled at either of his two greatest fellow-villagers, Thoreau or Hawthorne. Henry David Thoreau was called by Emerson *the* man of Concord, but he was little known during his lifetime and not so favorably then as later. With a conscience as sensitive as Emerson's, Thoreau, after graduating from Harvard, lost one teaching job because he refused to flog the pupils and gave up another because his purpose of making a living he considered unworthy. Emerson helped the younger man in writing and publishing poetry, gave him his friendship, and delighted in Thoreau's bristly independence. He tried literary life in New York under Horace Greeley's tutelage but decided that, as he told Emerson, he was made of Concord dust. Nor would he go to the "farthest Indies" by ordinary means. He walked a few miles to a woodlot of Emerson's at Walden Pond, built himself a cabin and lived there for two years. He did this in revolt against the greed and futility of conventional ways of life, and, as he wrote, "because I wished to live deliberately, to front only the essential facts of life, and see if I could not learn what it had to teach." Laborers building a railroad nearby, their bodies and minds permanently constricted by sixteen hours of toil per day for 60 cents, reminded Thoreau of what he opposed; and his intimate observations of seasons, animals, and plants, published as *Walden* (1854), recorded in prose more sinewy than Emerson's the great deal he learned of how man might live in union with nature.

This classical experiment in living Thoreau followed with an experiment in social protest against the government. As an abolitionist, he opposed the Mexican War, refused to pay his state poll tax, was arrested, and went to jail. From this experience he drew the doctrine of his essay, "Civil Disobedience," which became a guidebook of the route an individual may take when he opposes the state, and an inspiration to Mahatma Ghandi in his epochal campaign against British rule over India. An expert surveyor, Thoreau usually made his living by doing odd jobs for neighbors in Concord or making pencils for sale. Besides *Walden* only one other book was published during his lifetime, *A Week on the Concord and Merrimack Rivers* (1849). Emerson was disappointed that he was not the American scholar, great in action, he had hoped for, instead of captain of a huckleberry party. But Thoreau's protests reverberated. His last one, against the "slave power" for hanging John Brown, helped turn Massachusetts to abolitionism. After his death in 1862, further books of his essays, poems, and letters were published and his reputation slowly grew like the cairn on the bank of Walden Pond to which pilgrims from all over the world have added stones. His was the clearest of all American voices asserting the supremacy of the individual's moral imperative to dissent.

Hawthorne and Melville

Nathaniel Hawthorne created images of the evil that inheres in man rather than in society and did not pretend to exorcise it, like Emerson, or like Thoreau try to abolish it. Indeed he was unique among the New England intellectuals in adhering to the Democratic Party throughout the forties and fifties when they condemned it as the instrument of imperialism and slavery. No philosopher, he was the first American novelist to enter the highest rank of artists. His view of life was tragic and he had little faith in social reform. The fated consequence of guilt was his chief theme and his best work explored its operation among the Puritans who were his ancestors. Born in Salem, he graduated from Bowdoin College in 1825 and returned to Salem to live in seclusion and learn the craft of writing. In short tales he tried to please the taste for sentimental romance, lived for several periods in Concord among the Transcendentalists but aloof from them, and revealed his full stature only in 1850 with the publication of *The Scarlet Letter*. More than a romance, it was a profound portrayal of Puritans locked in expiatory relations to a sin. In 1851, Hawthorne published *The House of the Seven Gables*, showing Puritan guilt inherited as a family curse. European experience as United States Consul at Liverpool, an appointment Hawthorne received from his college friend, Franklin Pierce (after writing a campaign biography for him in 1852) and later as a resident in Italy, was most productively used in *The Marble Faun*. This suggests that the pagan past of the Old World also shadows its present.

Herman Melville, a New Yorker and a friend of Hawthorne, explored the power of evil in his masterpiece, *Moby Dick* (1851), in terms more universal than Hawthorne's. After voyages in the South Seas, Melville had won quick popularity with books of adventure which included reformist attacks against the misunderstanding of natives by missionaries and the brutalities of officers on warships and whalers. *Moby Dick*, however, left readers puzzled and the public indifferent until after the First World War, when the "Melville revival" placed it among the great books of all time. On its several planes it presented a mighty image of the whaling industry, a narrative of homeric chase of a legendary white whale, a drama of the humanly microcosmic crew of the whaler *Pequod*, and, in its ultimate symbolism, a tragic allegory of the enmity of nature against man. Sprawling in form and detail, and concealing its inner meanings in metaphysical imagery, totally contradictory of contemporary optimism in philosophy, *Moby Dick* was a strange production of the mid-century and earned for its author only obscurity during forty more years of life.

Edgar Allan Poe

Edgar Allan Poe was the darkest of American geniuses in private life as well as in literary creations. He identified himself with the Southern aristocracy by an exercise of imagination, and was quickly dismissed from both the University of Virginia and West Point. Dogged by poverty and tortured by alcoholism, he produced lyric poems and eerie short stories of haunting beauty and compelling power. His was the romanticism of esthetic egoism scorning social responsibility and democracy. His young bride died of consumption, and neither friends nor fame following the publication of "The Raven" in 1845 saved him from despair and early death. "The Gold Bug" and other stories turned intellectual ingenuity and grotesque emotional preoccupations to brilliant use. His poems initiated the modern school of Symbolism in which poets alienated from their societies create private mythologies. And his literary criticism was the first American attempt to judge art solely by mature artistic standards.

From Emerson to Poe this group of major writers presented in great works a spectrum of attitudes towards the eternal problems of man and society, ranging from complete acceptance and glorification of the common life of America to complete rejection of it as unredeemable except a-morally in art. With the addition of Mark Twain, who soon filled out the band with laughter, the leaders of the mid-century "renais-sance" provided archetypes for many subsequent developments in Amer-ican literature. It was to be expected that a maturing society should produce recollections of its past like those of Irving, Cooper, and Hawthorne, and that a radical democracy devoted to reform should evoke the protests of a Thoreau; but the optimism of Emerson and the Transcendentalists, the pessimism of Melville, and the despair of Poe, could be related to the conditions of their society only by virtue of the sunny reality of its promise which was bewilderingly offset by its equally real continuing evils.

Longfellow and Whittier

None of these greatest voices won audiences as large as those of writers whose ideas, language, and emotions were simpler. Henry Wads-worth Longfellow was the most popular of all American poets. A grad-uate of Bowdoin in Hawthorne's class of 1825, widely traveled in Europe, and professor of modern languages at Harvard, Longfellow's translation of Dante was scholarly, but his own poetry in sing-song rhythms made the past seem quaint, the present readily idealized, and human life ennobled by inexhaustible goodness and sweetness. His "Village Black-smith," "Wreck of the Hesperus," "Excelsior," "Evangeline," "Courtship of Miles Standish," and "Hiawatha" were for most Americans and masses of devoted readers in England all that poetry should be. A few of John Greenleaf Whittier's poems, notably "Snow-Bound," matched Longfel-low's in sweetness and popularity, but the Quaker poet spent his best energies on abolitionist propaganda and organization.

Newspapers and Magazines

Longfellow and Whittier are little read today; a host of their con-temporary purveyors of sentiment are wholly unreadable. Mass literacy and the growth of the middle class during this period created a market that expanded popular literature into an industry. More than books, newspapers and magazines were relished by the new mass audience. Horace Greeley's New York Tribune, founded in 1841, was a penny paper that remained intellectually respectable, if erratic, while building a mass circulation. But most of the new "penny dreadfuls," led off by James Gordon Bennett's New York Herald, frankly cultivated readers' tastes for sensation, crime, cloying sentiment, and flamboyant patriotism. The most popular magazines maintained higher standards than the penny papers, but here, too, the cleavage between the reading material of the masses and that of the cultivated minority became apparent. The North American Review (1815-1939), the Dial (1838-1844), and the

Atlantic Monthly (founded 1857) in Boston; *Harper's Magazine* (founded 1850) and *Knickerbocker Magazine* (1833-1865) in New York; *Graham's Magazine* (1838-1858) in Philadelphia; the *Southern Literary Messenger* (1834-1864) in Richmond: these strove for and sometimes achieved the authoritative standards of the great English reviews. Indeed, these genteel magazines on the two sides of the Atlantic, led by the *North American Review* and the *Edinburgh Review,* wordily fought each other to a standstill over the question of the relative merits of British and American civilizations. The most popular American magazines, notably *Godey's Lady's Book* (1830-1898) of Philadelphia, dealt in sentimentality so pervasive that it extended to "the old home," except on a few occasions such as when the beloved Charles Dickens, following an American tour in 1842, dared to describe flaws as well as pleasant aspects of the American scene.

Historians

Most indicative of cultural maturity, perhaps, was the work and the broad popularity of a new group of American historians. George Bancroft began in 1834 to publish his eleven-volume *History of the United States* on the basis of original research made palatable to readers by his lively style and rendered inspirational by his patriotic conviction that Providence presided over the birth of the United States. William H. Prescott in his histories of the conquest of Mexico and Peru did justice to the romantic possibilities of those fabulous episodes. John Lothrop Motley's *Rise of the Dutch Republic* defined Protestantism as the impelling force of liberty; and this theme was brought closer to Americans in the work of the greatest of the classical historians—the nearly-blind Francis Parkman, who took the struggle between Britain and France for mastery of North America as his subject. Parkman injured his health after graduating from Harvard by strenuous explorations of the West, but despite invalidism began in 1851 to publish the great series of which *Montcalm and Wolfe* is the most famous. His narrative power and imaginative reach made art out of fact. These historians wrote not for students so much as for the public at large and succeeded as no historian has done since.

THE ARTS

Architecture

Jacksonian America produced original work in other arts. The Greek Revival in architecture was the last stage of classicism. Roman buildings now began to look pompously aristocratic to Americans and, stimulated by the Greek Revolution, they turned to the simpler forms of ancient Athens. Spurning domes, arches, and baroque details, Benjamin Henry Latrobe convinced the public that Greek temples were suitable not only for governmental and commercial buildings but even for the homes of plain citizens. Pillared and pedimented facades sprang up in cities, and in the countryside wooden replicas looked out from knolls— suggesting that republicans dwelt there as gods. Ever since, government structures have been influenced by the Greek Treasury building in Washington and banks by Latrobe's Greek Bank of Pennsylvania in Philadelphia. But for their homes Americans, except in the South, quickly tired of wooden temples, and the creative phase of the Greek Revival lasted only from about 1820 to 1840.

Then the new middle classes in the North, including prosperous farmers, turned to the more "romantic" Gothic. This style was quickly adopted also for churches. Occasional factories sported battlements, but the most striking Early American Gothic completely revolutionized domestic architecture. Carpenters learned to avoid the boredom of squat white boxes by adding whimsical wings and towers, by emphasizing verticality with battens and high, pointed window frames, and by ornamenting the exterior with wooden imitations of intricate stone carvings. Naïve approximations of Gothic gave way steadily to more authentic copies of specific medieval European buildings, the accuracy of the copy being identified with artistry. Richard Upjohn's Episcopalian Trinity Church and James Renwick's Catholic St. Patrick's Cathedral, both in New York, showed the suitability of Gothic for those traditional communions. Why Gothic should also appeal to home-builders is suggested by one client's direction to his architect to design for him "a wild sweet cottage in the country." The style satisfied current romantic naturalism. It also gave newly-prosperous families a better opportunity than the classical styles to display high-toned extravagance.

Meanwhile, these impulses found happier expression in the improvement of country estates and public gardens. The most notable landscape gardener and horticulturist of the era was Andrew Jackson Downing (1815-1852), whose work was carried on by Frederick Law Olmsted and Calvert Vaux, designers of Central Park, New York. The sculptor Horatio Greenough vigorously attacked Gothic architecture as functionally unrelated to American needs, but on country estates and in public parks romantic naturalism was more congruous with the half-tamed American landscape than the formal gardens of the classical revival were.

Sculpture and Painting

The prestige of Greek and Roman sculpture grew while that of classical architecture declined. Greenough was the first American to make sculpture his profession. In the thirties he and other American sculptors and painters went to Italy for training and some of them stayed there to do their work. Greenough executed a statue of George Washington for the national capitol which bared that Virginia gentleman's torso above a toga as if he were a Roman senator. Hiram Powers, the first American sculptor to win a European reputation, departed from his ordinary portrait busts to carve a girl in chains as a Greek slave. Her expression of sweet nobility in suffering, her nudity, and the reference to contemporary American as well as Greek slavery made this a highly controversial piece of sculpture. She was carried from city to city for exhibition throughout the North, vast crowds paid admission to see her, with separate hours for men and women viewers, and everyone had an opinion on her spiritual meaning. Marble busts of noted Americans for placement in public buildings were the chief products of scuptors' studios. In 1853, the first equestrian statue cast in the United States resulted from the return of the Democrats to power. Clark Mills' *Andrew Jackson* was placed on a rearing horse in Lafayette Square, Washington, forever raising his hat to the occupant of the White House directly opposite.

American painting during these decades was rich in accomplishment. Historical subjects continued in high favor. Emmanuel Leutze's *Washington Crossing the Delaware* and *Westward the Course of Empire Takes Its Way* apotheosized those themes, while Washington Allston led a new school of historical romanticism which dealt mostly in Biblical scenes spread across gigantic canvases. The first original American group of landscapists, called the "Hudson River School," of whom Asher Brown Durand and Thomas Cole were most celebrated, invested rugged passages of American scenery with mystical glamor. Realism also flourished, however, in the form of anecdotal genre paintings of homely scenes and incidents. George Caleb Bingham's *Jolly Flatboatmen* and William Sidney Mount's affectionate rural dramas typified the genre painters' glorification of workaday America.

Advances in technology joined with the emergence of universal literacy to create new demands, forms, and markets in the graphic arts. Cheap "chromolith" color reproductions were a marvel of the era. Currier and Ives of New York made of these a big business, putting artists to work on an assembly line and spreading millions of copies of news pictures, genre scenes, and political posters throughout the land, while the new French art of photography gradually displaced almost all other techniques of reproduction.

Music and the Theater

Music also was now organized for mass audiences. Haydn and Handel societies in the leading cities provided occasional performances of those composers' works; symphony orchestras in Boston and New York performed Beethoven between renditions of less demanding composers; choral societies became popular, especially among German immigrants; and foreign grand opera companies in New York and New Orleans performed Mozart, Weber, Bellini, and Verdi. The foundations for an independent American musical culture were laid by schools for professional training in several cities. But American compositions were not yet attempted in forms more complicated than songs elaborated from folk tunes. Stephen Foster's compositions in the 1840's and early 1850's—such as "O Susanna" and "My Old Kentucky Home"—were great favorites.

In the theater a similar pattern was discernible. European plays and actors continued to dominate the American stage, although Edwin Booth and Charlotte Cushman proved that Americans could equal the best performers of Shakespearean roles. Rivalry between partisans of American and British actors reached the pitch of riots in Astor Place, New York (1849). Twenty-two people were killed in the argument whether the Englishman William C. Macready or the American Edwin Forrest was the better Hamlet. None of the dramas or comedies of the period has survived as more than a curiosity, but in the minstrel show Americans developed a popular theatrical form exploiting native folk music and humor, especially those of the Negro. In the cities and in the hinterland, "museums" of conglomerate art, curiosities and freaks salted education with amusement. Phineas T. Barnum's American Museum, opened in New York in 1842, delighted the public with fare ranging from frank hoaxes, the dwarf General Tom Thumb, and such spectacles as "The Burning of Rome" painted on a huge moving scroll, to Jenny Lind, "The Swedish Nightingale," whose concert tour was the chief artistic event of 1850.

Lyceums and Foreign Visitors

Such museums were gradually differentiated later in the century into public collections of art and traveling circuses, while the original mixture was perpetuated in the Chautauqua movement. In the Jackson era the most important effort at adult education was the National American Lyceum. Organized in 1831 at New York, within a few years 3000 local lyceums in fifteen states offered for modest fees series of lectures on any and all subjects. Touring the lyceum circuit became a normal reward of fame in every field, and a chief source of income for writers and savants. The tremendous popularity of lyceum lectures was pointed to as evidence that the whole people would absorb culture in quick gulps.

Particularly popular as lecturers were noted Englishmen. Americans eagerly demanded to hear the truth about themselves from representatives of Old World standards and then boiled over when it was not wholly complimentary. Captain Basil Hall, Mrs. Frances Trollope, and Charles Dickens deeply wounded American sensibilities when they showed in books that on their American tours they had observed the darker as well as the brighter sides of the lusty new civilization. That their criticisms were not ineffective is clear in the popular campaign to stop the spitting of tobacco juice in public places by crying "A Trollope!" at offenders.

But one of the best books ever written on the United States, *Democracy in America* (1835), was by a Frenchman, Alexis de Tocqueville. A keen observer and student of society and government, liberal in his sympathies, Tocqueville came to America without prejudice to judge on the evidence whether it offered hope for the future of human liberty. His considered answer was optimistic even while he warned that the tyranny of the majority in the New World might be as dangerous as that of the state in the Old World. He believed that the strengthening of society and self-government which democracy achieved by opening opportunity to all citizens was paid for by the lowering of cultural values from the best aristocratic standards to a mediocre popular level. His book was accepted as a genuine aid to self-knowledge by Americans and as a guide for liberals in many countries of the world. Its popularity to this day also bespeaks the truth that during the Jackson period the main characteristics of modern America—the glories and the hazards of liberty—came fully into view.

SELECT BIBLIOGRAPHY

General Statement

READING IN MORE DETAILED WORKS CAN ENORMOUSLY ENRICH AND ENLIVEN the story which is inevitably compressed in a book like this; and original sources can provide a vividness of impression that secondary narratives rarely convey. Part of the continuing appeal of historical study arises from the fact that there is always something more which anybody can learn about the past and that the closer one gets to the actual people and events the more vivid and real they become. To some extent every student can become an explorer in his own right, and in the investigation of some appealing topic can taste the joy of discovery.

The purpose of the present bibliography is to acquaint the student and reader with the most useful aids—stress being laid on those that are most accessible—and, without making any pretence of exhaustiveness, to mention selected books which can be read to advantage and sources which can be explored with relative ease. Comments are frequently attached—sometimes as a sort of warning but more often as an invitation to particular items in the historical feast.

First, there is a relatively brief list of works bearing on the whole or most of this volume; then, both general and specific suggestions are given chapter by chapter. These can be richly supplemented from the bibliographical items and suggestions in many of the listed books.

Basic Reference Works

The most important single bibliographical aid is the *Harvard Guide to American History* (1954), edited by Oscar Handlin. Besides excellent chapters on the materials and tools of American history and convenient lists of books in various categories, it contains suggestions for reading on the various periods and topics which go far beyond any that can be given here.

Every historical shelf should have the *Encyclopedia of American History* (1953), edited by R. B. Morris, a handy volume which is invaluable for facts and dates. The arrangement is both chronological and topical.

Among the larger reference works with which students should familiarize themselves is the *Dictionary of American Biography* (20 vols., 1928-36), edited by Allen Johnson and Dumas Malone; supplementary volumes edited by H. E. Starr (1944), and R. L. Schuyler (1958). This co-operative work provides rich personal materials for the whole of American history. A good way to turn mere names into real persons is to look them up in this collection of articles. Those desiring to read further will find suggestions in the bibliographies. (A selected list of biographies is given in the *Harvard Guide*, pp. 190-206).

Excellent examples of large collections of the writings of great Americans are Washington's *Writings*, edited by J. C. Fitzpatrick (39 vols., 1931-44); and

Lincoln's *Collected Works*, edited by R. P. Basler (9 vols., 1953). Among extensive collections now in process the pace-setter is Jefferson's *Papers*, edited by Julian P. Boyd, 16 vols. of which had appeared by 1964. A number of handy one-volume collections are mentioned hereafter.

The *Dictionary of American History* (5 vols., 1940), edited by J. T. Adams, is abridged in *Concise Dictionary of American History* (1962), edited by Wayne Andrews. The *Encyclopedia of the Social Sciences* (15 vols., 1930-34), edited by E. R. A. Seligman, is a work of much wider scope.

Fascinating statistical materials can be found in the publications of the Bureau of the Census, *A Century of Population Growth . . . 1790-1900* (1909), and *Historical Statistics of the U.S., Colonial Times to 1957: A Statistical Abstract Supplement* (1960). The *Biographical Directory of the American Congress, 1774-1949* (1950), besides giving the lists of members of the successive Congresses (and also of executive officers), contains brief biographical sketches.

Good maps are of the first importance. Two older collections have not yet been excelled for general historical use: W. R. Shepherd, *Historical Atlas* (1911), which deals with Europe as well as America; and *Harper's Atlas of American History* (1920), consisting of maps from the old *American Nation* series. Later school atlases of wide use include: C. E. and E. H. Lord, *Historical Atlas of the United States* (1944); and J. T. Adams, *Atlas of American History* (1943). The fullest and most authoritative work is C. O. Paullin, *Atlas of the Historical Geography of the United States* (1932), edited by J. K. Wright. While too big and cumbersome for frequent use, this is valuable for boundary disputes and other matters of concern to advanced students and specialists.

Much work has been done in making old and recent pictures available. The first extensive modern compilation was *The Pageant of America* (15 vols., 1926-29), edited by R. H. Gabriel. The *Harvard Guide*, pp. 65-66, has a list of later general collections. Some works of special value dealing with particular periods or subjects will be referred to hereafter at appropriate points. Naturally, pictorial records became more accurate as well as more extensive with the development of photography, but the older paintings and prints often convey a delightful sense of their own day.

Convenient Collections of Documents and Readings

The best general collection of documents in convenient form and a strong contender for any historian's bookshelf is *Documents of American History* (7 edn., 1963), edited by H. S. Commager. Besides official documents, this contains party platforms, important speeches, etc. It can be supplemented by L. B. Evans, *Cases on American Constitutional Law*, revised edition by C. G. Fenwick (1948), or by *Cases in Constitutional Law*, by Robert E. and Robert F. Cushman (1958), both of which are fuller in a more limited field. Treaties and diplomatic documents can be best consulted in R. J. Bartlett, ed., *The Record of American Diplomacy* (1950), a book which should stand on the shelf with Commager.

A rich collection of readings bearing especially on social and intellectual matters is *American Issues*, Vol. I, "The Social Record" (rev. edn., 1955), edited by Willard Thorp, Merle Curti, and Carlos Baker. Another good collection, which is more economic and political in emphasis, is *The Shaping of the American Tradition* (1947), edited by L. M. Hacker, whose relatively long introductions are illuminating and provocative. The older and less accessible work, G. S. Callender, ed., *Selections from the Economic History of the United States, 1765-1868* (1909), contains, besides readings, brief but unusually penetrating introductions which comprise a summary of economic history.

The Making of American History (rev. edn., 1954), edited by Donald Sheehan, is an anthology which contains 35 long extracts from historical writers dealing with major topics. Some of these will be specifically referred to hereafter. *Understanding the American Past* (1954), edited by E. N. Saveth, is a similar work.

Problems in American Civilization: Readings Selected by the Department of American Studies, Amherst College (1947-   ) comprise a useful series of paper-bound booklets. Each deals with a particular topic and contains selections from authors with varying views. Somewhat more than a dozen have been issued to date and they offer one of the best methods of studying controversial questions. Individual booklets will be mentioned hereafter.

Larger General Histories

Every student and serious reader should become acquainted with major long histories and series, and should dip into them to some extent. The present list is confined to works or sets covering the whole or most of American history.

Edward Channing, *History of the United States* (6 vols., 1905-25) extends through 1865. To some extent it reflects the author's Northeastern environment and at time his caprices, but generally it is judicious and temperate.

The Chronicles of America (50 vols., 1918-21), edited by Allen Johnson, comprise an unusually readable series of small volumes which inevitably vary in quality.

A History of American Life (13 vols., 1927-48), edited by A. M. Schlesinger and D. R. Fox, is the standard series for social history. The bibliographies are excellent.

The old series, *The American Nation: A History* (26 vols., 1904-08; additional vol., 1918), edited by A. B. Hart, has a distinguished position in American historiography and certain volumes are still of great value. *The New American Nation Series*, edited by H. S. Commager and R. B. Morris, to comprise about 40 vols., is in process. The volumes are of a handy size and contain full and up-to-date bibliographies.

A History of the South, edited by W. H. Stephenson and E. M. Coulter (1947-   ), projected in 10 vols., of which 8 fall in the period to 1877, is an admirable series, now almost done. The bibliographies are detailed and comprehensive.

Topical Histories

GEOGRAPHY AND ABORIGINES

There is need for a readable work on American historical geography in convenient size. The two following books are useful for reference: J. R. Smith and

M. O. Phillips, *North America* (rev. edn., 1940), a lengthy regional treatment of the United States, Canada, and Central America; R. H. Brown, *Historical Geography of the United States* (1948), a sound work, following the order of settlement. In the field of oceanography, Rachel Carson, *The Sea around Us* (1951), is fascinating. An excellent account of the Indians, written for the layman, is R. M. Underhill, *Red Man's America* (1953).

SETTLEMENT AND IMMIGRATION

Most general works pay considerable attention to the process of settlement and there are many specialized studies of particular areas. A comprehensive but compact book is R. A. Billington, *Westward Expansion; A History of the American Frontier* (1949), dealing also with transportation and land policies. *The Frontier in America* (1921), a collection of essays by F. J. Turner, is a classic.

The larger problems of immigration are illuminated by three books by M. L. Hansen: *The Atlantic Migration, 1607-1860* (1940), and *The Immigrant in American History* (1941), both edited by A. M. Schlesinger, and *The Mingling of the Canadian and American Peoples* (1940), completed by J. B. Brebner. A good general treatment is Carl Wittke, *We Who Built America: The Saga of the Immigrant* (1939). Works on the Negro and particular ethnic groups are cited hereafter.

ECONOMIC AND FINANCIAL HISTORY

Among general economic histories in one volume are H. U. Faulkner, *American Economic History* (8 edn., 1959); E. C. Kirkland, *A History of American Economic Life* (3 edn., 1951); F. A. Shannon, *America's Economic Growth* (rev. edn., 1961); and Robert R. Russel, *A History of the American Economic System* (1964). The older and more restricted works, D. R. Dewey, *Financial History of the United States* (12 edn., 1934), and F. W. Taussig, *Tariff History of the United States* (7 edn., 1923) are still useful handbooks.

AGRICULTURAL HISTORY

The standard works for the period covered by this volume are P. W. Bidwell and J. I. Falconer, *History of Agriculture in the Northern United States, 1620-1860* (1925), and L. C. Gray, *History of Agriculture in the Southern United States to 1860* (2 vols., 1933). While too detailed for general reading, these books are invaluable to those wishing to explore any part of this vital subject.

INTELLECTUAL HISTORY

Merle Curti, in *The Growth of American Thought* (2 edn., 1951), covers the whole period systematically and has unusually valuable bibliographies for his chapters. V. L. Parrington, *Main Currents in American Thought* (3 vols., 1927-30), is highly stimulating and a delight to read, even when one disputes the author's judgment. R. H. Gabriel, *The Course of American Democratic Thought* (2 edn., 1956), deals admirably with the period after 1815. Harvey

Wish, *Society and Thought in Early America* (1950), covers social as well as intellectual history to 1865.

LITERARY HISTORY

Abundant materials are available in R. E. Spiller and others, *Literary History of the United States* (3 vols., 1948), the third volume of which is an elaborate bibliography; and A. H. Quinn, ed., *The Literature of the American People* (1951).

LABOR

F. R. Dulles, *Labor in America* (1949), is a convenient general treatment.

CONSTITUTIONAL HISTORY AND PARTIES

For general use the best works on their subject are C. B. Swisher, *American Constitutional Development* (1943); and A. H. Kelly and W. A. Harbison, *The American Constitution: Its Origins and Development* (1948). A. C. McLaughlin, *A Constitutional History of the United States* (1935) becomes less valuable after the early national period. W. E. Binkley, *American Political Parties: Their Natural History* (3 edn., 1958), is a good survey.

DIPLOMACY

General treatments are: J. W. Pratt, *A History of United States Foreign Policy* (1955), a well-proportioned and judicious recent work; the old reliable, Bailey, *A Diplomatic History of the American People* (7 edn., 1964); Alexander De Conde, *A History of American Foreign Policy* (1963). There is much information and interpretation in S. F. Bemis, ed., *The American Secretaries of State and Their Diplomacy* (10 vols., 1927-29).

RELIGION, SCIENCE, AND EDUCATION

General treatments are disappointing, but the following works are useful: W. W. Sweet, *The Story of Religion in America* (rev. edn., 1939); D. J. Struik, *Yankee Science in the Making* (1948); E. P. Cubberly, *Public Education in the United States* (rev. edn., 1934) E. E. Slosson, *The American Spirit in Education* (1921, *Chronicles of America*). M. E. Curti, *Social Ideas of American Educators* (1935), is excellent. Richard Hofstadter and Wilson Smith, eds., *American Higher Education: A Documentary History* (1961), is basic. J. W. Smith and A. L. Jamison, eds., *Religion in American Life*, Vols. I, II, IV (1961) is a significant contribution.

ARCHITECTURE AND ART

The main lines of development are shown in T. F. Hamlin, *The American Spirit in Architecture* (1926); T. F. Tallmadge, *The Story of Architecture in America* (rev. edn., 1936); W. C. Andrews, *Americans, Ambition and Architecture*

(1955); Samuel Isham, *The History of American Painting*, supplemented by Royal Cortissoz (1927).

MILITARY AND NAVAL

The fruitfulness of scholarship in this field is best shown in specialized studies. General works do not yet fully reflect it, but the following are useful: W. A. Ganoe, *A History of the United States Army* (1942); O. L. Spaulding, *The United States Army in War and Peace* (1937); D. W. Knox, *A History of the United States Navy* (rev. edn., 1948); H. H. and Margaret Sprout, *The Rise of American Naval Power, 1776-1918* (1939). The old army textbook, M. F. Steele, *American Campaigns* (2 vols., last edn., 1922), with its maps, is still helpful.

Part I: Establishing the Republic, 1789-1815

1-4. FEDERALIST PERIOD, 1789-1801

General

This list for the period is followed by more specific suggestions for particular chapters.

NARRATIVE HISTORIES

Probably the best narrative in a general history is in Channing, Vol. IV, Chs. 1-8; but Ch. 9, describing the election of 1800, is not recommended. The most vivid is C. G. Bowers, *Jefferson and Hamilton* (1936), which accentuates the political duel between the two men and definitely sides with Jefferson. A. J. Beveridge, *Life of John Marshall*, Vol. II (1916), which is virtually a political history of the period, is just as strongly anti-Jeffersonian. Marshall himself belonged to the more moderate Federalist group, to whom Manning Dauer does justice in *The Adams Federalists* (1954). J. C. Miller, *The Federalist Era, 1789-1801* (1960) is moderate. Many of the nineteenth-century histories and biographies written in the Federalist tradition reflect the extreme point of view of J. C. Hamilton, *History of the Republic . . . as Traced in the Writings of Alexander Hamilton* (6 vols., 1857-60). This was unfair not only to Jefferson but to Adams and even to Washington, whom it tended to minimize.

BIOGRAPHIES

These are of the first importance in this period because of the great influence of a relatively small group of individual leaders on the conduct of public affairs. Biographers of Washington have generally dealt inadequately with his Presidency. D. S. Freeman, in *George Washington*, Vol. VI (1955), which covers the first term, is less penetrating and less convincing than in the earlier and more military volumes. Marcus Cunliffe, *George Washington: Man and Monument* (1958) is stimulating and witty. Gilbert Chinard, *Honest John Adams* (1933) needs to be supplemented by the work of Manning Dauer; S. G. Kurtz, *Presidency of John Adams* (1957); and Page Smith, *John Adams,*

II (1962). Nathan Schachner, *Alexander Hamilton* (1936), is readable and temperate. J. C. Miller, *Alexander Hamilton: Portrait in Paradox* (1959), is a colorful recent study. Broadus Mitchell, *Alexander Hamilton* (2 vols., 1957), 1962) is more detailed. H. S. Randall, *Life of Thomas Jefferson* (3 vols., 1858), has remained a classic, despite its partisanship, because of its scope and its thoroughness within the limits of knowledge available at the time of its writing. Dumas Malone, *Jefferson and the Rights of Man* (1951, Vol. II of *Jefferson and His Time*), extends through the year 1792; Vol. III, *Jefferson and the Ordeal of Liberty* (1962), covers the rest of the Federalist period. A convenient collection of Jefferson's writings is the edition of Adrienne Koch and William Peden (1944) in the Modern Library. Irving Brant, *James Madison* [III]: *Father of the Constitution, 1787-1800* (1948), is invaluable in this period. The relations between the two men are well treated in Adrienne Koch, *Jefferson and Madison: The Great Collaboration* (1950).

FOREIGN AFFAIRS

The general diplomatic histories can be supplemented by Bemis, *American Secretaries of State*, Vol. II (1927).

POLITICS AND PARTIES

Binkley, *American Political Parties,* continues to be useful. C. A. Beard, *Economic Origins of Jeffersonian Democracy* (1915), is hard reading but important. Joseph Charles, *Origins of the American Party System* (1956), is brief but challenging. N. E. Cunningham, Jr., *The Jeffersonian Republicans: The Formation of Party Organization, 1789-1801* (1958) is a sound study.

1. LAUNCHING A NEW GOVERNMENT, 1789-1793

Special

COUNTRY AND COURT

Rich information about the national scene can be gained from *A Century of Population Growth,* which says much about the Census of 1790. Washington's "Court" and the personalities of the times are described and commented on in R. W. Griswold, *The Republican Court: or American Society in the Days of Washington* (1855), a strongly Federalist work; Stewart Mitchell, ed., *New Letters of Abigail Adams, 1788-1801* (1947), and other correspondence of that highly articulate lady; *The Journal of William Maclay, United States Senator from Pennsylvania, 1789-1791* (1947), introduction by C. A. Beard, the acidulous and unfailingly interesting diary of the man described as the original Jeffersonian democrat. L. B. Dunbar, *A Study of "Monarchical" Tendencies in the United States, from 1776 to 1801* (1922), is a valuable monograph.

ORGANIZATION AND CONDUCT OF THE GOVERNMENT

L. D. White, *The Federalists: A Study in Administrative History* (1948), covers the entire period and throws fresh light on it. James Hart, *The American Presidency in Action, 1789* (1948), covers the critical first year.

HAMILTON'S POLICIES AND CRITICS: Hamilton's great reports and his opinion on the Bank can be conveniently consulted in Samuel McKee, Jr., ed., *Alexander Hamilton: Papers on Public Credit, Commerce and Finance* (1934). They are decidedly worth reading. His financial policies are described in financial and economic as well as general histories. W. G. Sumner, *Alexander Hamilton* (1890), is good in this connection. Bray Hammond, *Banks and Politics in America, from the Revolution to the Civil War* (1957), is learned and favorable. *Hamilton and the National Debt*, a booklet in the Amherst *Problems in American Civilization*, gives conflicting views. Lewis Leary, *That Rascal Freneau* (1941), is the best account of Hamilton's keenest journalistic critic; D. R. Anderson, *William Branch Giles* (1914), is a scholarly work on one of his most pugnacious Congressional foes.

2. THE NEW REPUBLIC AND THE OLD WORLD, 1789-1793

Special

BRITISH RELATIONS

S. F. Bemis, *Jay's Treaty* (1924), the standard study, is damaging to Hamilton and Jay but the author approves Federalist policies on the whole. The monograph of V. G. Setzer, *The Commercial Reciprocity Policy of the United States, 1774-1829* (1937), presents the policies of Madison and Jefferson more sympathetically. A. L. Burt, *The United States, Great Britain, and British North America* (1940), an able work extending through the War of 1812, is favorable to a pro-British policy and defends Jay. Frank Monaghan, *John Jay* (1935), is a friendly biography.

THE UNITED STATES AND THE FRENCH REVOLUTION

Zoltán Haraszti, *John Adams and the Prophets of Progress* (1952), presents in stimulating form Adams's criticism of French writers. C. D. Hazen, *Contemporary American Opinion of the French Revolution* (1897), is largely outmoded. Gilbert Chinard, *Thomas Jefferson: Apostle of Americanism* (1929), a good general biography, is specially good on Jefferson's relations with the French. These are discussed in considerable detail in Malone, *Jefferson and the Rights of Man* and *Jefferson and the Ordeal of Liberty*. Gouverneur Morris, *A Diary of the French Revolution*, edited by B. C. Davenport (2 vols., 1939), is full of wit and not without wickedness. Paine's "The Rights of Man," in *Representative Selections*, edited by Clark, shows the pamphleteer at his height. R. R. Palmer, in *The Age of the Democratic Revolution*, Vol. I (1959), ably synthesizes developments in the two worlds to 1791.

The monograph of C. M. Thomas, *American Neutrality in 1793* (1931), is the best single study of this important subject. The article on the fiery Genêt by M. H. Woodfin in *Dictionary of American Biography* offers a good shortcut.

The great plague of yellow fever in Philadelphia in 1793 is described in J. H. Powell, *Bring Out Your Dead* (1949). Its hero was the fabulous Dr. Benjamin Rush, whose *Letters,* ably edited by L. H. Butterfield (2 vols., 1951), are full of interest.

3. HAMILTON IN THE ASCENDANT, 1794-1796

Special

FOREIGN AFFAIRS

Important special studies are S. F. Bemis, *Jay's Treaty,* and *Pinckney's Treaty* (1926); A. P. Whitaker, *The Spanish-American Frontier, 1783-1795* (1927), and *The Mississippi Question* (1934). The article of Irving Brant, "Edmund Randolph, Not Guilty!" in *William and Mary Quarterly* (April 1950), is a convincing treatment of a confused and controversial episode. W. P. Cresson, *James Monroe* (1946), is sympathetic.

DOMESTIC DEVELOPMENTS

L. D. Baldwin, *Whiskey Rebels: The Story of a Frontier Uprising* (1939), and E. P. Link, *Democratic-Republican Societies* (1942), are studies of special interest. The attitudes of High Federalists can be seen in the early volumes of C. R. King, *Life and Correspondence of Rufus King* (6 vols., 1894-1900), and George Gibbs, *Memoirs of the Administrations of Washington and Adams* (2 vols., 1846), from the papers of Oliver Wolcott.

V. H. Paltsits, ed., *Washington's Farewell Address* (1935), a full account with documents, is also a moving story. The address itself is in Commager, *Documents,* and should by all means be read.

4. THE END OF FEDERALIST CONTROL, 1797-1801

Special

WAR WITH FRANCE

This is covered by general naval histories and G. W. Allen, *Our Naval War with France* (1909), with good bibliography. See also B. C. Steiner, *James McHenry* (1907).

FEDERALIST REPRESSION

The text of the Alien and Sedition Acts is in Commager, *Documents.* J. M. Smith, *Freedom's Fetters* (1956), and J. C. Miller, *Crisis in Freedom* (1951), give the story; Bernard Faÿ, *The Two Franklins* (1933), tells about the editor,

B. F. Bache; Dumas Malone, *Public Life of Thomas Cooper* (1925), Chs. 3-4, covers the trial of one victim; J. F. McLaughlin, *Matthew Lyon* (1901), describes another. L. W. Levy, *Legacy of Suppression: Freedom of Speech and Press in Early American History* (1960) takes an unfavorable view.

KENTUCKY AND VIRGINIA RESOLUTIONS

Text in Commager, *Documents*. Koch, *Jefferson and Madison*, Ch. 7, is the best account of the origins of the Resolutions. F. M. Anderson, in *American Historical Review*, Vol. V (Oct. 1899; Jan. 1900), describes contemporary opinion.

POLITICS AND THE ELECTION OF 1800-1801

Manning Dauer, S. G. Kurtz, and Beard, *Economic Origins of Jeffersonian Democracy*, are specially valuable here. Good use can be made of works on political developments in particular states, such as R. J. Purcell, *Connecticut in Transition, 1775-1818* (new edn., 1963), and H. M. Tinkcom, *Republicans and Federalists in Pennsylvania* (1950). Morton Borden, *The Federalism of James A. Bayard* (1954), is a good study of a man who played a crucial role in 1801.

CULTURE

Besides general works on architecture, religion, literature, thought, etc., see H. R. Warfel, *Noah Webster; Schoolmaster of America* (1936); F. L. Mott, *American Journalism* (1950); "The Age of Reason," in Thomas Paine, *Representative Selections;* W. B. Bryan, *History of the National Capital*, Vol. I (1914).

5-6. THE PRESIDENCY OF JEFFERSON

General

This general list for the two chapters is followed by specific suggestions for each of them.

NARRATIVE HISTORIES

Allen Johnson, *Jefferson and His Colleagues* (1921), and E. S. Corwin, *John Marshall and the Constitution* (1919), both in *Chronicles of America*, are excellent within their respective limits. Channing, *History*, Vol. IV, continues to be useful. C. G. Bowers, *Jefferson in Power* (1936), does not come up to *Jefferson and Hamilton* and is equally partisan but is good reading. Henry Adams, *History of the United States* (9 vols., 1889-91), covers the period 1800-1817 elaborately and brilliantly. The work is specially rich on the international side, and the description of the state of the country in Vol. I, Chs. 1-6 is notable. Adams is exceedingly critical of practically everybody.

SOCIAL HISTORY

This topic is covered by Krout and Fox, *Completion of Independence* (*History of American Life*). A sprightly work showing more liking for the Federalist New Englanders than for anybody else is *Jeffersonian America: Notes . . . Collected in the Years 1805-6-7 and 11-12 by Sir Augustus John Foster, Bart.* (1954), edited by R. B. Davis.

BIOGRAPHIES

Nathan Schachner, *Jefferson, Vol. II* (1951), is the only detailed recent biography of that statesman covering this period. Irving Brant, *James Madison* [IV]: *Secretary of State* (1952) is thorough-going and very critical of Henry Adams. The latter's *Albert Gallatin* (1879) is much more admiring of the Secretary of the Treasury than of the administration as a whole. A good supplement is Raymond Walters, Jr., *Albert Gallatin: Jeffersonian Financier and Diplomat* (1957). Beveridge, *Marshall*, Vol. III, is of the first importance. W. C. Bruce, *John Randolph of Roanoke* (2 vols., 1922), is a comprehensive treatment of that brilliant and erratic Congressional leader. W. E. Dodd, *Life of Nathaniel W. Macon* (1903), is a sympathetic account of a more consistently loyal Jeffersonian. S. E. Morison, *Harrison Gray Otis* (2 vols., 1913), and C. E. Cunningham, *Timothy Dwight, 1752-1817* (1942), are good studies of New England Federalists. William Plumer, *Memorandum of Proceedings in the Senate, 1803-1807*, edited by E. S. Brown (1923), reflects Federalist attitudes. Talbot Hamlin, *Benjamin Henry Latrobe* (1955), is an admirable biography of a major architectural figure.

5. JEFFERSONIAN LIBERALISM, 1801-1805

Special

THE MAN AND HIS MEANING

Jefferson and Jeffersonianism are interpreted variously by Beard, Beveridge, Bowers, Parrington, and others in works already cited. The *Jefferson Reader: A Treasury of Writings about Thomas Jefferson* (1953), edited by F. C. Rosenberger, contains a variety of comments and includes a thoughtful and delightful article, "Thomas Jefferson, Gentle Radical," from Dixon Wecter, *The Hero in America* (1941). See also Richard Hofstadter, "Thomas Jefferson: The Aristocrat as Democrat," in *The American Political Tradition and the Men Who Made It* (1949); C. M. Wiltse, *The Jeffersonian Tradition in American Democracy* (1935); M. D. Peterson, *The Jefferson Image in the American Mind* (1960). Other aspects of the man are shown in E. T. Martin, *Thomas Jefferson: Scientist* (1952); S. N. Randolph, *Domestic Life of Thomas Jefferson* (1871).

INAUGURATION AND SOCIAL REGIME

The description of the inauguration by Henry Adams is in his *History*, Vol. I,

Ch. 7; it is also in Sheehan, *Making of American History*, pp. 149-168. The first inaugural address can be profitably and easily read in Commager, *Documents;* Koch and Peden, *Writings* (Modern Library); and elsewhere. Margaret Bayard Smith gives interesting social description and sympathetic contemporary comments in *The First Forty Years of Washington Society* (1906), edited by Gaillard Hunt. Henry Adams plays up the ludicrous features of the regime in some of his sprightliest passages; see especially *History*, II, Ch. 16.

ADMINISTRATION AND PRESIDENTIAL LEADERSHIP

L. D. White, *The Jeffersonians: A Study in Administrative History* (1951), covers the period to Andrew Jackson. This fresh treatment can be supplemented by the monographs: C. R. Fish, *The Civil Service and the Patronage* (1903); and R. V. Harlow, *History of Legislative methods before 1825* (1917). E. S. Corwin, *The President: Office and Powers* (1948) is a standard work. N. E. Cunningham, Jr., *The Jeffersonian Republicans in Power: Party Operations, 1801-1809* (1963), is excellent.

JUDICIARY FIGHT

Beveridge, in *Marshall,* Vol. III, Chs. 1-4, gives a full and fascinating but biased account. Corwin, *Marshall and the Constitution,* is better balanced. See also Charles Warren, *The Supreme Court in United States History,* Vol. I, Chs. 4-6 (1927); Borden, *Federalism of James A. Bayard,* Ch. 9.

NEW ENGLAND OPPOSITION AND ATTACKS ON JEFFERSON

Theodore Dwight, *The Character of Thomas Jefferson* (1839), is a bitterly hostile view. Henry Adams, *Documents Relating to New England Federalism, 1800-1815* (1877), is an important collection. J. T. Adams, *New England in the Republic, 1776-1850* (1926), contains a general account. For the Paine episode see Adams, *History*, Vol. I. Ch. 12. F. L. Mott, *Jefferson and the Press* (1943), Ch. 9, shows his disillusionment.

6. EXPANSION AND DOMESTIC FACTION, 1803-1809

Special

WESTERN DEVELOPMENTS

A good over-all account is in Billington, *Westward Expansion*, Chs. 10-13, with bibliographies. See also the narrative of F. A. Ogg, *The Old Northwest* (1921, *Chronicles of America*). P. J. Treat, *The National Land System, 1785-1820* (1910) is a standard work, valuable for details. R. M. Robbins, *Our Landed Heritage: The Public Domain, 1776-1936* (1942), Part I, goes to 1850.

LOUISIANA PURCHASE

The best approach is through the general and diplomatic histories. Henry Adams, *History*, Vol. II, Chs. 1-6, has rich materials on this topic. More specialized works are: Whitaker, *Mississippi Question;* E. W. Lyon, *The Man*

Who Sold Louisiana: The Life of François Barbé-Marbois (1942); E. S. Brown, *Constitutional History of the Louisiana Purchase* (1920); I. J. Cox, *The West Florida Controversy* (1918). George Dangerfield, *Chancellor Robert R. Livingston* (1960), is an excellent biography.

EXPLORATIONS

Brebner, *Explorers of North America*, Ch. 24, is a general account. The condensed *Journals of Lewis and Clark* (1953), edited by Bernard DeVoto, give a readable first-hand story of a great adventure.

FACTION AND CONSPIRACY

The state of mind of die-hard Federalists is shown in Henry Adams, ed., *Documents Relating to New England Federalism*, pp. 331-381. H. C. Syrett and J. G. Cooke, eds., *Interview in Weehawken: The Burr-Hamilton Duel as Told in the Original Documents* (1960), is fascinating. T. P. Abernethy, *The Burr Conspiracy* (1955) is the latest study of that confused subject. Beveridge, in *Marshall*, Vol. III, Chs. 6-9, describes the conspiracy and is very detailed about the trial; Corwin, in *Marshall and the Constitution* is much more critical of the Chief Justice. R. B. Morris, in *Fair Trial* (1952), Ch. 5, is particularly concerned with procedure and tells a good story.

FOREIGN AFFAIRS AND EMBARGO

R. W. Irwin, *Diplomatic Relations of the United States with the Barbary Powers* (1931) is a monograph with bibliography. L. M. Sears, *Jefferson and the Embargo* (1927) is the fullest study of the subject and more favorable to Jefferson than most; it is particularly good on the effects of the Embargo on different parts of the country. General diplomatic and naval histories can be supplemented by Henry Adams, *History*, Vols, III, IV, and the noted work of A. T. Mahan, *The Influence of Sea Power upon the French Revolution and Empire, 1793-1812* (2 vols., 1892). A more favorable view of American diplomacy is taken by Brant in *Madison [IV]: Secretary of State*. Bradford Perkins, in *The First Rapprochement: England and the U.S., 1795-1805* (1955), and *Prologue to War: England and the U.S., 1805-1812* (1963), is critical. French Decrees, British Orders in Council, and American Acts for the years 1806-12 are in Bartlett, *Record of American Diplomacy*, Ch. 7.

7. THE WAR OF 1812

General

The story is told in Johnson, *Jefferson and his Colleagues*, and R. D. Paine, *The Fight for a Free Sea* (1920, *Chronicles of America*); Channing, *History*, Vol. IV, Chs. 16-20; F. F. Beirne, *The War of 1812* (1949); and, most fully of all, in Henry Adams, *History*, Vols. VI-IX. Irving Brant, *James Madison, The President, 1809-1812* (1956) and *Commander-in-Chief, 1812-1836* (1961), provide a modern corrective to Adams.

Special

CAUSES

On the part played by the West, the point of view of J. W. Pratt, in *Expansionists of 1812* (rev. edn., 1949), has been challenged by A. L. Burt, in *The United States, Great Britain, and British America,* Chs. 11-15. For the most conspicuous War Hawk, see Bernard Mayo, *Henry Clay* (1937), Chs. 9-13. See also Billington, *Westward Expansion,* Ch. 13.

OPERATIONS

Anyone wishing to go beyond general histories of the Navy and Army can find abundant materials in A. T. Mahan, *Sea Power in Its Relations to the War of 1812* (2 vols., 1905), and in Marquis James, *Andrew Jackson* [I]: *The Border Captain* (1933), Chs. 9-20.

NEW ENGLAND OPPOSITION

The best account is in Morison, *Harrison Gray Otis,* Vol. II, Chs. 21-28. For the Report and Resolutions of the Hartford Convention, see Commager, *Documents.*

DIPLOMACY AND PEACE

An excellent account is S. F. Bemis, *John Quincy Adams and the Foundations of American Foreign Policy* (1949), Chs. 9-10.

Part II: Nationalism, Sectionalism, and Democracy, 1815-1841

8. THE COMPLETION OF INDEPENDENCE: POSTWAR DIPLOMATIC TRIUMPHS, 1815-1823

General

The course of events is described in the general diplomatic histories of Bailey, Bemis, and Pratt, and more fully in Bemis, *John Quincy Adams and the Foundations of American Foreign Policy,* Chs. 11-19; and George Dangerfield, *The Era of Good Feelings* (1952), Part 4.

Special

Dexter Perkins, *The Monroe Doctrine, 1823-1826* (1923) is the standard treatment; this author carries the story through the following century in *Hands Off: A History of the Monroe Doctrine* (1941). Documents, including extracts from

Monroe's message of Dec. 2, 1823, to Congress, are in Bartlett, *Record of American Diplomacy*, Ch. 10. Other important works are: A. P. Whitaker, *The United States and the Independence of Latin America* (1941); E. H. Tatum, *The United States and Europe* (1936). See also W. P. Cresson, *James Monroe.*

9-10. ADMINISTRATIONS OF MONROE AND JOHN QUINCY ADAMS

General

NARRATIVES

F. J. Turner, *Rise of the New West, 1819-1828* (1906, *American Nation*), is excellent for sectional developments as well as political events. Turner's famous essay, "The Significance of the Frontier in American History," can be appropriately read at this point. It is in his book, *Frontier in American History*, Ch. 1; and in Sheehan, *Making of American History*, Vol. I, pp. 427-462. George Dangerfield, *The Era of Good Feelings*, is reliable and a pleasure to read. C. S. Sydnor, *The Development of Southern Sectionalism, 1819-1848* (1948, in *History of the South*), Chs. 1-6, is thorough and judicious. Krout and Fox, *The Completion of Independence (History of American Life)*, provides the social background to 1830.

TOPICAL HISTORIES

Dewey, *Financial History*, continues to be useful, and Taussig, *Tariff History*, becomes increasingly so in this period. Attention should again be called to the illuminating editorial introductions in Callender, *Selections from the Economic History of the United States.*

POLITICAL BIOGRAPHIES AND MEMOIRS

Besides Marquis James, *Andrew Jackson* [II]: *Portrait of a President*, and Wiltse, *John C. Calhoun [II]: Nationalist, 1782-1828*, see: M. L. Coit, *John C. Calhoun, American Patriot* (1950), a human and very friendly treatment; G. G. Van Deusen, *The Life of Henry Clay* (1937); Carl Schurz, *The Life of Henry Clay* (2 vols., 1887), old but still interesting; Allan Nevins, ed., *Diary of John Quincy Adams* (rev. edn., 1951), a selection from Adams's famous *Memoirs* (12 vols., 1874-77); C. M. Fuess, *Daniel Webster* (2 vols., 1930);   and T. P. Govan, *Nicholas Biddle: Nationalist and Public Banker, 1786-1844* (1959).

9. THE "ERA OF GOOD FEELINGS": NATIONS AND SECTIONS

Special

SECTIONALISM

F. J. Turner, *The Significance of Sections in American History*, edited by Max Farrand (1950).

Northeast

Agricultural developments are described in Bidwell and Falconer, *History of Agriculture in the Northern United States;* commercial developments in R. G. Albion, *The Rise of New York Port, 1815-1860* (1939), and Morison, *Maritime History of Massachusetts;* manufacturing in V. S. Clark, *History of Manufacturing in the United States, 1607-1860* (rev. edn., 4 vols., 1929). L. K. Mathews, *The Expansion of New England* (1906) describes New England migrations to the West.

Older South

For agricultural developments of all sorts, see Gray, *History of Agriculture in the Southern United States.* Works more restricted in scope are A. O. Craven, *Soil Exhaustion as a Factor in the Agricultural History of Virginia and Maryland, 1606-1860* (1926); and J. C. Robert, *The Tobacco Kingdom* (1938). The development of cotton culture is described more fully in Ch. 32 of the present work, but the biography, *Eli Whitney* (1952), by Allan Nevins and Jeanette Mirsky, should be mentioned here.

Transportation and Western Settlement

A. B. Hulbert, *The Paths of Inland Commerce* (1920, *Chronicles of America*) is brief and readable. R. A. Billington, *Westward Expansion*, Chs. 13-17, carries the story to and beyond the limits of the present chapter; the bibliographies give many suggestions for reading about particular localties. Other works of interest are: R. E. Riegel, *America Moves West* (1930); R. C. Buley, *The Old Northwest: Pioneer Period, 1815-1840* (2 vols., 1950); Everett Dick, *The Dixie Frontier* (1948).

10. JOHN MARSHALL AND JOHN QUINCY ADAMS

Special

Marshall and His Decisions

Constitutional histories of McLaughlin, Swisher, Kelly and Harbison; Beveridge, *Marshall*, Vols. III-IV; Corwin, *Marshall and the Constitution;* Warren, *Supreme Court*, Chs. 12-16, 19; C. G. Haines, *The Role of the Supreme Court, 1789-1835* (1944). The major decisions are in Commager, *Documents.* The struggle with Virginia is best described in Warren, Ch. 13, and in Sydnor, *Development of Southern Sectionalism*, Ch. 6. For a brilliant brief description of the "Old Republicans" in the Upper South, see A. M. Schlesinger, Jr., *The Age of Jackson* (1945), Ch. 2. The controversy between the federal government and the state of Georgia, which is referred to again in Ch. 12 of the present book, is described fully in U. B. Phillips, *Georgia and State Rights* (1902; *Annual Report of the American Historical Association* for 1901), Chs. 2-3. D. G. Morgan, *Justice William Johnson, The First Dissenter* (1955), is a good biography of the member of the Court who most opposed Marshall.

POLITICS AND THE TARIFF CONTROVERSY

These are well described in the general works and biographies already cited. Those interested in the rival philosophies of protection and free trade can make a good beginning by reading the articles on these topics in *Encyclopedia of the Social Sciences*. The important American thinkers are described in Joseph Dorfman, *The Economic Mind in American Civilization* (1946), Vol. II; see especially Chs. 28-31. J. A. Garraty, in *Silas Wright* (1949) casts fresh light on the motives of the Jacksonians in the Tariff of Abominations. The activities of an important early opponent of the tariff in South Carolina are described in Malone, *Thomas Cooper*, Chs. 9-10.

11-12. POLITICAL HISTORY OF THE JACKSON ERA

General

NARRATIVES

The posthumous publication of F. J. Turner, *The United States, 1830-1850* (1935), though incomplete, is the best single work on its period. A. M. Schlesinger, Jr., *The Age of Jackson* (1945) goes far beyond party politics and is an unusually stimulating book, though some other scholars do not see so close a parallel with the age of Franklin D. Roosevelt as the author does. C. G. Bowers, *Party Battles of the Jackson Period* (1922) is vivid and partisan. Sydnor, *Development of Southern Sectionalism*, Chs. 8, 9, continues to be good. An interesting interpretation is that of Richard Hofstadter in *American Political Tradition*, Ch. 3. C. R. Fish, *The Rise of the Common Man* (1932, *History of American Life*) covers social history. R. V. Remini, *The Election of Andrew Jackson* (1963), is the latest study.

BIOGRAPHIES

Marquis James, *Andrew Jackson* [II]: *Portrait of a President*, falls in this period, as does Wiltse, *Calhoun* [II]: *Nullifier, 1829-1839* (1949), which is particularly good for national politics, though too favorable to Calhoun and too severe on Jackson and Van Buren for many tastes. R. V. Remini, *Martin Van Buren and the Making of the Democratic Party* (1959), goes through 1828. Van Buren's *Autobiography* is available, edited by J. C. Fitzpatrick (1920: *Annual Report Amer. Hist. Asso.* for 1918, Vol. II). W. E. Smith, in *The Francis Preston Blair Family in Politics*, Vol. I (1933), presents an important member of the "Kitchen Cabinet." Other important biographies, besides those of Clay and Webster already mentioned, are C. B. Swisher, *Roger B. Taney* (1935); T. D. Jervey, *Robert Y. Hayne and His Times* (1909).

Special

JACKSONIAN DEMOCRACY

In its political aspects this is treated in general histories and biographies; in histories of parties, such as Binkley, *American Political Parties*, Chs. 6, 7; and in works on political thought, such as C. E. Merriam, *A History of American Political Theories* (1903), Ch. 5. A recent study of great suggestiveness is Marvin Meyers, *The Jacksonian Persuasion: Politics and Belief* (1957). See also E. M. Carroll, *Origins of the Whig Party* (1923); Chilton Williamson, *American Suffrage from Property to Democracy, 1760-1860* (1960); A. B. Darling, "Jacksonian Democracy in Massachusetts," *American Historical Review*, October 1923. A critical view of the "democracy" of Jackson himself is taken by T. P. Abernethy in *From Frontier to Plantation in Tennessee* (1932), Chs. 10-18. J. W. Ward, in *Andrew Jackson: Symbol for an Age* (1955), brilliantly argues that his age created him in its own image. Alexis de Tocqueville viewed American democracy in this era, in the large, not as a party movement. An admirable recent edition of his *Democracy in America*, first published in 1835, is that of Phillips Bradley (2 vols., 1942). Works dealing with expressions of the democratic spirit outside politics are mentioned later.

Administration

L. D. White, *The Jacksonians: A Study in Administrative History, 1829-1861* (1954), is a fresh and illuminating study; see esp. Chs. 1, 2, 8. The old work of C. R. Fish, *Civil Service and Patronage* is still useful for the origins and development of the spoils system. For the Presidency under Jackson, see W. E. Binkley, *Powers of the President* (1937), Chs. 4-5; Edward Stanwood, *History of the Presidency* (1921), Vol. I, Ch. 12.

The Bank and Panic

Besides Dewey, *Financial History*, and Hammond, *Banks and Politics in America*, the following more restricted works are suggested: R. C. H. Catterall, *The Second Bank of the United States* (1903); R. C. McGrane, *The Panic of 1837: Some Financial Problems of the Jackson Era* (1924); B. H. Hibbard, *A History of the Public Land Policies* (1939).

Nullification

Special studies are D. F. Houston, *A Critical Study of Nullification in South Carolina* (1906), and C. S. Boucher, *The Nullification Controversy in South Carolina* (1916), giving greater attention to the local fight. Calhoun's Exposition, the South Carolina Ordinance, and Jackson's Proclamation are in Commager, *Documents*.

Indians

Billington, in *Westward Expansion*, Ch. 15, gives a general account of the removal and numerous bibliographical suggestions. Events in Georgia, are well described in Phillips, *Georgia and State Rights*. See also M. L. Starkey, *The Cherokee Nation* (1946).

13. SLAVERY IS ATTACKED AND DEFENDED

General

The abolitionist movement is described in the general histories. A rather critical modern treatment is G. H. Barnes, *The Anti-Slavery Impulse* (1933). D. L. Dumond, in *Anti-Slavery Origins of the Civil War* (1939), Chs. 1-4, is more favorable, and in *Antislavery: The Crusade for Freedom in America* (1961) much more so. S. M. Elkins, *Slavery: A Problem in American Institutional and Intellectual Life* (1959), is a stimulating essay based on a comparative view of the subject. The best general account of developments within the South is in Sydnor, *Development of Southern Sectionalism*, esp. Ch. 10. References to slavery as an economic and social institution are given in the bibliography for Book 3, Ch. 4 of the present work. In the present chapter, the emphasis is on attitudes and ideas, agitation and repression, but general works on slavery provide a necessary background.

Among these are: Phillips, *American Negro Slavery*, based on notable scholarship but reflecting a conservative Southern point of view; K. M. Stampp, *The Peculiar Institution* (1956), emphasizing economics and directly opposing Phillips; Franklin, *From Slavery to Freedom*, the work of an able and conscientious Negro scholar; Gunnar Myrdal, *An American Dilemma* (2 vols., 1944), by a noted sociologist whose major interest was in the contemporary scene and whose chief concern was for the future.

Special

J. C. Robert, *The Road from Monticello: A Study of the Virginia Slavery Debate of 1832* (1941), corrects erroneous impressions of these events and gives significant extracts from speeches. C. H. Ambler, *Sectionalism in Virginia from 1776 to 1861* (1910) gives the background of internal politics. The unhappy position of the Free Negroes is described in Franklin, *Slavery to Freedom*, Ch. 14, and, more specifically, in several treatments of particular states. Among the best of these are J. H. Franklin, *The Free Negro in North Carolina, 1790-1860* (1943), and E. R. Turner, *The Negro in Pennsylvania* (1910). The accounts of the colonization movement in general works can be supplemented by the monograph of E. L. Fox, *The American Colonization Society, 1817-1840* (1919). For the foreign slave trade, see the early monograph of W. E. B. DuBois, *The Suppression of the African Slave Trade* (1896); for the domestic traffic, see W. H. Collins, *The Domestic Slave Trade of the Southern United States* (1904); Frederic Bancroft, *Slave-Trading in the Old South* (1931).

The individual abolitionist most emphasized by Barnes in *Anti-Slavery Impulse* is Theodore Dwight Weld; his article on Weld in *Dictionary of American Biography* offers a convenient shortcut. He is very critical of Garrison. There is no adequate biography of Garrison, since his biographers have largely accepted him at his own valuation. Richard Hofstadter, "Wendell Phillips: The Patrician as Agitator," Ch. 6 of *American Political Tradition*, is excellent. See also works on reform and reformers listed in the following chapter of the present work

The Southern proslavery philosophy is summed up in W. E. Dodd, *The Cotton Kingdom* (1917, *Chronicles of America*), and more fully described in W. S. Jenkins, *Pro-Slavery Thought in the Old South* (1935); see also A. Y. Lloyd, *The Slavery Controversy, 1831-1860* (1934), Chs. 4-7. The "Black Terror" and Southern repression of agitation are well described in the important book of Clement Eaton, *Freedom of Thought in the Old South* (1940), Chs. 4-5. See also R. B. Nye, *Fettered Freedom: Civil Liberties and the Slavery Controversy* (1949); and W. S. Savage, *The Controversy over the Distribution of Abolition Literature, 1830-1860* (1938). J. N. Norwood, *The Schism in the Methodist Episcopal Church, 1844* (1923), gives the details of that fateful occurrence.

14. JACKSONIAN REFORM MOVEMENTS

General

Much that bears on this and the following chapter can be found in Channing, *History*, Vol. V; Fish, *Rise of the Common Man;* Parrington, *Main Currents in American Thought*, Vol. II; Curti, *Growth of American Thought*, esp. Chs. 14-15; Schlesinger, *Age of Jackson*. Other books of general interest are: A. M. Schlesinger, Sr., *The American as Reformer* (1950); Daniel Aaron, *Men of Good Hope: A Story of American Progressives* (1951); A. F. Tyler, *Freedom's Ferment: Phases of American Social History to 1860* (1944). The underlying popular philosophy is nowhere better described than in R. H. Gabriel, *The Course of American Democratic Thought* (1940), Esp. Ch. 2.

Special

The following deal with education in this period and later: Paul Monroe, *The Founding of the American Public School System* (1940), Vol. I; B. A. Hinsdale, *Horace Mann and the Common School Revival in the United States* (1898); D. G. Tewksbury, *The Founding of American Colleges and Universities before the Civil War* (1932); Merle Curti, *Social Ideas of American Educators* (1935). Detailed suggestions for reading on various phases of education and particular institutions are in *Harvard Guide*, sect. 151, p. 350.

In the absence of good accounts of the movement for women's rights, it can be most easily approached, perhaps, by reading in the *Dictionary of American Biography* the articles on Susan B. Anthony, Elizabeth Gady Stanton, and other leaders. Mason Wade, *Margaret Fuller* (1940), is a good biography.

F. R. Dulles, *Labor in America*, Ch. 4, deals with this period. On socialistic experiments, see A. E. Bestor, Jr., *Backwoods Utopias* (1950); J. H. Noyes, *The History of American Socialisms* (1870); R. W. Leopold, *Robert Dale Owen* (1940).

J. A. Krout, *The Origins of Prohibition* (1925) is an excellent account of the temperance movement. On world peace, see Merle Curti, *The American Peace Crusade, 1815-1861* (1929), and *The Learned Blacksmith* (1937). Humanitarianism is well illustrated in Helen Marshall, *Dorothea Dix: Forgotten Samaritan* (1937). Interest in the reformers of this era has produced a luxuriant crop of good biographies. Others of these are: H. S. Commager, *Theodore*

Parker (1936); R. V. Harlow, *Gerrit Smith: Philanthropist and Reformer* (1939); A. M. Schlesinger, Jr., *Orestes A. Brownson* (1939); Odell Shepard, *Pedlar's Progress: A Life of Bronson Alcott* (1937); W. R. Waterman, *Frances Wright* (1934).

15. CULTURAL ACHIEVEMENTS IN A DEMOCRATIC ERA

General

Many books dealing with some particular aspect of American cultural history bear on this period without being restricted to it. The growing diversity of American culture is suggested by the following brief list.

RELIGION

W. W. Sweet, *Story of Religion in America;* and *Revivalism in America: Its Origin, Growth and Decline* (1944).

PHILOSOPHY

Curti, *Growth of American Thought,* esp. Ch. 13; H. W. Schneider, *History of American Philosophy* (1946); W. K. Berkmeister, *A History of Philosophical Ideas in America* (1949).

SCIENCE

Struik, *Yankee Science in the Making;* H. E. Siegerist, *American Medicine* (1934); F. R. Packard, *History of Medicine in the United States,* Vol. I (1931).

LITERATURE

Parrington, *Main Currents,* Vol. II; Spiller, *Literary History of the United States,* Vols. I, II; Quinn, *Literature of the American People,* Part Two; F. L. Mott, *A History of American Magazines* (3 vols., 1930-38), esp. Vol. I, and *American Journalism: A History of Newspapers in the United States* (1941).

ARTS

Larkin, *Art and Life in America;* Tallmadge, *Architecture in America;* Virgil Barker, *American Painting* (1950); Lorado Taft, *The History of American Sculpture* (1930); J. T. Howard, *Our American Music* (rev. edn., 1946).

Special

The topics which invite reading and investigation are very numerous, and the richness of the available literature can only be suggested here.

Unitarianism can be most readily viewed, perhaps, in a biography, such as H. S. Commager, *Theodore Parker.* Those wishing to explore evangelicalism further can find abundant materials in W. W. Sweet, *Religion on the American Frontier* (4 vols., 1931-46). For Mormonism see F. M. Brodie, *No Man Knows My History: The Life of Joseph Smith* (1945); and M. R. Werner, *Brigham*

Young (1925). Works on various religious groups and denominations are listed in *Harvard Guide,* p. 351.

An excellent approach to the difficult subject of Transcendentalism is provided in *The Transcendentalist Revolt against Materialism* (1949) in the Amherst *Problems in American Civilization.* See also biographies of Margaret Fuller, Bronson Alcott, and Orestes Brownson listed in Ch. 27.

Those wishing to explore works on specific sciences will find references in the bibliography of Curti, Ch. 13, and in *Harvard Guide,* p. 352. For individual scientists, see Bernard Jaffe, *Men of Science in America* (1944); J. F. Fulton and E. H. Thomson, *Benjamin Silliman* (1947); C. L. Lewis, *Matthew Fontaine Maury* (1927); and other biographies.

In literature, there is rich reading in F. O. Matthiessen, *American Renaissance: Art and Expression in the Age of Emerson and Whitman* (1941); great charm in Van Wyck Brooks, *The World of Washington Irving* (1944), and *The Flowering of New England* (1936). Biographies of special worth are: R. L. Rusk, *Emerson* (1949); H. S. Canby, *Thoreau* (1939); S. T. Williams, *Washington Irving* (2 vols., 1935); Newton Arvin, *Hawthorne* (1929), and *Melville* (1950); R. E. Spiller, *Fenimore Cooper* (1931); R. B. Nye, *George Bancroft* (1944). Emerson can be approached delightfully by dipping into *The Heart of Emerson's Journals* (1926), edited by Bliss Perry.

In the arts, a work of special interest is Carl Wittke: *Tambo and Bones: A History of the American Minstrel Stage* (1930). The stage as a whole is described in the pictorial *Pageant of America,* Vol. XIV.

APPENDICES

DECLARATION OF INDEPENDENCE

In Congress, July 4, 1776

A DECLARATION BY THE REPRESENTATIVES OF THE UNITED STATES
OF AMERICA, IN CONGRESS ASSEMBLED

When, in the course of human events, it becomes necessary for one people to dissolve the political bands which have connected them with another, and to assume, among the powers of the earth, the separate and equal station to which the laws of nature and of nature's God entitle them, a decent respect to the opinions of mankind requires that they should declare the causes which impel them to the separation.

We hold these truths to be self-evident:—That all men are created equal; that they are endowed by their Creator with certain unalienable rights; that among these are life, liberty, and the pursuit of happiness. That, to secure these rights, governments are instituted among men, deriving their just powers from the consent of the governed; that, whenever any form of government becomes destructive of these ends, it is the right of the people to alter or to abolish it, and to institute a new government, laying its foundation on such principles, and organizing its powers in such form, as to them shall seem most likely to effect their safety and happiness. Prudence, indeed, will dictate, that governments long established should not be changed for light and transient causes; and accordingly all experience hath shown that mankind are more disposed to suffer while evils are sufferable, than to right themselves by abolishing the forms to which they are accustomed. But when a long train of abuses and usurpations, pursuing invariably the same object, evinces a design to reduce them under absolute despotism, it is their right, it is their duty, to throw off such government, and to provide new guards for their future security. Such has been the patient sufferance of these colonies; and such is now the necessity which constrains them to alter their former systems of government. The history of the present King of Great Britain is a history of repeated injuries and usurpations, all having in direct object the establishment of an absolute tyranny over these states. To prove this, let facts be submitted to a candid world.

He has refused his assent to laws the most wholesome and necessary for the public good.

He has forbidden his governors to pass laws of immediate and pressing importance, unless suspended in their operation till his assent should be obtained; and when so suspended, he has utterly neglected to attend to them.

He has refused to pass other laws for the accommodation of large districts of people, unless those people would relinquish the right of representation in the legislature—a right inestimable to them, and formidable to tyrants only.

He has called together legislative bodies at places unusual, uncomfortable, and distant from the depository of their public records, for the sole purpose of fatiguing them into compliance with his measure.

He has dissolved representative houses repeatedly, for opposing, with manly firmness, his invasions on the rights of the people.

He has refused, for a long time after such dissolutions, to cause others to be elected, whereby the legislative powers, incapable of annihilation, have returned to the people at large for their exercise; the State remaining, in the mean time, exposed to all the dangers of invasions from without, and convulsions within.

He has endeavored to prevent the population of these States; for that purpose obstructing the laws for the naturalization of foreigners; refusing to pass others to encourage their migration hither, and raising the conditions of new appropriations of lands.

He has obstructed the administration of justice, by refusing his assent to laws for establishing judiciary powers.

He has made judges dependent on his will alone for the tenure of their offices, and the amount and payment of their salaries.

He has erected a multitude of new offices, and sent hither swarms of officers to harass our people and eat out their substance.

He has kept among us in times of peace, standing armies, without the consent of our legislatures.

He has affected to render the military independent of, and superior to, the civil power.

He has combined with others to subject us to a jurisdiction foreign to our constitutions, and unacknowledged by our laws; giving his assent to their acts of pretended legislation:

For quartering large bodies of armed troops among us;

For protecting them, by a mock trial, from punishment for any murders which they should commit on the inhabitants of these States;

For cutting off our trade with all parts of the world;

For imposing taxes on us without our consent;

For depriving us, in many cases, of the benefits of trial by jury;

For transporting us beyond seas, to be tried for pretended offences;

For abolishing the free system of English laws in a neighboring province, establishing therein an arbitrary government, and enlarging its boundaries, so as to render it at once an example and fit instrument for introducing the same absolute rule into these colonies;

For taking away our charters, abolishing our most valuable laws, and altering, fundamentally, the forms of our governments;

For suspending our own legislatures, and declaring themselves invested with power to legislate for us in all cases whatsoever.

He has abdicated government here, by declaring us out of his protection, and waging war against us.

He has plundered our seas, ravaged our coasts, burned our towns, and destroyed the lives of our people.

He is at this time transporting large armies of foreign mercenaries to complete the works of death, desolation and tyranny, already begun with circumstances of cruelty and perfidy scarcely paralleled in the most barbarous ages, and totally unworthy the head of a civilized nation.

He has constrained our fellow-citizens, taken captive on the high seas, to bear arms against their country, to become the executioners of their friends and brethren, or to fall themselves by their hands.

He has excited domestic insurrection among us, and has endeavored to bring on the inhabitants of our frontiers the merciless Indian savages, whose known rule of warfare is an undistinguished destruction of all ages, sexes, and conditions.

In every stage of these oppressions we have petitioned for redress in the most humble terms; our repeated petitions have been answered only by repeated injury. A prince whose character is thus marked by every act which may define a tyrant, is unfit to be the ruler of a free people.

Nor have we been wanting in our attentions to our British brethren. We have warned them, from time to time, of attempts by their legislature to extend an unwarrantable jurisdiction over us. We have reminded them of the circumstances of our emigration and settlement here. We have appealed to their native justice and magnanimity; and we have conjured them, by the ties of our common kindred, to disavow these usurpations, which would inevitably interrupt our connections and correspondence. They, too, have been deaf to the voice of justice and consanguinity. We must, therefore, acquiesce in the necessity which denounces our separation, and hold them, as we hold the rest of mankind, enemies in war, in peace friends.

We, therefore, the Representatives of the United States of America, in General Congress assembled, appealing to the Supreme Judge of the world for the rectitude of our intentions, do, in the name and by the authority of the good people of these colonies, solemnly publish and declare, That these united Colonies are, and of right ought to be, free and independent states; that they are absolved from all allegiance to the British crown, and that all political connection between them and the state of Great Britain is, and ought to be, totally dissolved; and that, as free and independent states, they have full power to levy war, conclude peace, contract alliances, establish commerce, and do all other acts and things which independent states may of right do. And, for the support of this declaration, with a firm reliance on the protection of Divine Providence, we mutually pledge to each other our lives, our fortunes, and our sacred honor.

The foregoing Declaration was, by order of Congress, engrossed, and signed by the following members:

JOHN HANCOCK

NEW HAMPSHIRE
JOSIAH BARTLETT
WILLIAM WHIPPLE
MATTHEW THORNTON

MASSACHUSETTS BAY
SAMUEL ADAMS
JOHN ADAMS
ROBERT TREAT PAINE
ELBRIDGE GERRY

RHODE ISLAND
STEPHEN HOPKINS
WILLIAM ELLERY

CONNECTICUT
ROGER SHERMAN
SAMUEL HUNTINGTON
WILLIAM WILLIAMS
OLIVER WOLCOTT

NEW YORK
WILLIAM FLOYD
PHILIP LIVINGSTON
FRANCIS LEWIS
LEWIS MORRIS

NEW JERSEY
RICHARD STOCKTON
JOHN WITHERSPOON
FRANCIS HOPKINSON
JOHN HART
ABRAHAM CLARK

PENNSYLVANIA
ROBERT MORRIS
BENJAMIN RUSH
BENJAMIN FRANKLIN
JOHN MORTON
GEORGE CLYMER
JAMES SMITH
GEORGE TAYLOR
JAMES WILSON
GEORGE ROSS

DELAWARE
CAESAR RODNEY
GEORGE READ
THOMAS M'KEAN

MARYLAND
SAMUEL CHASE
WILLIAM PACA
THOMAS STONE

CHARLES CARROLL, of
  Carrollton

VIRGINIA
GEORGE WYTHE
RICHARD HENRY LEE
THOMAS JEFFERSON
BENJAMIN HARRISON
THOMAS NELSON, JR.
FRANCIS LIGHTFOOT LEE
CARTER BRAXTON

NORTH CAROLINA
WILLIAM HOOPER
JOSEPH HEWES
JOHN PENN

SOUTH CAROLINA
EDWARD RUTLEDGE
THOMAS HEYWARD, JR.
THOMAS LYNCH, JR.
ARTHUR MIDDLETON

GEORGIA
BUTTON GWINNETT
LYMAN HALL
GEORGE WALTON

THE
CONSTITUTION
OF THE
UNITED STATES OF AMERICA

WE, THE PEOPLE OF THE UNITED STATES, IN ORDER TO FORM A MORE PERFECT union, establish justice, insure domestic tranquillity, provide for the common defence, promote the general welfare, and secure the blessings of liberty to ourselves and our posterity, do ordain and establish this constitution for the United States of America.

ARTICLE I
SECTION 1

ALL LEGISLATIVE POWERS HEREIN GRANTED SHALL BE VESTED IN A CONGRESS OF the United States, which shall consist of a Senate and a House of Representatives.

SECTION 2

The House of Representatives shall be composed of Members chosen every second Year by the People of the several States, and the Electors in each State shall have the Qualifications requisite for Electors of the most numerous Branch of the State Legislature.

No Person shall be a Representative who shall not have attained to the Age of twenty-five Years, and been seven Years a Citizen of the United States, and who shall not, when elected, be an Inhabitant of that State in which he shall be chosen.

[Representatives and direct Taxes shall be apportioned among the several States which may be included within this Union, according to their respective Numbers, which shall be determined by adding to the whole Number of free Persons, including those bound to Service for a Term of Years, and excluding Indians not taxed, three fifths of all other Persons.]* The actual Enumeration shall be made within three Years after the first Meeting of the Congress of the United States, and within every subsequent Term of ten Years, in such Manner as they shall by Law direct. The Number of Representatives shall not exceed one for every thirty Thousand, but each State shall have at Least one

* Repealed by Section 2 of Amendment XIV.

Representative; and until such enumeration shall be made, the State of New Hampshire shall be entitled to chuse three, Massachusetts eight, Rhode-Island and Providence Plantations one, Connecticut five, New-York six, New Jersey four, Pennsylvania eight, Delaware one, Maryland six, Virginia ten, North Carolina five, South Carolina five, and Georgia three.

When vacancies happen in the Representation from any State, the Executive Authority thereof shall issue Writs of Election to fill such Vacancies.

The House of Representatives shall chuse their Speaker and other Officers; and shall have the sole Power of Impeachment.

SECTION 3

The Senate of the United States shall be composed of two Senators from each State, [chosen by the Legislature thereof,]* for six Years; and each Senator shall have one Vote.

Immediately after they shall be assembled in Consequence of the first Election, they shall be divided as equally as may be into three Classes. The Seats of the Senators of the first Class shall be vacated at the Expiration of the second Year, of the second Class at the Expiration of the fourth Year, and of the third Class at the Expiration of the sixth Year, so that one-third may be chosen every second Year; [and if Vacancies happen by Resignation, or otherwise, during the Recess of the Legislature of any State, the Executive thereof may make temporary Appointments until the next Meeting of the Legislature, which shall then fill such Vacancies.]†

No person shall be a Senator who shall not have attained to the Age of thirty Years, and been nine Years a Citizen of the United States, and who shall not, when elected, be an Inhabitant of that State for which he shall be chosen.

The Vice President of the United States shall be President of the Senate, but shall have no Vote, unless they be equally divided.

The Senate shall chuse their other Officers, and also a President pro tempore, in the Absence of the Vice President, or when he shall exercise the Office of President of the United States.

The Senate shall have the sole Power to try all Impeachments. When sitting for that Purpose, they shall be an Oath or Affirmation. When the President of the United States is tried, the Chief Justice shall preside: And no Person shall be convicted without the Concurrence of two thirds of the Members present.

Judgment in Cases of Impeachment shall not extend further than to removal from Office, and disqualification to hold and enjoy any Office of honor, Trust or Profit under the United States: but the Party convicted shall nevertheless be liable and subject to Indictment, Trial, Judgment and Punishment, according to Law.

SECTION 4

The Times, Places and Manner of holding Elections for Senators and Representatives, shall be prescribed in each State by the Legislature thereof; but the Congress may at any time by Law make or alter such Regulations, except as to the Places of chusing Senators.

* Replaced by Section 1 of Amendment XVII.
† Changed by Clause 2 of Amendment XVII.

The Congress shall assemble at least once in every Year, and such Meeting* shall [be on the first Monday in December] unless they shall by Law appoint a different Day.

SECTION 5

Each House shall be the Judge of the Elections, Returns and Qualifications of its own Members, and a Majority of each shall constitute a Quorum to do Business; but a smaller Number may adjourn from day to day, and may be authorized to compel the Attendance of absent Members, in such Manner, and under such Penalties as each House may provide.

Each House may determine the Rules of its Proceedings, punish its Members for disorderly Behavior, and, with the Concurrence of two thirds, expel a Member.

Each House shall keep a Journal of its Proceedings, and from time to time publish the same, excepting such Parts as may in their Judgment require Secrecy; and the Yeas and Nays of the Members of either House on any question shall, at the Desire of one fifth of those present, be entered on the Journal.

Neither House, during the Session of Congress, shall, without the Consent of the other, adjourn for more than three days, nor to any other Place than that in which the two Houses shall be sitting.

SECTION 6

The Senators and Representatives shall receive a Compensation for their Services, to be ascertained by Law, and paid out of the Treasury of the United States. They shall in all Cases, except Treason, Felony and Breach of the Peace, be privileged from Arrest during their Attendance at the Session of their respective Houses, and in going to and returning from the same; and for any Speech or Debate in either House, they shall not be questioned in any other Place.

No Senator or Representative shall, during the Time for which he was elected, be appointed to any civil Office under the Authority of the United States, which shall have been created, or the Emoluments whereof shall have been encreased during such time; and no Person holding any Office under the United States, shall be a Member of either House during his Continuance in Office.

SECTION 7

All Bills for raising Revenue shall originate in the House of Representatives; but the Senate may propose or concur with Amendments as on other Bills.

Every Bill which shall have passed the House of Representatives and the Senate, shall, before it become a Law, be presented to the President of the United States; If he approve he shall sign it, but if not he shall return it, with his Objections to that House in which it shall have originated, who shall enter the Objections at large on their Journal, and proceed to reconsider it. If after such Reconsideration two thirds of that House shall agree to pass the Bill, it shall be sent, together with the Objections, to the other House, by which it shall likewise be reconsidered, and if approved by two thirds of that House, it

* Changed by Section 2 of Amendment XX.

shall become a Law. But in all such Cases the Votes of both Houses shall be determined by Yeas and Nays, and the Names of the Persons voting for and against the Bill shall be entered on the Journal of each House respectively. If any Bill shall not be returned by the President within ten Days (Sundays excepted) after it shall have been presented to him, the Same shall be a Law, in like Manner as if he had signed it, unless the Congress by their Adjournment prevent its Return, in which Case it shall not be a Law.

Every Order, Resolution, or Vote to which the Concurrence of the Senate and House of Representatives may be necessary (except on a question of Adjournment) shall be presented to the President of the United States; and before the Same shall take Effect, shall be approved by him, or being disapproved by him, shall be repassed by two thirds of the Senate and House of Representatives, according to the Rules and Limitations prescribed in the Case of a Bill.

SECTION 8*

The Congress shall have Power To lay and collect Taxes, Duties, Imposts and Excises, to pay the Debts and provide for the common Defence and general Welfare of the United States; but all Duties, Imposts and Excises shall be uniform throughout the United States;

To borrow Money on the credit of the United States;

To regulate Commerce with foreign Nations, and among the several States, and with the Indian Tribes;

To establish an uniform Rule of Naturalization, and uniform Laws on the subject of Bankruptcies throughout the United States;

To coin Money, regulate the Value thereof, and of foreign Coin, and fix the Standard of Weights and Measures;

To provide for the Punishment of counterfeiting the Securities and current Coin of the United States;

To establish Post Offices and post Roads;

To promote the Progress of Science and useful Arts, by securing for limited Times to Authors and Inventors the exclusive Right to their respective Writings and Discoveries;

To constitute Tribunals inferior to the supreme Court;

To define and punish Piracies and Felonies committed on the high Seas, and Offences against the Law of Nations;

To declare War, grant Letters of Marque and Reprisal, and make Rules concerning Captures on Land and Water;

To raise and support Armies, but no Appropriation of Money to that Use shall be for a longer Term than two Years;

To provide and maintain a Navy;

To make Rules for the Government and Regulation of the land and naval Forces;

To provide for calling forth the Militia to execute the Laws of the Union, suppress Insurrections and repel Invasions;

To provide for organizing, arming, and disciplining the Militia, and for governing such Part of them as may be employed in the Service of the United States, reserving to the States respectively, the Appointment of the Officers,

---

* Paragraphs 1-17 of Section 8 contain the "enumerated powers" of Congress.

and the Authority of training the Militia according to the discipline prescribed by Congress;

To exercise exclusive Legislation in all Cases whatsoever, over such District (not exceeding ten Miles square) as may, by Cession of particular States, and the Acceptance of Congress, become the Seat of the Government of the United States, and to exercise like Authority over all Places purchased by the Consent of the Legislature of the State in which the Same shall be, for the Erection of Forts, Magazines, Arsenals, dock-Yards, and other needful Buildings;—And

To make all Laws which shall be necessary and proper° for carrying into Execution the foregoing Powers, and all other Powers vested by this Constitution in the Government of the United States, or in any Department or Officer thereof.

Section 9†

The Migration or Importation of such Persons as any of the States now existing shall think proper to admit, shall not be prohibited by the Congress prior to the Year one thousand eight hundred and eight, but a Tax or duty may be imposed on such Importation, not exceeding ten dollars for each Person.

The Privilege of the Writ of Habeas Corpus shall not be suspended, unless when in Cases of Rebellion or Invasion the public Safety may require it.

No Bill of Attainder or ex post facto Law shall be passed.

No Capitation, or other direct, tax shall be laid, unless in Proportion to the Census or Enumeration herein before directed to be taken.

No Tax or Duty shall be laid on Articles exported from any State.

No Preference shall be given by any Regulation of Commerce or Revenue to the Ports of one State over those of another: nor shall Vessels bound to, or from, one State, be obliged to enter, clear, or pay Duties in another.

No Money shall be drawn from the Treasury, but in Consequence of Appropriations made by Law; and a regular Statement and Account of the Receipts and Expenditures of all public Money shall be published from time to time.

No Title of Nobility shall be granted by the United States: And no Person holding any Office of Profit or Trust under them, shall, without the Consent of the Congress, accept of any present, Emolument, Office, or Title, of any kind whatever, from any King, Prince, or foreign State.

Section 10‡

No State shall enter into any Treaty, Alliance, or Confederation; grant Letters of Marque and Reprisal; coin Money; emit Bills of Credit; make any Thing but gold and silver Coin a Tender in Payment of Debts; pass any Bill of Attainder, ex post facto Law, or Law impairing the Obligation of Contracts,§ or grant any Title of Nobility.

No State shall, without the Consent of the Congress, lay any Imposts or Duties on Imports or Exports, except what may be absolutely necessary for

° The "coefficient clause" (or "Elastic Clause" or "Necessary and Proper" clause) of the Constitution.

† This section imposes certain limitations on the powers of Congress.

‡ This section imposes certain limitations on the States.

§ The "Obligation of Contract" clause.

executing it's inspection Laws: and the net Produce of all Duties and Imposts, laid by any State on Imports or Exports, shall be for the Use of the Treasury of the United States; and all such Laws shall be subject to the Revision and Control of the Congress.

No State shall, without the Consent of Congress, lay any Duty of Tonnage, keep Troops, or Ships of War in time of Peace, enter into any Agreement or Compact with another State, or with a foreign Power, or engage in War, unless actually invaded, or in such imminent Danger as will not admit of delay.

ARTICLE II
SECTION 1

The executive Power shall be vested in a President of the United States of America. He shall hold his Office during the Term of four Years, and, together with the Vice President, chosen for the same Term, be elected, as follows:

Each State shall appoint, in such Manner as the Legislature thereof may direct, a Number of Electors, equal to the whole Number of Senators and Representatives to which the State may be entitled in the Congress: but no Senator or Representative, or Person holding an Office of Trust or Profit under the United States, shall be appointed an Elector.

[The electors shall meet in their respective States, and vote by ballot for two Persons, of whom one at least shall not be an Inhabitant of the same State with themselves. And they shall make a List of all the Persons voted for, and of the Number of Votes for each; which List they shall sign and certify, and transmit sealed to the Seat of the Government of the United States, directed to the President of the Senate. The President of the Senate shall, in the Presence of the Senate and House of Representatives, open all the Certificates, and the Votes shall then be counted. The Person having the greatest Number of Votes shall be the President, if such Number be a Majority of the whole Number of Electors appointed; and if there be more than one who have such Majority, and have an equal Number of Votes, then the House of Representatives shall immediately chuse by Ballot one of them for President; and if no Person have a Majority, then from the five highest on the List the said House shall in like Manner chuse the President. But in chusing the President, the Votes shall be taken by States, the Representation from each State having one Vote; A quorum for this Purpose shall consist of a Member or Members from two thirds of the States, and a Majority of all the States shall be necessary to a Choice. In every Case, after the Choice of the President, the Person having the greatest Number of Votes of the Electors shall be the Vice President. But if there should remain two or more who have equal Votes, the Senate shall chuse from them by Ballot the Vice President.]*

The Congress may determine the Time of chusing the Electors, and the Day on which they shall give their Votes; which Day shall be the same throughout the United States.

No Person except a natural born Citizen, or a Citizen of the United States, at the time of the Adoption of this Constitution, shall be eligible to the Office of

* Superseded by Amendment XII.

President; neither shall any Person be eligible to that Office who shall not have attained to the Age of thirty five Years, and been fourteen Years a Resident within the United States.

In Case of the Removal of the President from Office, or of his Death, Resignation or Inability to discharge the Powers and Duties of the said Office, the same shall devolve on the Vice President, and the Congress may by Law provide for the Case of Removal, Death, Resignation or Inability, both of the President and Vice President, declaring what Officer shall then act as President, and such Officer shall act accordingly, until the Disability be removed, or a President shall be elected.

The President shall, at stated Times, receive for his Services, a Compensation, which shall neither be encreased nor diminished during the Period for which he shall have been elected, and he shall not receive within that Period any other Emolument from the United States, or any of them.

Before he enter on the Execution of his Office, he shall take the following Oath or Affirmation:—"I do solemnly swear (or affirm) that I will faithfully execute the Office of President of the United States, and will to the best of my Ability, preserve, protect and defend the Constitution of the United States."

Section 2

The President shall be Commander in Chief of the Army and Navy of the United States, and of the Militia of the several States, when called into the actual Service of the United States; he may require the Opinion, in writing, of the principal Officer in each of the executive Departments, upon any Subject relating to the Duties of their respective Offices, and he shall have Power to grant Reprieves and Pardons for Offences against the United States, except in Cases of Impeachment.

He shall have Power,* by and with the Advice and Consent of the Senate, to make Treaties, provided two thirds of the Senators present concur; and he shall nominate, and by and with the Advice and Consent of the Senate, shall appoint Ambassadors, other public Ministers and Consuls, Judges of the supreme Court, and all other Officers of the United States, whose Appointments are not herein otherwise provided for, and which shall be established by Law: but the Congress may by Law vest the Appointment of such inferior Officers, as they think proper, in the President alone, in the Courts of Law, or in the Heads of Departments.

The President shall have Power to fill up all Vacancies that may happen during the Recess of the Senate, by granting Commissions which shall expire at the End of their next Session.

Section 3

He shall from time to time give to the Congress Information of the State of the Union, and recommend to their Consideration such Measures as he shall judge necessary and expedient; he may, on extraordinary Occasions, convene both Houses, or either of them, and, in Case of Disagreement between them, with Respect to the Time of Adjournment, he may adjourn them to such Time as he shall think proper; he shall receive Ambassadors and other public Min-

* The "Treaty Making Power" is contained in this sentence.

isters; he shall take Care that the Laws be faithfully executed, and shall Commission all the Officers of the United States.

SECTION 4

The President, Vice President and all civil Officers of the United States, shall be removed from Office on Impeachment for, and Conviction of, Treason, Bribery, or other high Crimes and Misdemeanors.

ARTICLE III

SECTION 1

The judicial Power of the United States, shall be vested in one supreme Court, and in such inferior Courts as the Congress may from time to time ordain and establish. The Judges, both of the supreme and inferior Courts, shall hold their Offices during good Behaviour, and shall, at stated Times, receive for their Services, a Compensation, which shall not be diminished during their Continuance in Office.

SECTION 2

The judicial Power shall extend to all Cases, in Law and Equity, arising under this Constitution, the Laws of the United States, and Treaties made, or which shall be made, under their Authority;—to all Cases affecting Ambassadors, other public Ministers and Consuls;—to all Cases of admiralty and maritime Jurisdiction;—to Controversies to which the United States shall be a Party;—to Controversies between two or more States;—between a State and Citizens of another State;—between Citizens of different States,—between Citizens of the same State claiming Lands under Grants of different States, and between a State, or the Citizens thereof, and foreign States, Citizens or Subjects.

In all Cases affecting Ambassadors, other public Ministers and Consuls, and those in which a State shall be Party, the supreme Court shall have original Jurisdiction. In all the other Cases before mentioned, the supreme Court shall have appellate Jurisdiction, both as to Law and Fact, with such Exceptions, and under such Regulations as the Congress shall make.

The Trial of all Crimes, except in Cases of Impeachment, shall be by Jury; and such Trial shall be held in the State where the said Crimes shall have been committed; but when not committed within any State, the Trial shall be at such Place or Places as the Congress may by Law have directed.

SECTION 3

Treason against the United States, shall consist only in levying War against them, or in adhering to their Enemies, giving them Aid and Comfort. No Person shall be convicted of Treason unless on the Testimony of two Witnesses to the same overt Act, or on Confession in open Court.

The Congress shall have Power to declare the Punishment of Treason, but no Attainder of Treason shall work Corruption of Blood, or Forfeiture except during the Life of the Person attainted.

ARTICLE IV

Section 1

Full Faith and Credit shall be given in each State to the public Acts, Records, and judicial Proceedings of every other State. And the Congress may by general Laws prescribe the Manner in which such Acts, Records and Proceedings shall be proved, and the Effect thereof.

Section 2

The Citizens of each State shall be entitled to all Privileges and Immunities of Citizens in the several States.

A person charged in any State with Treason, Felony, or other Crime, who shall flee from Justice, and be found in another State, shall on Demand of the executive Authority of the State from which he fled, be delivered up, to be removed to the State having Jurisdiction of the Crime.

No Person held to Service or Labour in one State, under the Laws thereof, escaping into another, shall, in Consequence of any Law or Regulation therein, be discharged from such Service or Labour, but shall be delivered up on Claim of the Party to whom such Service or Labour may be due.

Section 3

New States may be admitted by the Congress into this Union; but no new State shall be formed or erected within the Jurisdiction of any other State; nor any State be formed by the Junction of two or more States, or Parts of States, without the Consent of the Legislatures of the States concerned as well as of the Congress.

The Congress shall have Power to dispose of and make all needful Rules and Regulations respecting the Territory or other Property belonging to the United States; and nothing in this Constitution shall be so construed as to Prejudice any Claims of the United States, or of any particular State.

Section 4

The United States shall guarantee to every State in this Union a Republican Form of Government, and shall protect each of them against Invasion; and on Application of the Legislature, or of the Executive (when the Legislature cannot be convened) against domestic Violence.

ARTICLE V

The Congress, whenever two thirds of both Houses shall deem it necessary, shall propose Amendments to this Constitution,* or, on the Application of the Legislatures of two thirds of the several States, shall call a Convention for proposing Amendments, which, in either Case, shall be valid to all Intents and Purposes, as Part of this Constitution, when ratified by the Legislatures of three-fourths of the several States, or by Conventions in three fourths thereof, as the one or the other Mode of Ratification may be proposed by the Congress; Provided that no Amendment which may be made prior to the Year One thousand eight hundred and eight shall in any Manner affect the first and fourth

* The Amending power.

Clauses in the Ninth Section of the first Article; and that no State, without its Consent, shall be deprived of its equal Suffrage in the Senate.

ARTICLE VI

All Debts contracted and Engagements entered into, before the Adoption of this Constitution, shall be as valid against the United States under this Constitution, as under the Confederation.

This Constitution, and the Laws of the United States which shall be made in Pursuance thereof; and all Treaties made, or which shall be made, under the Authority of the United States, shall be the supreme Law of the Land; and the Judges in every State shall be bound thereby, any Thing in the Constitution or Laws of any State to the Contrary notwithstanding.

The Senators and Representatives before mentioned, and the Members of the several State Legislatures, and all executive and judicial Officers, both of the United States and of the several States, shall be bound by Oath or Affirmation, to support this Constitution; but no religious Test shall ever be required as a Qualification to any Office or public Trust under the United States.

ARTICLE VII

The Ratification of the Conventions of nine States, shall be sufficient for the Establishment of this Constitution between the States so ratifying the Same.

DONE in Convention by the Unanimous Consent of the States present the Seventeenth Day of September in the Year of our Lord one thousand seven hundred and Eighty seven and of the Independence of the United States of America the Twelfth. IN WITNESS whereof We have hereunto subscribed our Names.

G° WASHINGTON
Presid' and deputy from Virginia

NEW HAMPSHIRE	JOHN LANGDON NICHOLAS GILMAN
MASSACHUSETTS	NATHANIEL GORHAM RUFUS KING
CONNECTICUT	WM. SAML. JOHNSON ROGER SHERMAN
NEW YORK	ALEXANDER HAMILTON
NEW JERSEY	WIL: LIVINGSTON DAVID BREARLEY WM. PATERSON JONA: DAYTON
PENNSYLVANIA	B FRANKLIN THOMAS MIFFLIN ROBT. MORRIS GEO. CLYMER THOS. FITZSIMONS JARED INGERSOLL JAMES WILSON GOUV MORRIS

DELAWARE	{ GEO: READ GUNNING BEDFORD jun JOHN DICKINSON RICHARD BASSETT JACO: BROOM
MARYLAND	{ JAMES MCHENRY DAN OF ST. THOS. JENIFER DANL. CARROLL
VIRGINIA	{ JOHN BLAIR — JAMES MADISON JR.
NORTH CAROLINA	{ WM. BLOUNT RICHD. DOBBS SPAIGHT HU WILLIAMSON
SOUTH CAROLINA	{ J. RUTLEDGE CHARLES COTESWORTH PINCKNEY CHARLES PINCKNEY PIERCE BUTLER
GEORGIA	{ WILLIAM FEW ABR BALDWIN

Attest WILLIAM JACKSON *Secretary*

AMENDMENTS

ARTICLE I

Congress shall make no law respecting an establishment of religion, or prohibiting the free exercise thereof; or abridging the freedom of speech, or of the press; or the right of the people peaceably to assemble, and to petition the Government for a redress of grievances.

ARTICLE II

A well regulated Militia, being necessary to the security of a free State, the right of the people to keep and bear Arms, shall not be infringed.

ARTICLE III

No Soldier shall, in time of peace, be quartered in any house, without the consent of the Owner, nor in time of war, but in a manner to be prescribed by law.

ARTICLE IV

The right of the people to be secure in their persons, houses, papers, and effects, against unreasonable searches and seizures, shall not be violated, and no Warrants shall issue, but upon probable cause, supported by Oath or affirmation, and particularly describing the place to be searched, and the persons or things to be seized.

ARTICLE V

No person shall be held to answer for a capital, or otherwise infamous crime, unless on a presentment or indictment of a Grand Jury, except in cases arising in the land or naval forces, or in the Militia, when in actual service in time of War or public danger; nor shall any person be subject for the same offence to be twice put in jeopardy of life or limb; nor shall be compelled in any Criminal Case to be a witness against himself, nor be deprived of life, liberty, or property, without due process of law; nor shall private property be taken for public use, without just compensation.

ARTICLE VI

In all criminal prosecutions, the accused shall enjoy the right to a speedy and public trial, by an impartial jury of the State and district wherein the crime shall have been committed, which district shall have been previously ascertained by law, and to be informed of the nature and cause of the accusation; to be confronted with the witnesses against him; to have compulsory process for obtaining Witnesses in his favor, and to have the Assistance of Counsel for his defence.

ARTICLE VII

In suits at common law, where the value in controversy shall exceed twenty dollars, the right of trial by jury shall be preserved, and no fact tried by a jury shall be otherwise re-examined in any Court of the United States, than according to the rules of the common law.

ARTICLE VIII

Excessive bail shall not be required, nor excessive fines imposed, nor cruel and unusual punishments inflicted.

ARTICLE IX

The enumeration in the Constitution, of certain rights, shall not be construed to deny or disparage others retained by the people.

ARTICLE X

The powers not delegated to the United States by the Constitution, nor prohibited by it to the States, are reserved to the States respectively, or to the people.

[THE FIRST TEN ARTICLES PROPOSED 25 SEPTEMBER 1789; DECLARED IN FORCE 15 DECEMBER 1791]*

ARTICLE XI

[DECLARED RATIFIED 8 JANUARY 1798]

The Judicial power of the United States shall not be construed to extend to any suit in law or equity, commenced or prosecuted against one of the United States by Citizens of another State, or by Citizens or Subjects of any Foreign State.

ARTICLE XII

[DECLARED RATIFIED 25 SEPTEMBER 1804]

The Electors shall meet in their respective states, and vote by ballot for President and Vice-President, one of whom, at least, shall not be an inhabitant of the same state with themselves; they shall name in their ballots the person voted for as President, and in distinct ballots the person voted for as Vice-President, and they shall make distinct lists of all persons voted for as President, and of all persons voted for as Vice-President, and of the number of votes for each, which lists they shall sign and certify, and transmit sealed to the seat of the Government of the United States, directed to the President of the Senate;— The President of the Senate shall, in the presence of the Senate and House of Representatives, open all the certificates and the votes shall then be counted;— The person having the greatest number of votes for President, shall be the President, if such number be a majority of the whole number of Electors appointed; and if no person have such majority, then from the persons having the highest numbers not exceeding three on the list of those voted for as President, the House of Representatives shall choose immediately, by ballot, the President. But in choosing the President, the votes shall be taken by states, the representation from each state having one vote; a quorum for this purpose shall consist of

* These amendments bind only the National Government, but these rights are not infrequently binding against State authority because of the Court's interpretation of the "due process clause" of Amendment XIV.

a member or members from two-thirds of the states, and a majority of all the states shall be necessary to a choice. And if the House of Representatives shall not choose a President whenever the right of choice shall devolve upon them, before the fourth day of March next following, then the Vice-President shall act as President, as in the case of the death or other constitutional disability of the President. The person having the greatest number of votes as Vice-President, shall be the Vice-President, if such number be a majority of the whole number of Electors appointed, and if no person have a majority, then from the two highest numbers on the list, the Senate shall choose the Vice-President; a quorum for the purpose shall consist of two-thirds of the whole number of Senators, and a majority of the whole number shall be necessary to a choice. But no person constitutionally ineligible to the office of President shall be eligible to that of Vice-President of the United States.

ARTICLE XIII

[DECLARED RATIFIED 18 DECEMBER 1865]

SECTION 1

Neither slavery nor involuntary servitude, except as a punishment for crime whereof the party shall have been duly convicted, shall exist within the United States, or any place subject to their jurisdiction.

SECTION 2

Congress shall have power to enforce this article by appropriate legislation.

ARTICLE XIV

[DECLARED RATIFIED 28 JULY 1868]°

SECTION 1

All persons born or naturalized in the United States, and subject to the jurisdiction thereof, are citizens of the United States and of the State wherein they reside. No State shall make or enforce any law which shall abridge the privileges or immunities of citizens of the United States; nor shall any State deprive any person of life, liberty, or property, without due process of law; nor deny to any person within its jurisdiction the equal protection of the law.

SECTION 2

Representatives shall be apportioned among the several States according to their respective numbers, counting the whole number of persons in each State, excluding Indians not taxed. But when the right to vote at any election for the choice of electors for President and Vice-President of the United States, Representatives in Congress, the Executive and Judicial officers of a State, or the members of the Legislature thereof, is denied to any of the male inhabitants of such State, being twenty-one years of age, and citizens of the United States, or in any way abridged, except for participation in rebellion, or other crime, the basis of representation therein shall be reduced in the proportion which the

---

° Prior to date of ratification of the twenty-eighth state, Ohio and New Jersey "withdrew" their earlier assents to the amendment. Congress passed a joint resolution on July 21, 1868 declaring the amendment a part of the Constitution and directing the Secretary of State to promulgate it as such. On July 13th South Carolina ratified and on July 21 Georgia added its ratification.

number of such male citizens shall bear to the whole number of male citizens twenty-one years of age in such State.

SECTION 3

No person shall be a Senator or Representative in Congress, or elector of President and Vice-President, or hold any office, civil, or military, under the United States, or under any State, who, having previously taken an oath, as a member of Congress, or as an officer of the United States, or as a member of any State legislature, or as an executive or judicial officer of any State, to support the Constitution of the United States, shall have engaged in insurrection or rebellion against the same, or given aid or comfort to the enemies thereof. But Congress may by a vote of two-thirds of each House, remove such disability.

SECTION 4

The validity of the public debt of the United States, authorized by law, including debts incurred for payment of pensions and bounties for services in suppressing insurrection or rebellion, shall not be questioned. But neither the United States nor any State shall assume or pay any debt or obligation incurred in aid of insurrection or rebellion against the United States, or any claim for the loss or emancipation of any slave; but all such debts, obligations and claims shall be held illegal and void.

SECTION 5

The Congress shall have power to enforce, by appropriate legislation, the provisions of this article.

ARTICLE XV

[DECLARED RATIFIED 30 MARCH 1870]

SECTION 1

The right of citizens of the United States to vote shall not be denied or abridged by the United States or by any State on account of race, color, or previous condition of servitude.

SECTION 2

The Congress shall have power to enforce this article by appropriate legislation.

ARTICLE XVI

[PROPOSED 12 JULY 1909; DECLARED RATIFIED 25 FEBRUARY 1913]

The Congress shall have power to lay and collect taxes on incomes, from whatever source derived, without apportionment among the several States, and without regard to any census or enumeration.

ARTICLE XVII

[DECLARED RATIFIED 31 MAY 1913]

The Senate of the United States shall be composed of two senators from each State, elected by the people thereof, for six years; and each Senator shall have one vote. The electors in each State shall have the qualifications requisite for electors of the most numerous branch of the State legislature.

When vacancies happen in the representation of any State in the Senate, the executive authority of such State shall issue writs of election to fill such vacancies: PROVIDED, That the legislature of any State may empower the executive thereof to make temporary appointments until the people fill the vacancies by election as the legislature may direct.

This amendment shall not be so construed as to affect the election or term of any senator chosen before it becomes valid as part of the Constitution.

ARTICLE XVIII*
[DECLARED RATIFIED 29 JANUARY 1919]

After one year from the ratification of this article, the manufacture, sale, or transportation of intoxicating liquors within, the importation thereof into, or the exportation thereof from the United States and all territory subject to the jurisdiction thereof for beverage purposes is hereby prohibited.

The Congress and the several States shall have concurrent power to enforce this article by appropriate legislation.

This article shall be inoperative unless it shall have been ratified as an amendment to the Constitution by the legislatures of the several States, as provided in the Constitution, within seven years from the date of the submission hereof to the States by the Congress.

ARTICLE XIX
[PROPOSED 4 JUNE 1919; DECLARED RATIFIED 26 AUGUST 1920]

The right of citizens of the United States to vote shall not be denied or abridged by the United States or by any States on account of sex.

The Congress shall have power, by appropriate legislation, to enforce the provisions of this article.

ARTICLE XX
[DECLARED RATIFIED 6 FEBRUARY 1933]
SECTION 1

The terms of the President and Vice-President shall end at noon on the twentieth day of January, and the terms of Senators and Representatives at noon on the third day of January, of the years in which such terms would have ended if this article had not been ratified; and the terms of their successors shall then begin.

SECTION 2

The Congress shall assemble at least once in every year, and such meeting shall begin at noon on the third day of January, unless they shall by law appoint a different day.

SECTION 3

If, at the time fixed for the beginning of the term of the President, the President-elect shall have died, the Vice-President-elect shall become President. If a President shall not have been choosen before the time fixed for the beginning of his term, or if the President-elect shall have failed to qualify, then the Vice-President-elect shall act as President until a President shall have qualified;

* Repealed by section 1 of Amendment XXI.

and the Congress may by law provide for the case wherein neither a President-elect nor a Vice-President-elect shall have qualified, declaring who shall then act as President, or the manner in which one who is to act shall be selected, and such person shall act accordingly until a President or Vice-President shall have qualified.

SECTION 4

The Congress may by law provide. for the case of the death of any of the persons from whom the House of Representatives may choose a President whenever the right of choice shall have devolved upon them, and for the case of the death of any of the persons from whom the Senate may choose a Vice-President whenever the right of choice shall have devolved upon them.

SECTION 5

Sections 1 and 2 shall take effect on the 15th day of October following the ratification of this article.

SECTION 6

This article shall be inoperative unless it shall have been ratified as an amendment to the Constitution by the legislatures of three-fourths of the several States within seven years from the date of its submission.

ARTICLE XXI
[DECLARED RATIFIED 5 DECEMBER 1933]

SECTION 1

The eighteenth article of amendment to the Constitution of the United States is hereby repealed.

SECTION 2

The transportation or importation into any State, Territory or possession of the United States for delivery or use therein of intoxicating liquors, in violation of the laws thereof, is hereby prohibited.

SECTION 3

This article shall be inoperative unless it shall have been ratified as an amendment to the Constitution by convention in the several States, as provided in the Constitution, within seven years from the date of the submission hereof to the States by the Congress.

ARTICLE XXII
[DECLARED RATIFIED 1 MARCH 1951]

SECTION 1

No person shall be elected to the office of President more than twice, and no person who has held the office of President, or acted as President, for more than two years of a term to which some other person was elected President shall be elected to the office of the President more than once. But this article shall not apply to any person holding the office of President when this article was proposed by the Congress, and shall not prevent any person who may be holding the office of President, or acting as President, during the term within which this Article becomes operative from holding the office of President or acting as President during the remainder of such term.

SECTION 2

This Article shall be inoperative unless it shall have been ratified as an amendment to the Constitution by the legislatures of three-fourths of the several States within seven years from the date of its submission to the States by the Congress.

ARTICLE XXIII

[DECLARED RATIFIED 3 APRIL 1961]

SECTION 1

The District constituting the seat of Government of the United States shall appoint in such manner as the Congress may direct:

A number of electors of President and Vice President equal to the whole number of Senators and Representatives in Congress to which the District would be entitled if it were a State, but in no event more than the least populous State; they shall be in addition to those appointed by the States, but they shall be considered, for the purposes of the election of President and Vice President, to be electors appointed by a State; and they shall meet in the District and perform such duties as provided by the twelfth article of amendment.

SECTION 2

The Congress shall have power to enforce this article by appropriate legislation.

ARTICLE XXIV

[DECLARED RATIFIED 5 FEBRUARY 1964]

SECTION 1

The right of citizens of the United States to vote in any primary or other election for President or Vice President, for electors for President or Vice President, or for Senator or Representative in Congress, shall not be denied or abridged by the United States or any State by reason of failure to pay any poll tax or other tax.

SECTION 2

The Congress shall have power to enforce this article by appropriate legislation.

UNRATIFIED AMENDMENTS

Twenty-two Amendments have been ratified by the required three-fourths of the states, 5 others have been submitted to the States but have not been ratified.

In *Coleman vs Miller,* 307 U.S. 433, (1939) the U.S. Supreme Court ruled that the reasonableness of time for ratification was a political question to be determined by Congress.

THE TWO UNRATIFIED AMENDMENTS OF THE PROPOSED BILL OF RIGHTS (1789)

ARTICLE I

After the first enumeration required by the first article of the Constitution, there shall be one Representative for every thirty thousand, until the number shall amount to one hundred, after which the proportion shall be so regulated by Congress, that there shall be no less than one hundred Representatives, nor less than one Representative for every forty thousand persons, until the number of Representatives shall amount to two hundred; after which the proportion shall be so regulated by Congress, that there shall not be less than two hundred Representatives for every fifty thousand persons.

ARTICLE II

No law varying the compensation for the services of the Senators and Representatives shall take effect, until an election of Representatives shall have intervened.

THE UNRATIFIED AMENDMENT RELATING TO TITLES OF NOBILITY OF FOREIGN GOVERNMENTS
(proposed by 2nd Session of the 11th Congress)

Resolved by the Senate and House of Representatives of the United States of America in Congress assembled (two-thirds of both Houses concurring), That the following section be submitted to the legislatures of the several states, which, when ratified by the legislatures of three-fourths of the states, shall be valid and binding, as a part of the constitution of the United States.

If any citizen of the United States shall accept, claim, receive or retain any title of nobility or honour, or shall, without the consent of Congress, accept and retain any present, pension, office of emolument of any kind whatever, from any emperor, king, prince or foreign power, such person shall cease to be a citizen of the United States, and shall be incapable of holding any office of trust or profit under them, or either of them.

THE UNRATIFIED 13TH AMENDMENT (proposed by the 36th Congress, March 2, 1861)

This was signed by President Lincoln the day after the seizure of Fort Sumter. This is the only proposed amendment ever signed by the President. The President's signature is not considered necessary because of the constitutional provision that two-thirds of both Houses of Congress must concur before the amendment can be submitted to the States for ratification.

Resolved by the Senate and House of Representatives of the United States of America in Congress assembled, That the following article be proposed to the Legislatures of the several States as an amendment to the Constitution of the United States, which, when ratified by three-fourths of said Legislatures, shall be valid, to all intents and purposes, as part of the said Constitution, viz:

ARTICLE XIII

No amendment shall be made to the Constitution which will authorize or give to Congress the power to abolish or interfere, within any State, with the domestic institutions thereof, including that of persons held to labor or service by the laws of said State.

THE UNRATIFIED CHILD-LABOR AMENDMENT (proposed by the 1st Session of the 68th Congress in June 1924)

Resolved by the Senate and House of Representatives of the United States of America in Congress assembled (two-thirds of each House concurring therein), That the following article is proposed as an amendment to the Constitution of the United States, which, when ratified by the legislatures of three-fourths of the several States, shall be valid to all intents and purposes as a part of the Constitution:

ARTICLE ———

SECTION 1. The Congress shall have power to limit, regulate, and prohibit the labor of persons under 18 years of age.

SECTION 2. The power of the several States is unimpaired by this article except that the operation of State laws shall be suspended to the extent necessary to give effect to legislation enacted by the Congress.

STATES OF THE UNION, 1787–1841

State	Date Admitted	Rank in Population 1790	1820	1850
THE ORIGINAL THIRTEEN*				
Delaware	1787	13	22	30
Pennsylvania	1787	3	3	2
New Jersey	1787	9	13	19
Georgia	1788	11	11	9
Connecticut	1788	8	14	21
Massachusetts	1788 (& Maine)→	2	7	6
Maryland	1788	6	10	17
South Carolina	1788	7	8	14
New Hampshire	1788	10	15	22
Virginia	1788	1	2	4
New York	1788	5	1	1
North Carolina	1789	4	4	10
Rhode Island	1790	12	20	28
Vermont	1791		16	23
Kentucky	1792		6	8
Tennessee	1796		9	5
Ohio	1803		5	3
Louisiana	1812		17	18
Indiana	1816		18	7
Mississippi	1817		21	15
Illinois	1818		24	11
Alabama	1819		19	12
Maine	1820		12	16
Missouri	1821		23	13
Arkansas	1836			26
Michigan	1837			20

* Arranged in the order of their ratification of the Constitution.

POLITICAL PARTIES, 1796-1840

	FEDERALIST	REPUBLICAN
1796	J. Adams (1797-1801)	
1800		Jefferson (1801-09)
1804		
1808		Madison (1809-17)
1812		
1816		Monroe (1817-25)
1820		
1824		

J. Q. Adams (1825-29)
Jackson-candidate

	NATIONAL-REPUBLICAN	DEMOCRATIC-REPUBLICAN
1828	Adams-candidate	Jackson (1829-37)
		DEMOCRATIC
1832	Clay-candidate	Jackson elected again 1832
	WHIG	
1836	Coalition candidates in 1836	Van Buren (1837-41)
1840	Harrison (1841) Tyler (1841-45)	

MAJOR EXECUTIVE OFFICERS
OF THE
UNITED STATES, 1789-1841

President		*Term*
GEORGE WASHINGTON of Virginia		1789-97
Vice-President	John Adams of Mass.	1789-97
Secretary of State	Thomas Jefferson of Va.	1790-93
	Edmund Randolph of Va.	1794-95
	Timothy Pickering of Pa.	1795-97
Secretary of the Treasury	Alexander Hamilton of N.Y.	1789-95
	Oliver Wolcott of Conn.	1795-97
Secretary of War	Henry Knox of Mass.	1789-95
	Timothy Pickering of Pa.	1795
	James McHenry of Md.	1796-97
Attorney General	Edmund Randolph of Va.	1789-94
	William Bradford of Pa.	1794-95
	Charles Lee of Va.	1795-97
Postmaster General	Samuel Osgood of Mass.	1789-91
	Timothy Pickering of Pa.	1791-95
	Joseph Habersham of Ga.	1795-97
JOHN ADAMS of Massachusetts		1797-1801
Vice-President	Thomas Jefferson of Va.	1797-1801
Secretary of State	Timothy Pickering of Pa.	1797-1800
	John Marshall of Va.	1800-01

Secretary of the Treasury	Oliver Wolcott of Conn.	1797-1801
	Samuel Dexter of Mass.	1801
Secretary of War	James McHenry of Md.	1797-1800
	Samuel Dexter of Mass.	1800-01
Attorney General	Charles Lee of Va.	1797-1801
Postmaster General	Joseph Habersham of Ga.	1797-1801
Secretary of the Navy	Benjamin Stoddert of Md.	1798-1801

THOMAS JEFFERSON of Virginia   1801-09

Vice-President	Aaron Burr of N.Y.	1801-05
	George Clinton of N.Y.	1805-09
Secretary of State	James Madison of Va.	1801-09
Secretary of the Treasury	Albert Gallatin of Pa.	1801-09
Secretary of War	Henry Dearborn of Mass.	1801-09
Attorney General	Levi Lincoln of Mass.	1801-05
	John Breckinridge of Ky.	1805-07
	Caesar Rodney of Del.	1807-09
Postmaster General	Gideon Granger of Conn.	1801-09
Secretary of the Navy	Robert Smith of Md.	1801-05
	Jacob Crowninshield of Mass.,	1805-09

JAMES MADISON of Virginia   1809-17

Vice-President	George Clinton° of N.Y.	1809-12
	Elbridge Gerry† of Mass.	1813-14

° Died 1812.
† Died 1814.

Secretary of State	Robert Smith of Md.	1809-11
	James Monroe of Va.	1811-17
Secretary of the Treasury	Albert Gallatin of Pa.	1809-14
	George Campbell of Tenn.	1814
	Alexander Dallas of Pa.	1814-16
	William H. Crawford of Ga.	1816-17
Secretary of War	William Eustis of Mass.	1809-13
	John Armstrong of N.Y.	1813-14
	James Monroe of Va.	1814-15
	William H. Crawford of Ga.	1815-17
Attorney General	Caesar Rodney of Del.	1809-11
	William Pinckney of Md.	1811-14
	Richard Rush of Pa.	1814-17
Postmaster General	Gideon Granger of Conn.	1809-14
	Return J. Meigs of Ohio	1814-17
Secretary of the Navy	Paul Hamilton of S.C.	1809-13
	William Jones of Pa.	1813-14
	Benjamin Crowninshield of Mass.	1814-17

JAMES MONROE of Virginia		1817-25
Vice-President	Daniel D. Tompkins of N.Y.	1817-25
Secretary of State	John Quincy Adams of Mass.	1817-25
Secretary of the Treasury	William H. Crawford of Ga.	1817-25
Secretary of War	John C. Calhoun of S.C.	1817-25
Attorney General	Richard Rush of Pa.	1817
	William Wirt of Va.	1817-25
Postmaster General	Return J. Meigs of Ohio	1817-23
	John McLean of Ohio	1823-25
Secretary of the Navy	Benjamin Crowninshield of Mass.	1817-18
	Smith Thompson of N.Y.	1818-23
	Samuel L. Southard of N.J.	1823-25

JOHN QUINCY ADAMS of Massachusetts   1825-29

    Vice-President   John C. Calhoun of S.C.   1825-29

    Secretary of State   Henry Clay of Ky.   1825-29

    Secretary of the Treasury   Richard Rush of Pa.   1825-29

    Secretary of War   James Barbour of Va.   1825-28
                                Peter B. Porter of N.Y.   1828-29

    Attorney General   William Wirt of Va.   1825-29

    Postmaster General   John McLean of Ohio   1825-29

    Secretary of the Navy   Samuel L. Southard of N.J.   1825-29

ANDREW JACKSON of Tennessee   1829-37

    Vice-President   John C. Calhoun* of S.C.   1829-32
                                Martin Van Buren of N.Y.   1833-37

    Secretary of State   Martin Van Buren of N. Y.   1829-31
                                Edward Livingston of N.Y.   1831-33
                                Louis McLane of Del.   1833-34
                                John Forsyth of Ga.   1834-37

    Secretary of the Treasury   Samuel Ingham of Pa.   1829-31
                                Louis McLane of Del.   1831-33
                                William Duane of Pa.   1833
                                Roger B. Taney of Md.   1833-34
                                Levi Woodbury of N.H.   1834-37

    Secretary of War   John H. Eaton of Tenn.   1829-31
                                Lewis Cass of Ohio   1831-37

    Attorney General   John M. Berrien of Ga.   1829-31
                                Roger B. Taney of Md.   1831-33
                                Benjamin F. Butler of N.Y.   1833-37

    Postmaster General   William Barry of Ky.   1829-35
                                Amos Kendall of Ky.   1835-37

* Resigned in Dec. 1832.

Secretary of the Navy	John Branch of N.C.	1829-31
	Levi Woodbury of N.H.	1831-34
	Mahlon Dickerson of N.J.	1834-37

MARTIN VAN BUREN of New York   1837-41

Vice-President	Richard M. Johnson of Ky.	1837-41
Secretary of State	John Forsyth of Ga.	1837-41
Secretary of the Treasury	Levi Woodbury of N.H.	1837-41
Secretary of War	Joel R. Poinsett of S.C.	1837-41
Attorney General	Benjamin F. Butler of N.Y.	1837-38
	Felix Grundy of Tenn.	1838-40
	Henry D. Gilpin of Pa.	1840-41
Postmaster General	Amos Kendall of Ky.	1837-40
	John M. Niles of Conn.	1840-41
Secretary of the Navy	Mahlon Dickerson of N.J.	1837-38
	James K. Paulding of N.Y.	1838-41

JUSTICES OF THE UNITED STATES
SUPREME COURT, 1789-1841

Name

John Jay of N.Y. (CHIEF JUSTICE)	1789-95
John Rutledge of S.C.	1789-91
William Cushing of Mass.	1789-1810
James Wilson of Pa.	1789-98
John Blair of Va.	1789-96
James Iredell of N.C.	1790-99
Thomas Johnson of Md.	1791-93
William Paterson of N.J.	1793-1806
John Rutledge of S.C. (CHIEF JUSTICE)	1795
Samuel Chase of Md.	1796-1811
Oliver Ellsworth of Conn. (CHIEF JUSTICE)	1796-99
Bushrod Washington of Va.	1798-1829
Alfred Moore of N.C.	1799-1804
John Marshall of Va. (CHIEF JUSTICE)	1801-35
William Johnson of S.C.	1804-34
Henry B. Livingston of N.Y.	1806-23
Thomas Todd of Ky.	1807-26
Joseph Story of Mass.	1811-45
Gabriel Duval of Md.	1812-35
Smith Thompson of N.Y.	1823-43
Robert Trimble of Ky.	1826-28
John McLean of Ohio	1829-61
Henry Baldwin of Pa.	1830-44
James M. Wayne of Ga.	1835-67
Roger B. Taney of Md. (CHIEF JUSTICE)	1836-64
Philip P. Barbour of Va.	1836-41
John Catron of Tenn.	1837-52
John McKinley of Ala.	1837-52

INDEX